W9-DEU-256

Environmental Gardening

by Karen Arms

with illustrations by

Thom Smith

and

Bitterroot Studios

Copyright © 1992, by Halfmoon Publishing.

All rights reserved. No part of this publication may be reproduced
or transmitted in any form or by any means without permission in
writing from the publisher:
Halfmoon Publishing
P. O. Box 30279
Savannah, GA 31410-0279

Production manager: Marta E. Rodriguez
Cover art: Thom Smith
Illustrations: Thom Smith and Bitterroot Studios
Typesetting: Savannah Color Separations

This book is printed on recycled paper.

Environmental Gardening

Library of Congress Catalog Card Number: 91-92926

ISBN 0-9629275-6-2

To the memory of
my grandfather,
Will Yeo,
whose hydrangea walk
and tomato-scented greenhouse
are never far from my garden

PREFACE

As a biologist, I am often asked which gardening practices are environmentally sound and which are dangerous or unethical. Am I poisoning the neighborhood when I spray the roses for fungus? Is lawn care hazardous to your health? How can I attract (or get rid of) butterflies? This book is at least a partial answer to a torrent of questions from gardeners old and new. It is also my excuse to write, for once, about the hobby I love.

This is not a textbook on environmental science. It is not even a book of instructions for environmentalists or a manual on perfect lawns without pesticides. It is, rather, a guide to understanding how a garden is part of a larger environment. Most gardeners are environmentalists at heart, even as they take arms against a sea of squirrels and kudzu. We provide habitat for native plants, and coexist, if sometimes reluctantly, with other animals that share the garden. But we often lack accurate information. Bombarded on the one hand with the message that good gardeners fight insects wherever they find them, and on the other with advertisements for dubious "green" pesticides and soil amendments, what is the conscientious gardener to believe? I hope that this book provides some of the answers.

An understanding of how and why wildlife and weeds are, and should be, always with us, makes life easier for those of us with full-time jobs and no hired help. Our gardens may never be seen in the pages of glossy magazines, but they can bring us great satisfaction: supplying us with decorations for the house and tasty food, an outlet for artistic ambitions, and a retreat from the cares of the day—or at least confronting us with different cares.

In my talks with other gardeners, I have discovered that gardeners are modest people and do not realize how important their efforts can be. Hundreds of species of native and exotic plants are not going to survive into the twenty-first century unless gardeners and other volunteers save them. Then there are heirloom garden plants to be rescued. The other day I was holding forth about the disappearance of open-pollinated petunias when a listener told me that her mother's petunias were still seeding themselves in the bed where they have lived for fifty years. She had rather scorned these determined plants for their small flowers and weedy habits and was excited to learn that rescuing old garden plants is a valuable enterprise. This same group of gardeners has been planting trees and shrubs along streets and around public buildings. As government agencies slide further into the red, more and more gardeners are taking on the work of reforesting urban areas, beautifying our communities and slowing global warming. These efforts are enormously important.

Many plants are mentioned in this book and I hasten to confess that I have not grown all of them, despite many years of gardening in England, California, New York, and Georgia, where my career as a biology teacher and writer has led me.

The people who have helped with this book are many. They have introduced me to other enthusiasts, traveled with me and given me plants, fed me and housed me, argued with me about gardening and grammar, and even offered to weed my neglected garden while I wrote. My heartfelt thanks to Ann and Holden Bowler, Bruce and Beth Bowler, Bill Dilger, Martin and Eleanora Fry, Mary Ann Gephart, Peggy Gregory, Patti King, Laura Belle Macrae, Peter Marks, Gwen Schrader, Mary Stoller, Simone Van Stolk, Tricia Smith, Connie Wingard, Hazel Whitmyre, and Louisa Farrand Wood, to John Ambrose, Jerral Mayes and all our 'Wilmington 96' volunteers, and especially to my husband, Thom Smith.

I hope that gardeners everywhere will find in this book at least some of the fun and stimulation that I have found in writing it.

Karen Arms
Savannah, May 1992.

CONTENTS

CHAPTER 1

Introduction

The son and heir blew in the other day, with the college sailing team, dirty laundry, and hair that looked as if he had joined a reggae band.

"The garden looks great," he said as he changed the oil in their long-suffering van.

"You know, I have to thank you guys for introducing me to plants and animals. We drove to New Orleans last month and I'm going, 'Wow, what redbuds! Look, turkey vultures: we're in the South! Amazing azaleas!' And the others didn't know what I was talking about."

"You'll be scratching your own patch of dirt before your hair falls out," I predicted: another environmental gardener, with field guides by the kitchen window, a six-foot poke salad weed in the vegetable garden ("Just to see how big it'll get"), and swallowtail butterflies feeding on Queen Anne's lace in the wild garden.

Gardening has many attractions for today's harried workers. It is about the best exercise we can get; it gives a feeling of control over lives that often seem to be spinning out of control, and it satisfies the urges of many a frustrated artist.

Gardening, like cooking, creates art that is here today and gone tomorrow—or at least when the next weed germinates. Unlike the painter's, or even the cook's, the gardener's art is at the mercy of every vagary of the weather and the general cussedness of living things. As Hugh Johnson put it, "On this flapping canvas an amateur without previous experience, holding the instruction book in one hand, tries to daub his vision of a better world—or if that is flying a bit high, at least to grow vegetables and feed his family."

WHAT IS ENVIRONMENTAL GARDENING?

Henry David Thoreau once planted a bean patch at Walden Pond and then tore it out because it was an intrusion on the environment. It was all very well for him; he didn't depend on the bean patch for food or a pleasant place to sit after a hard day at the office. The rest of us are not going to give up gardening because it interferes with nature. But these environmental days, we do feel a responsibility to see that our gardens don't harm the world around us. Perhaps we merely feel twinges of worry that the way we care for the lawn may be covering the family with pesticides. Or perhaps we are curious about what organic gardening is, and wonder whether its proponents are showing common sense or peddling snake oil.

An environmental gardener wants to garden in harmony with nature—to create habitat for wildlife, eat pesticide-free vegetables, save water and energy, and generally become part of the solution rather than the problem. An environmental approach to gardening can do much more than prevent damage. It can provide solutions.

One spring day, a Georgia couple walked their property, trying to decide what to do about a large marshy area. Should they dig out a small lake and stream, with a bridge and water-loving plants, or drain the whole lot? Somehow, they did not like the idea of drowning or uprooting the many tall, tubular plants that were pushing their heads up in the marsh. They decided to find out more about the plants before going further. After consulting local experts, they found that they owned a bog full of endangered pitcher plants (*Sarracenia*). These insect-eating plants live in isolated bogs, hundreds of which have been destroyed or built over. The proud owners saved the marsh and listed it with a conservation registry.

Pitcher plants, *Sarracenia flava*.
This particular species has been bred for use in the garden and will grow in ordinary moist garden soil. Pitcher plants are carnivorous. They are adapted to wet, acid areas where little nitrogen is available from the soil. They obtain their nitrogen from insects that are trapped in the water-holding pitcher. Here the insects are digested by the plant and absorbed, supplying the plant with nitrogen.

Now they are experts on pitcher plants and their habitat, and host parties of students and botanists who come to admire the beautiful spot where at least some of these fascinating and specialized plants have found a safe home.

Even if your garden never becomes a preserve for endangered plants, it is remarkable how many interesting animals and plants will become our neighbors if we give them a chance. Giving them a chance may mean taking positive steps to attract birds, butterflies, and native plants or it may just mean opening our eyes to the life that is all around us if we look for it. This usually means avoiding the use of pesticides and fertilizers that could damage wildlife and understanding why our gardens will not go to hell in a handbasket if we allow an occasional weed in the lawn.

GOALS OF AN ENVIRONMENTAL GARDENER

Any gardener wants to create a beautiful setting for the house, a place of recreation for the family, and, above all, a retreat for the gardener. Most of us also want a place where we can enjoy entertaining fellow gardeners who will, we hope, at least occasionally, drool with admiration and envy.

The difference between an ordinary gardener and an environmental gardener is that the ordinary gardener battles with nature, in an endless struggle to eliminate weeds from the border, moles from the lawn, tree seedlings from the bog garden, and anything else that threatens the gardener's vision of precisely how the garden should look. The environmental gardener is curious about the natural world inside and outside the garden, leaves in place an unknown plant to see what it will turn out to be, calls the family to marvel at the blind eyes and burrowing limbs of the mole the dogs have dug up, and doesn't bother to fight futile battles, such as trying to rid the garden of medflies or squirrels. The environmental gardener appreciates the other creatures that share the earth with us, enjoys the sight of a raccoon washing its food in the swimming pool, of bees humming over the sweet alyssum, or of a wren darting by with an insect almost as big as itself.

The environmental gardener experiments. The books say phlox needs sun, but you live in the South where the sun is hot. You will try a division of your favorite phlox in the woodland garden this year to see if it will bloom in shade. Above all, the environmental gardener learns how and why the other organisms that inhabit the garden with us, from bacteria to beech trees, from nematodes to nightingales, can work with, rather than against, our attempts to create a place of beauty—or even grow a few vegetables. This is the basic premise of organic gardening.

I realized that I had become a more-or-less organic gardener one autumn as I surveyed my hi-tech gardening aids. Most of my pesticides, weed-killers, plant hormones, pruning paint, lime, lawn fertilizer, vegetable fertilizer, acidifiers, hoses, and sprinklers stood on their shelves, unused that year and indeed for many years. I wasn't sure whether I was scared of poisoning the family and local wildlife, or if I was too lazy to load a sprayer. Whatever the reason, it was clear that many of the expensive adjuncts of modern gardening were never going to play a major role in my life.

There is no precise definition of "organic gardening" or "organic farming." Some states have legal definitions of "organically grown" fruit and vegetables, but that is only so that consumers know precisely what they are getting when they pay the high prices organic produce often commands. To aficionados, organic gardening means gardening without using anything not produced by living organisms (organically). True evangelists may even eschew power tools, thereby avoiding energy loss, air pollution, and noise. Don't despise fanatical organic gardeners. Without the message that they have been preaching to a largely deaf world for many decades, we

Green Thumbs Tip
Misnamed Plants

One of the more infuriating difficulties that arises sooner or later for a gardener is that plants are sometimes misidentified. The climbing lily *Gloriosa Rothschildiana* is staring at me from a recent catalogue, firmly labeled *"Gloriosa superba,"* which is the choicer species and has smaller yellow flowers. The result is that you see a lovely thing in a friend's garden, order it from your favorite nursery, and when it arrives it is something completely different. There is nothing much you can do about this except scold the nursery. And most of us think we are more likely to have the plant wrong than the nursery is so we end up doing nothing about it.

Also on my desk is a British article describing how to grow gloriosa lilies (correctly identified) in pots so that you can bring them indoors when frost threatens. I assure the writer that if the gloriosa lily is hardy in my part of the world, where winter temperatures drop below 20 °F, it is hardy in most of Britain as long as it is planted deeply, as it should be.

The moral is that you cannot believe everything you hear or read and that a gardener embarks upon a lifetime of learning and experimentation, finding out what plants grow well in the garden, where they grow best, and even what their names may be.

Gloriosa Rothschildiana.
This is an unusual member of the lily family that climbs using tendrils at the tips of its leaves. The flowers are red with yellow margins.

should not today have some of the miracles of modern research, many biological pest controls, or so many drought-tolerant annuals.

But most organic gardeners and farmers are not fanatical; they bring common sense to bear. There are many gardens in which a hand mower will control the lawn just as fast and with much less expenditure of money and energy than a power mower. On the other hand, if you are stuck with vast areas of lawn to mow or sweet corn to harvest, common sense dictates the most powerful and efficient power tools you can afford. For this reason, agriculturists usually prefer the term "low-input farming" to "organic farming." High-input farmers pour more water, fertilizer, and pesticide on their fields each year as their soil becomes poorer and birds that eat pests disappear from the countryside. Low-input farmers rotate crops to control pest populations and they build fertile soil by adding plant residues and manure. Because they have fertile, water-retaining soil, they use less water, fertilizer, and pesticide than their high-input neighbors. Low-input farming or gardening do less damage than their high-input equivalents to the local waterways and wildlife, and perhaps to people who eat whatever the farm or garden produces.

I am not a "pure" organic gardener. I am addicted to my power lawn-mower, edger, and tiller. I use trace elements on chlorotic plants, biological insecticides on fire ants and fleas. But these aids are useful only when there is no alternative and not when we use them just because everyone else does. Water is plentiful where I live and the soil is dry, so most people water their gardens early and often—and then wonder why their camellias and daphnes die. Both shrubs are adapted to dry conditions and are easily killed by kindness. Plants have been around for a long time without people to fuss and fertilize and a little benign neglect goes a long way, even in the finest garden. When gypsy moths defoliated the maple trees, the neighbors panicked and called the mayor. I swept up the mess and waited for predators and disease to decimate the moth population—which they did. Understanding natural checks and balances can save a lot of environmental damage—and a lot of energy.

 Understanding the Environment
Xeriscapes and Xerophytes

"Xeriscape" is a confusing name coined in Colorado to describe gardens that need less water than the usual gardens found in dry areas. I find the word "xeriscape" misleading because it is so similar to "xerophyte," the botanist's term for plants adapted to desert life. There is nothing xerophytic about a "xeriscape" in the southeastern United States with its 50 inches of rain a year.

The National Xeriscape Council does not actually advise not watering a garden. It advocates practices such as grouping plants with similar water needs so that part of the garden needs little water, replacing water guzzlers with drought-tolerant plants, efficient watering, soil improvement, and energy-efficient landscaping. The term is now loosely used to describe everything from a garden that is never watered to a desert garden.

Perhaps the goals of environmental gardening are best illustrated by examples. Sometimes a garden impresses you by its appropriateness. It seems part of the larger environment and a happy home to gardener, plants, and animal visitors.

• In Idaho, Bruce and Beth Bowler live in a house built into a steep hillside. Theirs is a dry part of the world, with about eleven inches of precipitation a year, nearly all of it in the form of snow. In front of the house is a conventional garden with a small lawn that they water in summer, small trees and an arbor to provide shade, and a choice collection of ferns, penstemons, and annuals that are well adapted to this shady oasis. Behind the house is a hot, steep hill with a view over Boise, which had been a problem for many years. The lawn was too steep to mow properly and flowers around the edges of the lawn never seemed to get enough water.

Then Beth read a book on dry gardens and was inspired. She would create a garden that reflected the surrounding hills, where choice plants from dry habitats around the world would flourish and that would not need watering. She enlisted male muscle to help her build a zigzag path that divides the hill into a series of terraces. Then she found a seed company in Montana that specializes in native plants and set to work. Now, you look from the house over a serene picture of colorful flower and foliage plants, widely spaced as desert gardening demands so that each is seen to best advantage.

The garden will never be finished because it is full of experiments. As each plant is tried out, it may be a success and moved to the formal beds near the house, it may be a disaster and relegated to the compost pile, or it may be deemed an informal sort of plant that belongs further down the hill in the "wild" area where birds and insects cluck and hum contentedly in the heat of an Idaho summer. This is a garden that feels completely right and brings endless excitement and pleasure to its owners and their visitors.

• Dyanna Byers holds open house for local birds, without precisely intending to. She went away for the weekend, leaving the door of her screened porch propped open so the dog could get in and out. When she returned, wrens had nested in a hanging basket on the porch, so she had to leave the door open for another two weeks until the babies fledged. The house got rather full of bugs, but she had a fine view of wren family life since the birds did not seem to mind people enjoying the cocktail hour on the porch. The parents would land on the open door, with large struggling insects in their bills, then hop from plant to plant until they reached the nest.

Recently, a group of mallards wintering on a local pond have taken to visiting Dyanna's swimming pool for a paddle in the evening. Dyanna worries about their sex life since the group consists of three males and one female. The female laid an egg beside the pool—but the shell never hardened. The next day they followed a

Leucojum autumnale,
autumn snowflakes.

cat into the house and started eating from the cats' food bowls. There is something about Dyanna and birds. She's raised an injured brown thrasher and helps herons—who sometimes seem disoriented when they leave the nest—to find the marsh. It all makes suburban life a lot more interesting than it might otherwise be.

• In Arizona, Carol and Frank Naylor decided to create an oasis, where garden plants would create a lush and colorful surrounding for house and people, but where the desert's other inhabitants would also be welcome. They attract wildlife by supplying food, as well as that rare staple of desert life, water. At the edge of the garden, they dug a pond beside a small tree and planted a shrubbery where animals can hide and nest. Although the garden is not large, rabbits, squirrels, chipmunks, coyotes, and javelinas visit the pond regularly. The Naylors have even attracted cougars, bobcats, and mule deer. Dozens of bird species are attracted to feeders and to running water circulated by a pump. Of course there are snags: rabbits eat the garden and pack rats cart off valuable plants to build their nests. But looking at the healthy plants and billows of color, you would never guess that dozens of animals are feeding in this garden.

ETHICAL GARDENING

Environmental gardeners are interested in plants that are native to their own parts of the world as well as plants from similar areas elsewhere that will probably flourish in the garden; and this often leads to ethical problems. We do not want to cause environmental problems elsewhere while building our own gardens. Can I transplant a wild flower from nearby woodland to my own garden without damaging the woodland habitat? Am I helping to destroy tropical forest if I buy teak garden furniture? There is no avoiding these questions once you start to think about environmental problems.

We even have to worry about the damage we may be doing when we purchase plants from commercial sources. There are always people more concerned with making a buck than worrying

ECOLOGICAL SUCCESSION

As an ecologist sees it, gardening is a constant battle against ecological succession, the changes that would occur if we left the land alone. Imagine what would happen if you stopped looking after the lawn. In most parts of the world, the space would eventually fill up with shrubs and trees, and succession would have turned the lawn into forest. The forest, prairie, chaparral or other plant community that forms if land is left alone for long enough is the climax community. By mowing and weeding we constantly interrupt succession, preventing the climax community from forming.

Succession occurs because different plants are adapted to different conditions. For instance, when a farm in New England is abandoned, weeds quickly move in, clothing the earth with a colorful carpet of black mustard, wild carrot, and dandelions. These plants are fugitive pioneers of newly available sunny habitat. They grow rapidly and produce seeds adapted to disperse long distances to wherever they find new patches of open ground.

Plant succession in an abandoned farm field in North Carolina.

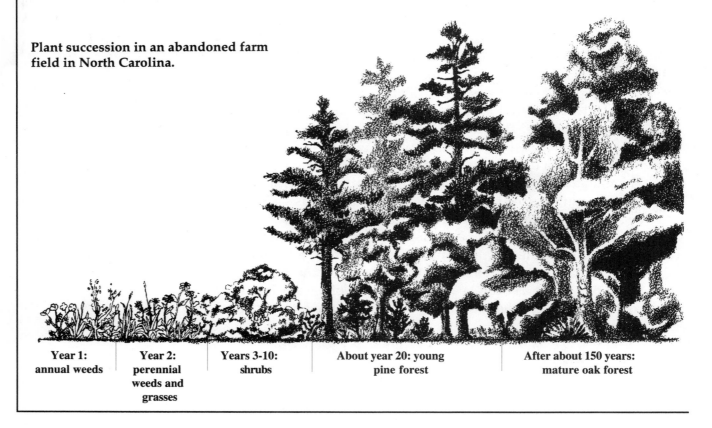

| Year 1: annual weeds | Year 2: perennial weeds and grasses | Years 3-10: shrubs | About year 20: young pine forest | After about 150 years: mature oak forest |

about the environment. When these people are starving peasants trying to feed a family, it is hard not to sympathize. But just as the drug trade would not exist without consumers to buy the drugs, so we as gardeners try to discourage practices we consider unethical by the power of our wallets. Take the trade in small bulbs.

For many years, most of the little bulbs so popular in gardens were dug up in the wild and trucked by the million to Holland to be marketed under "Product of Holland" labels. Few of the buyers realized that these bulbs were dug from the wild (often illegally). In Turkey alone, during the 1980s, 71 million anemones, 20 million cyclamen, 62 million leucojums, 111 million winter aconites, and 200 million snowdrops were dug and exported, with no attempt to leave behind populations large enough to

Soon, slower-growing perennial plants, such as goldenrod and grasses, move in. These newcomers shade the ground and their long roots monopolize the soil water. It becomes difficult for the seedlings of the pioneer species to grow. But even as the tall weeds choke out the sun-loving pioneer species, they are in turn shaded and deprived of water by the seedlings of pioneer shrubs and trees, such as pin cherries and aspens, which take longer to become established, but command most of the resources once they reach a respectable size. Succession is still not complete, for the pioneer trees are not members of the species that make up the mature climax forest. Slower growing oak and hickory or beech and maple trees will eventually move in and take over, shading out the saplings of the pioneer tree species. After perhaps a century, the land returns to the approximate species composition of the original forest.

In any tract of land, we can always find at least small patches that are undergoing succession following disturbance—a spot where a tree has fallen, a slope where a landslide has occurred, a burned forest, or a bulldozed roadside. The existence of various patches undergoing succession ensures a steady supply of fugitive plants, the fast-growing, here-today-and-gone-tomorrow weeds.

Animals, as well as plants, may be fugitive species. Insects that specialize in eating a particular plant may travel far and use their keen senses to smell out new patches of their food plant. Some of our agricultural pest problems stem from the fact that many crop plants originated as fugitive species, depending on their sparse distribution and their nomadic habits to protect them from insects. By planting fields exclusively to one crop year after year, farmers and gardeners create a paradise for such fugitive animals as tomato worms and cucumber beetles, which no longer have to spend energy to find food and have nothing to do but eat and multiply.

Succession in a lawn or abandoned field occurs relatively rapidly because it uses the existing soil. The soil may already contain the seeds of some successional species and others will blow or be carried in from surrounding areas. Succession is much slower when the habitat is some distance from a source of seeds and animal colonizers. The extreme case is succession on rock or sand when there is no soil.

Some microorganisms and lichens can grow on sand or rock, surviving mainly on the nutrients in rain. Water may freeze and thaw in cracks, breaking up the rock. Soil will slowly form as dust particles are trapped in cracks and as the dead bodies of organisms accumulate. Mosses and ferns may gain a foothold in even a thin layer of lichen remains and rock dust. As these plants add their own dead bodies to the pile, the seeds of small rooted plants are able to germinate and grow, beginning a process much like that of old-field succession.

Succession can be seen in any street. Mosses, lichens, and weeds establish themselves in cracks in the street or driveway; quite large plants may grow in a corner where leaf litter and dirt have been deposited by a gutter, and fungi and mosses invade a roof that needs repair. If we stopped cleaning and repairing it, even the center of Manhattan would turn into a rock-filled woodland within our lifetimes.

Succession comes to the aid of the gardener who wants to create

sustain future harvests. This is what is known as depleting our natural resources.

As a result of digging from the wild in the Mediterranean and Middle East, many species of bulbs are endangered. This is not merely an environmental disaster in itself, it also endangers the sources from which new bulb varieties can be developed. Modern tulips and narcissi, after all, are the descendants of species that once clothed hillsides in Asia and Europe.

Steps are now being taken to ensure that at least consumers know when they are plundering wild populations. In 1991, the Dutch bulb industry, the World Wildlife Fund, and the British Flora and Fauna Preservation Society signed an agreement protecting 31 species of bulbs usually dug from the wild, packaged, and passed off as

Dutch. These bulbs will now be labeled "Bulbs from Wild Source." By 1995, all bulbs will carry labels describing their origins.

Of course, labeling plants will not save wild populations if gardeners continue to buy plants dug from the wild, but the push for ethical gardening is on and many concerned plant sellers are getting in on the act. You will see catalogues guaranteeing that none of the plants offered are collected from the wild. Unfortunately, some of these claims are themselves suspect, but we are taking steps in the right direction. It is possible to have a beautiful garden, full of interesting native and exotic plants without endangering the habitats they come from.

WHAT BIOME DO YOU LIVE IN?

Do you garden in prairie or temperate forest, desert or chaparral? To an ecologist, these are all biomes, types of habitat described by their vegetation, and the main thing that determines this is climate: temperature and precipitation. Climate and vegetation vary with latitude and altitude. The temperature falls as you move further from the equator and as you move up a mountain. Rhododendrons grow in temperate forests and mahogany trees in tropical forests because rhododendrons cannot survive in hot wet conditions and mahogany trees cannot survive cold or dry weather. Large trees grow only where there is plenty of moisture, while progressively drier conditions support plant communities dominated by small trees, shrubs, grasses and finally scattered cactuses or other desert plants. The map opposite shows the main biomes in North America. Once you know which biome your garden lies in, you will have a good idea of the type of vegetation that flourished in your area before the advent of civilization. This will tell you the types of plants that are most likely to thrive without your fussing over them. For instance, the chaparral biome occurs in California as well as the coast of the Mediterranean. Not surprisingly, many Mediterranean plants do well in much of California.

You can learn more about your own biome by studying field guides, such as *Plants of the Northern Prairie,* or *Guide to Rocky Mountain Wild Flowers.* Field guides are often ignored by gardeners, but they contain a wealth of ideas for plants that will do well in your garden.

THE IMPORTANCE OF EXPERIMENTS

I think the most important thing a gardener can learn is to experiment—with plants, techniques, and designs. One of the problems with reading too many gardening books is that we find ourselves accepting other people's answers instead of discovering our own.

When I moved from New York to Georgia and found myself in the same climate zone as most of England, I was thrilled with the

Major biomes. Trees occur only where there is plenty of water. Western deserts lie in the rain shadows of mountains, where there is little rain. Grassland is found where there is slightly more rainfall. Coniferous trees are tougher than deciduous trees and can survive where the soil is frozen for much of the year (taiga) and where the soil is sandy and holds little moisture (Southeast). Notice the effect of rivers and their drainage basins. Deciduous forest occurs around the Mississippi and its western tributaries, while only grasses can survive further from the river.

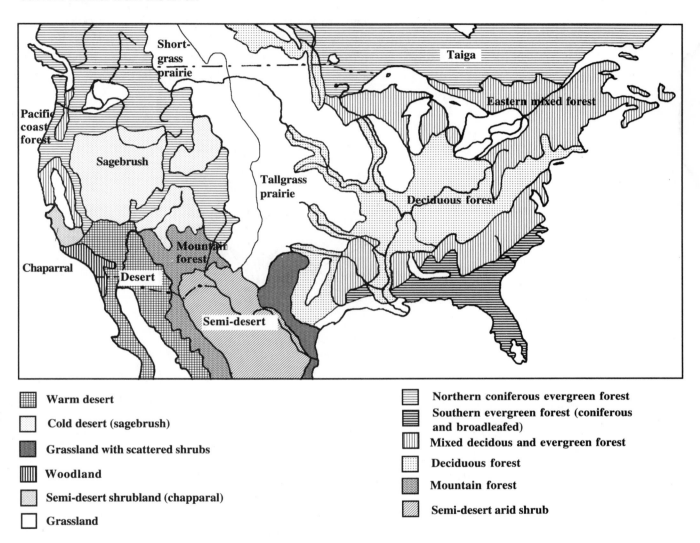

▦ Warm desert	▤ Northern coniferous evergreen forest
☐ Cold desert (sagebrush)	▦ Southern evergreen forest (coniferous and broadleafed)
▓ Grassland with scattered shrubs	▥ Mixed decidous and evergreen forest
▥ Woodland	▒ Deciduous forest
▨ Semi-desert shrubland (chapparal)	▓ Mountain forest
☐ Grassland	▨ Semi-desert arid shrub

idea of growing the plants I remembered from English gardens. I imagined aubretia, dahlias, rhododendrons, lilacs, bluebells, and delphiniums fighting for space in my garden. So I planted some of them, and they died in August or refused to flower. Why? And what could I do about it?

I am now convinced high nighttime temperature in summer is the main culprit. And the solution is to search for plants adapted to this particular climatic quirk. But there are many more of these than are generally grown in southern gardens and I still cannot predict which plants will be happy in my garden, or where. In the South, many plants like a lot more shade than suits them further north. When planted in shade they may need no water, whereas in a sunny spot they die without it. The only way to discover these things is by trial and error, by keeping your eyes open for discoveries when you visit other people's gardens, and by maintaining a healthy skepticism to what you read in catalogues and books.

Once we develop the urge to learn for ourselves, we find ourselves growing plants that are not supposed to be hardy, "difficult" plants that die for our neighbors, and discovering gardening adventures we never knew existed.

CHAPTER 2

Landscaping

Whether you have just moved into a new house or feel the urge to make changes to your existing garden, you are about to undertake the fairly major task of designing a garden. The task seems particularly overwhelming if you have just moved into a house on an abandoned farm surrounded by large areas of absolutely nothing or surrounded by the few trees and shrubs that builders often install as "landscaping."

I think the general goal of garden design is to produce good "bones" and then clothe them with plants. The bones of a garden are its major, long-lived features, such as driveway, large trees, hedges, fences, paths, and buildings. If these are well arranged to begin with, the gardener's job becomes the pleasant one of planting the exuberant flowers and foliage that turn the place from a yard into a garden. If the bones are poorly designed or non-existent, even sophisticated planting will not show to best advantage and the gardener will be perpetually irritated by the garden's shortcomings.

It is no good thinking you can just sit down as soon as you move in, design the garden, and then carry out the design. You will change your mind about all kinds of garden features as time goes by. Lifestyles also change, and with them demands on the garden, as children, spouses, pets, jobs, money, and energy come and go. But here is a general plan of campaign that was once suggested to me and that seems to make sense.

•Find out what you have. Buildings and driveways are fairly obvious, but even in an ex-hayfield you will probably find other features on closer examination, including dry and boggy areas, sunny and shady spots. Parts of the property may have different soil from the rest, slight slopes will appear, or you may find a corner with some interesting wild flowers that could be preserved as a wild garden.

•Identify problems. Does the drive turn into a mud hole when it rains? Does foundation planting block the view from the house? Do you feel as if you're living in a goldfish bowl? Make a note of problems when you think of them and you'll remember to solve them when you plan—

or perhaps you will have to decide how to live with them. Our garden never looks tidy. Our old evergreen oaks are very beautiful but, unlike civilized trees, they drop their leaves for about six months every year. And even when they are not shedding leaves, they drop branches and Spanish moss whenever it rains. We refuse to prune them into well-behaved street trees because the dead branches support several species of woodpecker. So the lawn and drive are permanently littered with bits of trees. What sort of landscaping goes well with untidy trees?

Are there areas where the grass looks even more scruffy than elsewhere? There is probably a reason. We found that our gutters overflow, wiping out the grass underneath. We shall have to replace the grass under the gutters with ground cover that will hold the soil in place and can stand drought or deluge.

•Decide what you want and make an overall plan. It is amazing how many different types of garden you can cram into even a small space, so you have to make some decisions about what you want first, remembering that you can usually change your mind later.

Almost every garden includes a few basics: somewhere to park the car, somewhere to sit and enjoy the garden, plantings that enhance the appearance of the house, and a work area where you can make compost and keep garden tools. But beyond this, the choices are endless. Now is the time to let your imagination loose and to pencil in the wild area, bog garden, butterfly garden, swimming pool, and knot garden. It may be hard to imagine a formal fountain when what you see out of the window is a hayfield, but if you have always wanted one, include it in the design. The world's great gardens were all carved out of forest or farmland and they too must have been pretty hard to imagine when they were merely lists and sketches on paper.

•Start work on one part of the project and go back and revise the master plan as you go. Not that the order in which you do things really matters much; most of the things that you care about will get done eventually.

SOIL TYPE AND NATIVE VEGETATION

The soil and native vegetation determine what will be easy and what will be difficult in creating your dream garden. Just because you know what biome you live in, doesn't mean you know all about the natural vegetation. In our suburb, a pine forest on clay soil with poor drainage lies across the road from an oak forest on dry sand. Even if you are planning a roof garden, one location may be windy, dry, and sunny, while another nearby is shady, sheltered, and gets much more rain.

Dig holes in various parts of the garden to find out what type of soil you have and watch the holes after its rains to see how fast the water drains away. Make an inventory of trees and shrubs and, if you can, find out something about them—whether they are full-grown or juveniles, what their final size will be, whether they will soon need replacing or can be relied on for years. Don't feel bad if you cannot identify everything. Three years after moving into this garden, I know we have several species of oaks I but still cannot identify all of them. I await a visit from a botanist who will, I hope, enlighten me.

Nobody ever takes this advice; I certainly don't, but it is good advice so I repeat it anyway: when faced with a new garden, study and plan for at least a year before making major changes. If you plunge in without planning you will eventually find that you have made expensive mistakes such as planting a weeping willow where its roots invade a septic tank. You will find that your vegetable garden lies in deep shade until midsummer, or that you have planted desert shrubs in an area that turns to marsh when the snow melts. Even if you cannot bear to wait for a full year, perhaps you could avoid major construction projects until you have time to learn a little more about the site.

There are plenty of things you can usefully do while waiting. You can brighten up the front door with hanging baskets or beds of annuals. You can, and probably should, start a nursery for plants that you've brought from the old garden or acquired because you know you will want them somewhere. You can even crawl around weeding the lawn, something you may never feel like doing again.

Meanwhile, study the garden and the way it changes with the seasons. Make plans and see if they still look good as the seasons pass. Garden books always seem to advise drawing up scale plans on graph paper and if that is the way you like to work, why not? Or you can buy one of those computer programs that permits you to move plants around on the screen, see how large your trees and shrubs will be in 30 years and tricks of that kind.

I become more and more convinced that there is a lot to be said for taking photographs of your house and garden, preferably in black and white so that the outlines are simplified. Photographs are particularly good at revealing areas of muddle and confusion. I was amazed when I looked at a photograph of a cherished clump of lilies to see that the picture was marred by a confused background of road, fence, and scattered trees, which I had never noticed in the garden. It was photographs that convinced me I had to plant sheared hedges to cut off the driveway from the vegetable garden and provide a background for the mixed border. Unless you have a real artist's "eye," I think you will find photographs very useful at the design stage. Identify things you don't like, or bad shapes, and then use grease pencils or wax crayons to block in features you are considering.

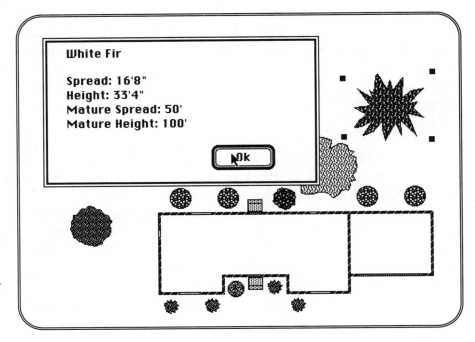

White Fir

Spread: 16'8"
Height: 33'4"
Mature Spread: 50'
Mature Height: 100'

Ok

Computer landscaping.
There are many types of programs and ways to use them. You may be able to list your existing major plants and find out roughly how large they will be in ten years' time, try out new plantings, or keep track of your landscaping as you go.

What to Remove and What to Keep

What do you like and what don't you like in the garden as it is? Are there major features that you'd like to get rid of, such as a lawn so steep it's difficult to mow or a view of your neighbor's back yard?

Do you enjoy entertaining outdoors or relaxing in the garden when old Casper's work is done? In that case you probably need a patio, terrace, or wooden deck as a dry stable surface for chairs and tables. You want the patio to be shaded in summer and sunny in winter. Perhaps you have the patio, but need to chop down a tree or plant a tree to provide the necessary sun and shade.

Problems with the existing landscape may be practical or aesthetic. Practical problems include things like overgrown planting that blocks the view from a window, and potential hazards, such as damp spots that are slippery to walk on or a large tree with branches overhanging the house. Hazardous situations may require major surgery such as taking down a tree or rerouting a path. Aesthetic problems are often the result of poor proportions or inappropriate plants: a large house surrounded by teeny weeny plants that reveal ugly architectural lines, or a desert landscape in a British suburban street. You will have to decide whether plants need to be removed or whether you can add plants that will solve the problem.

An early step should be to figure out drainage patterns. On many properties these are disastrous and you cannot imagine how the previous owners lived with water that drains straight into the basement or washes half the lawn away in a thunderstorm. In our garden, the driveway is built so that all the water that lands on it drains down a concrete path beside the house, across a flower bed (I use the term loosely), and onto the back lawn, which dumps fresh water and soil into a salt marsh, to the detriment of garden and salt marsh. For a year and more I couldn't really believe that this was happening since I knew the previous owner had worked on the drive only a few years before. But it is. The driveway should be cambered so that most of the rain that falls on it runs off into the lawn and shrubs that border it; and the concrete path and the flower bed are a bog garden, whether I like it or not. When I finally hauled all this on board, it caused some major changes in the Master Plan. Am I really going to dig up the concrete in that path? Or am I going to look for shallow-rooted bog plants that can grow in the mud on top of it?

PLANNING THE GARDEN

It is best to start by identifying your own particular needs. There is no point in falling in love with some garden pictured in a coffee table book that bears no relation to your life with teenagers, a large dog, and a few hours each week to devote to the garden.

Work Area

Lucky and rare is the gardener with a large enough work area. You need somewhere to keep your tools, which may eventually include not just trowels and watering cans, but sprayers, garden carts, lawn mowers, chain saws, and tractors. These can take up an awful lot of space, even evicting cars from the garage. (Then you need some swift landscaping to hide the cars in the driveway.) You need somewhere to store bags of wood chips that you bought while they were on sale, and all the paraphernalia for propagating plants: seeds, potting mix, flats, and pots. You need somewhere to make compost, preferably a space large enough for a cart to load and unload. If you are not the world's tidiest person, it is a joy to have a work area that is hidden from public view so that you can abandon tasks and return to them later without worrying that visitors will stumble over your mess.

Once you have lived with electrical outlets and water taps in the garden, it is hard to imagine how gardeners a few decades ago survived without these conveniences. If you are thinking of paving a driveway or building paths, consider whether you should run electric lines and water pipes underneath first and where they should go. Perhaps you might one day want a greenhouse, which will need water and electricity. How about lights and a fountain at the far end of the garden?

Where will you arrange flowers you have cut for the house? Perhaps it will have to be the kitchen sink, but wouldn't it be delightful to have a sink and shelves in the tool shed or garage where you could keep vases and chicken wire and create your creations without messing up the kitchen? If you grow vegetables, this might also be the place to chop off carrot leaves and wash potatoes before you bring them into the house. Perhaps the same area can be used to wash bird feeders and store bird food. The sink from this work area could drain into a bog garden or stream.

Traffic Patterns

Traffic patterns in the garden involve everything from car parking to making gateways wide enough for carts. Safety first: when you drive out into the street, do trees and shrubs block your view of the traffic? If so, they must go or be pruned back. It is much safer to drive forward into the street than to back out into traffic. If cars drive onto your property, can they turn around to go out forward? A turning area takes little space; or perhaps you could make a garden feature of a drive-through driveway that comes to the front door and back to the road again.

People walk through gardens, frequently where you wish they wouldn't. Children take short cuts through shrubbery and across lawns when walking home from school. When carrying heavy loads from car to kitchen, most people take the shortest path even if it means stepping through flower beds and over hedges. "Keep off the grass" notices do not work, as keepers of public lawns and parks have known for a long time. Some lawn grasses can take a lot of foot traffic. With others, you can see beaten paths of dead grass where one person walks twice a week.

First find where people actually walk and decide whether or not you can live with these traffic patterns. If you cannot, you must force people to walk somewhere else. This takes a bit of doing because children, in particular, are not easily deterred by hedges and slopes, although fences and walls will work. Adults are better behaved and you can route them around things by visual obstructions such as berms (humps planted with grass or shrubs) or low hedges.

When you've decided where the foot traffic goes, plan to build paths in areas where feet may damage the lawn or other plantings. Garden paths are nearly always too narrow. How many times have you walked along a path or battled to a front door, ducking wet branches and trying not to step on plants, in no position to enjoy or even look at the garden? You'll find paths that are irritatingly narrow even in large well-known gardens that should know better. Sometimes this is a function of time. A path that was once wide enough has been narrowed by plants growing in from either side. It should be rebuilt, or at least weeded. A path should be at least four feet wide to take a wheelbarrow and six feet wide for two people to stroll along it side by side.

Things to Hide

Decide what you would like to hide from view by examining your property from behind every window and from outdoor areas such as the lawn and patio. If you're lucky, you'll have nothing to hide but an ugly view, the tool shed, and cars. More likely, you would like to hide your husband's collection of old windows and the boat your daughter will sell when someone offers her enough money for it, or the tricycles, fire engines, and carts that come with small children. Make a few measurements or dust off your trigonometry to calculate what height of barrier you'll need to block out particular views.

The farther away a barrier, the taller it has to be to block a view. A hedge at the boundary of your garden might have to be 15 feet tall before it would block a view of the neighbor's house from your living room. Consider planting a cherry tree outside your living room window instead. This might give you a view of cherry blossoms instead of neighbors almost as soon as you plant it. A fence even six feet high at one side of the patio where you sunbathe would give you plenty of privacy while a hedge grows to full size.

Consider what you want to hide from neighbors and from the street, which probably includes you in not-very-many clothes on a summer day weeding the shrub border. Americans are finally recovering from the dicta of nineteenth century midwestern designers that it is unpatriotic to block the view of your house from the street or the house next door. Under this dogma, the herb gardens, parterres, and cottage gardens of colonial houses were replaced by "front yards" containing nothing but lawn and trees. The very word "garden" came to mean "vegetable garden." Everything else on the property was merely "landscaping" for the general public. This was vandalism on a par with Humphrey Repton and 'Capability' Brown's eighteenth century vision of British gardens as cow pastures sprinkled with trees and streams. Britain has had longer to recover; the Englishman's home is once again his castle and this includes, if he wants them, castle walls along the boundary lines so that nobody can report on what he gets up to in his swimming pool.

The moral is that fashion in garden design can cause just as much personal discomfort as fashion in clothes. We don't realize that we are following fashion when we design our houses and gardens, but we cannot help being products of our time. There is less excuse for us than for our ancestors if we jump thoughtlessly on the latest bandwagon. We have access, as they did not, to books and films that show us gardens from every country in the world for the past thousand years and more. These include enough ideas so that we need never run short of ways to design the garden around our own individual lives and our own individual desires. Don't be a garden sheep!

Things to Enhance

Meanwhile, back at the ranch, somewhere on your property there is probably a view that is worth framing, especially if you can visually remove the junk that surrounds it. Suppose you are on a hill with a view of town or fields in the distance that is spoiled by a road and telephone lines in the foreground. You can probably design your garden so as to obscure the road and lines while keeping the distant view.

Look long and hard at any trees on neighboring property. If the view from your terrace includes a path that disappears in the direction of those trees, your garden can be made to feel much larger than it really is. Or perhaps the view is unabashedly urban and you should chop down an old hedge and design the garden with white, scented flowers and patio lighting so that you can sit out and enjoy the city lights in the evening.

PRINCIPLES OF DESIGN

You don't have to reinvent the wheel when designing a garden. Over the centuries, certain principles of garden design have evolved. There is little obvious similarity between Versailles and a Japanese temple garden, but if you think about all the gardens you find attractive, you will find they have certain things in common. It's worth asking *why* you find a particular garden appealing or unappealing, in a photograph or in the flesh. This is one of the best ways to learn about your own taste.

•**Invitations for the eye.** Some gardens are nothing but vistas, static pictures designed to be viewed from a distance. Many American properties consist of merely front and back vistas: a view of the house and surrounding plants, designed to be seen from the road, and a back garden designed to be viewed from the house or patio. This is the least complex type of garden design, which does not mean it is easy. Landscapers have diverted rivers and built mountains to create the pictures they were after, often to achieve effects that the viewer does not realize are not natural. A botanist in Ontario, who spent ten years lovingly recreating a tallgrass prairie behind his house was slightly stunned when an ignorant visitor remarked, "I see you haven't landscaped the back yard yet."

I think a garden should invite you to walk through it, to view it from different angles, to get close to some plants so that you can smell them or admire their texture, to stand back from other areas so that you can appreciate particular garden pictures from a distance. The building blocks of garden invitations are paths that lead the eye, visual barriers that stop the eye, and focal points that attract the eye.

If your living room looks out across a lawn surrounded by shrubs to a statue at the far side, the lawn is the visual path, the shrubs are the barriers that stop the eye at the edges of the path, and the statue is the focal point. Without the statue, this would be a boring picture, however perfect the lawn or well-tended the shrubs.

Let us start with the front of the house which is often poorly landscaped, not to mention anonymous since many people never check to see whether the number of the house or other identification is visible from a car in the street even during the day, let alone at night. But supposing you have overcome this initial hurdle and people can find your house and see where they are supposed to park, how do you assure that they can find and reach the front door (another surprisingly difficult task at many houses)?

You want to lead people straight to the front door from wherever they step out of their cars or enter your front garden. Sometimes the front door is not even visible from where you park the car, especially in houses that have driveways at the side. From the car park, you want a wide path to the front door, with visual barriers on both sides and a focal point at the end. The focal point says, visually, "this is where you're going." It might be a large pot of flowers by the front door. The visual barriers edging the path don't have to be tall hedges because visitors are, presumably, trying to reach the door and not planning to stroll around the rest of the garden first. These visual barriers are merely designed to draw attention along the path to the focal point at the end of it. Straight front paths lined by matching low hedges of lavender or box are a classic way of achieving this effect. Or you can copy Monet's design at Giverny and have a wide path with rose arches overhead and banks of flowers on either side. Or you can stop messing around with plants and make the path overwhelmingly wide, sweeping up to the front door. This is how the visitor is led to stately homes where the architecture is spectacular and designed to be viewed from a distance.

When it comes to the view from the house, paths and visual blocks should invite the viewer to step out into the garden and stroll along a path. If you have a long narrow back garden with a lawn down the middle, use barriers so that the lawn looks as if it disappears round a corner. A large shrub that sticks out from one side of the garden hides the lawn beyond it and invites the visitor to walk round the shrub and explore the area beyond.

• **Surprise.** In a well-designed garden, you cannot see everything at once. We want garden visitors to feel a bit like children unwrapping presents: pleasurable anticipation followed by surprised delight. So the path that tempts the viewer to walk should not end at the compost pile or a fence. Ideally, the path should not end at all. It should lead through a series of garden areas and bring you back to your starting point without requiring you to retrace your steps. The path might go right round the house, or it might go down one side of the garden, round something, and back the other side. A tiny town garden might have a pool in the middle that you can walk around before coming back to the house.

As you walk, you should stumble upon sights that surprise and delight. Beyond the tall shrub, you are rewarded by a view that was hidden from the house. This might be a view over the countryside, a view of the vegetable garden or wild garden, a pond, or a grassy path leading to a garden seat. Each new vista as it opens up should contain a focal point that stops the eye and makes the visitor pause and contemplate the scene.

• **Focal points with backgrounds.** Anything that stands out from its surroundings sufficiently clearly can act as a focal point. And because it needs to stand out in a garden, the focal point is often not a plant. It may be a bench, a pond, a statue, sundial, bird bath, or fountain. For that matter, it can be a pink flamingo, a concrete gnome, or a tire painted red and filled with marigolds.

Focal points look best against simple backgrounds such as walls and hedges. Perhaps it is also true that artificial things like statues look best against backgrounds of plants and plants look best against artificial backgrounds. For visual impact it is hard to beat a few red lilies against a pink stucco wall in the Nevada sun or a gray stone bench against a clipped yew hedge in a British park. The more you can isolate your focal point from its surroundings, the greater its effect. A pot of geraniums packs a lot of punch

UNDERSTANDING THE ENVIRONMENT

WATER: WHAT GOES UP COMES DOWN

Have you even wondered how come, if we are constantly adding pollutants to all the water on earth, there is any clean water left at all? The answer is that water is continuously purified in a giant solar still: the water cycle, powered by the sun's energy.

Molecules of water vapor, the gas that evaporates into the air, are pure water and nothing else, no matter how polluted the river or ocean from which the water evaporates. As water vapor in the air rises, it eventually reaches altitudes so cold that it condenses on dust particles, forming liquid water or ice, which make up clouds. When the water is liquid, gases and other substances dissolve in it as it travels through the atmosphere, so that rain and snow are not pure water but dilute solutions of various chemicals. When conditions are right, the contents of clouds fall to earth again as rain or snow, completing the water cycle.

The water cycle is driven by the sun's heat, which causes water to evaporate. Some of the water evaporates from plants, which give off water when they exchange gases with the air, but most of it comes from the ocean, which covers 70% of the earth's surface. About 10% of the water evaporated from the oceans each year blows inland and eventually descends on the land as rain or snow. About the same amount runs from the land back into the oceans. This volume makes up our "water income," the recycling supply of purified water upon which life depends.

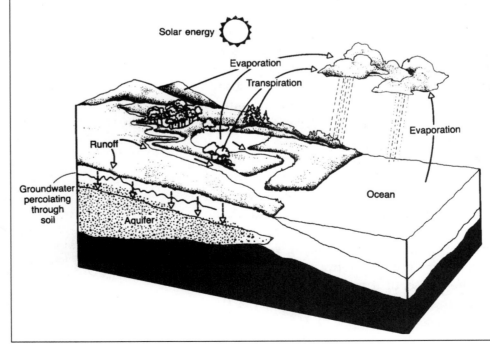

standing by itself in the middle of a lawn, very little when it stands at the edge of a flower bed.

Almost everything in a garden looks better if it is seen against a background that isolates it visually. A flower bed that looks stunning against the background of a lawn or wall has little impact if you look across it at parked cars or even driveway and house.

• **Balancing simplicity and complexity.** This is the most difficult balancing act in gardening, or in designing anything for that matter. If you make things too simple, they are boring; if you make them too complex, they are ugly. You want your garden to contain many different textures, because this adds interest. But if you have paths of concrete, brick, and paving stones as well as gravel around a house made of wood, what you've got is a mess. The same applies to plants.

In this context, it is worth pondering some of the principles that give good Japanese gardens a sense of harmony. The first of these is that a garden should be a celebration of the natural landscape. This is the reason a desert garden in a British suburb looks odd. If you live in the arid west, invite the rocks, dry water courses and scattered plants of the desert into your garden. When you build a pool, let it reflect the brown water of the streams and marshes in your area rather then the blue waters of the Caribbean. Avoid incongruity by using local materials. If you live on a sand bank, don't import flagstone for your garden paths. Don't even fight the prevailing style of your suburban street. If the style is clapboard houses and wooden fences, pink stucco with brick walls is going to look out of place.

Since you are reading this book, you probably have, or are planning, a pretty complex garden containing wild areas, native flowers, shrubs to attract wildlife, water, and many species of plants,

Visual invitiations.
This is a view from a living room, across a patio, through an arch, and onto a lawn surrounded by plants. The lawn continues beyond the shrubs you can see. The view invites you to stroll out onto the lawn and see where the lawn goes. The design is also clever in that you cannot tell from this view how large the garden is. In fact, it is a small town garden, but it might be any size.

Focal points. A bench (above) makes an attractive focal point in a garden, inviting the viewer to rest and enjoy the view. (Make sure the view from the bench is not of the neighboring junkyard.) You can give the bench added importance and a formal touch (below), by adding paving underneath and vertical accent plants on each side (perhaps 'Skyrocket' junipers).

so your problem is more likely to be trying to tie the design together than overcoming too simple a landscape. Oddly enough, the best design for a bird-lover's naturalistic garden may be a severely formal design that ties the multitude of different plantings together.

FORMAL AND INFORMAL

Josephine Nuese suggested that tidy people should have informal gardens and untidy people should have formal gardens. The theory is that tidy people would be driven to drink by a branch out of place in a formal garden but accept this as a necessary part of an informal

Paths should suit their environments. This path through a woodland garden should be made of nothing more formal than wood chips or sand. It would look most peculiar if it were a straight line of concrete or brick.

design, whereas an untidy person needs the discipline of formal design if the garden is not to become a shambles. After much musing, I have come to the conclusion that she was right. Of course there are always the untidy people who think it is fine if the garden becomes a visual mess, but these people don't need the assistance of this chapter in designing their gardens.

When we think of formal gardens, we think of sheared hedges on either side of straight paths, trees lined up in rows like soldiers on parade, square or oblong ponds, statues, and hedges of box. This style of gardening almost disappeared when the fashion for "natural" or "landscape" gardens swept Europe at the end of the eigh-

teenth century and North America in the nineteenth.

Landscapers of today urge us to create informal gardens by leaving shrubs unpruned and avoiding straight lines in paths, edgings, and hedges. A little thought, however, convinces that there is nothing informal about such a garden. Le Nôtre, the French landscape architect who designed the gardens at Versailles and the park of St. Cloud, would have recognized modern gardens as formal by their lawns alone (which he would have called *tapis verts*, green carpets). Lawns mowed with machines and with edges trimmed to uncompromising right angles are as formal as formal can be. And they look incongruous beside the studied "informality" of flower beds edged in carefully irregular curves and kidney-shaped garden ponds.

There is a lot to be said for letting the bones of our gardens be formal and letting the plants provide the informality. People with small gardens usually know this already. Town gardens tend to consist of circular and rectangular beds, hedges, ponds, and paths, with plants tumbling over the edges to provide a balanced and harmonious picture. So why is it that the minute we move to the suburbs we start putting wiggly edges on our flower beds and failing to prune our hedges?

GARDEN ROOMS

Supposing you are convinced by all of this, how does one go about imposing formality on a design, especially when faced with an odd-shaped garden and house, several mature trees, chain link fence on one side and a brick wall on the other?

You can start by thinking of the garden as a series of "rooms," rather like an extension of the house. Most gardens start with at least two rooms: front and back. You are probably planning to add additional areas such as a wild garden, vegetable garden, work area, flower bed with a path beside it, bog garden, and shrubbery. Each of these can be considered a separate room. The design challenge is to make each room an appealing one, with attractive walls, floor, and ceiling.

The ceiling of the room is usually the sky (although in an arbor it might be wood slats and grape leaves). Is the view of the sky messed up by television antennae which you might be able to disguise with a suitable tree? Would the ceiling of the room be better if it were partly covered by foliage, and do surrounding plants and structures give the ceiling a pleasing shape? The finest garden rooms have "walls," which you can see through only where the designer chooses to let you. And the designer chooses that the entrances to the room, through which you can look, frame attractive sights. The rest of the room consists of solid, though decorated, walls.

Another Japanese principle is useful here, which is that everything should have, or should appear to have, a reason, even if the reason is a fairly trivial one. A rose arch isolated in the middle of a lawn looks wrong; a rose arch shading the front door looks right. An irregularly shaped pond looks right on a hillside, where it conforms to the contours of the hill, but it looks all wrong in the middle of a flat lawn, where water would naturally form a circular puddle. If you really want a wiggle in the edge of a lawn or pond, plant a shrub in the wiggle to give the illusion that the lawn or pond has been forced to flow around the shrub. There are plenty of other good reasons for curves. When you build a hedge alongside a curving driveway, it would look most unnatural if the hedge didn't follow the same curve as the drive.

When you do build curves into the design, to take the lawn around a tree, to take a path down a slope or around a sundial, why not make the curves symmetrical? The bed around a tree can be circular, the sundial in a circle in the middle of the path. Circles and ovals are good simple shapes and avoid the irrationality of irregular curves. Symmetry is formal. If you've decided to plant trees along the drive, plant them in lines both sides of the drive and equally spaced, even if they are not all of the same species. If you've edged one bed with brick, don't edge the next bed with cement blocks; and build paths and patio from brick as well.

Symmetry. On the left, an irregular pool, bordered by odd-shaped stones, such as may be found in many a suburban lawn. It is supposed to look natural but it doesn't. Why not make the pool symmetrical, like the one on the right, creating an attractive work of art instead of a poor imitation of nature?

There's no need to be obsessive about formality. It's just worth bearing in mind. When you build a path, consider a straight one. When you want a background for a flower bed or a windbreak for the vegetable garden, consider a clipped hedge. However formal the garden you create, it is going to get more informal with time. Entropy is at work ensuring that disorder increases. Bricks fall out of walls, the bed round the tree turns from a perfect circle to an imperfect oval, and the path slides down the hill.

Naming Garden Areas

Vita Sackeville-West believed in choosing romantic names for parts of the garden. You have to call borders and garden rooms something, and "the rondel" certainly sounds better than "the bed behind the garage." But it is not always easy to come up with good names. Simone van Stolk christened one side of our driveway "Hydrangea Allée" because it is lined by hydrangeas, and that is the best name we have so far. I tend to refer to areas by the name of some prominent plant, but "the ardisia bed" is not very helpful when talking to members of the family who wouldn't know an ardisia if it jumped out and bit them. I can only hope that you are better at choosing names than I am.

Slopes

If your property is as flat as a pancake, you could consider building berms or sinking ponds to vary the terrain a little. But this is not usually necessary for visual interest because as your plants grow up they will introduce many differences of height into the picture.

A much more common problem is slopes that are too steep for comfort. Major hills and hollows repay careful thought. Perhaps you have a hole where the basement of a barn or a swimming pool once stood. This might make a delightful sunken garden. A steep rocky hillside might be made into a series of graceful terraces linked by steps. Look for inspiration in the surrounding countryside and in books before ordering a bulldozer to flatten out your humps and hollows.

Permanent or Temporary?

Great gardeners look to the future. They plant yew hedges that will reach their full beauty when the gardener is long gone. They plant oaks that will be landmarks in 200 years time. But as well as making our marks on posterity, many of us live much of our lives in gardens that are ours only until the next transfer or until we can afford something better. We have inherited someone else's idea of a garden and we want rapid fixes to the obvious problems.

The solution, I think, is to plant both for the here and now and for the future. Plant the baby oak or maple that will one day shade the terrace, and the yew or hemlock hedge that will take many years to reach full beauty. But also build a cheap fence for privacy and plant a poplar, locust, or willow that will produce shade within a year or two. The idea is that in about ten year's time, you can cut down the willows, get rid of the rotting fence, and have the nucleus of a permanent landscape. If you plant fast-growing things, however, you must be prepared to prune and eventually to remove them, painful though this will probably be when the time comes. Fast-growing trees tend to have weak wood and one day your overgrown poplar will drop a huge limb on the roof and cost you large sums for repairs. Your once-sunny garden will be dank and gloomy from the shade of a big untidy tree and you will be fighting your way to the front door through a large wet hydrangea that cuts off all the light from the dining room window. Stroll down any established suburban street with a critical eye and you will see lots of places where planting would improve the landscape, but you will also see many places where removing overgrown shrubs and trees would

HOW ONE SUBURBAN GARDEN ACQUIRED GARDEN ROOMS

These diagrams show the conversion of a one-third acre garden from the wide open spaces of the usual American suburb to a series of garden rooms.

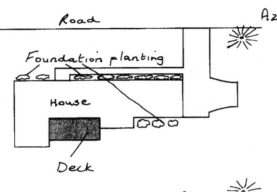

1

1. The builders left the house with foundation planting, a few juvenile pines around the edges, and a wooden deck outside the living room windows.

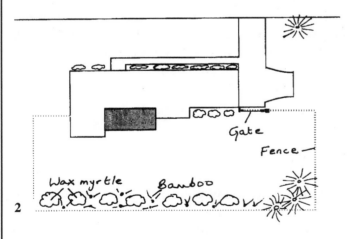

2

2. The first owners had dogs and young children, so they fenced the back yard. Then construction started in the area behind the house. The owners planted fast-growing wax myrtles and bamboos to hide the building site.

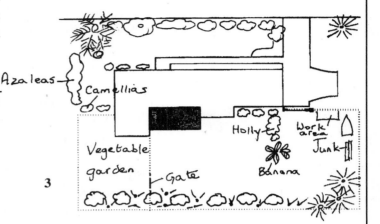

3

3. The next owners had pets and teenagers. They planted a vegetable garden behind the master bedroom and found they had to build a dog fence to keep the puppy from digging up the vegetables.

The family moved a collection of beams, windows, boats, and bicycles into a corner of the garden and the gardener planted a screen of banana and holly to hide the horrible mess from the house. This "room" of the garden became the work area and out of bounds to visitors.

The gardener wanted privacy when she puttered in the front garden, so she moved some of the overgrown foundation plants out to the street and added some trees and shrubs. Then she installed shrubs and a flower border to the south of the front lawn to partly hide the cars that were always parked in the driveway because the garage was full of woodwork and gardening tools. The neighbor to the north got into the act by installing some large azaleas along the boundary.

Now the front garden was fully enclosed and the gardener further separated the side garden to the north of the house by planting shrubs on either side of the entrance to this space and moving her camellias to this partly shaded area.

The next owners were also gardeners, and have added their touch by enlarging the small arbor over the patio into a large arbor covered with climbing roses, creating a shady area where their collection of house plants spends the summer.

open up views or provide air and space for a desirable plant that is now choking in the jungle.

THE CASE FOR LESS LAWN

We are often told that American lawns consume more time and money than any other part of the home landscape. This pseudo-statistic is misleading, however, because many homes are surrounded by nothing but lawn and shrubs so that caring for the lawn is the only garden task for the owner. Getting rid of part of your lawn is not going to save you time and money if you replace it by a high-maintenance flower garden. If your garden contains any lawn to mow, reducing that area is going to save maintenance time only if you replace it with something, such as a shrubbery or wild garden, that is easier to look after.

In much of the United States, water shortages provide a compelling reason for getting rid of as much lawn as possible. It is impossible to keep *tapis verts* looking as they should without watering the lawn during the frequent dry spells of a hot summer. In many areas, you are rewarded with a tax cut if you replace lawn by plants that do not need watering. This may be the incentive you need to create a wild garden. Gardeners in western and midwestern areas sometimes just stop watering parts of the lawn. The lawn grass dies and native grasses and wild flowers take over the area. In wetter parts of the world, however, a jungle rapidly develops if you just abandon part of the garden. This is desirable if you are trying to increase the habitat for wildlife but it may look terrible. Perhaps you can plant trees or shrubs that hide the wild area from the more formal part of the garden. Or perhaps the answer is to create a rough meadow, which needs mowing only twice a year and is never watered. More on wild gardens in later chapters.

GARDEN STRUCTURES

To people who want to spend their limited gardening time growing plants, it is irritating to realize that building things is sometimes more worth doing. Weeding the vegetable garden just needs to be done again next week. A well-built path gives satisfaction forever.

Unfortunately, most worthwhile garden structures are expensive. A brick or stone wall, which is one of the loveliest features a garden can have, is a big investment even if you have the skill to build it yourself. You can make the expense feel less, however, if you calculate how much money and time you would have to spend on a hedge or shrubbery to produce the same visual barrier. Even if you cannot afford a wall, you are almost certainly going to have to build a patio or terrace and some paths if they don't already exist.

A little ingenuity can sometimes substitute for cash. Materials can often be recycled. If you live in an area with lots of brick, you may be able to scrounge old bricks from structures that are being demolished. Builders throw away lots of wood and you may be able to beg some from a building site. Then what about the waste you generate yourself? If you are forced to take down a tree or even some branches, perhaps the wood can be used for a rustic arbor or rose arch.

You have probably seen attractive paths made of concrete slabs or stones set into the lawn with lawn between them. Before you leap into this apparently cheap solution to the path problem, consider your lawn grass. If the grass spreads rapidly, the stones will be overgrown with grass in no time and it would be much cheaper in the long run to build a solid path which you can easily edge.

If you live in a sandy area, you may be able to create paths by merely removing lawn or weeds to reveal the sand underneath. A dirt path edged with wood can be very attractive. If drainage is a problem, you might fill the path with wood chips for a dry surface. It may take a long time to fill a path with chipped Christmas trees, but it can be done.

In a woodland garden, fallen or pruned tree branches make a good edging for an informal path. Ferns, hostas, and trilliums that you plant in the woodland will droop attractively over the branches and the edging serves several useful functions. If you have old trees that often lose limbs, using them for edging permits you to dispose of rotting branches without accumulating a huge pile of them. And decaying wood is some of the best wildlife habitat there is. Frogs and toads will hibernate under it and woodpeckers will love the insects that live there. Plants may also arrive as spores and seeds and start growing, because leaves and decomposing wood provide perfect soil for woodland ferns and other plants.

Benches make attractive garden features but they don't need to be of teak, and perhaps they shouldn't be. Although most reputable garden suppliers now guarantee that their teak is not cut from natural tropical forest but grown in plantations, somebody chopped down a tropical forest to make room for the plantation. You can build your own simple garden benches from local lumber and even from your own wood. A plank of treated lumber set on two large logs makes an attractive seat in a rustic part of the garden.

On a hillside, a wooden deck cantilevered out from the house may be the answer to the seating problem. But think twice before you build a sitting area from which you need a staircase to reach the garden. Most gardeners want to be in the garden rather than looking out over it and feel more comfortable with a terrace at ground level from which they get a close view of their plants. You can reduce the feeling of isolation on a deck by building containers into the edge of the deck. These can be beautiful, but they take a lot of maintenance and you are still not in contact with the garden proper.

PLANTS THAT CHANGED HISTORY

Many plants have changed the course of history, a thought that adds a glamorous glow to some of the plants we grow. The Americas were discovered by Europeans as a byproduct of their search for pepper, valued with other Asian spices for its ability to mask the flavor of salted meat, stinking fish, and boring vegetables. A prosperous trade in spices once flourished between Europe and Asia. But by 1480, the Turks had blocked the overland trade route. In reaction, Italian, Portuguese, and Spanish explorers sailed west or south in their attempt to reach the East, and that was when they found the New World.

The discovery of a plant that controlled malaria had even more dramatic effects. Carried from one person to another by blood-sucking female mosquitoes, malaria was endemic in southern Europe, Asia, and northern Africa during the Middle Ages. European travelers took it all over the world. Thousands died of it during the settlement of the United States. Even in this century, ten million cases were reported during an epidemic in the Soviet Union in the 1920s and more than two million people die from it each year.

What is still the only partly effective treatment for malaria was discovered in Peru in the seventeenth century when the Countess of Cinchon recovered from malaria after drinking tea made from bark of the Cinchona tree. Peruvians had recommended this to Jesuit missionaries as a cure for fever. The bark was eventually imported to Europe, but many Protestants, such as English leader Oliver Cromwell, distrusted the Jesuits, refused their drug, and died of malaria.

West African and some southern European populations had evolved sickle cell hemoglobin, which affords some protection from malaria. Genetic resistance to malaria was a major reason west Africans were prized as slaves in the southern United States and the Caribbean, before quinine was widely available.

Tonic water is quinine dissolved in carbonated, sweetened water. Few who enjoy gin and tonic realize that the drink was invented to make their daily dose of bitter quinine palatable to Northerners living in malarial areas. Quinine permitted northern Europeans, who had no natural defenses against the disease, to establish vast empires in tropical areas more ably defended by malaria than by any human agency. It also permitted

CONTAINER PLANTS

There are lots of good reasons for growing plants in containers. Many town gardens are completely paved and all the plants are in tubs and window boxes. A container raises and emphasizes a plant, which may be just what you need for a focal point in the garden. I once lived with a puppy who dug up everything planted in the ground. Window boxes were the only way to have any flowers at all until we got her trained. But there are also many disadvantages to container gardening. Plants in containers are more susceptible to cold in winter than plants set in the ground because their roots get colder. But I think the worst problem is that most containers are so small that they need watering almost constantly. An English couple with a wonderful garden in the ground also had dozens of plants in containers, which they said needed water up to three times a day! These people could hardly go out to lunch, let alone take a trip. If you do use containers, make them as large as possible, and use them for drought-tolerant plants.

When planting containers, try out water-absorbing polymers. These really do reduce the need to water and they are cheap. Obey the instructions to the letter or you will find polymer oozing out of the container and all over the countryside. The best technique seems to be to put about one-third of the potting mix into the container untreated and then mix the hydrated polymer thoroughly with the next third. Then plant in the top third. That way the polymer is not too near the top of the container although the plant roots can reach it easily. Then water as you normally do but much less often: highly recommended.

Europeans to move about 20 million Indians and Chinese from their homes to tropical areas where they would have died without quinine. The European empires of the nineteenth century in Africa, Madagascar, Malaysia, and Sri Lanka were based on plantations worked by the cheap labor of these immigrants, many of whom became the ancestors of large modern populations in these areas.

Huge new industries were based on these population movements: sugar in the Indian Ocean and the Caribbean, tin and rubber in Malaysia, and tea in India and Sri Lanka were all made possible by quinine. The drug also probably permitted the Allies to win World War II in the Pacific. During that war, 25 million people in the Allied armed forces traveled to areas where malaria was epidemic, areas where many of them would not have survived without quinine.

Extracting quinine from a forest tree was expensive until plantations were established in other countries with seed stolen from the Peruvian Indians, who understood its value. Most quinine is still extracted from Cinchona bark. The natural product is cheaper and pleasanter tasting than the synthetic variety and remains one of the world's most important drugs. The malaria parasite has so far defeated all attempts to produce a vaccine against it and quinine remains the most effective treatment, although many varieties of the parasite are resistant to it.

If one tree affected world history in these ways, no wonder scientists sure that in destroying unexplored tropical forest, we are depriving ourselves of valuable plants. Closer to home, American loggers under the control of the U.S. Forest Service are still burning that byproduct of clear-cutting old

Cinchona: a branch of *Cinchona officinalis* with flowers and fruit.

growth forests, the Pacific yew, source of taxol, the most important cancer-fighting drug discovered in many years, whose production is limited by the shortage of yew trees.

WATER AND DRAINAGE

Water for wildlife is a vital part of any environmental garden. At many times of year, animals are more likely to be short of water than they are of food. If you are not yet ready to build ponds and streams, rig up a simple bird bath with water dripping into it to attract birds. The bath itself can be any shallow dish with a rim to perch on. Set it off the ground to give a little protection from prowling cats and beside a largish shrub in which frightened birds can hide and in which you can hide the drip system. This you create by taking a plastic container, such as a large soft drink bottle, filling it with water and poking a small hole in it with a needle. If the drip is slow enough (about a drop a minute), the bottle will not need refilling for days. Suspend the bottle above the bath and use your ingenuity to hide it—or convince your-

self that it is an attractive focal point in the garden.

Draw up a wish list of water features you would like to see on your property: perhaps a bird bath, a decorative fountain, a pond for fish and water lilies, and a bog garden. Each of these can be very small. With a bit of ingenuity, you can fit the whole lot into a tiny town garden. Since you don't want dozens of different plumbing projects, try to run water from one feature into the next. Perhaps your fountain could be a stone lion's head attached to a wall, from which a little spout of water falls into a shallow bowl to act as a bird bath. The overflow from the bird bath might trickle down over rocks between ferns and irises and other water lovers into a little pond in the sun. Here fish may hide under the water lilies. The overflow from the pond might trickle through a tiny acid bog designed for carnivorous plants and natives of peat bogs. Finally, any remaining trickle of water could be absorbed in a low corner of the garden made exotic by the gorgeous leaves of gunneras or bananas.

Before installing any water features, consider the natural drainage patterns on your property and see whether you can use the rain that falls on it to better effect. Where does water from the roof go? Could you lay a drainage pipe from a gutter to the bog garden? If water is really short in your area, consider installing an underground tank to collect rainwater from the roof. Add a small pump and you may have enough water for all your garden needs.

Muddy paths make the garden less appealing in wet weather and few plants can survive for long with their roots in water. Unless you want to grow nothing but water cress, your vegetable garden has to be well drained, and most flowers and shrubs also need reasonable drainage. So if there are many damp areas on your property after it rains, you might as well bite the bullet and install drainage tile, leading the water down to what will eventually be a pond or bog garden.

LANDSCAPING TO SAVE ENERGY

Unless you are rich enough not to worry about energy bills, it makes sense to design your landscape so as to keep the house warmer in winter and, unless you live in a very chilly part of the world, cooler in summer. The main things you can control are wind speed and shade.

Windbreaks

Winter winds can add enormously to heating bills and a windbreak will permit you to grow many plants that cannot stand to be buffeted by the wind. Trees and shrubs are better windbreaks than walls and fences because they don't completely cut off the wind, they merely slow it down. Wind speed drops dramatically in the lee of a solid windbreak so that snow collects in a drift on the leeward side of an exposed fence or house. Trees or shrubs, on the other hand, slow down the wind and may prevent the snowdrift from forming at all.

You will also want to plant trees and shrubs between road and house to cut down noise and reduce air pollution. Perhaps these can be part of the windbreak. You don't need tall trees for noise control. Shrubs and small trees are best because they create a barrier that deflects sound at human height.

Temperature Control

Trees are efficient air conditioners. The air temperature under a tree on a hot day is often more than 15 °F cooler than elsewhere. This is not just the effect of shade, as you can prove to yourself by standing in the cool shade of a tree and the less-cool shade of a porch or walkway on the same hot day. It is the effect of evaporation. For a plant to make food by photosynthesis, it must let water evaporate through pores in its leaves. A large tree may transpire tons of water on a hot day, pulling the water up from its roots to evaporate from its leaves. Water absorbs heat when it evaporates (which is why the human body sweats when it overheats).

The ideal tree for house-cooling purposes is one that shades the house. But this is not easy to achieve because the sun is so high overhead in midsummer that branches have to stretch right over the house to shade it. (It is much easier to plant a tree that casts shade on a house in winter when you don't want it.) If your house is low to the ground, by all means plant trees with spreading branches that will eventually shade the roof. You don't want anything with brittle branches or you'll spend your life worrying that a branch is going to come through the roof.

More practical than completely covering the house with tree is shading particular hot spots. Of course you need shade over the deck or patio if you like to sit there in summer. (But not over the swimming pool where leaves will fall into the water.) All hard surfaces near the house absorb heat and warm the house in summer. Shade as many of them as you can.

The west side of a house is often uncomfortable as the sun sinks on a summer's day. Does the dining room window face west so that evening sun makes the room intolerable? Quite a small tree near the window might solve the problem. How about people waiting for you to answer the door? Do they have shade to stand in while you turn off the pots boiling over in the kitchen? Do you have an outdoor heat pump that sits in full sun? Save on your energy bills by shading it with trees and shrubs. Vines growing up a house wall or a tree espaliered against the wall will also insulate the house and save on heating and cooling. By the same token, heavy vegetation to the north of a house where there is little sun can trap damp air near the house, rotting wood and making paths slippery.

COLOR SCHEMES

Color is not something that most people take into account when starting a garden and this is surprising since we are highly visual animals. Only birds and our ape and monkey relatives have color vision as good as ours. But if you consider the color schemes in gardens in your neighborhood, you will probably find them very dull at most times of year.

The main problem is probably the gap between vision and execution. When bulbs flower in spring, you realize that white daffodils would look better than purple and white fritillaries against the red brick of the front path. By the time bulb-planting time arrives, you have forgotten this bright idea as well as where the fritillaries are. Which leads us to the necessity of keeping a garden notebook if the garden is ever to live up to expectations. Then, when you view your midsummer border, you note "move all coreopsis in the holly border to the front near the coneflowers" and remember to do it in the autumn—if you remember to look at your notebook before renovating the border. And even if you do, you tend to come across cryptic remarks such as "plant something white by the Lady Banks rose" and wonder what you meant by that.

If your garden has enough in the way of background, you may be able to get away without worrying about color schemes at all. A neutral-colored house, stone walls, or yew hedges provide enough background to support the riot of colors found in a cottage garden. If you have not yet built or grown your backgrounds, you are often advised to restrict the garden to a simple color scheme until you learn what goes with what. Perhaps this is good advice if you are planting flowering shrubs, but is not really practical with flowers, since the first thing you need to do in a new garden is to find how things grow. You want to know if chrysanthemums, crinums, and hundreds of other things do well in your garden, whether they crowd out their neighbors or are consumed by insects. If they don't do well in the sun, you move them to see if they prefer shade. You tear the mistakes out and replace them with plants you hope will do better. While you are in this experimental stage, you might as well forget about harmonious color schemes, at least in the flower bed. A few years down the road, you will start to dislike the muddle and work on the color scheme.

A garden should provide refreshment from daily life so a first step might be to decide the dominant color scheme of your neighborhood and emphasize the opposite in your own garden. Squint down your street with eyes half closed so that you cannot see the details. What is the color scheme? Glaring desert ochre and silver? Red brick with white trim, tastefully set off by dark gray road? The overall color scheme will be even more obvious on an overcast day. Our neighborhood is full of evergreen oaks, with dusty green leaves, that cast heavy shadows. This gloomy environment is reinforced by the local preference for mud-colored houses with black roofs. The garden cries out for light and color—any color but dark green.

If your neighborhood is desert, or predominantly concrete, brick, and sunlight, you might aim for a shady oasis in the garden. If it is apple green farmland, you may want a garden full of splashes of color to counteract the feeling that you are living in a field. If your neighborhood reminds you of Sherwood Forest, you probably long for yellow stone walls and sunny open spaces.

Most of the world's gardens are enough to give anyone agoraphobia from too much staring at green. The problem is particularly acute if you are like me and green is your least favorite color. The worst time of year is summer, after the spring flowers are over and before autumn color—if there is any autumn color in your area. If you live in a dry part of the world, you may suffer from the opposite problem: most of your native vegetation has a silver or gray cast and you long for lush greens.

If you suffer from this color problem, you develop a hawk's eye for plants that display unusual colors without the aid of flowers. There are things with maroon and purple leaves: purple-leaved plums, sand cherries, Japanese maples, redbuds, beeches, and perennials to add color to the summer garden. There are plants with gray and silver leaves, such as Russian olives, variegated pittosporum, and artemisias. And then there are the invaluable plants with interesting colors in winter. Look for trees and shrubs with reddish bark and those that retain white, yellow, or red berries through much of the winter: hollies, cherries, mountain ash, many roses, and pyracantha. If you have ever experienced New England autumn color but now live elsewhere, you will never be satisfied with autumn in your garden and will find yourself tracking down plants such as sumac and euonymus that will add a little autumn color. If you live in New England, on the other hand, you may find that you are stunned by the reds and yellows of maples and spend your time planting ash trees for the wonderful purple-gray leaves that tone down the autumn color scheme.

It helps to grasp a little color theory. The primary colors are blue, yellow, and red. All colors can be made from these three with the addition of white and black. Something is white when it reflects all colors in the spectrum and black when it absorbs all light. The brightest visual effects come when contrasting colors are seen together: blue with orange, green with red, or yellow with purple. Remember contrasting colors by thinking of the primary colors: the contrast to each primary color is the mixture of the two others. So a mixture of blue and red (purple) is the contrasting color to yellow.

Gardeners usually think of flower colors as either warm or cool. The warm colors are yellow through orange; the cool colors are blue through a red that has no hint of yellow in it. Pure white can go in either group but if the white has a touch of pink, it is a cool color and if it is creamy, it belongs with the warm colors. The colors within each group are harmonious, not contrasting. Some of the most effective garden color schemes are made up of plants within one color group with a few from the other for contrast. A couple of yellow day lilies in a bed of dark purple ones is a stunning sight.

When the colors in a garden jangle your nerves, it is often from an excess of warm colors. Beds full of bright yellow, orange, and orangey-red flowers can be exhausting. You probably wouldn't want to live in a room with this color scheme either. One secret of handling warm colors is to mass them together. Yellow coreopsis scattered though a bed can make it look messy, while a dozen coreopsis next to a dozen orange marigolds is effective. Blue goes well with contrasting orange although it tends to disappear into the background when on its own. Gardeners tend to add blue to a warm bed to show it off and to "cool down" warm colors.

On the other hand, perhaps you live in an area where hot sounds like heaven and warm colors are always welcome. A Scottish gardener was heard to remark that she hated snowdrops, the small white bells that are the first sign of spring, because "no sooner has the snow melted than you've got white spots all over the place again." She would undoubtedly be happier if orange California poppies were the first sign of spring in Scotland.

The bright sunshine of midsummer saps color from the landscape; cool colors tend to disappear and only warm colors have much impact. Since plants flower at different times of year, it is not impossible to design a flower bed that changes from cool-colored in the spring to warm in the summer and back again in the autumn. Garden colorist Gertrude Jekyll (rhymes with "treacle") designed single flower beds that went from cool colors at one end to hottest of hot at the other by gradations, with no contrasting colors next to each other. You need a huge flower bed and enormous knowledge to pull this one off, however.

A rather limey yellow is the most visible color in the spectrum and the reason that red fire engines are being replaced by yellow ones. If you want the first flowers of spring to catch your eye after a winter spent indoors, plant lime-colored hellebores, yellow crocuses, and winter aconites. Even in a distant corner of the garden, a splash of yellow is noticeable, while blue flowers would be invisible. For the same reason, if you want your shady garden to show off from a distance, yellow flowers are the way to go.

White lightens a landscape. A dark corner can be made less gloomy by planting it with shrubs with variegated (white-striped) leaves instead of with green-leaved varieties of the same thing. Finding the right color at the right time preoccupies you more and more as your gardening skill grows. Indeed life in a small garden would become too easy once the paths are laid and backgrounds created were it not for the endless search for better color schemes, more interesting textures.

Westerners tend to be rather conservative with color. The Japanese may paint a bridge or gateway bright red for a splash of color in a predominantly green landscape. Even Claude Monet, Impressionist painter that he was, could not bring himself to go as far as this and painted the Japanese-style bridge and half-sunk boat at his lake in Giverny a dull turquoise instead of anything brighter—although when it came to flowers, Monet let colors run riot.

C H A P T E R 3

Getting
Started

Gardening would not be gardening without a succession of unexpected disasters and equally unexpected triumphs. Nonetheless, many problems can be avoided by a little forethought before you start work on a new garden or renovate an old one.

Take the complications caused by local climate, even in an area you know well. I once built a patio behind a new house, installing a wooden fence for privacy. I planned to use the fence as backdrop for an early summer show. Three clematis 'Henryi' would display starry white flowers and green leaves against the rust-colored wood, this rather demure picture to be enlivened by hot pink and yellow 'Neon' peonies with white arabis at their feet.

It didn't work out that way because the clematis did not all flower together and they did not flower at the same time as the peonies. I had failed to allow for the shadow of the house, which meant that the plants further from the house got more sun. The peonies liked this and those farthest from the house bloomed first.

The clematis preferred more shade and those at the other end of the fence grew faster and flowered earlier. All the plants flowered well and were very decorative, but they never produced the overall picture I had imagined.

HARDINESS AND MICROCLIMATES

Inducing things to flower at the same time depends on an understanding of climatic conditions within the garden. You also need this knowledge to decide whether a plant you covet in a garden center or nursery catalogue will do well for you. The first consideration in this case is hardiness, meaning whether or not the plant will survive your winter cold and summer heat.

In North America, a huge land mass produces severe winters over much of the continent, with a major effect on what will grow where. This was early recognized by Harvard's Arnold Arboretum, whose staff drew up plant hardiness maps based on the annual average minimum temperature. These

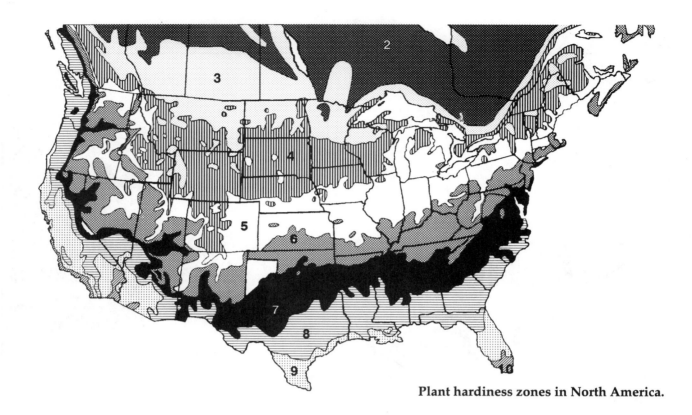

Plant hardiness zones in North America.

evolved into the U.S. Department of Agriculture's Plant Hardiness Zone Map and a similar map for Europe.

In catalogues, "Hardy to Zone 5" means, or should mean, that you can grow the plant in question if you live in Zone 5 or a warmer area. Of recent years, nurseries have got better about also listing the warmest zone in which a plant will survive, so that you often see a plant listed as "Zones 4-7," meaning that it cannot take the heat of a Zone 8 summer or the cold of a Zone 3 winter.

Since nurseries want to sell to as many people as possible, they tend to push their luck with hardiness zones. It is, therefore, safer to purchase plants that are advertised as hardy one zone beyond you. I live in Zone 8 and I prefer to purchase unfamiliar plants only when they are listed as hardy to Zone 9—and the average catalogue contains almost nothing that is hardy to Zone 9. People living in Zones 2 and 3 face the same dearth of choice. (I am convinced the average catalogue has more plants for Zones 2 and 3 than for Zones 9 and 10, but that may be just sour grapes.)

Many factors not addressed by the official zone classifications affect whether a plant will thrive in your garden even if you provide ideal soil and moisture. They include:

1. Summer minimum temperature. When the hardiness zone maps were started, most Americans lived in the northeastern United States, and their main concern was the winter cold that prevented them from growing plants they knew from Europe. Summer heat was not a big problem and nobody took much notice of it.

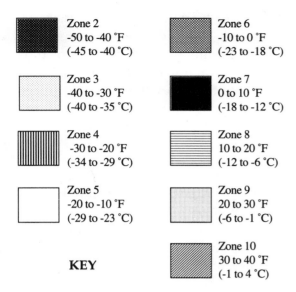

Zone 2
-50 to -40 °F
(-45 to -40 °C)

Zone 3
-40 to -30 °F
(-40 to -35 °C)

Zone 4
-30 to -20 °F
(-34 to -29 °C)

Zone 5
-20 to -10 °F
(-29 to -23 °C)

KEY

Zone 6
-10 to 0 °F
(-23 to -18 °C)

Zone 7
0 to 10 °F
(-18 to -12 °C)

Zone 8
10 to 20 °F
(-12 to -6 °C)

Zone 9
20 to 30 °F
(-6 to -1 °C)

Zone 10
30 to 40 °F
(-1 to 4 °C)

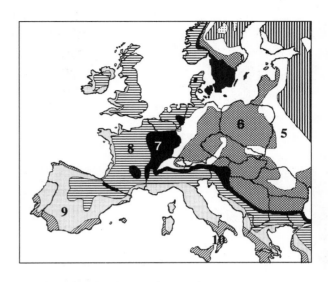

Plant hardiness zone map for western Europe.

Many plants cannot survive high minimum (nighttime) temperatures in summer for any length of time. They do not mind the heat as such. You will find many of these plants growing in desert gardens where summer temperatures are as high as anywhere in the world—but where the temperature drops rapidly at night because the air is dry. So if you live in the southern United States or Hawaii, your plant selection is more likely to be limited by the minimum temperature in summer than in winter.

2. Number of hot days in summer. Things like grapes, tomatoes, peaches, and peppers need a fairly long period of warm weather for the fruit to ripen. If you live high up in the Rockies or in most of Britain, you cannot grow these things outdoors unless you provide them with extra heat—by growing them under glass or against a warm wall. The law of natural cussedness being what it is, no sooner have you gone to great trouble to provide these growing conditions than along comes a summer so hot you could grow eggplants outdoors.

3. Winter chill. Apples, tulips, and hyacinths are among the many plants that are adapted to fairly long winters. If they do not get enough cold weather in winter, their hormones are not prepared for spring and they do not produce fruit and flowers. Especially if you live in warmer parts of the world, you are in for a sad disappointment if you buy fruit trees and bulbs that are not adapted to mild winters.

4. Average length of drought. When California severed water supplies during a drought, orchards of avocados and citrus shriveled up and died. A four-month period without rain in the southern United States killed thousands of azaleas that had survived without care for decades. Lilacs, on the other hand, don't mind going for months without water after they have flowered.

The average length of drought may be almost impossible to calculate. Britain, for instance, tends to jump between summers in which it rains every other day and summers with no rain for three months. But it is worth doing some local research. Even if you live in an area with very low rainfall, does the rain fall when it does most good? Many plants can survive without rainfall in late summer and winter. Few can survive without water while they are actively growing in spring.

Local Climate

Hardiness zone maps give only the vaguest approximation of the climate in your garden and what will grow there because local variations abound. For instance, the staff of *Sunset* magazine has divided the western United States into 24 biomes, with large variations in precipitation, temperature, and native plant life. It helps to find a local soil and climate map and do some research on your own.

• The single biggest influence on local climate is altitude. We used to live 1000 feet above sea level and in spring everything in the garden flowered about three weeks later than it did in the nearby town some 400 feet lower.

• Northerners may be disappointed when peppers and other hot-weather crops flourish one year but fail the next—because the growing season is barely long enough for these vegetables. In this situation, look for varieties that will mature during your growing season—the number of days each year with average temperature above 43 °F (6 °C). Incidentally, you cannot be sure a vegetable will be ready to harvest in the time listed on the packet, which assumes almost ideal growing conditions. As the advertisement says, your mileage may differ.

• A large town is usually warmer and drier than the surrounding countryside because it lies within an "urban heat bubble." This bubble forms as the heat generated by energy use in the town rises into the air. A large urban heat bubble can make a dramatic difference to the climate. For one thing it can prevent rain. Low-flying clouds, such as those that bring most summer rain, tend to bounce off heat bubbles so that clouds travel around the town instead of over it. Phoenix, Arizona has recorded a steady decline in rainfall as the town has grown in the last few decades, although the rainfall in the surrounding countryside has not altered. Wind tends to dissipate urban heat bubbles, so towns in windy areas are less affected.

• Any body of water moderates the climate. Temperatures near the sea are higher in winter and lower in summer than in inland areas. The most dramatic example of this is in the climate of western Europe, which is controlled by the continental landmass to the east, generating cold east winds, and the Atlantic Ocean with its warm Gulf Stream to the west, producing warmer west winds. The effect of the Atlantic is so strong that climate zones in Europe

UNDERSTANDING THE ENVIRONMENT SLOPES AND SOIL MOISTURE

In dry areas where melting snow provides much of the moisture, north-facing slopes contain most soil moisture. You can observe this in dry mountainous areas where north-facing slopes bear trees and shrubs and all other slopes are grass-covered. North-facing slopes are cool so the snow melts slowly in spring and much of the moisture sinks into the soil where plants can use it. On a south-facing slope, in contrast, the snow melts so rapidly that the ground cannot absorb all of it and much of it runs uselessly off the surface.

tend to run north-south instead of east-west. Ireland seldom suffers from frost although it is further north than Winnipeg. Even a small lake has a moderating effect on the climate.

Indicator Plants

One way to check whether you are in a warmer or a cooler area than appears from the zone map is to check the neighborhood for indicator plants. The indicator plants for a zone are common, well-studied plants that are difficult to grow in a colder zone. Thus, if your neighborhood is full of privet hedges and dogwood, you live in Zone 5 or warmer. Indicator plants for Zones 2 to 10 are listed on pages 44 and 45.

Microclimates

Even if you live near sea level firmly in the middle of a zone, you will probably find that there are several different microclimates within your garden. It is worth discovering where and what these are because they may permit you to grow things that the official zone map says you cannot grow. And they permit you to grow plants so that they give their best display instead of merely surviving. Southerners find, for instance, that growing tomatoes under the cooling shade of a tree lengthens the tomato season by as much as a couple of months. In Ohio, tender rhododendrons may survive against the warm brick wall of a house but die in a distant corner of the garden.

There are several ways to test for microclimates in your garden. Dashing around with a thermometer on a February night is one of them. But there may be easier ways. One is to plant tender annuals, such as marigolds, in many parts of the garden and watch them carefully after the first killing frost of the year. Probably most of the marigolds died, but one clump survived. These are sitting in a warm spot.

You can plant seeds of poppies in autumn and watch them germinate with the first rain and warm weather in spring. Where do the seeds germinate first? That may well be another warm spot. Watch how frost evaporates on the morning after a freeze. What parts of the lawn warm up first? Are these the same as the areas that the sun strikes first? Where does snow melt last? Where is the snow deepest? (Probably in the lee of a fence or shrubbery where the wind speed drops suddenly.)

It is particularly worthwhile bearing microclimates in mind when planning a garden because otherwise you can make such maddening mistakes. It is very disappointing to plant an expensive fruit tree in a frost-pocket where the fruit seldom sets and never ripens.

Then consider the man who one summer built a little patio at the sheltered northwest corner of the house. He imagined himself

GREEN THUMB TIP

MICROCLIMATES

Try using a warm spot in the garden for a display of spring bulbs. Snowdrops, crocuses, squills, early daffodils and irises flower in early spring and you want them up and about as soon as possible because they fade rapidly when warm weather arrives.

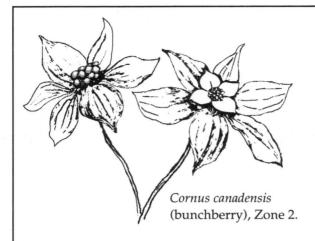

Cornus canadensis (bunchberry), Zone 2.

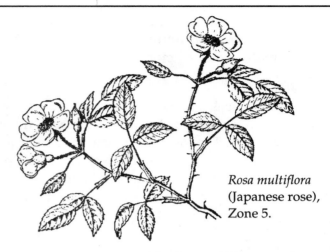

Rosa multiflora (Japanese rose), Zone 5.

Juniperus communis (common juniper), Zone 3.

INDICATOR PLANTS

These are representative, long-lived plants that are often present in gardens, listed under the coldest zone in which each normally succeeds.

Zone 2 -50 to -40 ℉ (-45 to -40 ℃) *Betula papyrifera* (paper birch), *Cornus canadensis* (bunchberry dogwood), *Elaeagnus commutata* (silverberry), *Larix laricina* (eastern larch), *Potentilla fruticosa* (bush cinquefoil), *Viburnum trilobum* (American cranberry)

Zone 3 -40 to -30 ℉ (-40 to -35 ℃) *Berberis thunbergii* (Japanese bayberry), *Elaeagnus angustifolia* (Russian olive), *Juniperus communis* (common juniper), *Lonicera tatarica* (Tatarian honeysuckle),

Malus baccata (Siberian crabapple), *Thuja occidentalis* (American arborvitae)

Zone 4 -30 to -20 ℉ (-34 to -29 ℃) *Acer saccharum* (sugar maple), *Hydrangea paniculata* (panicle hydrangea), *Juniperus chinensis* (Chinese juniper), *Ligustrum amurense* (Amur River privet), *Parthenocissus quinquefolia* (Virginia creeper), *Spiraea* x *Vanhouttei* (Vanhoutte spirea)

Zone 5 -20 to -10 ℉ (-29 to -23 ℃) *Cornus florida* (dogwood), *Deutzia gracilis* (slender deutzia), *Ligustrum vulgare* (common privet), *Parthenocissus tricuspidata* (Boston ivy), *Rosa multiflora* (Japanese rose), *Taxus cuspidata* (Japanese yew)

Hydrangea paniculata (panicle hydrangea), Zone 4.

Acer palmatum (Japanese maple), Zone 6.

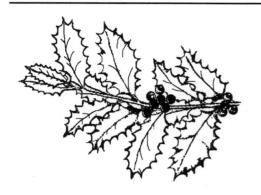

Ilex aquifolium (English holly), Zone 7.

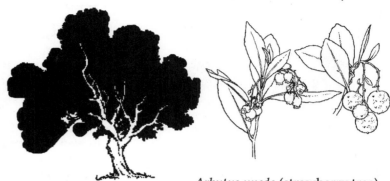

Arbutus unedo (strawberry tree), Zone 8.

Zone 6 -10 to 0 °F (-23 to -18 °C) *Acer palmatum* (Japanese maple), *Buxus sempervirens* (common box), *Euonymus fortunei* (winter creeper), *Hedera helix* (English ivy), *Ilex opaca* (American holly), *Ligustrum ovalifolium* (California privet)

Zone 7 0 to 10 °F (-18 to -12 °C) *Acer macrophyllum* (bigleaf maple), *Rhododendron* Kurume hybrids (kurume azalea), *Cedrus atlantica* (Atlas cedar), *Cotoneaster microphylla* (small-leaf cotoneaster), *Ilex aquifolium* (English holly), *Taxus baccata* (English yew)

Zone 8 10 to 20 °F (-12 to -6 °C) *Arbutus unedo* (strawberry tree), *Choisya ternata* (Mexican orange), *Olearia haastii* (New Zealand daisy bush), *Pittosporum tobira* (Japanese pittosporum), *Prunus*

laurocerasus (cherry laurel), *Viburnum tinus* (laurestinus)

Zone 9 20 to 30 °F (-6 to -1 °C) *Asparagus setaceus* (asparagus fern), *Eucalyptus globulus* (Tasmanian blue gum), *Syzgium paniculatum* (Australian bush cherry), *Fuschia* hybrids (fuschia), *Grevillea robusta* (silk oak), *Schinus molle* (California pepper tree)

Zone 10 30 to 40 °F (-1 to 4 °C) *Bougainvillea spectabilis* (bougainvillea), *Cassia fistula* (golden shower) *Eucalyptus citriodora* (lemon eucalyptus), *Ficus elastica* (rubber plant), *Ensete ventricosum* (ensete), *Roystonea regia* (royal palm).

Berberis Darwinii (Darwin barberry) Zone 8.

Fuschia hybrids, Zone 9.

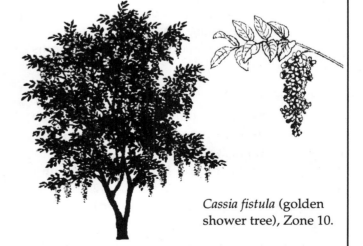

Cassia fistula (golden shower tree), Zone 10.

WHAT IS AN ECOSYSTEM?

We often hear that pesticides and herbicides are bad for the environment because they disrupt ecosystem food webs and have unforeseen effects. One example was documented by ecologist Lamont Cole.

In the 1950s, the World Health Organization (WHO) tried to eliminate malaria from Borneo by spraying with the insecticide DDT. The spray did indeed kill the mosquitoes that transmit malaria, but it also poisoned cockroaches. Geckoes (insect-eating lizards) ate the cockroaches and suffered nerve damage from the DDT. Their reflexes became slower, and more of them than usual were

A gecko.

caught by cats. Because most of their gecko predators were now gone, caterpillars eating the local thatched roofs multiplied unchecked, and the roofs started to collapse. In addition, the cats were soon dying of DDT poisoning. Rats moved in from the forest, and with them came rat fleas carrying the bacteria that cause plague. Most people would rather have malaria than plague, and so the WHO stopped spraying DDT and, in an attempt to remedy the damage already done, parachuted large numbers of cats into the jungle—an expensive lesson in the importance of understanding a food web before you start pulling out its strands!

An ecosystem is a group of organisms and the habitat they live in. A Borneo village is an ecosystem; so is your perennial border. Ecologists treat ecosystems as units because things within an ecosystem interact. Each biome is made up of many ecosystems.

Although things move from one ecosystem to another, a natural ecosystem is self-sufficient. It produces its own food and disposes of its waste. To do this, every ecosystem needs mineral nutrients, water, air, and living organisms. It also needs a continuous supply of energy which comes from the sun.

Consider a pond containing plants but no animals. Microorganisms are also present. The plants use sunshine to turn water and carbon dioxide into carbohydrates by photosynthesis, releasing oxygen as a byproduct. Chlorophyll, the green plant pigment, is the extraordinary molecule that traps energy from the sun for photosynthesis. We have only recently learned to use the sun's energy to power solar batteries. Plants have used it to power much more complicated reactions for millions of years.

The plants combine some of their carbohydrates with mineral nutrients, converting them into other molecules they need for growth and reproduction. The energy for these conversions comes from respiration, the breakdown of carbohydrate that uses up oxygen and releases carbon dioxide. Plants produce more oxygen by photosynthesis

---

sitting in this warm spot on a sunny February day planning his gardening year. You've guessed by now that he had not realized that that corner of the house was in complete shade throughout February and several other months of the year.

Beating the Cold

Here are some of the things to remember when deciding where to plant within the microclimates in your garden:

• The position of the sun is different in winter and summer. In winter the sun is lower in the sky, rising in the south-east and setting in the south-west. In summer it rises and sets considerably further north. As a result, a wall that faces due north gets some sun in summer but none in winter; and in winter it also throws a shadow.

One autumn I planted sweet peas twenty feet from a north-facing wall in a spot that was in sun all summer. They produced only one or two flowers—because they were in the shadow of the house for most of their winter growing season.

• A south-facing slope warms up faster than level ground. In winter, a 15° slope to the south gets twice as much sunshine as level ground, while a 15° slope to the north gets essentially no sunlight. A sunny south-facing slope may be ideal for an early spring vegetable garden, but is not the place for

than they use in respiration so that, overall, plants add oxygen to the air and remove carbon dioxide. In fact, all the oxygen we breathe has been released into the air by plant photosynthesis over millions of years.

Plants are the route by which energy from the sun gets into an ecosystem. They are the producers (of food). An ecosystem would be doomed, however, if it contained only producers because eventually the plants would use up all the mineral nutrients. Decomposers are the solution to this problem.

Decomposers are the many organisms, particularly fungi and bacteria, that break down dead bodies and parts of bodies, extract nutrients and energy for their own use, and release minerals into the soil and water where they can be reused.

Most ecosystems contain more than just producers and decomposers. Some of the green plants are eaten by plant-eating herbivores, which in the pond

KEY
→ Movement of nutrients
⇒ Energy flow

Energy (Light from the sun)

Inorganic nutrients (Nitrate, potassium, etc., in soil or water)

This box contains what is absolutely necessary for a self-sustaining ecosystem

Producers (Green plants)

Decomposers (Mostly bacteria, fungi, and insects)

Energy loss (Heat)

Energy loss (Heat)

Primary consumers (Herbivores; organisms that eat plants)

Secondary consumers (Carnivores; organisms that eat herbivores and other carnivores)

might be water snails or fish. These are the ecosystem's consumers. In turn, these may either die and be broken down by decomposers, or they may be eaten by carnivores, which are secondary consumers.

Energy is lost from an ecosystem as heat whenever organisms use energy. Thus an ecosystem needs a constant supply of energy from the sun. But molecules—in mineral nutrients or body parts—are recycled, passing from one organism to another within the ecosystem. Many things can disrupt this recycling of

molecules. Erosion is one of them. If soil or leaves wash or blow out of the ecosystem, nutrients and organisms are lost. If we use fungicides in the garden, we may kill off the fungi that decompose a particular waste material. Then the waste accumulates. Or insecticides may kill parasitic wasps. Then populations of their maggot prey explode and wipe out our melons.

Every organism depends on dozens of other members of its ecosystem, many of them so small we never see them, but nonetheless essential.

doubtfully hardy shrubs. This is because winter damage is often caused by alternate freezing and thawing. A frozen shrub that thaws out in the winter sun may be killed, while its neighbor in the shade remains frozen and survives.

• On a very cold day, the temperature inside a snow bank is higher than the air temperature. Snow is a good insulator and a cold winter with little snow kills more plants than one with heavy snow cover. The message again is not to plant tender things where they receive winter sun which may melt their snow cover.

• Cold air runs downhill and collects in hollows. If your garden is on a slope with a hedge at the bottom, the area by the hedge will be a cold spot on a winter night, no matter which way it faces.

• Wind dries plants as it dries the washing, a the higher the wind speed, the greater the dryi effect. Wind is particularly damaging in co winters and dry summers. When the soil frozen, plants cannot replace water lost fro their leaves by absorbing more water from t soil. Similarly, summer wind can dehydrate plant faster than the plant can absorb water fro the soil.

Wind is often surprisingly strong even apparently protected spots such as the base o wall. When wind hits a wall, some of it deflected up and some of it is deflected dowr causing a draft where the wall meets the groun

HOW PLANTS ARE NAMED

We need internationally recognized names for organisms because common names are not precise. Busy Lizzie, sultana, patient Lucy, impatiens, and patience are all common names for the popular shade-loving plant *Impatiens Wallerana*. Similarly, "cornflower" means many things to many people.

The system we use to name plants was devised by the Swedish botanist Carolus Linnaeus in the eighteenth century. Linnaeus gave every species its own two-word name. The first word gives the genus (*Impatiens*) and the second the species (*Wallerana*).

Each genus contains one or more species. For example, the genus *Impatiens* contains the species *Impatiens capensis* (jewelweed) and *Impatiens Balsamina* (balsam) as well as *Impatiens Wallerana*. (Species names are capitalized only when the species is a proper noun.)

Linnaeus classified plants by

Impatiens Wallerana

their flower parts, which are sexual organs. He used group names such as *Polyandria*, which he said meant, "twenty or more males in bed with the same female." This emphasis on sex shocked some of his contemporaries. The Bishop of Carlisle wrote, "To tell you that nothing could exceed the gross prurience of Linnaeus's mind is perfectly needless," and Goethe worried about the embarrassment chaste young people might suffer when reading botany textbooks. One can imagine how these worthies would have felt about the names of the cactus *Mammillaria* and the fungus *Phallus impudicus*.

Scientific names are Latin (often with Greek roots) because, for hundreds of years, Latin was the common language of European scholars. Many Latin names are full of information and folklore. For instance, *Gypsophila* (baby's breath or chalk plant) means "chalk-lover" a reference to this plant's fondness for alkaline soil. Medieval folklore taught that, as an early herbal put it, "God maketh grass to grow upon the mountains, and herbs for the use of man, and hath given them particular signatures, whereby a man may read, even in legible characters, the use of them." Thus, *Hepatica*, a spring flower whose name means "liver," was believed to cure diseases of the liver because its leaf is liver-shaped. You can imagine how *Ilex vomitoria* (yaupon holly) affects the

Impatiens Balsamina

human body.

Linnaeus classified organisms in a hierarchy of ever larger and more inclusive categories, a system borrowed from the Swedish military of his day. The most inclusive categories (taxa) are the kingdoms (plants, animals, protists, fungi, and bacteria). The lowest taxon is the species, a group of organisms that resemble one another closely in appearance, chemistry and, ultimately, the genes they contain, and that usually breed only with each other. Each successively higher taxon generally includes a larger number of more distantly related species. The classification for two plants is shown opposite.

This classification is undoubtedly not quite what you learned in high school botany. Botanists change their minds about how things should be classified and named. For instance, the genus

Winter Protection

Gardeners sometimes go to great lengths to preserve plants from winter cold. Occasionally, you see a garden in which every shrub is wrapped in burlap and climbing roses have been removed from their trellises, laid on the

ground, and covered with soil. This is definitely high-maintenance gardening.

Several easier steps will increase the chances that tender plants will survive a cold winter. Plants suffering from water stress have less resistance to cold, so it helps to ensure that

Hymenocallis caroliniana

Taxon	Meadow lily	French marigold*
Kingdom	Plantae	Plantae
Division	Anthophyta	Anthophyta
Class	Liliopsida (monocots)	Magnoliopsida (dicots)
Order	Liliales	Asterales
Family	Liliaceae	Asteraceae (=Compositae)
Genus	*Hymenocallis*	*Tagetes*
Species	*caroliniana*	*patula*

*Actually native to Mexico and Guatemala.

Tagetes patula

Chrysanthemum has now been subdivided. The spray chrysanthemums often grown in gardens are now correctly *Dendranthema*. The names used in this book are from *Hortus Third*, the dictionary of plants cultivated in North America, prepared by the Liberty Hyde Bailey Hortorium at Cornell University. New editions of this mammoth tome are not published very often, however, and I have adopted some of the changes that the International Commission on Botanical Nomenclature has adopted since the 1976 edition.

Species and genus names are conventionally italicized or underlined: the human species is *Homo sapiens* or <u>Homo sapiens</u>. The genus is often abbreviated after it has been used once. Thus, *Homo sapiens* can be repeated as *H. sapiens*. When you name a species, you must use the names of both both genus and species: *Tagetes patula*. The species name is often trivial (*patula* means "spread out"), and many organisms have the same species names.

We often have to go beyond species in naming garden plants because many have been bred and selected to improve on the original species. The most common horticultural category is a cultivar (from *cultivated variety*).

An "x" indicates a hybrid, a cross between two or more species (or cultivars). When the parents are known, their names are often given. Thus a plant labeled *Camellia sasanqua x C. japonica* 'Flirtatious' is a cultivar named "Flirtatious," which was produced by crossing the two species *Camellia sasanqua* and *Camellia japonica*. A hybrid may merely be called *Iris x*, *Iris hybrida*, or *Iris x hybrida*. In fact many species hybridize with each other so readily that they are not even labeled as hybrids. A group of irises may be called "Pacific Coast Iris" (or "Pacificas") or "Louisiana Iris." You would have to be in the know to understand that the Pacific Coast irises offered for sale are selected from populations of hybrids between various iris species.

Popular annuals are often the results of many hybridizations. Sometimes botanists are not even sure of all the species in the ancestry. These plants are usually listed by the generic or common name and the cultivar: *Verbena* 'Cheers' or Pansy 'Pacific Giant.'

everything is well watered when really cold weather is forecast. Second, a thick mulch will protect young plants from cold until they have grown roots down to below the level to which the soil freezes. When you rake up leaves in the autumn, lay them down in a thick mulch around young plants.

In spring, when you inspect plants for frost damage, don't be in a hurry to assume a plant is dead. A shrub that has had branches killed during the winter frequently looks as dead as the dodo in spring. It may continue to look hopeless even when the same species in another part of the garden has developed leaf and flower buds. But sometimes "dead" shrubs belatedly come to life.

FINDING THE PLANTS YOU NEED

Most keen gardeners go to ridiculous lengths to grow difficult plants. I am into my tenth attempt in as many years to get cyclamen established in the garden. That's the way gardeners are. But if your hedges, large trees, and major shrubs are cast-iron hardy, you can wrestle with a few tender specimens without spoiling the look of the garden.

Beside hardiness, a good shape may be the greatest asset of a backbone plant because the first impression that we get of a garden is of shape: the outline of trees and shrubs, the shape of the lawn, of structures, and of beds. Attractive shapes are a lot easier to achieve if you start with shapely plants.

Plants that look good in more than one season are also desirable. There are so many plants that are deadly dull except when in flower, and many of them flower for only a week or two each year. Especially in a small garden, a plant should earn its place in the garden even when it is not in flower. Look for trees with leaves that change color in autumn and that have unusual shapes or berries in winter. Look for perennials with colorful foliage or interesting leaves when they are not in bloom.

Japanese gardeners might tackle this problem by emphasizing the appearance of the plant when it is not in flower. Consider evergreen azaleas. In American gardens these are usually left unpruned, and they are unappealing shrubs except when covered with flowers for a week or two in spring. In Japan, azaleas are often tightly sheared, with flattish spreading tops and foliage cut away at the bottom to reveal the trunk. To maintain this shape, you have to shear several times a year, which removes flower buds, so that the bushes have only a sprinkling of flowers in spring. But a Japanese azalea garden in midsummer looks much better than its American equivalent. It is worth thinking about.

If you are new to gardening or new to an area, you have to do a certain amount of research to discover plants that will do well in your garden. Walks in your neighborhood will introduce you to the plants most people use for shade trees, hedges, and spring color. These are undoubtedly the hardy dependables of your area.

Knowing which biome you live in will suggest other well adapted plants. A local bookstore, university, or extension office may have a list of trees, shrubs, and wild flowers native to your county and even field guides with pictures.

Your first source of well-adapted plants is a garden center or nursery run by someone who knows the area. There is nothing wrong with buying cheap plants and nursing them back to health but, until you are a fairly experienced gardener, go to a good nursery for major plants.

There is an amazing amount of ignorance out there, even among professionals. I heard the owner of a local herb shop tell a customer that rosemary and bay would not survive winters outdoors in our area—which they will. A store near us has a large garden department where they sell peach and apple varieties, yews, and lilacs, that will not grow as far south as this.

The next step to finding interesting plants is to subscribe to a gardening magazine or two, partly for the numerous advertisements that will tempt you to send for catalogues. In the United States, *Fine Gardening, Horticulture,* and *National Gardening* are colorful publications that will keep you in touch with the latest developments in horticulture and plant breeding. In Britain, *The Gardener* and *Gardeners' World* also have folksy, easy-to-read styles. Once you have ordered from a few widely advertised catalogues, you will find yourself flooded with garden catalogues every year. Many of these are gorgeous productions full of color photographs, seducing you with page after page of perfect plants in glorious flower. These are particularly tempting in January, when the weather is miserable and you plan a year in which every corner of the garden will be weed-free and filled with flowers and wildlife. In catalogues, every plant is hardy from Zones 2 to 9, is untouched by pests, and flowers from spring to frost. You pore over the pages, circling every other picture. It is a heady process that brings stars to the eyes and mush to the mind. You send in lengthy orders for randomly chosen plants, which arrive the day that you are leaving on a skiing trip and perhaps you'll be wiser next year but probably not because it is the inalienable right of gardeners to make their own mistakes.

If you were really afflicted with catalogue fever when you ordered, planting will probably consist of wandering around the garden with trowel in one hand and plant in the other, wondering where to put it. Competent gardeners never do this. Their new plantings are laid out on graph paper complete with color scheme and precise calculations of how many plants are needed to fill the area. Then they do the research needed to discover the well-adapted shrub with white flowers in June and good autumn color that grows to a final size of six feet by six feet. They track down a nursery that sells the shrub and buy only as many as they need. When the garden is full, they stop buying plants.

The rest of us resolve that one of these days that is exactly what we will do but meanwhile how can we resist trying this new plant with enticing flowers? Our gardens are individual and inter-

GREEN THUMB TIP

HEELING IN

If dozens of plants do arrive at an inconvenient time, the only thing you can do is unpack them and "heel them in," hoping they will survive until you can plant them properly. Heeling in just means sticking them roughly in the ground. Dig a shallow trench, preferably in a shady, damp corner of the garden, lay the plants on their sides with their roots in the trench, cover the roots and parts of the stems with soil, and tread the earth firmly into the roots. If the plants are in the sun, shade them. Most plants will survive for a week or more if they are well heeled in, but plant them as soon as you can.

esting even if overall design sometimes seems slightly lost in the vegetation. And we console ourselves with the thought that it is not difficult to move even quite a large tree or shrub if we decide we have made a mistake. There are, however, ways of reducing the number of mistakes we make.

• **Visit as many gardens as you can.** Many of these will be public gardens or the gardens of historic houses. Keep an eye open for private gardens that are opened to the public for a day or two in aid of some good cause. Since the time of year is carefully chosen and the owners have tidied up for the occasion, you can see a garden looking as good as it gets in your area. With luck, you will also see a few horticultural mistakes that will make you feel superior. And you are almost bound to see a few ideas that appeal: a fence covered with jasmine that scents a hidden garden, a little pond with ferns and primulas, hot red petunias with white azaleas, a climbing rose trained to creep over a bank as a ground cover, a few white lilies set off by a red brick wall, or a bed of annuals edged by sheared box. You reel home filled with so many ideas for your own garden that you don't know where to start.

• **Visit wildlife refuges.** Bird sanctuaries often have field guides to local flora and fauna as well as booklets on what to plant to attract birds to the garden. They may even sell plants and seeds.

• **Visit, or get the catalogues of, local specialist nurseries.** These are the small places where dedicated gardeners breed and sell one or a few genera of plants. For instance, there is almost certainly someone growing wild flowers and other natives somewhere in your part of the world. There may also be a seed savers' exchange where you can buy or exchange seeds of hard-to-find plants. These small operations are not always easy to find because they seldom advertise.

• **When you buy seeds, order them from catalogues** rather than buying them in a shop: the seeds will be fresher and you will get more choice and cultural information. (The Stokes catalogue is a mine of useful information.) Seeds get old and die, some faster than others, so you want to plant seeds that are as fresh as possible. Distribution to retailers is a lengthy process and it is impossible for seed producers to supply shops with reliably fresh seeds; better to buy straight from the producer or distributor whenever you can.

HEIRLOOM PLANTS AND GENETIC DIVERSITY

A sad fact of modern life is that we are losing so many plants (and animals, for that matter). I am not thinking of species destroyed when tropical rain forest is cut down, but of ordinary garden plants. If you fall in love with one of Gertrude Jekyll's garden plans from the early 1900s, you find that you cannot duplicate it today because many of the cultivars she used are no longer grown. They have been lost to horticulture in less than a century. If you try to recreate an eighteenth century garden, you are in even worse trouble. Once a plant is no longer grown and propagated regularly, it eventually disappears.

Many new cultivars are undoubted improvements on those that have been lost, but many are not. After a steady diet of huge double flowers, many gardeners long for the simple cultivars of yesteryear—and then cannot find them.

Preserving Genetic Diversity
In the last fifty years, geneticists have raised the alarm about the disappearance of plant species and cultivars. Many lost plants undoubtedly contained genes and gene combinations that breeders need to develop new cultivars.

People heeding geneticists' warnings, and others with an academic or aesthetic interest in old plants, have swung into action to save what is left of our disappearing heritage. They have found many "heirloom" flowers and vegetables that have been preserved by being passed down through families or garden clubs.

In my own family, heirloom seeds include a marigold and a strange-looking squash, both of unknown origin. Every year, seeds of these two have been saved and planted. A neon pink phlox and a purple dahlia, both at least 50 years old, have been passed to neighbors as divisions.

Some of the plants handed down through families and friends are not long-lost varieties. I suspect that our family marigold is 'Queen Sophia.' Nevertheless, plants propagated for generations far from the commercial mainstream have usually accumulated adaptations and gene combinations not found in commercial varieties. They may be useful sources of genetic diversity for plant breeders and for genetic research.

Some heirloom plants are hardier and easier to grow than their modern relatives. I know an English village where a nameless rose, propagated through the years by cuttings, grows on almost every cottage wall. Read Thomas Christopher's *In Search of Old Roses* for the story of a group of Texans who track down and identify old roses in that part of the world. Many of the found roses have grown untended in cemeteries or abandoned homesites for 50 years and more.

Many recent cultivars are hybrids between two species. Like a mule, which is a hybrid between a horse and a donkey, many (but not all) hybrid plants are sterile and do not reproduce. If they do produce seeds, these seeds grow into plants that are different from their parents. Only "open-pollinated" plants come true from seed and fewer and fewer of these are available commercially with every year that passes.

ADAPTATIONS OF PLANTS
Through many generations, different species of plants evolve

UNDERSTANDING THE ENVIRONMENT GENETIC DIVERSITY AND FOOD

In the United States, about 700 plant species are in critical danger of extinction, according to the Center for Plant Conservation. As these plants become extinct, they take with them irreplaceable combinations of genes. This is particularly worrying in the case of food plants because new, high yielding cultivars are badly needed. Today, more than 20 million people die of malnutrition every year. We face widespread starvation unless the production of food (particularly grains) grows at unprecedented speed—the human population is expected to double within the next 50 years.

In the 1980s, geneticists attempting to breed grain varieties suitable for low-input agriculture in tropical areas, searched Asian villages for drought-resistant cereals. They found, to their horror, that these older varieties had disappeared, replaced in cultivation by modern varieties that produce well only when grown with large quantities of water and fertilizer. In contrast, plant hunters in a Mexican forest in 1982 discovered a type of wild corn (maize) which is now an ancestor of several productive, disease-resistant hybrids worth billions of dollars a year to North American farmers.

Conservationists in many countries are collecting plants in "germ plasm banks" in a race to save as much genetic diversity as possible. Gardeners all over the world are taking part in this effort.

different adaptations. If all plants were adapted to the same conditions, some habitats would be crowded with plants competing for space and others would be empty. Instead, sunny prairie and shady forest, clay soils and sand, wet and dry areas, all have their own well-adapted groups of plants.

When we bring plants into cultivation, we may alter plant adaptations. The average garden plant gets better soil and more water than plants in a nearby forest. Some plants will die under these conditions, but others will have genetic variations that permit them to thrive in the garden. Plant breeders are constantly on the lookout for seedlings with genes that make them better garden plants. For instance, northern rhododendron growers watch for seedlings that come unscathed through unusually cold winters. Then they breed from these plants in the hope of producing rhododendron cultivars that can survive further north than any now available.

Wild flowers are usually selected in cultivation for large flowers with strong stems so that the plants will make a better show in the garden. Even if the common fire-wheel or blanketflower, *Gaillardia pulchella* or *G. lanceolata*, is native in your area, the gaillardias you grow from commercially bought seed will have larger flowers on sturdier plants than the flowers growing wild on nearby roadsides. (Most cultivated gaillardias are hybrids, known as *G. x grandiflora*.)

As a result of all this selective breeding, commonly available garden plants tend to be adapted to a wide range of conditions. Nevertheless, you will find that most plants have their preferences. They will thrive in some places and merely survive in others. A continuing search for plants that are particularly well adapted to your area and to various parts of your garden is one of the things that raises a distinguished garden above the ordinary.

NATIVE PLANTS

As I write this in July, my neglected perennial border is bright with gaillardias and black-eyed susans (*Rudbeckia hirta*). Another splash of color is a large clump of yellow cannas (*Canna flaccida*) on the far side of the lawn (far enough so that I cannot see the mess that leaf rollers have made of the leaves). These plants are natives. Hardy, happy, and drought-resistant, they brighten the garden even after months of neglect and they multiply to form larger pools of color each year.

Gardeners will never stop fighting to grow plants that are not well suited to their gardens—plants that need conditions of soil or climate found only on mountain peaks or foreign shores. We thrive on eternal optimism and know no greater thrill than bringing some novel exotic into flower for the first time. But many of the plants an environmental gardener grows should be either native to the region or so long-adapted that they seem native. There are many reasons for this:

Blanketflower, *Gaillardia pulchella*.
Gaillardia species and hybrids are short-lived perennials, hardy in Zones 3-10. They prefer dry sandy soil and sun, bloom from spring to frost, and self-seed freely wherever they are happy.

•**Well-adapted plants grow better.** My garden contains hybrid clematis and forsythia—all permanently on the verge of death from heat stroke. Each spring they put out a few flowers and grow a handful of leaves. When I think of the billowing forsythia hedges and cascades of purple and white clematis in New England gardens, I bleed for my long-suffering plants and resolve yet again to replace them. (Of course such is human contrariness that I never valued forsythia when I grew it; I thought it common and messy.)

Well-adapted plants don't have to be the boring species found in every garden. Your neighborhood may be full of azaleas and redtips imported from Asia while the woods nearby and a specialist nursery in the next county are full of attractive natives seldom seen in local gardens.

•**Natives need less care.** Californians and Londoners struggling with drought, and forbidden to water except by hand on alternate Thursdays, have learned the hard way that gardens full of natives remain fresh and lovely while flower beds full of foreigners wither and die.

•**Native plants are what your native wildlife needs most.** If your garden is even vaguely reminiscent of the vegetation that occupied the area before civilization, you may be thrilled to find yourself host to a rare bird species or even an endangered mammal. If the pileated woodpeckers we see in our trees ever nest in our garden, I shall know I have died and gone to heaven.

Once you get interested in native plants, you will find yourself lusting after the rarer species. These can sometimes be acquired, legally and ethically, from a nursery that propagates them without endangering wild populations. With care and planning, your garden could become a refuge for some endangered plant, a mecca for botanists and conservationists.

Some of your best buys may be plants that are native to your area but have been improved during cultivation, a fact brought home to me by the case of the oakleaf hydrangea (*Hydrangea quercifolia*). When I moved to Savannah I was delighted to find a wild specimen of this lovely shrub in the garden. With cone-shaped white flowers in spring and big palmate leaves the rest of the summer, I wanted more of this beauty, so I ordered a cultivar named 'Snowflake' and was delighted at the improvement. 'Snowflake' blooms when it is an infant, and has flower heads twice the size of the wild type's, that arrive a week earlier and last two weeks longer. Now I yearn for 'Snow Queen,' described by the Wayside catalogue as discovered as a seedling in New Jersey and holding its blooms up better than 'Snowflake.'

With improved natives, you usually get the hardiness and pest resistance of a native combined with better shape and growth habits. Europeans have long bred goldenrods (*Solidago*) as garden flowers. Since North America is home to more than 130 species of goldenrod,

Oakleaf hydrangea, *Hydrangea quercifolia*.
In Latin, *quercus* means "oak" and *folia* means "leaf." This deciduous shrub grows to about 6 feet and is covered with white flowers in spring. It is hardy in Zones 5-9.

Franklinia Alatamaha.
This small deciduous tree has red autumn foliage and produces white flowers with bright yellow stamens from late summer to frost. (Zones 5-8 or 9). I think it prefers moist soil and part shade in the Deep South, but I have not had mine for long enough to be sure. Farther north, it appears to be happy almost anywhere.

Americans tend to despise it as the housefly of horticulture. But it's worth taking another look. There are some gorgeous goldenrods out there and many of them make a colorful and well-behaved change from the endless daisies of the midsummer border. (Despite popular misconception, it is not goldenrod that causes hay fever; it is ragweed.)

When looking for native plants, you cannot just buy anything described in a catalogue as "native." Particularly in North America, which contains so many biomes, "native" may describe a plant adapted to a Quebec forest, the Utah desert, or a midwestern prairie. What you want is plants native to your own biome, and the only way to discover what these are is to look at field guides designed to help you identify the local vegetation. Keep an eye open for small books with names such as *Guide to the Roadside Flowers of Oregon*, or *Flowers of the Hedgerows of Sussex*. Plants that grow wild in local road verges and hedges are well-adapted to your area and are natives for your purposes, even if they were actually introduced from elsewhere many years ago.

You might imagine that using native plants as the backbone of your landscape would solve all problems of hardiness. Remarkably, this is not so. Some plants, like the goldenrods, have been cultivated in foreign climates for so many years that they may wither and die when returned to their native turf.

The Franklin tree *(Franklinia Alatamaha)*, a small tree with flowers rather like those of a magnolia, is native to Georgia but now extinct in the wild. Luckily, botanist John Bartram took specimens to his Philadelphia garden in the eighteenth century. Nowadays, Franklinia is so well-adapted to its adopted home in the North that it is considered a challenge to grow in the South.

For this reason, there is a lot to be said for buying plants that have actually been propagated in your part of the world. For instance, gardeners in the North in search of old roses would be well advised to buy them from Pickering Nurseries in Ontario, rather than from the Antique Rose Emporium in Texas.

A HOME NURSERY

When you start collecting plants, there is a lot to be said for setting aside one corner of the garden as a nursery—a temporary home for plants. Perhaps you can use part of the vegetable garden for this purpose because plants in a nursery do better if they are watered and weeded regularly.

The most amazing home nursery I have ever seen looks like a huge metal greenhouse with a built-in irrigation system. Instead of glass, the walls and sides are made of shade fabric, which can be rolled up to expose the plants to full sun. In this structure, the owner grows every newly acquired plant. Plants that suffer badly from pests are dug up and tossed on the compost pile, but the real moment of truth comes when a plant flowers for the first time. Then the gardener cuts a flowering stalk and wanders round the garden with it, holding it up against other flowers to decide where the new plant will contribute most to the color scheme.

You don't have to be a perfectionist of this persuasion to use a home nursery for many purposes:

• Save money by growing your own ornamentals either from cuttings or by buying them in bulk in small sizes. Tiny privets or yews will look like nothing when they arrive, but after a few years in your nursery they will be sturdy plants that will make a believable hedge when you plant them in the garden. If you plan to convert the children's play area into a parterre in a few years' time, you can save money and give slow-growing box plants for your miniature hedges a head start in the nursery.

• The nursery is the place to heel in things you can't plant yet and to store all those plants you bought and can't decide where to put. Stick them in the nursery until you realize where they should go.

• Most of us now and then acquire a plant we cannot identify so we have no idea where it should go in the garden. Pop it in the nursery until it flowers or does something that permits you to find out what it is and how it is going to behave.

WEEDING

Weeding is an unavoidable chore en route to the garden of your dreams. I am always amazed by interviews with experienced gardeners who say, "We don't have many weeds because this area has been cultivated for so long." I suppose if you had a roof garden in the middle of Manhattan such might be the case, but even there I would expect weed seeds to shower on my garden with every wind that blew and every bird that visited. For most gardeners, I suspect that weeding is second only to lawn care as the chore that eats up time we would prefer to devote to more exciting pursuits such as propagating plants and renovating the shrubbery.

Weeds compete with garden plants for light, water, and nutrients so there is no way to avoid weeding if you want healthy plants. There is also no avoiding the fact that a nicely edged and weeded flower bed looks much better than one in which grass and nettles tower over the flowers. Some people minimize weeding by planting things very close together. It is certainly true that as your baby marigolds grow fat and sassy they will shade out many weeds. But plants that are too close together also compete with one another and will never reach the size and beauty of plants that are properly spaced.

It is worth taking thought to make weeding as painless as possible. First, design your plantings so that all areas are reasonably easy to get at. We have a huge azalea hedge that is ten feet wide, backed by a fence, and a nightmare to weed. Every year it is choked by grape, honeysuckle, and Virginia creeper, which are almost impossible to get out because we can't reach their roots in the interior of the hedge. I am not sure there is a perfect solution to this problem, but a path between the hedge and the fence would certainly make life much easier and I may yet take machete in hand and create one.

It is worth experimenting with different methods of weeding. For years, I used a little garden fork and thought it was fairly efficient at getting out the roots of weeds. Recently I have found myself using a clawed affair that someone gave me and I think the weeding gets done faster. Give new methods a try and don't be a stick-in-the-mud about this.

Those with bad backs may prefer weeding tools that permit them to stand or sit. A friend uses a long-handled spade with a tiny blade to dig up weeds and then rakes them off the bed with a narrow lawn rake. Find out what works for you. For the nursery and vegetable garden, the easiest way to kill most weeds is to plant things in rows and hoe between the rows fairly frequently.

For those of us who are always behind with our weeding, there are consolations. Native plants of great beauty will occasionally pop up in our gardens. This year a lantana arrived in my vegetable garden and was three feet high and covered with flowers by the time I even thought of weeding that bed. One spring I was late cleaning up a flower bed. By the time I got to it, it was full of zinnia seedlings, self-sown by plants from the previous year. Since I had no great plans for the bed I left the seedlings and was rewarded by a spectacular display of flowers, which brightened up a rather dull border. A neglected lawn even produced native orchids, to my great delight.

Which brings us to the importance of learning to recognize weed seedlings. This isn't as big a task as it sounds, since you will probably find that a very few species make up the bulk of your garden weeds. When I am weeding, I leave any seedling I don't recognize. Sometimes it turns out to be a new and invasive weed, but more often it is an attractive wild flower or the seedling of some plant already in the garden. The seedling can be transplanted to the nursery bed to grow until it is large enough to take its place in the garden proper.

Mulches and Landscape Fabrics
Although some people find weeding soothing, most of us search for ways to avoid it. Mulches, usually stones or organic matter spread on the ground between plants, are the usual weed-suppressors. For starters, you can just buy bags of wood chips or other mulch and scatter it between your plants to help keep the soil moist and slow down the weeds. (The uses and abuses of mulches are discussed in Chapter 4.)

Similar to mulches are artificial substances, such as the sheets of black plastic often used in vegetable gardens. Landscape fabrics are a modern improvement. Unlike black plastic, these are permeable to water (and dissolved nutrients) and air. They prevent weeds from growing by forming a physical barrier and by keeping light off the soil. The fabric degrades in sunlight so you have to lay a sunshield mulch over it if it is to last any time. (The fabrics also look pretty awful unmulched.) On the other hand, mulched fabrics develop weeds. Weed seeds get trapped in the mulch or are carried in by rain or irrigation water and send roots down through the fabric. When you pull the weeds, you tear the fabric.

Still, landscape fabrics do reduce weed growth so what are the snags? First, using the fabrics around perennials and woody plants for any length of time may leads to carbon dioxide buildup in the soil. This is not good for plant roots, which need oxygen. Second, the roots of your plants will grow up through the fabric (probably in search of oxygen) and when you pull up the fabric you damage the roots. The take-home message is that landscape fabrics are ideal only for certain situations. One of these is erosion control. Suppose you have cleared a steep bank that you plan to hold in place with a fast-spreading ground cover such as crown vetch. Cover the slope with landscape fabric, cut small X-shaped slits in it through which you plant your ground cover, water, and leave. The fabric will keep the soil relatively weed-free until the ground cover spreads, by which time the fabric will be disintegrating and will eventually disappear.

Tools

It is amazing for how long one can garden equipped only with a cheap fork, a trowel, and a lawn mower. At some point, however, everyone buys new tools and it is worth doing this carefully because tools are expensive and it is easy to end up with a shed full of gadgets you never use. When you get serious about gardening, only the best tools will do. Happily, the best are not necessarily the most expensive. I would not be without my dibble (a sharpened broken spade handle) or my line for laying out rows of plants (two stakes joined by 30 feet of string).

Do not get seduced by the snobbery that holds European tools superior to American ones. It ain't necessarily so. I spent the first years of my gardening life using forks and spades with the short T- and D-shaped handles so beloved of English gardeners. Only when I first used long-handled American shovels and compost forks did I realize why so many English gardeners have permanent back problems. On the other hand, I can't imagine why anyone would ever use any but European pruning shears, despite their high price. My Wilkinson Sword secateurs have been with me for many years.

Even a lawn mower does not have to cost an arm and a leg. I once lived in a lakeside community where the lawns were small and

Pruning shears.
With this tool, it is worth paying for quality. Sturdy pruning shears will permit you to prune large shrubs and even small trees without using loppers or a pruning saw.

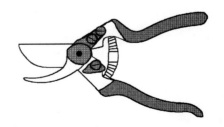

rough, filled with rocks and rabbit holes. The local farm and garden shop took old lawn mowers in part exchange for new ones, serviced them, and sold them. One summer we passed round the hat and collected $30 for a communal power mower from this source. This small but efficient mower lived outdoors and performed its function admirably for three years until the wheels rusted off. Then we passed the hat again for a replacement. Now, however, I live with an acre of lawn, permanently covered with a layer of palm fronds and oak twigs, and our lawn mower cost more than my car. After wrestling with various cheap mowers, we decided that the top-of-the-line Toro riding mower would save both time and temper. It has been worth every penny.

If you have a small lawn, investigate the new push-powered reel mowers. These are vast improvements over the exhausting monsters I remember from my teens and much easier to maintain than power mowers. They are also quieter and don't belch pollutants into the summer air.

If you have a large garden, you probably have, or want, a power tiller. However, these have disadvantages in addition to cost and pollution. A tiller churns up the top few inches of soil but it compacts the soil below this. If your soil contains a lot of clay, a tiller may be the death sentence to any hope of decent drainage.

Tillers divide into large and small. Large ones are wide and heavy and should always have tines at the rear, which makes them easier to use. Small tillers have tines less than a foot wide and are light enough to carry around the garden in one hand. They are easy to use whatever the position of the tines. I have a little Mantis, which I use occasionally to dig the vegetable garden and occasionally to start a new bed in the lawn. But its chief use is to dig planting holes for shrubs and trees, a task it accomplishes at high speed.

Maintaining Tools

If you invest in power tools, you must also invest in figuring out how to maintain them or they will spend most of their time broken down. Your most important task is keeping dirt out of the innards. This means replacing air and fuel filters at frequent intervals, changing the oil, and replacing any leftover fuel with fresh fuel after the machine has stood unused for more than about two months. Cleaning and sharpening blades also makes an amazing difference, as you know if you have ever replaced the beaten up blades on your lawn mower with new ones. Cleanliness and sharpness are equally important for hand tools. Use a file or a belt sander to sharpen spades and edgers, and wipe damp tools with an oily cloth before putting them away.

RECYCLING GARDEN WASTE

Before you have been gardening for very long, you will find that you are always short of organic matter to use for mulch, to improve the soil, and to use as fertilizer (Chapter 4). So you might as well start collecting organic matter by recycling garden waste.

One autumn day, near the center of Cambridge, I saw ahead of me a thick haze, which I assumed to be mist rising over the River Cam. It turned out to be smoke from a huge bonfire of leaves in the garden of one of the Cambridge colleges. Smoke from similar bonfires drifts through our Savannah suburb on most days during the winter. It is remarkable that in this environmental age people on both sides of the Atlantic are still polluting the air with bonfires and burning organic matter that their gardens need. An environmental gardener ensures that waste organic matter returns to the soil where it belongs and doesn't contribute to our air pollution or solid waste problems.

One of the most satisfying aspects of gardening is that essentially everything can, or should be, recycled. Disposable pie dishes, milk cartons, and instant dinner containers make bird feeders or pans for seedlings; plastic bottles that admit light can be used to cover small vegetables, warming them up and speeding them on their way. In fact the garden of a dedicated recycler could look like a lot like the local dump.

Recycling gives you the Earth Mother feeling that your life is somehow entwined with the land's—which may sound like bean dip on the brain, but may equally be a reflection of the thousands of years for which our species has been tilling the soil. Whatever the reason, recycling organic matter is a gardening necessity and environmentally vital.

Brush Pile

Most waste material in the garden falls into two categories: small stuff that goes on the compost pile and larger things that go on the brush pile and require more effort to recycle. Even wood decomposes, given enough time, but unless you make an effort to use up the material in the brush pile, the pile will grow faster than it decomposes. This may be acceptable if you have enough space, because a

Long-handled shovel.
For heavy digging, you may find this type of shovel easier on the back than a short-handled spade.

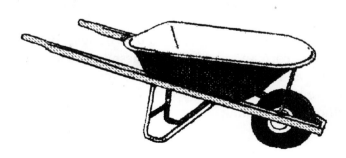

A wheelbarrow.
A large wheelbarrow or garden cart that you find comfortable to use is a garden necessity. A large tire makes for easier pushing when it is muddy. I also find a small wheelbarrow very useful. This is easier than a large cart to maneuver in small spaces and so light that I can transport it in the car when I need it for community projects. A neighbor has a small plastic cart that she uses for similar purposes.

Long-handled fork for compost or hay.

D-handled nursery spade.
A sharp nursery spade can be used to edge beds and to root-prune trees and shrubs before moving them.

brush pile is fine habitat for wildlife. Ours is home to several families of wrens and thrashers as well as miscellaneous snakes and rodents.

One approach to reducing the pile is to buy, rent, or borrow a chipper, a machine that chops branches into wood chips. The snag is that unless you have a large and expensive chipper, it will not take anything except tiny twigs and makes no dent in your collection of branches.

The brush pile can supply kindling for the fire in winter, pea brush for climbing plants, and driftwood for flower arrangements. If it contains large branches, you might also consider using them to build rustic garden structures, such as arbors, seats, or rose arches.

Compost

Compost is vegetation that has decomposed into crumbly dark brown stuff with a pleasant earthy smell. Compost is the most useful form of organic matter because it is high in nutrients, looks good, and is more or less free. You can feed it to your vegetables or scatter it around the pansies by your front door and make them look more beautiful. A layer of oak leaves and grass clippings here would have little social class.

A mystique surrounds compost, which many people view as an expensive nuisance to make. In fact, compost is nothing but the pile of decomposing waste in a corner of the garden. Weeds, leaves, twigs, grass clippings, vegetable remains from the kitchen, are thrown onto the pile. When you want the compost, you burrow into the bottom of the heap and dig it out.

The advantage of a simple pile like this is that it takes no upkeep. You can add a ton of leaves in the fall, then let the pile shrink as you use up the compost in spring. The disadvantage is that the pile does not decompose very fast. Big or woody things, such as twigs, pampas grass, tomato and corn stalks take at least a year to decompose if they are merely thrown on the pile. There are several ways around this.

You can speed up decomposition by separating things that decay rapidly from those that do not. You can use piles, or you can make the whole procedure neat and tidy with bins made of wood, cement blocks, or wire. Bins should be at least three feet in all dimensions for fast composting. These are the piles that we find most useful:

1. The coarse compost pile is the place for tough things, such as old houseplants with soil, corn and okra stalks. These things are slow to decompose and are allowed to take their time. You have to start a new coarse pile every year or two or you never get a chance to use the compost without dismantling a huge pile.

2. The regular compost pile is home to quick-rotting things, such as weeds, chopped leaves, turf, and vegetable leftovers from the kitchen.

3. A leaf mold pile is for everything that the lawn mower picks up— which means chopped up grass, twigs, and leaves. I find this the most useful pile of all because the organic matter is already chopped up and relatively weed-free so it can be used on the garden at any time.

   You can leave these piles to compost at their own speed or you can hurry things along by making a pile with layers of different material. Put down about a six-inch layer of material containing soil, add a six-inch layer of leafy things, and repeat until your heap is about four feet high. Make a bit of a dent in the top to hold water, sprinkle the pile with water occasionally if you think of it, and you will have compost after six months or so.

   When you come to use the compost, it may not look very beautiful. The material on the outside of the pile tends to dry out without decomposing and weeds grow on the pile. Just toss this unusable material onto the bottom of your next compost heap to uncover the compost in the middle of the pile.

   If you have enough room, it is a good idea to move your compost every few years by starting new piles in different parts of the garden. The earth underneath an old compost pile is so fertile that it will grow marvellous plants. Or plant a fruit tree nearby to take advantage of the nutrients that wash out of the compost.

   Most gardeners find they need more compost than they can make from their own garden waste. This is why, in areas where municipalities still collect garden waste, you may see gardeners at the roadside, loading the neighbors' bags of leaves into their cars. (You're performing a public service by reducing the amount of waste that goes to the dump.) We avoid houses where we know

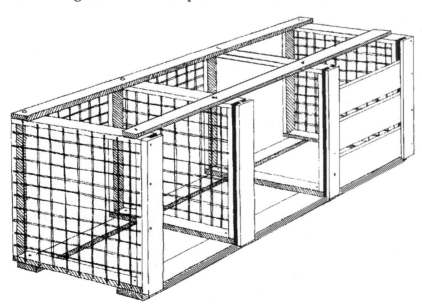

A compost bin.
The wire has been removed from two panels to show how the bin is constructed. The front is made of boards that slide into slots and are easily removed when you want to get at the compost. Build this bin of treated lumber and it will last for may years.

   There are several ways of organizing the three bins. One bin might contain completed compost for use now, the second might be where you collect waste to be composted, and the third might contain a completed pile that is decomposing.

GREEN THUMB TIP

COMPOST STARTERS

Compost starters are powders or solutions containing bacteria. They are supposed to act as the nucleus of the populations of decomposers that create your compost. You don't need them. Every leaf, every twig, and every handful of soil is laden with the spores of bacteria and fungi all ready to grow, reproduce, and form populations of decomposers to go to work in your compost pile.

Furthermore, these organisms are adapted to your climate and your soil and are much more likely to thrive in your compost than are immigrant microorganisms. Why pay money for what nature provides for free?

pesticides are used, and we save pine needles for mulch, but everything else (except the beer cans and hamburger wrappers) goes onto the compost pile.

Space-Saving Compost

Compost piles are an aesthetic problem in small gardens, but there are numerous solutions. My sister-in-law has one of those plastic compost bins that looks a bit like a rain barrel. You put the organic matter in at the top and pull the compost out through a little door at the bottom. She says it makes good compost, is just about large enough for her purposes, and is good looking enough to stand in full view against the house wall.

Martin Fry solves the same problem by composting on the spot. He leaves an unplanted strip of ground at the back of flower and vegetable beds and dumps weeds, leaves, and lawn clippings on this strip. The compost strip is not visible from the front of the bed and the system has the extra advantage that you don't have to carry your weeds any distance to dispose of them.

Then there is trench composting. The idea here is to dig a trench and use it as a compost repository until it is full. Then you cover the compost with soil and have a fertile area ready to plant. However, compost shrinks as it decomposes so, unless the compost is well rotted before you cover it with soil and plants, the bed will also sink. And it is certainly arguable that digging trenches is a lot of unnecessary effort that doesn't put the compost where it will do most good, which is near the soil surface so that the nutrients trickle down to the plant roots.

Fast Compost

If you are really into compost-making, you can make compost in only a few weeks. This involves giving decomposers plenty of water and warmth. One way of doing this is to chop all your raw material into small pieces, water it well, and place it in a black plastic bag in a sunny spot. A bag of leaves treated in this way will decompose in a month or two (depending on the temperature) and will contain most of the plant nutrients that were present in the original leaves. Since there is little air in the bag, this method encourages anaerobic decomposers, those that can survive without oxygen. These are also the decomposers that produce smelly gases, which may give you a slight shock when you open the bag, but will disperse rapidly.

An even faster method of making compost uses aerobic decomposers, which must be supplied with oxygen. You chop everything up into tiny pieces, add water, and stir the stuff every day in a pile or rotating drum. (Stirring increases the air supply.) The compost will be ready to use in a few weeks. It will have a higher nutrient content than compost made by slower methods but a lower nutrient content than compost made anaerobically.

CHAPTER 4

Growing Healthy Plants

The first secret of healthy plants is to choose plants suited to your climate. No amount of tender loving care is going to make a lilac on the Gulf Coast produce the masses of flowers of even a neglected lilac in Wyoming or Britain. Having chosen the right plants, however, a certain amount of attention is still necessary if most plants are to become sturdy specimens with healthy foliage, flowers, and fruit. This attention includes weeding and pruning, as well as providing soil in which the plants will thrive.

One of the most important contributions of organic gardeners has been to emphasize the importance of soil, which suffered severe neglect in the avalanche of inorganic fertilizers upon which gardeners came to depend after World War II. A 70-year-old Iowa gardener said the other day, "It has taken me 40 years to realize that the most important job of a gardener is improving the soil. If the soil is good, the plants are healthy, and healthy plants are seldom troubled by pests and seldom need watering."

Soil is an all-important variable in gardening. We cannot do much about the quality of the local air or water, but we can alter what goes on in the soil. The soil in most gardens contains more living organisms than there are people on earth and a gardener constantly alters the soil ecosystem.

Different plants are adapted to different soils but the vast majority of garden plants like moderately fertile soil that is neither very wet nor very dry. Leaving aside areas of the garden for plants with special requirements, the gardener's goal is to create and constantly renew a nice thick layer of fertile loamy soil everywhere in the garden.

Living with Your Soil

Before you start improving your soil, find out what grows well in the soil you already have and grow it. I learned this lesson the hard way a few years ago. Living in the Southeast for the first time, I inherited a garden in which Louisiana irises, ginger lilies, and flowering cherries bloomed abundantly and bananas, wax myrtle,

Berberis, among the attractive shrubs that thrive on clay soil.

and bald cypress grew at high speed. A few years later, I moved all these plants or their offspring to our new house nearby. And there they languished, refused to flower, and generally sulked.

I soon realized that we had moved from a swamp to a high and dry sand bank and the plants didn't like the change at all. The old garden lay on what was undoubtedly card-carrying wetland. The builders had filled the area with sand and shells dredged from a river bottom (thereby raising the soil level around several trees and killing them). After a thunderstorm, water stood in puddles throughout the garden for 48 hours and more, draining away slowly through the layer of clay that lay close beneath the surface. In the new garden, the clay was absent and the sandy soil was bone dry within a day of heavy rain. Now I mourn the scent of the ginger lilies and plan a bog garden so that I can have my irises back. Meanwhile, I search for plants that can survive humid summer heat while their roots bake in dry soil.

Life on clay soil is probably easier in the long run, even if the soil is poorly drained because clay soil is fertile. Willows, birches, firs (try *Abies koreana*), and all the maple family *(Acer)* enjoy clay soil. Among the shrubs, mountain laurel, rhododendrons, and azaleas will produce spring color if you are on acid soil, yellow-flowered Darwin barberry *(Berberis Darwinii)*, if you are not. Roses of all types and sizes will flower throughout the summer and smokebush *(Cotinus coggygria)*, sumac *(Rhus typhina)*, and European cranberry *(Viburnum opulus)* could brighten the autumn.

There are plants adapted to every conceivable combination of soil and climate. Try and find a few lovely things that like your garden just the way it is. These can keep you smiling while you drain part of your bog or turn your sandbank into dark organic soil.

Much of the world's soil has been eroded by deforestation and poor farming; and builders usually remove most of what is left when they build houses. My first garden in upstate New York lay on a hill that had lost essentially all its soil in less than a century. The area was described on the county soil map as "Volusia Channery silt loam, 90% eroded." This was forested country where nineteenth century settlers had felled trees and plowed the hills as best they could to plant corn and pasture grasses. The soil washed down the hills until only the valley floor retained enough soil to produce crops. The farmhouses on the hills were abandoned or sold to commuters working in a nearby town.

Whether you're gardening on former farmland, a coastal sandbank, or western semidesert, you've probably inherited poor soil. Many people in this position buy loads of topsoil. Unless your soil is really impossible, this is an expensive non-answer to the problem. To understand why, it helps to understand how soil forms and what makes soil fertile .

HOW SOIL FORMS

Soil doesn't just appear; it is made by living organisms. Mosses and ferns can live in even a thin layer of organic matter and rock dust. The organisms add their own dead bodies to the gathering soil, in which the seeds of small rooted plants can germinate and grow. Decomposers break down the organic matter in the forming soil, releasing nutrients. Many fungi grow close around, or even into, the roots of plants, in symbiotic associations called mycorrhizae. These fungi absorb soil minerals and pass some of them on to the plant roots. This supplies the plant with more nitrogen, phosphorus, and potassium than it would otherwise get, and so allows it to grow much more rapidly. As the rock breaks up and the bodies decompose, soil slowly accumulates. Depending on the climate, it takes several hundreds to several thousands of years to produce a thick layer of fertile soil naturally, but we can easily speed up this process in the garden.

CLAY AND SANDY SOILS

Soil ends up as a mixture of rock particles, decaying organic matter, living organisms, air, and water. The smaller the rock particles, the more tightly the soil holds water. Clay soils, with the smallest particle size, are said to be "light." They tend to hold water so tightly that plants cannot withdraw much of it. The other main snag with clay soils is that the spaces between the rock particles are usually filled with water and there is little room for air, which plant roots also need. At the opposite extreme, light sandy soils have large particles that hold lots of air and little water. Mineral nutrients and water drain rapidly out of sandy soil.

Fertile soil, such as the original soil of the prairies, is made up largely of organic matter. Manure, dead leaves, and bits of wood act like sponges, soaking up water and swelling when it rains, and later releasing the water slowly as the soil dries out. This alternate swelling and shrinking helps keep the soil loose, allowing roots to

UNDERSTANDING THE ENVIRONMENT

CLIMATE DETERMINES SOIL TYPE

Climate is the main thing that determines what type of soil forms because climate determines which soil-forming organisms can survive and how fast they work. The organisms produce a soil type that is typical of the climate rather than of the underlying rock. A particular type of rock will give rise to one kind of soil in a temperate region with high rainfall and to a completely different kind of soil in a semitropical arid region. In moist parts of the tropics, deep soil never does build up because decomposition is so rapid that organic matter decomposes as fast as it hits the ground. In the prairies, in contrast, soil may be six feet deep because the weather is relatively cold and dry so that organic matter accumulates faster than it decomposes.

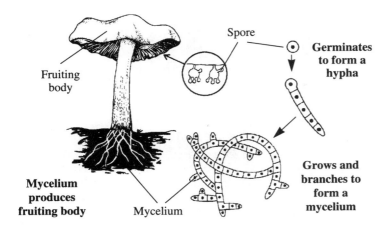

The life history of a fungus.

grow through it easily. Organic matter on top of the soil acts as a sunshield, reducing evaporation. And the organic matter in soil is a reservoir of nutrients, which are released slowly by decomposition. The take-home message for the gardener is that adding organic matter makes both sandy and clay soils more fertile.

If you add organic matter to poor soil on a regular basis, you will see improvement in quite a short time. The soil turns darker in color and eventually, one triumphant day, you will find earthworms as you dig, a sure sign that the soil contains a good supply of organic matter. Soil formation is a continuous process. Organic matter decomposes so, if you stop adding it, the soil will revert to its original clay or sandy consistency. This is why buying topsoil is no solution. When the organic matter in the topsoil has all decomposed, you'll be back to rock particles, which is probably what you had before you added the soil. The main exception to this is that sand, together with gypsum (calcium sulphate), is sometimes recom-

UNDERSTANDING THE ENVIRONMENT
NITROGEN FIXATION

In general, plants take oxygen and carbon dioxide from the air, water and minerals from the soil. The exception is nitrogen, a mineral nutrient that comes from the air. Air is about 70% nitrogen gas (N_2) so there is plenty of it around. Nevertheless, nitrogen is not readily available to plants because the only organisms that can absorb it from the air are a few species of bacteria in the soil. These bacteria fix nitrogen by converting nitrogen gas into salts of ammonia (NH_3).

It has been known for centuries that you can improve soil fertility by growing plants of the legume family. These include peas, beans, clover, and vetch, as well as trees and shrubs such as mesquite *(Prosopis)* and acacias. These plants add nitrogen to the soil because nitrogen-fixing *Rhizobium* bacteria live in nodules on their roots. The bacteria feed on sugars that the plant produces. In return, they supply the plant with nitrogen. Legumes have an almost unlimited supply of nitrogen, which they need to make proteins. As a result, legumes make rather more of their body parts from proteins than do most plants, making legumes nutritious high-protein plants for animals to eat.

Plant breeders and microbiologists are trying to induce *Rhizobium* to grow on plants other than legumes. Agriculture would benefit if more plants could produce their own nitrogen. Breeders also aim to produce a human food plant that contains "perfect" protein. Proteins are made up of twenty amino acids and humans need large amounts of some of these.

Legumes contain a lot of protein, but they contain too little of several amino acids needed in the human diet. These amino acids are produced in large amounts by plants such as potatoes, maize, and wheat. If breeders could produce *Rhizobium*-hosting varieties of potato, wheat, or maize, these plants might produce a complete human food and be enormously helpful in feeding the burgeoning human population.

Rest harrow, a European legume (*Ononis campestris*) with flowers enlarged in the box. Many legumes share this type of flower, which looks like that of a garden pea.

mended as an additive that makes clay soil easier to work. This may be a reasonable fix for a small raised bed, but if you have a large area of clay, it is impractical. (Gypsum also leaches out rapidly in areas with high rainfall.)

ACID AND ALKALINE SOILS

Herewith a little elementary chemistry: even in soil containing plenty of minerals, plants may not be able to absorb all the nutrients they need if the soil is either very acid or very alkaline. Many minerals come apart, or dissociate, into ions when they dissolve in water. Soils are said to be acid or alkaline, depending on the ions they contain. An acid is a substance that releases hydrogen ions (H^+) when it dissociates. An alkali (or base) is a substance that releases hydroxyl ions (OH^-). A salt is a substance that gives off neither hydrogen nor hydroxyl ions when it dissociates. Table salt, sodium chloride ($NaCl$), is an example of a salt.

The acidity or alkalinity of a solution is indicated by its pH. The pH scale goes from 0 to 14. A pH of 7 is neutral (neither acidic nor alkaline). pH values below 7 are acidic and above 7 are alkaline. Pure water is neutral, with a pH of 7, because it gives off equal numbers of hydrogen ions and hydroxyl ions when it dissociates. The pH scale is logarithmic, so a solution with a pH of 5 is ten times as acidic as a solution of pH 6 and 100 times as acidic as a solution of pH 7.

Soil pH determines the mix of nutrients that dissolve in the soil water and so are available to plants. Most plants do best at a soil pH

UNDERSTANDING THE ENVIRONMENT
MINERAL NUTRIENT CYCLING

Organisms require six elements in relatively large quantities: carbon, hydrogen, oxygen, nitrogen, phosphorus, and sulphur. All are present in rocks and are released, by erosion and weathering, into soil, rivers, lakes and the oceans. Some elements, such as nitrogen, oxygen, and carbon, are also present in the air. The movements of nutrient elements through the biosphere are called biogeochemical cycles. They are called cycles because minerals may be used over and over again by living things. Some statistician calculated that, on average, every breath you breathe contains several million atoms once inhaled by Plato—or by any other person who lived for 65 years.

Nutrients may cycle rapidly through ecosystems, entering and leaving plants every few hours or days, or they may become involved in such long term cycles that it is millions of years before an atom in one organism enters the body of another.

In terrestrial ecosystems, carbon cycles rapidly between living organisms and the atmosphere, taken in during photosynthesis and released during respiration. Some carbon, however, enters a long-term cycle, forming insoluble compounds (such as the calcium carbonate in a snail's shell). This carbon may be incorporated into rock which may be heaved to the surface millions of years later. Deposits of limestone, coal, oil and natural gas formed in this way. As we burn fossil fuels, we release their carbon back into the atmosphere as carbon dioxide.

Lack of nitrogen often limits the rate at which plants and animals can grow because the only organisms that can fix nitrogen gas are a few species of bacteria. The only source of nitrogen except the air is a limited pool of nitrogen in soil water, rivers, lakes, and oceans. Ecosystems on land continually lose nitrogen as it washes away in ground water and streams. This nitrogen is eventually returned to the atmosphere by bacteria that live in anaerobic mud at the bottom of oceans, lakes, and bogs, and release nitrogen gas.

Dianthus
Dianthus, *Heuchera* (coral bells), and *Aquilegia* (columbine) are among the plants that like a little lime occasionally if you have acid soil.

of 6.0 to 7.5, which is also the range in which nutrients tend to be most available. However, there are plenty of plants adapted to higher or lower pH ranges. A pH of not much more than 5.5 or thereabouts is vital for acid-loving gardenias, mountain laurel, cranberries, heaths, and heathers. (Rhododendrons and azaleas, although they are acid lovers, are not as fussy and can stand a slightly higher pH.)

Soil pH often varies considerably from one part of the garden to another and if plants are looking unhealthy, pH is one of the first things to check. You can do this by taking soil samples to a lab to analyze or you can buy an inexpensive pH meter.

CHANGING SOIL pH

Soil pH can be adjusted to suit the plants we wish to grow. As a rough rule, adding organic matter makes alkaline soil more acid and has little effect on acid soil. The leaves of most trees, for instance, decomposes into compost with a pH of about 6.5. Lime (calcium carbonate) is applied to acid soils to raise the pH.

Lime comes in various forms. Hydrated lime, also known as slaked lime or builder's lime, is lime that has been heated, crushed, and ground. It alters soil pH rapidly. Ground limestone alters pH more slowly. It usually takes the form of ground oyster shells or ground marl. Wood ash also raises pH since it is up to 40% lime and it is also valuable as a fertilizer since it contains 2-10% potash. Where soils are naturally deficient in magnesium (as in parts of the eastern United States), gardeners use dolomitic lime to raise pH because it contains calcium magnesium carbonate. The amount of lime you need to raise pH by a given amount depends on the soil type and rainfall. You can find out by experimentation or consult your extension service for advice.

As well as changing the pH, lime improves the texture of both sandy and clay soils. It clumps clay particles together making them larger and it packs sandy soil, slowing drainage. Since concrete and cement contain lime, remember that soil near a brick wall or concrete walkway will be more alkaline than soil further away, at least when the structure is new. Don't go planting gardenias next to a new brick wall.

If an acid soil's pH is raised too much, iron may precipitate out of the soil solution. Plants often show you when they are suffering from iron deficiency and the pH needs to be lowered. They develop chlorosis, a condition in which the foliage loses its green color, becoming paler and eventually yellowish, while the leaf veins become more and more apparent. The long term solution is to lower the pH with lots of organic matter but, for a quick fix, add chelated iron or an acidic mineral to the soil. You can use sulfur powder (most effective) or aluminum, ammonium, or iron sulphate. If you keep using aluminum sulphate, aluminum will build up in the soil, which won't bother your azaleas but may be toxic to less acid-happy plants if you ever tear out the azaleas and replace them with something else.

Chemical acidifiers are only a quick pick-me-up, like a glass of champagne for a bride's exhausted father. If you grow acid-lovers, and most of us do, you should embark on a long term program of lowering the pH by incorporating organic matter into the soil. Then everything will be happy.

On the subject of pH, another point to remember is that manure, even if well-rotted, may be surprisingly alkaline so don't go tossing it around your acid-loving plants.

ARID LAND AND SALINITY

All this discussion of soils gets a bit more complicated if you live in an arid part of the world. Arid lands are those where more water evaporates each year than falls as rain. These are warm areas with little rainfall. Plant roots pull water up from below the soil surface into their leaves, where it evaporates into the air faster than rain falls to replace it. As a result, the solution of minerals in the soil water gets more concentrated as time goes by. Then you are left with a salty (saline) soil. Most plants cannot grow in very saline soil because the salt solution actually drags water out of their roots by the same process that causes fertilizer burn when you give plants too much chemical fertilizer.

Probably no one needs native and other plants adapted to the existing soil as badly as a gardener on the saline soils of the western United States. And a rewarding collection of plants they are. Brittlebush (*Encelia farinosa*), desert lavender (*Hyptis Emoryi*), fairy-duster (*Calliandra eriophylla*), palo brea (*Cercidium praecox*), and acacias such as *Acacia Smallii* and *A. Baileyana* are at home even in heavy alkaline clay. Coreopsis, gaillardias, native lupines, yarrows (*Achillea* spp.), fleabane (*Erigeron karvinskianus*), with various sunflowers and evening primroses will give you a colorful flower bed where your neighbors have nothing but a couple of cactuses. Mulch the whole lot with crushed granite or whatever stone is cheap in your area and worry about the vegetable garden later—or give up vegetables altogether and get serious about native plants.

Saline soils are alkaline and they get more so when you water them with the local alkaline water. In limestone areas, soil and water may be incredibly alkaline. A gardener near Tucson, Arizona killed an orchard of fruit trees in six months by watering it with well water which, he discovered too late, had a pH of nearly 9. If your soil has a pH of more than about 8, you might as well forget trying to lower the pH. (One British magazine could think of nothing but "paprika" to recommend for growing in soils with a pH of more than 8.1!) The soil acidifiers you would need every year to

Most acacias have attractive fluffy yellow flowers.

reduce pH will cost more than building artificial beds and filling them with the most acid topsoil you can find. Even these beds will need acidifiers every year if your water is alkaline. If your native soil contains a lot of clay, use it to build the beds. Sunken beds lose moisture less rapidly than level ground or raised beds. Dig about two feet of soil out of a bed that is narrow enough to reach across and use the soil to build a walkway around the bed. Fill the bottom of the bed with topsoil and organic matter, and you will find you can grow even thirsty vegetables, such as corn and squash, using very little water. In this situation, don't even try to improve the drainage; you want the bed to hold water.

If your soil is alkaline but the pH is below 8, lowering the pH and breaking up the often rock-like soil is tough, but it can be done.

IMPROVING THE SOIL

Improving soil always means adding organic matter to increase fertility. Depending on your soil, you may also need to add lime to raise the pH, sulfur to lower it, or gypsum and sulfur to loosen clay. All these additives eventually vanish from the soil, so they have to be added at regular intervals. People with clay soil probably have it easiest because clay is already full of nutrients which merely need to be released. Usually, conscientious mulching alone will be

---

UNDERSTANDING THE ENVIRONMENT
SOIL SALINATION

Salination (or salinization), is the accumulation of salts in the soil and a major cause of soil infertility in many parts of the world, including California's Imperial Valley, which grows a large part of the United States' fruit and vegetables. Worldwide, about 5000 square kilometers of irrigated land each year goes out of production, its fertility destroyed by salination.

Soil salination has destroyed civilizations. Grain records in southern Iraq show that equal amounts of wheat and barley were grown there in 3500 BC. Fifteen hundred years later barley, the more salt-tolerant of the two, accounted for almost all the crop. Temple records show that the yield per acre had been more than halved. Cities such as Ur and Uruk, where writing and mathematics were invented, dwindled to mere villages or were abandoned as salination destroyed the soil.

Salts enter the soil naturally as rock particles dissolve. Salts are also present in all the water that falls on soil, either from rainfall or from irrigation. Salts leave the soil when they are absorbed by plants and when soil water slowly drains away. In most biomes the balance between these processes is such that the salt content of the soil remains about the same from one year to the next. But in some places, the balance between input and output is upset and the soil becomes increasingly salty.

Arid lands have naturally salty soil because more water leaves the soil than enters it. In practice, land is arid if it receives 20 to 25 centimeters of rainfall a year and semiarid if it receives 25 to 60 centimeters.

Irrigation is the most important cause of salination. When land is irrigated, much of the water evaporates, leaving the salts it contained behind. Calcium and magnesium tend to precipitate, leaving sodium as the main ion in the soil solution. Sodium is adsorbed onto clay particles, turning the clay into a cement-like solid that neither water nor roots can penetrate.

Altering the position of the water table can also contribute to salination. Sprinklers, irrigation canals, reservoirs, wells, and deforestation can all raise the water table. Trees absorb more water than crop plants. When they are cut down, rain water may penetrate deeper into the soil, raising the water level. In Australia, an estimated 500,000 acres of deforested land which once supported crops and pasture has been destroyed by salination caused by deforestation. In North America, the same problem has surfaced in Manitoba, Alberta, Montana, and North Dakota.

sufficient. Those on sandy soil, especially in warm areas, have the toughest job. This soil turns from healthy loam to sand dune in the twinkling of a bedpost if you omit to replenish the organic matter twice a year.

Whatever your soil, you can start by covering the surface with a thick layer of compost, leaves, wood chips, straw, or whatever organic matter you can scrounge, and digging it into the surface soil when you plant. The traditional method of converting lawn into garden is to dig up the grass, add organic matter, dig again, leave the whole lot over winter, weed in the spring, and finally plant. This is awfully labor-intensive. I add a new square to my checkerboard vegetable garden by using the designated area of lawn as a compost pile for a year or more. Lawn clippings, weeds, leaves, and any other organic matter I can find are just piled on the bed-to-be. This pile grows a fine crop of potatoes, mint, and weeds. (I call them "wild flowers" to make them more socially acceptable.) When the pile is high enough, we kill all the plants by covering the area with a thick layer of leaves for six months, then plant. The patch is relatively weedy during its first year and is never smooth so I use it to grow viny-weedy things like melons and tomatillos. But the soil is of marvellous quality and by the second year many of the weeds have gone. A tidier approach is to kill the lawn by covering it with black plastic or leaves and then to plant green manure.

GREEN MANURE

Green manure is a crop that is dug into the soil to add organic matter. Planting green manure is an amazingly potent way of improving the soil. A couple of crops of green manure is the only thing known to horticulture that will eradicate witch grass from a vegetable patch. Many people call green manures "cover crops" on the assumption that every bare patch of soil should be covered by something. And indeed, this is a good way to think of it. If you are preparing a vegetable bed or an area for a new hedge, do it a few months in advance, and plant a cover crop that will be dug in before you start planting. You prevent soil erosion and give your vegetables or shrubs a head start in fertile soil.

Seed catalogues today list green manures adapted to particular areas. Buy your seed from a wholesaler or farm store if possible so that you can buy it in volume. Green manure gets awfully expensive if you buy the seed in little packets. Some of the best green manures are legumes, such as alfalfa or beans, which add more nitrogen to the soil than other plants.

Manure

How about ordinary manure, everybody's favorite fertilizer since the Hanging Gardens of Babylon? It is depressing to learn that

Crabgrass, quackgrass, witchgrass.
Call it what you will, this European weed that spreads by stolons deep underground, is now a serious pest in most parts of the world.

modern research doesn't think much of it. It turns out that hay contains more nutrients before it has passed through a horse or cow than afterwards. Even the nitrogen from the urine and feces in manure does not make up for the nitrogen the animal has removed from its feed.

That said, I confess that the best vegetables I ever grew appeared the year we shoveled two large loads of well-rotted horse manure on the garden before planting. And I wasn't going to listen when people told me that two similar-sized loads of compost would have been even more effective. If you can lay your hands on manure in bulk, do so, just don't assume that you have thereby supplied your soil with everything plants could possibly need. It is essential that the manure be well-rotted, preferably left to decay for a year or more. Otherwise the ammonia in it may burn plants and any hay seeds in it will germinate in the garden. If you are offered fresh manure, accept with thanks, but add it to your own compost pile to decompose.

Rosemary Verey's inspired solution was to put the compost pile in the chicken run—not for the sake of the egg production, but for the sake of the compost. The chickens add their own contributions to the decomposing weeds and leaves, leaving high quality compost to be shoveled onto the garden.

MULCHES AND CULTIVATION
Back in the bad old days, gardening invariably involved lots of digging, tilling, hoeing, and other methods of disturbing the soil. Many of the world's great gardeners still engage in the back-breaking practice of double-digging a new or renovated bed. This involves digging the whole area two spades deep, mixing fertilizer, lime, manure or whatever into the soil and replacing all the soil. This is a heroic undertaking and far be it from me to knock the practices of the many gardeners who grow prize-winning plants in soil prepared in this way. They have my whole-hearted admiration. And I admit that it is a very satisfying experience to contemplate a newly dug and raked bed, lying there waiting for seeds or plants. But there are snags to all this stirring up of the soil. One is that you usually uncover thousands of seeds, which germinate into a fine crop of weeds when exposed to light and air. Another is that digging and walking over the soil tends to break down earthworm tunnels, nematode holes, and other air spaces, and you end up with compacted airless soil that is hard for plant roots to penetrate. In addition, every time you expose bare soil to the air, you increase the chances of it eroding—blowing away in the wind or washing away when it rains.

Modern labor-saving practice on the farm and in the garden advises disturbing the soil less often than in the past. After harvesting a crop, farmers can drill seeds of the next crop into the ground, leaving the roots and stalks of the old crop to decompose where they are. In the garden, we can supply the soil with organic matter by putting it on the surface as a mulch instead of digging it in.

Most plants benefit from a mulch of whatever organic matter is cheapest and easiest in your area. A neighbor of mine carefully rakes up the leaves that blow under her bushes and burns them, then sighs wistfully that I have a green thumb. I am trying to summon the courage to tell her that her thumbs would be greener if she would let nature mulch her camellias. Mulching is, after all, nature's way of recycling nutrients. Leaves, petals, seed pods and dead plants fall to the ground where they decompose. Worms, insects, and rain pull the decomposing plant material into the soil where it supplies nutrients to plant roots. Leaves that blow under bushes and into corners are also habitat for wildlife, such as hibernating frogs, toads, and hedgehogs.

UNDERSTANDING THE ENVIRONMENT

UNETHICAL MULCHES

There are some mulches and soil conditioners best avoided for environmental reasons. One is salt marsh hay which is valued because it contains no weed seeds. But it is harvested from a salt marsh. The food web of a salt marsh depends on last year's cordgrass (*Spartina* spp.) decomposing in the marsh to provide nutrients. If the cordgrass is harvested for mulch, the algae and bacteria in the marsh reproduce more slowly. Then there is less food for the oysters, shrimp, baby flatfish, menhaden, herons, and thousands of other creatures that feed in the marsh.

It is also environmentally unethical to use many types of seaweed, popular with organic gardeners. For instance, eelgrass beds on the east coast of the United States forms highly productive ecosystems that are home to millions of marine creatures. Seaweeds beds have already suffered great losses from development and pollution and the environmental gardener will avoid adding to the problem.

In Europe, peat moss is a severely depleted resource (although most of it is burned as fuel, not used by gardeners). Peat moss is dug from a peat bog, a wetland ecosystem characterized by acid soil that contains little air. Like all wetlands, peat bogs are disappearing from the face of the earth and with them carnivorous pitcher plants, sundews, venus fly traps and other marvellous plants adapted to life in this unusual environment. Europeans have severely

depleted their peat bogs and the push is on to protect what is left.

North American peat comes mainly from Canadian bogs and the Canadian Sphagnum Peat Moss Association assures us that it is still perfectly ethical to use Canadian peat. The industry says that although peat forms slowly, each year more peat moss forms than is harvested and less than one percent of Canada's peat bogs are harvested to produce horticultural peat moss. Bog owners encourage peat formation by leaving border strips of the original vegetation when they harvest a bog and cooperate with conservation organizations to preserve bogs for posterity. Let's hope it's true.

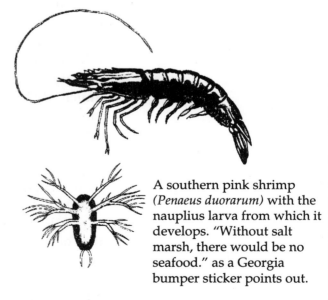

A southern pink shrimp (*Penaeus duorarum*) with the nauplius larva from which it develops. "Without salt marsh, there would be no seafood." as a Georgia bumper sticker points out.

In dry areas, stone and gravel mulches can actually add water to the soil. Dew condenses on the stones in the cold night air and runs down into the soil. Stone mulches are also useful for decoration. One Pennsylvania garden sports a group of pollarded willows in a gravel island. The yellow-green of the willow leaves, the gray of the trunks, and the silvery color of the gravel make a wonderful splash of color in the middle of a wide lawn.

Artificial materials, such as plastics and landscape fabrics, can be used as mulches in special situations. Black plastic is particularly useful in spring vegetable gardens in cold areas. Because dark substances absorb solar energy, soil under black plastic warms up faster than the surrounding soil. When the soil is warm enough, you cut small holes in the plastic to plant your early vegetables. Black and clear plastic are also used to "solarize" soil which means partly sterilizing it with heat from the sun. This is a common practice in warm areas where root-rot nematodes and similar nasties interfere with vegetable gardening. If the soil is covered with plastic for a month before planting, much of the nematode population dies.

I am prejudiced against artificial mulches except in special situations like the vegetable garden. I inherited one garden in which some landscaping firm had gone mad with sheets of black plastic. They had laid it right round the house, planted shrubs in holes in the plastic, and then covered the surface with wood chip mulch. A fine crop of weeds had seeded itself in the mulch and many of the weeds had rooted through the plastic. When I pulled out the weeds, swaths of plastic came out too. We moved before I got rid of all the bits of plastic that floated round the garden. Fabrics can kill a tree if they are wrapped tightly around its base so you can't use them to deter weeds round newly planted trees. They slow down the growth of roots so it is inadvisable to use them round shrubs or perennials. In fact, in my undoubtedly jaundiced view, they are more trouble than they are worth.

The mulches you do need are organic. An organic mulch looks tidy, smothers weeds, moderates soil temperature, slows evaporation of water, and supplies nutrients. Depending on where you live, the mulch of choice may be pine needles, sawdust, chipped bark, leaf mold, coco hulls, or one of a dozen other possibilities. (But not peat moss, which produces a hard crust that water cannot penetrate.) I can't imagine anyone being able to make enough compost to use it for mulch except in a few select positions. But if you've really got your compost-making organized, then compost is absolutely the best mulch.

A lot of nonsense has been written about mulches. You are told that decomposing wood takes nitrogen from the soil so you should add nitrogen fertilizer when you use sawdust as mulch. You are told to pull mulch away from the stems of annuals lest their stems rot, and on and on until you decide mulch does more harm than good.

Forget it. It's really pretty hard to go wrong heaving all the mulch you can find onto the garden.

RAISED BEDS

Raised beds are fashionable at the moment. But think this thing through before you mortgage the ranch to buy railroad ties, concrete blocks, or bricks and start building. Of course, a bed may be raised, as my cousin's vegetable garden is, because you add organic matter faster than it decomposes so that the soil level rises. This does not count.

In arid areas, we have seen that sunken beds are more use than raised ones. And if you live in a sandy area with heavy rainfall, a raised bed will merely make bad worse. Here, the problem is to keep nutrients and water in the soil. My soil is bone dry within a day of a heavy rain. In a raised bed, it would be dry in hours. Raised beds also tend to take a lot of maintenance. For instance, you can't mow right up against a raised bed so you have to provide a flat barrier between lawn and wall or spend hours weeding and edging. If your raised bed is surrounded by lawn, sink bricks or timbers into the ground around it. This will slow down the grass and permit you to mow right up to the bed.

Raised beds can, however, serve several useful functions. A rock-garden enthusiast with clay soil may find a raised bed full of sand and gravel the easiest way to provide the rapid drainage that most alpine plants demand. On soggy soil, even vegetables may do better in raised beds.

A raised bed may be one answer to an aching back. Make the wall high enough to sit on comfortably and the bed narrow enough to reach across easily and you can slide into a creaking old age while still growing exquisite primulas and other small plants. The wall can also provide decorative seating. Many an elegant formal terrace is separated from a lawn by raised flower beds surrounded by walls topped with stone slabs for sitting on.

In a flat garden, raised beds can provide height. Many tiny urban back yards are best landscaped by building a high wall around the whole thing—perhaps topped with trellis or treillage for extra privacy. Then you can pave most of the ground and surround this area with raised beds. Perhaps the far end of the garden will have a big raised bed containing a tree and a couple of shrubs, or a tiny pond with a fountain built into the wall.

NUTRIENTS AND FERTILIZERS

Clay soils are full of nutrients which only need to be unlocked by adding organic matter and lime to the soil. When I gardened on heavy clay, I never even thought about plant nutrients and fertilizer. You have enough to worry about in a garden full of clay without bothering about fertilizers. On sandy soil, it's another story.

Everywhere you look, you see plants with discolored foliage and spend much of your gardening life trying to correct multiple nutrient deficiencies.

We tend to talk about "feeding" plants with fertilizer. Purists object, maintaining that you cannot feed a plant because, unlike animals and fungi, plants make their own carbohydrate food. However, carbohydrates contain nothing except carbon, hydrogen, and oxygen which come from air and water. Other plant molecules contain additional elements, which plants obtain as minerals dissolved in water in the air and soil. When we fertilize plants, we supply these nutrients, either by spraying a mineral solution on the leaves or by adding the minerals to the soil. It is worth remembering, however, that a plant needs a lot more carbohydrate than any other type of molecule, so all the fertilizing in the world will not substitute for giving your plants enough light and water.

Most minerals are components of molecules needed in many parts of the plant, such as proteins (nitrogen and sulphur), nucleic acids (nitrogen and phosphorus), and chlorophyll (nitrogen and magnesium). An inadequate supply of any one of these minerals may result in rather general deficiency symptoms, such as chlorosis and poor growth. It is, however, difficult to diagnose an ailing plant

GREEN THUMBS TIP

CONNING CONSUMERS

What about these proprietary enzyme products and "soil activators" that seem to be popular at the moment? It seems unlikely to this biologist that these are anything other than another snake oil scam. Enzymes are special types of proteins, found in every living cell, which speed up particular chemical reactions. We ourselves contain thousands of enzymes.

Every organism makes the enzymes it needs to perform all its life processes. Most of these soil activator products probably contain bacteria spores and soluble fertilizer, although it is hard to be sure since they don't list their ingredients. They are not likely to contain enzymes that have been isolated from their cells, an expensive and difficult task. Bacteria, like all other living cells, contain enzymes so it is true that these products contain enzymes. But all you are really doing when you add them to the soil is adding a bit of fertilizer and some bacteria. The idea is that these will break down organic matter in the soil, releasing nutrients, which they may or may not, depending on the type of bacterium or enzyme. But the soil ecosystem will achieve the same result on its own without you spending money on useless additives.

Remember the story of the food coloring sold at high price as a rose booster. You added it to water and sprinkled it on the rose once a week. Did it work? Of course it did. The buyers were watering their roses regularly for the first time!

Another example of misleading advertising in a recent gardening magazine? "Kick the chemical habit with our best all natural organic and mineral fertilizers." That cleverly deceptive sentence suggests that if you use the fertilizers in question, you will join the good guys and dissociate yourself from the villains who pollute our waterways with fertilizer runoff. But what does it actually say?

A chemical is any combination of atoms, and chemicals are either organic (made by living organisms) or inorganic. A mineral is a rock with a particular chemical composition and inorganic fertilizers are minerals because they are made from rocks. A mineral is "natural" in that it was produced by nature. In fact, many of the rocks used as fertilizer were produced by living organisms. Limestone is usually made up of the shells of marine organisms that lived millions of years ago; so is phosphate rock.

So what is this advertisement offering? A mixture of organic matter with inorganic fertilizer. And you can bet that it costs more than it would cost you to make the same substance by sprinkling a handful of lime and ammonium sulphate on a pile of leaves. Save your money to buy plants!

since too much water and fertilizer produce many of the same symptoms as too little.

Plants need fairly large amounts of nitrogen, phosphorus, potassium, calcium, and magnesium. Calcium and magnesium are plentiful in most soils but the other elements often need to be added. Commercial fertilizers are rated by the percentage of nitrogen, phosphorus, and potassium they contain. A 5-10-5 fertilizer contains 5% nitrogen, 10% phosphorus, and 5% potassium, by weight. The remaining 80% is "inert" matter (meaning, I suppose, that it is not useful to plants). Plants also need various minerals in small amounts, including sulfur, iron, boron, zinc, manganese, chlorine, molybdenum, and copper. And when we say small amounts, we mean small; whereas nitrogen may be applied to the soil at the rate of several hundred pounds per acre per year, the treatment for molybdenum-deficient soils in Australia is two ounces of molybdenum per acre, applied once every ten years.

So how do we supply our plants with all the nutrients they need? The common method is to sprinkle dry fertilizer around in a random fashion and hope for the best. But this system has many snags and will not do for the environmental gardener. Inorganic fertilizers kill organisms in the soil. Soil that has been treated only with inorganic fertilizer for many years is essentially dead, the ecosystem of microorganisms and invertebrates that create fertile soil hopelessly disrupted. Some of the nutrients in inorganic fertilizers wash rapidly out of the soil after each treatment. This wastes money and pollutes nearby waterways. Especially in dry periods, too much fertilizer may make the soil mineral solution so concentrated that plants lose water by osmosis. Such "fertilizer burn" dehydrates and kills the plant. Too much fertilizer can actually deprive a plant of nutrients. For instance, excess potassium can prevent a plant from absorbing calcium and magnesium. In fact, many experts believe that more plants are killed by too much inorganic fertilizer than by any other means. One garden designer said flatly, "I have never seen a container-grown plant that wasn't over-fertilized."

You never get fertilizer burn from organic matter. So the first task for the gardener who wants to avoid the pitfalls of inorganic fertilizers is to add organic matter to the soil, constantly and in large quantities. This doesn't mean that every inch of the garden should be turned into a fertile loam. Save some areas for plants that prefer a leaner diet. One gardener consulted me about sickly camellias. It seemed that he was killing them with kindness in rich organic soil with lots of moisture. Camellias come originally from dry hillsides and cannot stand all this attention. Plenty of natives and even common garden plants prefer their soil dry and infertile and you can save your precious compost and water for those that like it.

Those of us on very sandy soil find it hard to lay hands on enough organic matter to keep the soil fertile, so we have to supply

GREEN THUMBS TIP

BUYING FERTILIZER

Consumers often pay much too much for chemical fertilizer—as much as thousands of dollars per pound for some brands of houseplant fertilizer, while others are selling for less that $50 per pound. How can you avoid being sold down the river? The simplest method is to find out roughly how much you are paying for nitrogen.

I have here two bottles of liquid house plant fertilizer: 5-10-5 costing $2.49 and the same volume of 12-24-12 costing $3.10. The first figure is the percentage of nitrogen in the fertilizer so I have paid 49¢ for each 1% of nitrogen in the first bottle and 31¢ for each 1% of nitrogen in the second bottle. The second bottle is much the better buy. You will also find that it is usually much more expensive to buy liquid fertilizer than to buy the solid and dissolve it yourself—although you'll probably need a calculator for that one.

our plants with extra nutrients occasionally. If you see plants looking yellow, examine a leaf for signs of insect damage or fungus disease which might have caused the problem. If there is no apparent pest or disease damage, and if you're convinced the plant is not suffering from too much fertilizer, you are probably looking at nutrient deficiency.

The nutrient most likely to be deficient is nitrogen. Research on crops growing in many different types of soil have shown that the best yields come from fields treated with organic matter together with a *small* amount of nitrogen fertilizer. The equivalent for a gardener is always to keep a supply of nitrogen fertilizer on hand and use it on any plant that looks a bit yellow. High-nitrogen fertilizers include urea, ammonium sulfate, ammonium chloride, ammonium nitrate. Follow the directions for use if you purchase these because they can cause fertilizer burn if used in excess. Nitrogen that is not used immediately by a plant is converted by soil bacteria into nitrates and nitrites, which are poisonous in high concentrations. These may build up in your vegetables or they may wash away and pollute the water supply. And don't go dolloping nitrogen on any plant that doesn't look sick, especially in the flower bed, since nitrogen encourages the growth of leaves at the expense of flowers.

Some complex organic fertilizers contain a lot of nitrogen, although you probably don't want to go to the trouble of burying an old leather shoe or dead fish under every sickly plant. Anyway, this high-nitrogen plant fertilizer is most useful if it is in the form of a dilute solution that the plant can absorb immediately and that doesn't need to be watered in. Some people drop a little house plant fertilizer into the watering can. Others keep a tub of "compost tea" to to carry to the aid of any yellowing specimen. This is a tub full of water into which you occasionally dump a shovelful of compost. Dip a watering can of the tea-colored solution from this tub for plants that aren't in perfect health. There is now some evidence from tests on tomatoes that compost and manure tea make plants more pest-resistant. The dilute but complex solution of nutrients in compost tea may well be the best fast-acting fertilizer there is.

You may or may not need trace elements, depending on your soil type and rainfall. If you live on clay, you probably don't need them. Sandy soil loses nutrients so rapidly that magnesium and iron are often in short supply and things like hydrangeas and gardenias may turn yellow from iron deficiency when they are growing rapidly. Epsom salts are a cheap source of magnesium, and why this mineral should often be cheaper when sold for human consumption than as a fertilizer is beyond me.

Is organic fertilizer better than inorganic? Well, yes and no. Organic matter releases its nutrients slowly and improves the soil's structure and water-holding capacity at the same time. Inorganic fertilizers used incorrectly are an environmental scourge, destroy soil organisms, and kill many plants. However, many organic gardeners will not buy inorganic fertilizers as a matter of principle and this has led to great inflation in the price of commercial organic fertilizers. I really cannot see buying bat guano, seaweed extract, or enzymes at hideous cost to the management when all I really need is a little ammonia, Epsom salts, a bottle of trace elements, or lots of compost tea.

MAKING DO WITH LESS WATER

Water seems to get scarcer and more expensive with every day that passes. You cannot even assume that you can use all the water you want if you are prepared to pay for it, because water rationing affects more people every year.

We waste much of the water that falls as rain. It is undoubtedly time we built houses like those in the Caribbean, with cisterns to catch water that falls on the roof. Roof cisterns are not practical

The nitrogen content of some fertilizers.

Source	Approximate analysis (%Nitrogen-Phosphorus-Potassium)
Ammonium nitrate	34-0-0
Ammonium sulphate	21-0-0
Bat guano	11-1-1
Blood meal (dried blood)	14-0-0
Compost	4-2-8
Cottonseed meal	7-2-2
Cow manure	2-1-1
Fish emulsion	5-2-2
Fresh grass	5-4-6
Hoof and horn meal	10-2-0
Horse manure	2-1-1
Leather dust	10-2-1
Leaves	2-1-1
Legume hay	10-4-6
Poultry manure	3-2-2
Straw (dried)	1-0.5-2
Urea	46-0-0

except in new houses because the house has to be specially strengthened to hold the great weight of the water. But people are beginning to build underground cisterns and to lead pipes from gutters into them. If your cistern can be located uphill of at least part of the garden, you can use gravity to get the water onto the garden. Otherwise you need a pump. A pond loses more water to evaporation than a cistern (which has a roof), but it may still be used to store any rain that can be led into it. And it has the advantage that it becomes a garden ornament and wildlife habitat as well. At the very least, make sure that your gutters empty into a rain barrel so that you catch at least some rainwater. (And then you have to tackle the problem of mosquitoes that breed in the barrel; there's no such thing as a free lunch.)

The usual rule for adequate watering is one inch of water every week from irrigation or rainfall. Vegetable gardens need at least an inch of water a week and often more. In the United States, most of the water on a garden goes on a lawn but, oddly enough, this is often unnecessary. Many lawn grasses go brown in a drought but they don't die.

The ultimate luxury is an underground irrigation system with sprinkler heads that can spread water to all parts of the garden. This sounds as if it would waste a lot of water, but if properly designed it may do just the opposite. It is important to have separate regulators on the water supply to different parts of the garden unless you're growing only one species of plant. Many gray-leaved plants, such as lamb's ears *(Stachys byzantina)* and mesembryanthemum will plain old die if they are watered regularly. Some plants just need more water than others and a single regime will not do for all of them. Ideally, you have timers to control the various parts of the system. Then you experiment to find out how little water you can get away with. Unnecessary water merely washes nutrients out of the soil. One western gardener in an area where it never rains in summer has his system set to deliver 15 minutes' worth of water to the irrigated part of the garden at 4 o'clock every other morning. This uses a lot less water than a couple of sprinklers in the middle of the day when about one-third of the water evaporates before touching the ground.

If you have a watering system on the surface of the soil, try out the new drip and soaker systems. Instead of spraying water in the air, these drip water onto the soil, again reducing the amount lost to evaporation. You attach a soaker hose to a tap and lay it in place in a bed, leaving it there more or less permanently and turning it on as necessary or controlling it with an automatic timer. There are a few snags, however. If your water is very hard, mineral deposits will block the tiny holes in the hose (or the emitters of a drip system). Even if you don't encounter this problem, I learned the hard way that you must cover soaker hoses completely with a coarse mulch such as wood chips. If the hose is exposed to sunlight for any length of time it

GREEN THUMB TIP

GRAY WATER

There is nothing wrong with using gray water from the bath, sink, or washer on the garden although it is, ridiculously, illegal in some places. If you use gray water, always use a liquid laundry detergent. Some of the powdered ones contain as much as 30% sodium and much too much phosphate for garden plants. Oasis is a brand of detergent developed in California specifically for gray water systems. It even has a useful fertilizer analysis of 4-3-6.

will deteriorate and holes will form which are almost impossible to repair. These hoses are particularly useful when you have just planted a hedge and want to give it a swift start in life. A summer next to a soaker hose may double the size of your baby yew hedge. When you wean it from the water, do so in autumn so that it has the cool winter months to adjust. Cutting it off cold turkey in midsummer would be too much of a strain.

Planting at the right time of year can save a lot of water. The vast majority of trees, shrubs, and perennials are best planted in the autumn. This is particularly essential in the Deep South where many plants die if planted in spring, no matter how much you water them, but survive if planted in autumn. In order to draw water for photosynthesis up from the roots, plants have to let water evaporate from their leaves (the process called transpiration). But photosynthesis, like all biochemical reactions, proceeds rapidly at high temperatures and almost stops when it gets cold enough. So a tree planted after the weather has cooled and after deciduous plants have lost their leaves will lose little water during the winter. The plant will use its

UNDERSTANDING THE ENVIRONMENT

FERTILIZERS AND POLLUTION

Oil and chemical spills make the headlines when they pollute rivers and lakes. But much more water pollution is caused by fertilizer that runs off gardens and farms.

Biologists define pollution as any undesirable change in the characteristics of an ecosystem. This usually means that pollution injures or kills living organisms. Or it may mean that pollution makes the ecosystem unfit for the use we want to make of it, as when the water in a river becomes undrinkable. Sometimes fertilizer poisons water directly. For instance, water polluted with fertilizer contains nitrates. In the digestive tract, nitrates are converted into toxic nitrites which reduce the blood's ability to carry oxygen, causing methemoglobinemia ("blue babies"). Nitrate pollution has caused the deaths of hundreds of babies, mostly in rural areas where a well used for drinking water is polluted by fertilizer from a farm.

More often, fertilizer pollutes water indirectly. When a body of fresh water is polluted with fertilizer or sewage, or naturally contains a lot of organic matter, it is said to be eutrophic (full of food). The opposite, a river or lake containing few organisms is said to be oligotrophic. Oligotrophic lakes and rivers contain few plant nutrients or lack one nutrient that plants need. Few plants can survive and there is little organic matter in the water. The water is usually clear and contains enough oxygen to support fish such as trout.

In eutrophic water, the many decomposers use up most of the oxygen. At the bottom live decomposers that do not need oxygen, including sulfur bacteria, which produce hydrogen sulphide gas, smelling of rotten eggs and characteristic of polluted ponds. When fertilizers run off a garden or field into water, they supply nutrients so that more vegetation can grow. As nutrient pollution increases, weeds start to grow in an oligotrophic river and you may wonder what has happened to the trout fishing.

Lack of phosphorus often limits plant growth in an oligotrophic lake. Many of our lakes and rivers now receive phosphorus continuously in the form of sewage, high-phosphate detergents, and fertilizer runoff. As a result, they are becoming steadily more eutrophic.

Oligotrophic waterways are much more appealing and useful than eutrophic lakes covered with algae, clogged with weeds, and stinking from the by-products of anaerobic bacteria. For this reason, there has been strong pressure to ban the use of detergents containing phosphorus and to speed the installation of sewage treatment plants which remove nutrient molecules from the water. In some cases, these measures have brought lakes back toward a more oligotrophic condition. (Liquid detergents usually contain no phosphate; check the label.)

food reserves to grow new roots that push through the soil, equipping it to absorb water from the soil more efficiently when the weather warms in the spring.

We are often advised to water deeply and thoroughly because sprinkling a plant when the spirit moves induces it to grow roots near the surface that will dry out quickly. I find this argument unconvincing. The vast majority of feeding roots, even of large trees, are in the top few inches of soil anyway. If your plants are well mulched, roots near the surface are protected from drying out. Furthermore, some of the world's great gardens grow in areas like the English midlands where nature does most of the watering in little dribs and drabs rather than in torrential downpours. And I also believe in wandering around the garden with a hose or watering can, sprinkling a little here and there when I feel the urge. This is when I do most of my casual weeding, discover that aphids are devouring my favorite rose (and wash them off with a squirt of the hose), and discover that the endangered fringed campion (*Silene polypetala*) that I have been nursing for years has finally produced a flower—not the dainty endangered bloom I was expecting but a blousy pink thing that reminds me of a chorus girl in a feather boa.

Most plants, especially those with soft leaves, wilt when they need water. But wilting is not always a sign of water shortage. In hot weather, even some well-established plants wilt in the middle of the day no matter how much water you give them. They simply cannot draw water up from the roots as fast as it evaporates from the leaves. Hydrangeas and impatiens often suffer from this midday wilt. They need extra water only if they wilt in the cooler morning or evening.

PESTS

There is no escaping the fact that trillions of valuable plants are killed every year by pests. There is also no escaping the fact that most of the sprays commonly used to control pests are poisonous to people and other animals or do lots of environmental damage. Pesticides include insecticides to kill insects, fungicides to kill fungi, nematocides to kill nematodes, and herbicides to kill plants. Perhaps surprisingly, more herbicides are used than any other type of pesticide.

Most modern pesticides are organic compounds produced from petrochemicals. These first became widespread during the 1940s with the advent of DDT to control mosquitoes that carry malaria. But there were plenty of poisonous plant sprays before that date. A 1939 book on vegetables from the Cornell College of Agriculture points out the dangers of sprays containing arsenic, nicotine, cyanide and various other poisons. (It also describes rotenone and pyrethrins, insecticides that are mainstays of modern biological pest control.)

In this age of ever-increasing protection for the consumer, why are we still exposed to hazards from pesticides? Part of the reason is that pesticides are inevitably hazardous: many are designed to kill animals, and humans are animals too. Part of the reason is the sheer volume of the problem. Of the thousands of organic compounds sold in pesticides, only a few hundred have ever been tested for toxicity. Often a lot is known about the properties of the active ingredient in a pesticide but nothing is known about the "inert" ingredients. Recent research on the weed-killer glysophate has disclosed that one of the inert ingredients causes nerve damage in mice. Although cancer gets a wider press, the greatest danger to human health from pesticides is nerve damage, because many of these chemicals work by paralyzing the nervous system. Another recently recognized problem is that pesticides may interact with other substances that make them more dangerous. An American died recently of complications that developed after he used 2 4, D on his lawn, apparently properly. Researchers believe that the chemical interacted adversely with the common drug Tagamet that the man was taking to control an ulcer. 2 4, D, the most commonly used weedkiller for lawns, is also almost certainly responsible for numerous cases of lymphoma in dogs and, probably, in children.

Most of the damage done by pesticides cannot be blamed on the compounds themselves. We are exposed to dangerous things like cars and lawn mowers every day of the week but we have learned to use them with care so as to minimize the damage they do. People seem to find it much harder to learn the safe use of dangerous things they cannot see, like the chemicals in pesticides. Farmers are more careful with fertilizers and pesticides than homeowners, probably because they work with them every day and because wasting them is costly. (They also have higher cancer rates than people in other lines of work although the jury is still out on whether this can be blamed on farm use of chemicals.) But gardeners spend relatively little money on chemicals and studies show that more than 50% of the chemicals applied to home gardens and lawns are wasted. They run off the soil and never reach the plant or pest they are supposed to affect.

So what is the gardener to do? The low-maintenance approach is to cultivate a philosophic attitude and to remember that pests are part of life's rich tapestry. Aphids are unsightly, but they don't do much damage to plants. Why not leave them alone? There is no need to aim for a perfectly manicured garden. Such a garden is a sterile environment, anyway. Without insects, you won't have insect-eating snakes, toads, wrens, mockingbirds, or robins either. If you can't stand a little caterpillar damage, your garden will never be gay with butterflies. It *is* disappointing when you have grown decent melons for the first time, to find that caterpillars have appeared overnight and destroyed every fruit, but the happy gardener reflects that it will all be the same in a hundred years. Remember too that many plants are tougher than they look. A few chewed up leaves are unlikely to kill a plant. I have a lovely rose that flowers in spring but loses all its leaves to black spot fungus by midsummer. Despite its defoliation, the bush gets bigger and the flowers more beautiful every year. I solved the problem of the bare summer branches by planting a climbing gloriosa lily next to the rose. The lily is a late starter in spring and doesn't get going until the rose has lost its leaves. Then it covers the rose with leaves and flowers until replaced by the rose's new leaves and big orange hips in fall. In a cooler climate, a clematis might perform the same function just as beautifully. For those whose laissez-faire is less well developed, however, there are approaches to protecting plants from pests that don't involve poisoning the neighborhood.

A first rule is that healthy plants sustain less damage from pests than those that are barely alive. Keep your plants growing strongly and they will shrug off minor pest attacks. A second rule is to consider pest problems when you decide where to plant things. For instance, cannas are native to our part of the world and so are their pests. So the cannas flower abundantly with no care but their foliage is brown and shredded by midsummer. My solution is to place them a long way from the house, behind other plants, so that from my desk I can see the splash of color they make and ignore the pest damage. Fremontodendron and ceanothus are popular in Britain where they are troubled by few pests; they probably suffer more damage in their native California. Planting bug-ridden things in a distant corner won't work in a tiny garden where every plant is on stage all the time. Here, you would undoubtedly be better off avoiding plants that get particularly pest-ridden in your area.

LESS-TOXIC PESTICIDES

Some gardening books provide lists of pests after each plant discussed. This seems to me a terrible idea. The lists are so long that the reader could be pardoned for thinking that every plant will be consumed by pests and that the only solution is to give up gardening altogether. The reason the lists are so long is that the same plant is attacked by different pests in different parts of the world and at different times of year. If you list every pest that attacks pelargoniums (geraniums), you'll have a long list. But nothing ever attacks my pelargoniums except a neurotic blue jay that tears up the petals. The place to learn about your own particular pests is a local nursery, cooperative extension service, or similar agency. Most extension services will identify pests that you bring to them and also tell you how to control them. Universities and government agencies also publish hundreds of free pamphlets on growing fruit, vegetables, and other plants in particular areas. Collect these pamphlets whenever you can. They will list the main pests you're likely to encounter and how to control them.

Damage to plants does not always mean you have a pest problem. For instance, air pollution may cause leaf damage that looks like a fungus infection. In many urban areas, brown spots on tomato leaves are caused not by pests but by high levels of ozone in the air. Various air pollutants are lowering crop yields in all parts of the world, not merely in towns. Pests are particularly unlikely to be the cause if only one or two plants are affected while others of the same species look fine. For a while, I was convinced that heat from a heat pump was killing two of our Indian hawthorns (*Raphiolepis indica*). Then I realized that a plant on the other side of the pump was unaffected. Plunging into the shrubbery, I discovered that the dogs had

Some less-toxic pesticides.

Compound	Uses	Notes
Bacillus thuringiensis (BT)	*Various strains target the larvae of mosquitoes, gypsy moths, cabbage worms, and other garden caterpillars*	*A bacterium that is harmless to humans, birds, fish and worms and most beneficial insects. Plants with BT genes built into them are now being produced by genetic engineering.*
Diatomaceous earth	*For control of cockroaches and ants*	*An inert, non-toxic desiccant; try not to inhale it. Loses its effectiveness in wet conditions.*
Dormant (horticultural) oil	*As dormant sprays to control scales and insect eggs, or summer sprays to control aphids, mites and scale. Use only on woody plants.*	*Petroleum based; can damage some plants. Avoid contact with skin or inhaling vapor. Toxic to fish.*
Insecticidal soap	*For control of soft-bodied pests, such as aphids, thrips, whiteflies, and mites.*	*Generally not toxic to humans.*
Milky spore	*For control of Japanese and other beetle larvae. A single application increases in effectiveness with time if the bacteria are happy in your garden and reproduce.*	*Bacteria that cause disease in larvae. Considered harmless to humans, birds, fish and beneficial insects.*
Pyrethrins	*Kills many pests such as mosquitoes, aphids, flies and beetles. Also used in household insect sprays and in flea and tick sprays for pets.*	*Isolated from several species of Pyrethrum (chrysanthemum). Breaks down quickly and leaves no toxic residue Toxic to fish and most beneficial insects. Avoid contact with skin.*
Rotenone	*Controls caterpillars, weevils, flies, mosquitoes, beetles, and many other pests. Also used to control lice and ticks on pets.*	*A plant derivative that breaks down quickly and leaves no harmful residue. Not toxic to bees but highly toxic to fish. Avoid contact with skin.*
Sabadilla	*Controls aphids, caterpillars and several species off bugs and beetles.*	*A plant derivative; not highly toxic to humans, but avoid breathing dust. Kills bees and other beneficial insects.*
Sulfur	*As a dust or spray; controls mites and some fungal diseases.*	*Can injure plants in hot weather. Relatively non-toxic, but some people are allergic to some sulfur compounds and the dust may irritate the skin. Avoid inhaling it.*

excavated a huge pit under one of the plants, exposing its roots and piling the dirt so that it covered eight inches of the stem of the other shrub. Ten minutes with the hose washed the soil back where it belonged and saved one of the shrubs, at least. (Or perhaps this really was pest damage because I should count the dogs as pests.)

In the case of fruit and vegetables, covering plants so that birds and insects cannot reach them is a big help in controlling pests. Spun bonded row covers and various kinds of netting are used for this purpose. But this solution doesn't work on the flower garden which is not designed to look like the washing line.

One of the troubles with many methods of pest control, organic and inorganic, is that they don't work and you have just spent all that money and time for nothing. People who sell these things are out to make money and there is as much quackery in the garden-supply industry as there ever was in the patent medicine business. Forget about those electric fences and underground sonic systems that are supposed to stop your dog, deer, gophers, or the neighbor-

---

UNDERSTANDING THE ENVIRONMENT
WHY MANY PESTICIDES DON'T WORK:
EVOLUTION OF RESISTANCE

The average useful life of a new agricultural fungicide these days is about four years. After four years, most fungi will be immune to the fungicide and spraying will no longer preserve plants from fungal disease. This is an example of the evolution of resistance to pesticides, a dramatic example of evolution in action. Consider this case.

A scale insect feeds on citrus trees in California. In the early 1900s, growers sprayed the trees with cyanide gas, and this killed the scale. But by 1914 some of the insects survived the spraying. The cyanide did not kill them because they possessed a single gene that permitted them to break cyanide down into harmless compounds. Insects without this gene died, but insects with the gene survived to reproduce, and they passed on the gene to their offspring. The frequency of the gene in the population increased with every generation until the whole population was resistant to cyanide. Scale insects, like many insects, reproduce frequently, so they evolve quickly.

Pests don't have things all their own way; the organisms they attack evolve resistance to their pests. At one point nearly all the oysters in Malpeque Bay of Prince Edward Island were killed by a bacterial disease. However, a few oysters contained genes that permitted them to survive the infection. These flourished and reproduced. Fifteen years later, the bacteria were still present, but most of the oysters were now resistant. Within twenty years, the oyster harvest was higher than it had been before the disease struck, and when the disease appeared elsewhere, Malpeque oysters were sent to contribute their genetic resistance to the newly afflicted populations.

If you have ever used a chemical weed-killer regularly, you have probably watched pesticide-resistance evolve in your own garden. At first, when you spray a herbicide on a gravel drive or a patio, it works beautifully, killing every plant it touches. But after a while, you notice that one type of weed, which used to be rare, is becoming more and more common until eventually it covers much of the area and the herbicide has no effect on it. That weed is genetically resistant to the herbicide. By removing all the other weeds, you are also removing its competition, so the weed takes over the area.

The genes that protect pests from pesticides do not appear in the population as a result of the pesticide. The genes have always been present, serving other functions. For instance, a gene that causes pesticide-resistance in oak moths also causes the moths to reproduce particularly early in the spring. This is not usually a good thing, since moth families containing this gene may be killed by cold, so the gene is not very common—until gardeners start spraying the moths with insecticides. Then the gene means the difference between life and death because oak moths without it are killed by the insecticide. Soon, the gene will be present in nearly every member of the moth population.

hood rabbits. There is no evidence that they work. I used to be enamored of those bright yellow Japanese beetle traps that lure the beetles with pheromones. They certainly catch hundreds of beetles. But several studies now show that plants get just as badly damaged by the beetles whether there are traps nearby or not. In this case, you can improve your success rate. Since the traps attract beetles, don't put them near the plants you are trying to protect. Hang them downwind and a long way away. If you have a real Japanese beetle problem and it persists for several years, you may want to increase your plantings of things that the beetles seldom touch, such as euonymus, rhododendron, boxwood, pears, magnolias, and dogwoods—which all sound pretty attractive so this might be a good idea anyway.

Sometimes garden writers say such silly things that you wonder if they really read what they write. For instance you are advised to spray camellias with dormant oil in autumn to control scale. This may be feasible if you have two tiny camellias, but if you have more than a few plants, you could spend all winter spraying. If you don't completely cover the top and bottom of every leaf, the scale will be back in force within no time at all. As a matter of fact, it will be back in no time at all, anyway, whether you spray or not. In this case, as in many others, the solution is to rip out any scale-ridden camellia and replace it with a variety that isn't susceptible. Pest-resistant plants are one of the best answers to pest problems. Plant breeders are working madly to select pest-resistant varieties of all the most popular garden plants. When you buy a plant, look for mildew-resistant phlox and crape myrtle, roses that don't get black spot, and disease-resistant vegetables. And if you don't know which these varieties are, your local nursery or favorite gardening maga-zine will often tell you. Don't trust catalogues on this point; since they are in the business of selling plants, they would have you believe that every rose is fragrant and resistant to disease.

Sometimes you pretty much have to use pesticides; for instance, when the house is full of fleas, or when you return from a trip to find the garden invaded by poison ivy, kudzu, fire ants, or something you're allergic to. I suppose you could move or give up gardening, but most of us reach for the weed killer or insecticide. The secret then is to use the pesticide that will do the job while causing as little peripheral damage as possible.

Biological pest controls are becoming popular as generally safer than other forms of pesticide. Some of these, like pyrethrins and rotenone, are chemicals produced by plants for their own protection. The fact that they are natural products does not make them automatically safe for children and pets, however. It is still important to follow the directions scrupulously. But it does mean that they are broken down by decomposers so that they don't remain in the environment for very long. Other biological controls

Crape myrtle, a summer-flowering small tree for Zones 7-10 which is prone to mildew unless you buy a new, resistant variety.

are predators or parasites of the pest you are trying to get rid of. Parasitic wasps, ladybugs, and various bacteria fall into this category. Most of these really are harmless because they attack only particular target pests that are their natural prey. Another safe group of pest controls are things like diatomaceous earth, a dust that works by abrading the waterproof cuticle of insects so that they die of dehydration. Sprinkling ashes that deter slugs falls in the same category. The trouble with both these pest controls is that they have to be reapplied if it rains—but the same is also true of most pest sprays which wash off the leaves if it rains.

The next offerings in our arsenal of biopesticides will probably avoid this problem. Plants genetically engineered to contain the genes of Bt toxins have the toxin built right into their leaves so it cannot wash off. Then there is the Indian neem tree, which produces azadirachtin, a terpenoid that mimics insect hormones and interferes with the insects' molting, reproduction, and digestion, and is also a bactericide. The advantage of azadirachtin (marketed in the United States as Margosan-O) is that it is absorbed into the leaves of anything it is sprayed onto, poisoning insects that eat the leaf but not beneficial insects, which eat other insects and not leaves.

Rose growers in our area insist that changing the mulch under their roses each year reduces pest problems. This is an example of "garden hygiene," cleaning pest-infected plants and debris out of the garden. You are told to remove every black spot-tainted rose leaf and throw it away (rather than adding it to the compost where the fungus will survive). If you have more than a few roses that's another bit of hopelessly optimistic advice like spraying both sides of every camellia leaf, but never mind. I must confess that I am not completely convinced by the logic of all this cleanup advice. It is true that fungal spores and insects overwinter in mulch and other dead vegetation. But if your soil is reasonably fertile, a little digging will convince you that they also overwinter quite deep in the soil and you are not going to get rid of soil pests by throwing out the mulch. And the spores of fungi and bacteria are in the air and on the plants around us all the time. On top of all this, trying to clean out dead plant material makes it difficult to also supply your plants with all the organic matter they need. Perhaps the thing to do is perform a few experiments in this area and to use common sense about your own situation. For instance, removing the mulch round your roses can't possibly prevent pests if your rose garden lies cheek by jowl with that of a neighbor who leaves the mulch in place.

CHAPTER 5

Trees

Trees and shrubs are the skeleton of the garden. They determine its character and the background against which other plants will be seen. Perhaps you have inherited a garden full of lovely old trees and you will have to live with the character that they impose on the place. Perhaps you have a new house with a barren landscape which needs trees in a hurry to give it character, shade, and shelter from the wind. Or you may have an overgrown lot where trees planted by previous owners are now too big for their sites and the most urgent need is to thin the jungle to let in some light.

Whether or not you keep existing trees, it is important to plant new trees. Not only will you be doing your bit for global reforestation and pollution control, but you will have up-and-coming replacements on their way if any of your old trees are destroyed by old age or severe weather. When lightning and hurricanes hit, old trees are the first to go. If no one has planted young trees over the years, the result may be a landscape that looks as if someone had dropped a bomb on it.

Trees do not have to cost much. A neighbor has husband and children give her a tree each year for Mother's Day. They give her large trees in containers and she now has an attractive mixed woodland in the garden. In most communities, small trees are given away by community organizations celebrating Arbor Day or some such occasion. Government conservation and forestry departments often have free trees to give to those who can use them. These tend to be small seedlings in large quantities, but the local garden club may pot them up and give them away separately.

Don't assume that you can't use a tiny tree because it will grow too slowly. Trees are usually listed as fast, slow, or medium-speed growers, but most trees are not as simple as this. They are more like children: they grow in spurts. A tree may take a while to settle into a new home, apparently not growing at all while its root

Sabal palmetto.
The palmetto, or cabbage palm, is native to the coastal southeastern United States. (Carol Johnson)

system develops. Then it puts on an adolescent spurt that takes it from three to thirty feet in a few years. As it ages, its growth slows down again.

I transplanted three black cherry seedlings (*Prunus serotina*) from under the old black cherry in our garden. Less than three feet high when I moved them, a year later the seedlings are nine feet tall and will provide partial shade for the house within a few years. Moved from crowded woodland to an open space by the house, they have taken on a rounded shape, with leaves close together and nice straight trunks. Tree seedlings can grow amazingly fast when given enough space, a good mulch, and some extra water. Roadsides, woodlands, vacant lots, overgrown gardens, and your friendly neighborhood park are all possible sources of seedling trees that will grow beautifully for you. Thousands of tree species can be grown from seed and many are hard to grow *except* from seed. If you want a palmetto (*Sabal palmetto*) or a longleaf pine (*Pinus palustris*), pop seeds in a large container in your home nursery and eventually you will have a plant that the neighbors envy.

DESIGNING WITH TREES

If you have a fairly large property, you want trees to provide energy savings, wildlife habitat, and visual effects. Trees may frame or block views, add shape and color to the ceilings of your garden "rooms," or stand as focal points in open spaces.

There is no such thing as the perfect tree for a situation because trees change all the time. Most mature trees, however, remain roughly the same size and shape for many years and it is this mature size and shape that has to be taken into account when you plant. Trees, like people, have the vices of their virtues. A fast-growing tree will shade the patio within a year or two—and shade the vegetable garden in three or four. A tree with lovely flowers and fruit will delight you with its beauty—and drop petals and nuts all over the front path a little later.

If your garden is small, you will do most of your landscaping with shrubs, perhaps adding height and shade with one or two small trees. I particularly like small trees with somewhat horizontal branches that appear to embrace the shrubs and flowers beneath them. Dogwoods and magnolias grow in this way as do many fruit trees—but not things like Bradford pears, which develop graceless, almost spherical, heads. Choose a Kousa dogwood in preference to an American dogwood to avoid dogwood anthracnose, a disease that is now spreading in the eastern United States.

Another way to landscape a small garden is to forget graceful, horizontal lines and concentrate on a mixture of textures. Suppose you step out of the living room onto a small stone terrace with a fountain in the wall on one side with ferns and hostas under it, and an evergreen cherry laurel (*Prunus laurocerasus*) or Brazil cherry

(*Eugenia brasiliensis*) pruned to a mophead and arranged to partly block the view of the garden on the other. Beyond the cherry laurel, you can see the spiky shape of the cabbage palm, *Cordyline australis* (summering in a pot where it is not hardy) in front of an informal hedge of shrubs that surround the rest of the garden. Add clematis and ivy to one side and pelargoniums, daylilies, lobelia, and sweet alyssum for color, and you have a lush garden with a multitude of interesting textures.

You can control the shape of a small tree by thoughtful pruning, but large trees have wills of their own and you'll be happier if you like the shapes they adopt naturally. There are enormous variations. The branches of some oaks actually grow downward. The effect of horizontal, drooping branches is stunning, but the pruning costs will get you down if you have to keep the tree from blocking your drive. Elms have dramatic vase shapes, which are best viewed from a distance, while a corkscrew willow has wiggly branches that are a delight in closeup. Beware of the unexpectedly upright shape of some ornamental cherries (*Prunus* spp.). I once bought a cherry guaranteed by the catalogue to spread wide branches over a path. The flowers were as lovely as promised but the branches refused to do anything but grow straight up despite all my careful pruning. I even resorted to wedges between trunk and branches and hanging weights on the branches in an attempt to make them go sideways. But trees have much more staying power than humans and usually win battles of this type.

Gymnosperms (conifers such as spruces, pines, and firs) are even more variable in shape than angiosperm trees. (Angiosperms are the flowering plants.) Gymnosperms frequently produce "sports," mutant offspring very different from their parents. So a

Creating a mophead or umbrella-shaped tree.

Use a tree with small leaves. Tie it to a stake (with soft ties such as old pantyhose) to keep the trunk straight and prune unwanted growth from the trunk each year until the tree reaches the desired height. At the same time, shear the top growth lightly to make it thick and bushy. When the tree is tall enough, you can either leave the top as a sphere (mophead) or trim it flat underneath to produce the umbrella shape shown here. A group of mopheads makes a fine formal accent in the middle of a lawn or you might use a pair to emphasize a front door.

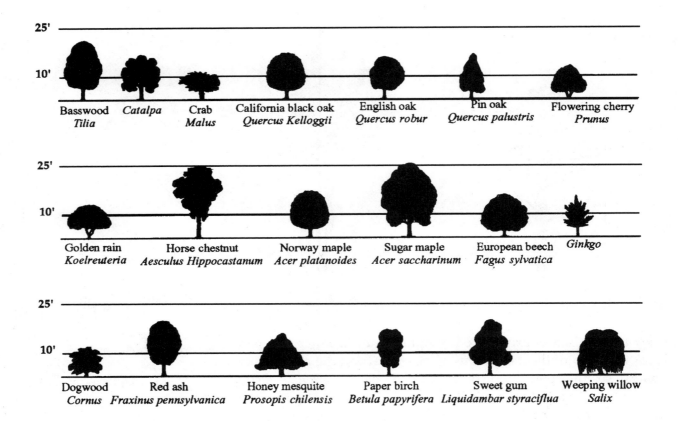

Basswood *Tilia*	*Catalpa*	Crab *Malus*	California black oak *Quercus Kelloggii*	English oak *Quercus robur*	Pin oak *Quercus palustris*	Flowering cherry *Prunus*

Golden rain *Koelreuteria*	Horse chestnut *Aesculus Hippocastanum*	Norway maple *Acer platanoides*	Sugar maple *Acer saccharinum*	European beech *Fagus sylvatica*	*Ginkgo*

Dogwood *Cornus*	Red ash *Fraxinus pennsylvanica*	Honey mesquite *Prosopis chilensis*	Paper birch *Betula papyrifera*	Sweet gum *Liquidambar styraciflua*	Weeping willow *Salix*

The shapes of some popular trees with the approximate size they reach in eight to ten years.
In some cases, this bears little relation to the tree's final size. For instance, a ginkgo grows to about 80 feet but starts slowly whereas a crab or cherry is almost full grown after ten years.

single species of juniper may include varieties that grow to 60 feet at the drop of a hat, ones that produce neat little evergreen muffins without pruning, and ground-hugging creepers. Most gardeners have gone into shock on at least one occasion when their "low-growing junipers" blocked the windows in a couple of years.

It is difficult to bring ourselves to cut down a tree, but sometimes you have to harden your heart and call in the tree service. The Northeast contains many farmhouses that look as if they are being pushed over by huge Norway spruces (*Picea abies*) planted close to the house a century ago by people anxious for rapid shelter. Years later, the trees are undermining the foundations and blocking the view. And, if the tree were felled, the house would stand naked on its hillside because no one has planted any trees since the house was built so there is no grove of young trees ready to take over.

TREES FOR ALL SEASONS
Landscape designers tend to use many trees of the same type to produce a coherent picture, but the prudent gardener never plants too many of any one species. That way lies disaster by disease. When Dutch elm disease wiped out millions of elm trees, towns, universities, and homeowners with quadrangles and avenues of elms lost all their landscaping in a few horrible years. Those with plenty of other species in their streets and gardens only had to

replace a few trees. If your trees are of various ages and several species, neither hurricane, gypsy moth, chestnut blight, nor too much salt on the road will ruin your garden.

For my money, most of the trees in most gardens should be natives. These are the ones that grow well, look right, and persuade the local wildlife to make their home with you. But there is no reason that you cannot have trees that add interest to the garden in all seasons. This is more difficult if you have to do it with one or two trees in a small garden, but it can be done.

Anyone who has driven through Virginia in spring must yearn for redbuds. Acres of these little purple-flowered trees at the forest's edge look down on highway medians planted with forsythia by a highway department with more romance in its heart than you expect from highway departments. The result is a symphony in purple and yellow. A redbud has flowers in spring, good foliage color in summer and fall, and shapely limbs in winter—at least if it has been properly pruned. Before you plunge into the local woods looking for baby redbuds, however, you need to know that redbuds are very difficult to transplant so you will be better off with one grown in a container. In addition, there are many different species and varieties and if you don't live in redbud country, you may need especially hardy specimens.

Fall leaf color is an obvious seasonal feature, but consider the color of leaves when buds break in spring as well. Some trees have lovely yellow and lime green colors in their young leaves; in others, new leaves and even twigs are red. Then there is trunk color. Sycamores, birches, and cherries are often more memorable for their lovely bark than for their foliage. Silver bark doesn't pack much of a punch against a background of snow, but the mahogany color of cherries does. And don't forget possible disadvantages of seasonal interest. Mulberries on the front path can ruin your carpets; conkers and hazelnuts, beautiful as they are, can make a mess of a lawn mower.

Coniferous Trees

When choosing trees, the first decision is whether you need deciduous trees or evergreens. For climate control, deciduous trees are usually better. These cut out the sun in summer and then lose their leaves so that the sun can reach the house and warm it in winter. On the other hand, traffic does not stop in winter, so most of the trees and shrubs that cut off the sight and sound of the road should be evergreen.

There are lots of evergreen angiosperms, often called broad-leaved evergreens to distinguish them from needle-leaved gymnosperms. Many of these come from China and Japan and were assumed to be too tender for northern areas. Now, experiments at places such as Boston's Arnold Arboretum are showing that many

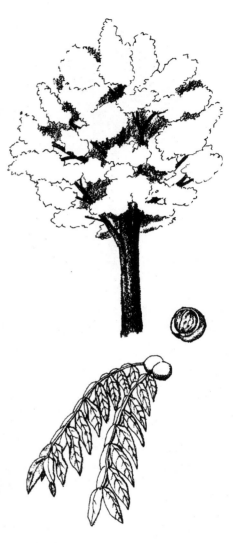

Walnut tree, *Juglans regiae.*
Walnuts make lovely shade trees. They produce valuable timber and edible nuts.

Many pine trees have graceful, irregular crowns.

broad-leaved evergreens tolerate cold weather better than expected, so don't rule them out if you have cold winters. But the widest range of evergreens is still to be found among the gymnosperms. Most gymnosperms are native to northern temperate areas, but they come in every conceivable shape and size, adapted to almost every corner of the earth. Some, such as larches and bald cypresses, are even deciduous, their leaves turning an attractive rust color before they fall in autumn.

If you want a thick screen between you and the road or an ugly view, your best bet is probably a cypress or fir with fairly small needles that doesn't lose its lower branches as it ages as most conifers do. If the tree loses only the branches nearest the ground you can fill the gap with broad-leaved evergreen shrubs. But many pines lose at least the lower 30 feet of branches and do not make a satisfactory screen.

Pines

I confess to a soft spot for the many species of pine with handsome, irregular crowns. These throw filtered shade on the ground, perfect for shade-loving beauties such as dogwoods, redbuds, azaleas, and rhododendrons. And pine trees obligingly mulch the shrubs beneath them by dropping a layer of pine straw every year. Queen of the pines is *Pinus palustris*, the longleaf pine, native to the southern United States, with needles more than a foot long. This, like many

REFORESTATION AND THE GREENHOUSE EFFECT

We are often urged to plant trees to save the world from overheating. How does this work?

Nitrogen and oxygen make up about 99% of clean, dry air. In addition, air contains small amounts of water vapor, carbon dioxide, and methane. These gases, however, are very important because they absorb infrared radiation (heat) from the earth. They trap this heat within the atmosphere, preventing it from escaping into space. This "greenhouse" of gases warms the earth's surface from minus 18 °C to habitable temperatures. Without the greenhouse effect, the earth would be too cold for life. However, the more of these gases the atmosphere contains, the more heat is retained. Human activities add small quantities of water vapor to the atmosphere but, much more important, they add lots of carbon dioxide and methane, and these are increasing temperatures on earth.

The methane comes mainly from "flatulent cows," since cows, sheep, and other ruminants contain bacteria that produce methane. This is not a trivial source of greenhouse gas. Methane is much more effective than carbon dioxide at retaining heat and the earth's livestock population is exploding even faster than the human population—partly because of widespread soil erosion that leaves soil unsuitable for crops but still able to grow scattered grass and shrubs on which livestock can feed. Carbon dioxide is added to the air when we burn wood and fossil fuel. It leaves the air when it dissolves in water and when it is used by plants for photosynthesis.

Scientists cannot predict how fast the earth will warm because there are too many variables to build an accurate model. But there is no question that we can help to slow global warming by planting trees—or any other plant, but trees are more effective because they are larger. From the Pacific Northwest to the tropical forests of Indonesia, millions of acres of forest a year are cut down and the remnants burned. It is unrealistic to hope that this rate will slow before most of the world's natural forest has gone. Our only chance of having enough forest in the twenty-first century to slow climate changes and support rural economies is to plant trees.

pines, is adapted to surviving forest fires. Its seeds need extreme heat to germinate. When young, a longleaf pine goes through a "grass" stage, resting at only a few feet high for years. It is too short to be injured by crown fires flashing though the forest canopy overhead. The short stalk with a bushy crewcut of needles is a familiar sight by southern roadsides where our children christened it the "punk pine." Eventually, with food stored in roots and leaves for the big breakout, the pine shoots upward, growing as much as six feet a year until its crown is well above the undergrowth where forest fires are hottest. This pine, by the way, is hard to transplant because it develops an enormous tap root. And I don't like the look of the scale insects on the grass stage longleaf in my garden, so perhaps it is also rather fussy about where it lives.

Although pines occupy little space in the garden when they mature, young ones are as bad as palm trees for occupying large areas when their crowns are spread out at ground level. An exception is the Japanese black pine (*Pinus thunbergii*), which gets its branches off the ground early in life. This is the pine that Japanese gardeners train into tortured shapes so that even a young tree looks centuries old. This is fun to try. You thicken up the trunk and branches by cutting each candle in half in spring. (Candles are the candle-shaped buds of the new year's needles.) Then prune the branches so that they are well-spaced and more-or-less horizontal. Remove any twigs and leaves that hide the shape of the trunk and

The world is not fiddling while our forests burn. An estimated 15 million acres of land are now planted with trees each year (although this is still less than the 28 million acres of forest that are felled each year). By 2000, the area reforested each year is expected to grow to 42 million acres. In 1970, the forest area of New England, though smaller than in precolonial times, was 40% greater than in 1890. China has doubled its forested area in less than 20 years.

Many programs have increased the tree cover in developed countries, particularly in urban areas. Arbor Day is an American institution, a day when people and organizations are encouraged to plant trees in their communities. The College of William and Mary in Virginia lacked the space to establish a separate arboretum. So the College documented all the trees and shrubs that already existed on campus then encouraged various groups to pay for particular species of trees that would add to the collection. The result is a campus forested with native trees and exotic species, with an educational program to match. The University of Idaho has a similar collection of trees and shrubs with labels that identify the species and the donor.

In India, one state instituted a program of planting windbreak trees on state land beside roads and canals. In the past, such trees were rapidly destroyed by villagers desperate for firewood. But now nearby villages protect the saplings, and in return can cut the grass under the trees and take a share of the profits when the trees are harvested. The trees thrive. The most popular forestry in dry areas is planting green belts, large windbreaks which protect towns and villages from winds, dust storms, or encroaching sand dunes, and which can be harvested for firewood, poles, or fodder. More trees go into the town itself, providing shade and improving air quality. The once dusty desert town of Bouza in Niger is now famous for its cool tree-lined streets.

Imaginative forestry programs have reforested large areas, using the latest research to choose appropriate trees for different purposes. The trees serve dozens of useful functions as well as slowing global warming.

presto! An instant, gnarled "old" pine tree, small enough for a city courtyard. By pruning once a year you can keep it to any size you want.

A Warning on Size

It is horribly easy to plant trees that are too big for their sites and then not remove them when you should. Our landscapes are full of disasters waiting to happen. For instance, Leyland cypresses are popular at the moment, but this is partly because they haven't been around long and they are very pretty in their young years. But if you looked at roadside plantings of Leyland cypress in Britain, you would shudder and rip out your own. These huge trees are rapidly shooting skyward past 50-year old pines and have lost all their lower limbs. They are also susceptible to various pests including the charmingly named bagworm. Leyland cypress is only suitable for hedging for five years or so while slower growing plants catch up. A better choice is red cedar (*Juniperus virginiana*) or Rocky Mountain juniper (*Juniperus scopulorum*) especially if you buy one of the excellent varieties with fastigiate (upright) growth that gets only about 30 feet high.

CREATING A WOODLAND GARDEN

A woodland garden imitates a corner of a forest. Here you can stroll among trees, admiring the dappled light and the many lovely shrubs, flowers, and ferns that flourish in rich humusy soil in shade. Woodland is often the best low-maintenance alternative to lawn. Florida gardeners are beginning to create such woodland gardens, using the native trees and shrubs that are disappearing so rapidly from that lovely state. British gardeners may plant a garden hedgerow, with a few trees and a dense thicket of shrubs, rescuing another endangered habitat that is home to many wild flowers and animals.

If your garden is in forest, most of it is probably woodland already and merely needs to be pulled into shape. Thin out crowded trees to give each room to develop naturally and to let in light for other plants. If you are gardening in an ex-potato field, you will need to plant the trees as well as everything else. Plant them reasonably far apart so that you will have open woodland, rather than a jungle, when the trees mature.

The next consideration is a path and here you abandon all pretensions to formality because a path through a wood should look like little more than a deer track. The path should meander, so that you cannot see the whole of the area at once and it should not be made of anything more formal than wood chips. If your soil is well drained, there is no need to lay anything on the path at all. Just plan the route the path will take over fallen leaves, perhaps marking the edges with branches. If you are lucky enough to have a major

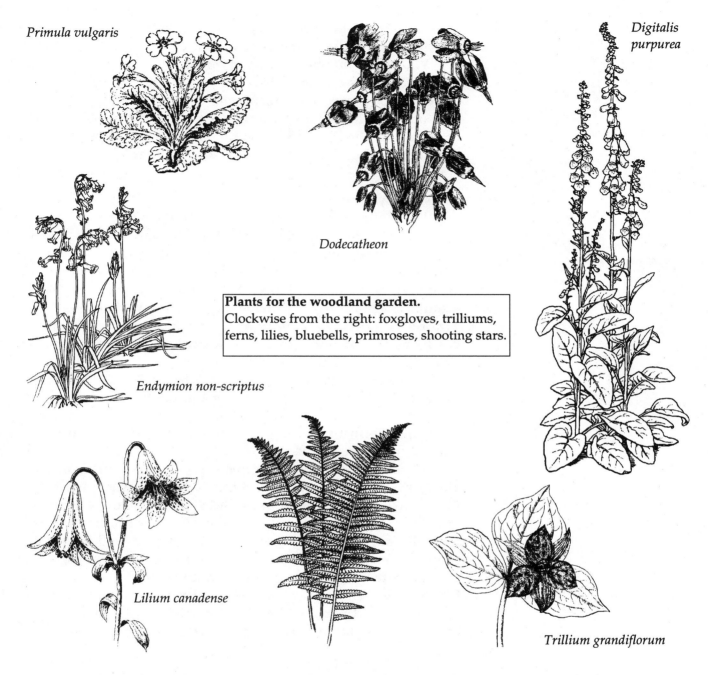

Primula vulgaris

Digitalis purpurea

Dodecatheon

Plants for the woodland garden.
Clockwise from the right: foxgloves, trilliums, ferns, lilies, bluebells, primroses, shooting stars.

Endymion non-scriptus

Lilium canadense

Trillium grandiflorum

rock in your future woodland, make sure the path goes right by it so that you can plant ferns and primroses or other woodland natives where they will be seen against the gray stone.

Next, you will want to plant shrubs to block the view straight through the wood and to provide color and texture that contrasts with the trunks and leaves of the trees. Rhododendrons and azaleas are classic subjects for the woodland garden because they will flower in shade. If all the shrubs are deciduous, the woodland will look much more open in winter than in summer and maybe that is

A western tiger swallowtail,
Pterourus rutulus.

the way you want it. But don't forget to provide some dense shrubbery in which wildlife can hide in winter.

When choosing trees for your woodland, dig out the butterfly field guide and see what native trees are butterfly food plants. Most butterflies don't really lay their eggs on your passionflowers and potatoes, even if they appear to; they lay them on trees, shrubs, and grasses. With the right trees, you may be able to watch male swallowtail butterflies fighting for territory in your garden. (Yes they do, honestly!)

Forest Ecosystems

For those living in forest biomes, it is worth bearing the natural structure of a forest in mind. Tall trees, members of the climax community, are usually slow-growing and their leaves eventually form a canopy high overhead. In dry areas, the trees are fairly far apart and the canopy is thin so that quite a bit of light reaches the ground. Such a forest will have an understory of shrubs. If the canopy is dense, as it is in an English beech wood, and in beech/maple/hickory forests of New England, the ground may be almost empty of plants in the summer.

These are deciduous forests and light reaches the forest floor when the trees are without leaves. As a result, the forest is home to many species of flowers which pop up rapidly with the first warmth of spring, flowering and setting seed before the trees leaf out and cut off their light.

All forests, whether evergreen or deciduous, contain areas along the edge, or where an old tree has fallen, where more light than usual reaches the ground. These openings are where most flowering small trees are found. Things like cherries, amelanchiers, redbuds, hawthorns, dogwoods, sumacs, and the wild progenitors of most domestic fruit trees are native to forest clearings, where they grow rapidly so that they reproduce before being choked out by slower growing shade trees. Many of them set seed that falls to the ground and remains dormant for years until another disturbance admits light, upon which they germinate and grow.

ATTRACTING WILDLIFE

Your woodland garden will be very attractive to wild plants and animals and an environmental gardener encourages such an invasion. Don't plant the whole of your woodland with domesticated plants. Leave an area untended and see what arrives by itself. It may take a long time or it may happen within the first year, but eventually your wild garden will become home to native flowers, shrubs, and trees, and the animals that live on them. Orchids, primroses, foxgloves, roses, deer, lizards, martens, weasels; who knows what might appear?

The first rule in attracting woodland wildlife is to plant at least some native trees and shrubs and to leave them alone. Don't remove fallen branches. Don't cut off dead branches. Don't even cut down dead trees (unless they become dangerous). Dozens of species of birds, ferns, and flowering plants depend on dead wood for food. Many of these species are threatened with extinction as humans run around tidying and cleaning up. Owls, woodpeckers, bobcats, raccoons, wood ducks, and chipmunks are just some of the animals that like to nest in holes in trees; and carefully pruned trees don't have any holes. When a tree or a branch dies in the garden watch how quickly it develops dozens of large and small holes. You may not see the animals that dig these holes but you will probably hear them, especially at dusk and dawn, as you stroll through your woodland. Include somewhere to sit where you can wait quietly in the hope of seeing a flying squirrel or family of raccoons.

A raccoon. (Carol Johnson)

You are often advised to attract wildlife by planting things that produce a lot of fruit, such as hollies, blueberries, hawthorns, and cherries. This obviously helps out the food supply. But in many areas fresh water would be even more inviting. Here's how one couple in Colorado catered for wildlife in their garden:

Sitting on a bench, you look across a pond into a little wildlife refuge, a dense thicket of trees and shrubs where animals can nest, or just hide while deciding that it is safe to drink from the pond. A person sitting quietly on the bench becomes part of the scenery to an animal in the thicket, especially if the animals learn that you hardly ever set foot in the area. From this bench, its owners have seen snakes, rabbits, raccoons, deer, and even a mountain lion, come to the pond to drink. You may never see a mountain lion in your wildlife refuge if you live in the middle of a city, but you will certainly see birds you had no idea lived near you. In a wooded suburb you may see dozens of species which have adapted to life within arm's length of civilization although we hardly ever see them.

PLANTING TREES

Tree people seem to agree that it is a waste of money to plant a tree more than eight feet high. The roots of a larger tree take so long to become established that the smaller tree will get to ten feet first. My experience with seedlings transplanted from around the garden certainly bears this out. It is amazing how fast a seedling tree gets going if it is happy in your garden—and if it is not, you haven't lost much when you tear it out and replace it with something else. Gardening is constant experimentation and it is nice to know that we can experiment even with trees without spending a lot of money. I don't think most people experiment enough. One of the best gardeners I know kept an unhappy (diseased?) dogwood on her front lawn for years, fussing over it with fertilizer, sprays, and mulch. Why bother? There are plenty of other trees. If she had replaced it within a couple of years of it starting to look sick, she could have had a fifteen foot cherry, plum, crape myrtle, or redtip (*Photinia* x *fraseri*) flowering away merrily in the same spot by now.

Before you plant a tree, it is wise to test the drainage at your chosen spot. Dig a hole about two feet deep where you plan to plant and fill it with water. If all the water drains away within 24 hours, the drainage is good enough. If there is still water in the hole the next day, it would be safer to plant your tree in a better drained spot or choose a tree, such as a bald cypress or willow, that can live with wet feet.

In the bad old days, we were told to "plant a $1 tree in a $5 hole." This meant digging a huge pit and mixing organic matter with a ton of soil to backfill the hole. But then an observant guardian started running a North Carolina arboretum on a shoestring. J. C. Raulston could not afford peat moss for planting holes, so he merely planted the arboretum's rare and beautiful trees in unimproved soil and mulched them with all the organic matter he could lay hands on. They flourished. Then someone did some studies and decided that trees treated in this cavalier fashion actually grew better than those given improved soil. Apparently the roots of a pampered tree tend to choke themselves by growing round and round in the good earth of the planting hole while underprivileged trees send their roots out far into unimproved soil in search of nutrients and water. The pleasant result of all this is that we don't have to feel guilty when we plant trees in small holes in poor soil.

There seems to be one exception to this rule. If you are planting acid-loving trees or shrubs in heavy clay soil, adding organic matter to the hole to acidify the soil is a good idea. Tests show that pine bark is a better acidifier than peat moss in this situation. (I am convinced that peat moss is not a very good soil conditioner, anyway. I would rather have a bushel of leaves or pine straw any day.)

There is another reason for planting trees in small holes. An arborist said recently that he had seen more trees killed by having the soil level around the trunk changed than by any other means. Trees cannot survive soil piled around their trunks or having many roots exposed. So it is important that a newly planted tree does not sink down into the soil after planting. This is quite likely to happen if you have dug a huge hole and piled loose soil in the bottom. The recommended planting hole nowadays is the same depth and about twice as wide as the tree's root ball.

Trees come in several forms. They may be bare-rooted, in which case they have to be shipped and planted while they are dormant, which means in the winter or very early spring. They may be balled and burlapped, which means the roots have been dug up with a ball of earth and the whole root system wrapped in sacking, which can be watered to keep the roots moist. Such trees can be planted at any time; so can trees grown in containers. However, I am a firm believer in autumn planting. It saves you having to water.

Autumn Planting

The usual reason a newly planted tree dies is that its leaves pull water up from the roots faster than the roots can supply it from the soil. Since roots contain stored food, they can grow in winter even though there are no leaves on the tree. The roots will grow whenever the soil is not frozen and will be well established by the time new leaves arrive to make demands in spring. This reasoning does not apply to evergreens, which continue to photosynthesize throughout the winter. But even evergreens metabolize much more slowly in winter than in the heat of summer and need less water and clucking over if planted in autumn. The exception to autumn planting seems to be that evergreens are better planted in spring in areas with very cold winters. Here the danger is that alternate freezing and thawing will crack the soil, exposing the roots to air that could kill them.

Your goal is to get the roots growing strongly in their new home as rapidly as possible. This is not usually a problem with bare-root trees. You just spread the roots out as far as possible in the planting hole, backfill the hole, and then water thoroughly to make sure that all the roots are touching the soil. You seldom encounter root problems with balled and burlapped trees either. But roots that have been in containers often need a little help.

When you are ready to put it in its hole, take the tree out of its container and examine the root ball. If you can see hardly any roots, go ahead and plant the tree. If a lot of roots are visible, treatment now will speed growth later. First cut off any roots that have started to circle the root ball. Then use a knife to make several fairly deep vertical cuts around the root ball. Experts use a viscious technique known as "butterflying." They cut right through the root ball, starting at the bottom and going about two-thirds of the way up it. Then they spread the two root flaps out more or less horizontally in the planting hole. As long as you don't slice off all the roots, this is not as drastic as it sounds because when a root is cut, it grows lots of the baby roots that matter—little feeder roots. Butterflying speeds the formation of feeder roots in the new site.

If the plant is balled and burlapped, put it in the hole without unwrapping it. Roots will grow out through string, burlap, and baskets. Remove the burlap from around the trunk and cut away as much burlap and string as you can from the root ball. Don't try to remove the burlap completely because this may disturb the roots too much. Leave plastic baskets in place but punch four or five holes in them and remove the top rim. If the root ball is wrapped in plastic sheeting, put the root ball in the planting hole first and then pull the plastic out from under it.

Backfill the hole by replacing the soil around the root ball without letting this extra soil touch the trunk. Use leftover soil to build a substantial dike around the tree to direct water down to the roots. This is a water-saving device. With a dike, a single bucket of water will be enough for quite a big tree or shrub because the water goes straight to the roots. Without the dike, you can run a hose on a tree for ages without giving the roots much water because the water runs off the surface.

Spread a layer of mulch around the tree stretching at least two feet from the trunk. Use a layer up to four inches deep but be careful not to destroy the dike. Pull the mulch away from the trunk, leaving

Tree planting.

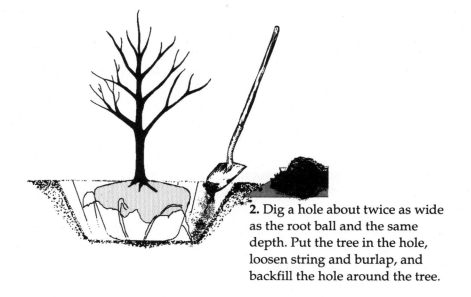

1. Test that the drainage at your chosen spot is adequate.

2. Dig a hole about twice as wide as the root ball and the same depth. Put the tree in the hole, loosen string and burlap, and backfill the hole around the tree.

3. Build a dike around the trunk to hold water.

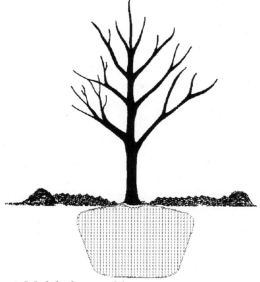

4. Mulch thoroughly.

about a six inch mulch-free ring. Use your hands or a plastic or bamboo rake for this job so that you don't damage the bark.

Should trees be staked? Yes if they keep falling over! Staking is not recommended because it can damage bark. Plants also develop stronger roots and stems if they are allowed to move in the wind. Staking should not be necessary unless your tree has an unusually small root ball so that it is very top heavy. If this is the case, don't try to stake the tree too tightly and do use lengths of hose to protect the bark from whatever wire or rope you use to attach it to its stakes. I sometimes put a single stake to one side of a young tree that isn't growing straight, with a rope to pull it in the right direction.

MAINTENANCE

If you choose trees and shrubs that are adapted to your soil and climate, they will live for many years with no care at all as long as you maintain them properly for the first year or two.

The most important maintenance is watering during hot dry spells and adding more mulch. Trees don't need much water in the winter unless it is unusually warm and dry. In summer, however, it is usual to water newly planted trees about once a month if it doesn't rain. The main thing is to keep an eye on them and water rapidly and heavily if you see the slightest sign of wilting leaves.

I have never fertilized a tree and I don't plan to start now. A good mulch is all most trees need. However, people who know about trees tell me that many trees suffer from nutrient deficiencies and would grow faster and stronger if they were fertilized. The two guidelines are not to fertilize when the tree is planted and not to fertilize by digging holes around the tree and putting fertilizer in the holes. You will still find "tree care" companies who will charge you large sums to treat your trees in this way. The holes damage the roots, the concentrated fertilizer in the hole burns the roots, and most of the roots have no access to fertilizer in the holes anyway. The way to fertilize a tree (or any plant) is to place the fertilizer on the surface so that the nutrients wash down to the roots in dilute form over a period of time. Fertilize your tree by spreading compost or manure on top of the mulch in a large circle around the trunk and letting rainfall wash it down to the roots.

If you are like me, and tend to change your mind about where plants should be, you'll find yourself moving trees, which is heavy labor and reveals a disorganized mind and lack of planning.

This chore is made easier if you root prune the tree a few months to a year before moving day. To root prune a tree of about human height, go right round the tree and make a vertical cut with a nursery spade to the full depth of the spade, a bit more than a hand span from the trunk, chopping through any roots you encounter. This induces the tree to grow new feeder roots. By the time you come to dig up the tree with its root ball, the root ball will be full of little feeder roots which will keep the tree nourished in its new home. There is no need to dig a vast trench around the tree unless some of the roots are too big to cut with a spade. In this case you need to dig a trench so that you can get at the roots with an axe. If you do go the trench route, refill the trench with compost or mulch until moving day.

I know this all sounds drastic, but trees are resilient and put up with a lot of abuse. We have a Southern magnolia (*Magnolia grandiflora*) that we have moved four times in the last ten years. And I'm still not sure it is in the right place or that there is really room for it in the garden at all.

How to Prune

The new wisdom says that trees should not be pruned when they are planted. There used to be a theory that you removed about one-third of the top of a tree at planting time to balance any loss of roots. But this is apparently unnecessary. Young trees need all the leaves they can keep for photosynthesis and should not be pruned until they are well established—perhaps a year after planting.

Many trees would be much more beautiful if pruned carefully when they were young. The scraggly little branches on your tiny tree will one day be thick limbs and the time to train them is now, while they are easy to cut. If your tree is one that develops a naturally graceful shape as it ages, you don't need to prune at all. This applies to most conifers, the vast tribe of flowering cherries and crabapples, most oaks, maples, and beeches. Even with these trees, however, it is a good idea to take a critical look at the branch structure once a year decide if you like the form that is developing, and remove one of any pair of crossed branches that are rubbing against one another.

But there are many trees, including the small magnolias, figs, Russian olives, acacias, and sophoras, with irregular branching structure, that can either become an ugly jumble or elegantly gnarled with age, depending on how you prune them.

There are two main things to remember about pruning. First, branches stay in the same place as the tree grows. If you tie a ribbon around the branch of a young tree at shoulder height, the ribbon will still be at shoulder height a century later (unless the branch falls off first). Second, pruning stimulates buds on the stump to develop into branches. And each bud points in the direction in which it will grow. This is easiest to observe with something like a cherry, rose, or privet where the buds are easy to see. If you are new to pruning, practice on one of these. Cut the end off a branch above a bud that points into the center of the bush and watch how the bud grows into a branch that points in the same direction. So, if you have a branch that is growing straight up and you want it more horizontal, cut it above a bud that points away from the center of the tree. When removing a branch, leave a short stump, rather than cutting the limb off flush with the trunk. This prevents disease organisms from entering the trunk and helps the wound heal faster. And don't paint the wound with that tar-like pruning paint. Research shows that it slows wound-healing.

Most young trees have a leader, a single main stem. If the top of the leader is cut or damaged, two or three branches will form in its place. If you do not want a major fork in the trunk at this height when the tree is full grown, remove all but one of these branches and the remaining branch will straighten up to become a new leader. Unless the tree is growing where no one ever walks, you will want to keep a leader and remove lower branches at least until you can walk under the tree without bumping your head.

Buds are easiest to see in spring but some difficult trees have few visible buds. The chances are that such a tree will grow many new branches from the stump when you cut a branch. Then you really need to start pruning to prevent uglification. For instance, if you cut the branch of a crape myrtle or willow, a forest of shoots appears from the branch just below the cut. Choose a shoot that points in the direction you want the branch to go and remove all the other shoots. You may have to keep removing shoots for a while, but eventually your chosen shoot will develop into the branch you want.

When it comes to pruning or felling a larger tree, you just have to take out a second mortgage and call in the tree service. It is much too dangerous for the untrained to attempt. Make sure the tree people are qualified, licenced, and insured. There are some charlatans running around out there. Discuss what you want them to do in detail. Do you want the stump ground down to ground level, or do you want to leave a tall stump for decoration and wildlife? If the tree people chip the wood they remove, make sure you get to keep the wood chips for mulch. Perhaps you could also rescue some branches to build a rustic arbor or bench. There are lots of choices to be made.

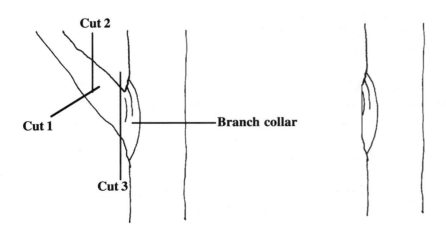

Sawing off a large limb.
If you simply cut from the top down, the weight of the branch will pull it loose before the cut is finished, tearing bark off the trunk. Prevent this by making the first cut part way through the branch from underneath. Then cut down to your first cut. Finally tidy up the stump by cutting it parallel with the trunk, but far enough from the trunk to leave the branch collar intact.

Pollarding

Pollarding involves cutting off all the main branches of a deciduous tree every year. It takes advantage of the forest of shoots that develops from a cut branch to give a tree a head like a mop. Pollarding is used to keep a tree from getting any bigger or for decorative effect. It is frowned on by the "back to nature" crowd. I don't know where people get this attitude to gardening which is, after all, a pretty unnatural activity. You must start pollarding a tree when it is young; cutting all the branches off an old tree will probably kill it. As the years go by, the trunk of a pollarded tree will thicken, and a knobby base will form at the point where you remove the limbs. Prune a pollarded tree in winter.

With a small-leaved tree, you can achieve an effect rather like tidy pollarding by pruning the tree as a mophead. Mopheads makes lovely formal accents near entrances or a group of mopheads can be used as an accent in the middle of a lawn.

Diseases of Trees

When trees become diseased or pest-infected, you really have only two choices: put up with it or chop the tree down. Millions have been spent on spraying trees in attempts to protect them from diseases, such as Dutch elm disease, and attacks of pest such as gypsy moths. But this is usually money down the drain. The tree will either survive the attack or die anyway—no matter what you do. If a tree does die on you, look on it as an opportunity, not a disaster. We are waiting for a small tree to die so that we can stick it out in the middle of a nearby marsh. Egrets like to roost on snags in open areas and the dead trees they traditionally use are become scarce in our part of the world as *Homo suburbiens* trims and prunes and chops.

A dead tree is also your opportunity to grow some of the lovely climbing things that are too large for most arbors and trellises. A dead tree is the perfect support for big roses, such as 'Paul's Himalayan Musk Rambler,' Lady Banks rose, or a Cherokee rose, or for a wisteria or climbing hydrangea, *Hydrangea anomala petiolaris* (anomalous, as its name suggests, because most hydrangeas don't climb). The wildlife won't in the least mind sharing their habitat with a climber or two.

UNDERPLANTING

Some trees do a good job of keeping the ground beneath them free of weeds and grass by casting such dense shade that nothing can grow. Some, like walnuts, produce chemicals that inhibit the growth of other plants. If this is how your trees behave, give thanks and leave them in peace.

But more likely, you have trees in the lawn with untidy tufts of grass sticking up around the trunk where the lawn mower won't reach. And you have vaguely thought of using the string trimmer on this untidy mess. Don't. The living cells of a tree trunk are in the cambium, a thin layer lying just beneath the bark (the rest of the trunk is dead wood cells). If you damage the bark you are liable to slice through the cambium and if you do this right round the trunk the tree will die. This is why a rabbit can kill a young tree overnight; it munches right round the tree, eating all the bark it can reach and "girdling" the tree. If you see damage to the bark of a young tree, protect it by wrapping it in paper. The best solution to the weeds-around-the-trunk problem is to plant trees in beds of ground cover or surround them by mulch or paving with many cracks in it (so that water can penetrate). But this bed-making has to be done rather carefully or you may cause another problem—suckers.

Suckers are thin mini-trunks that often grow straight up from the roots of things like lilacs. Suckers can start from any root so one tree can produce dozens of them. They are difficult and time-consuming to get rid of and it doesn't help at all to realize that you probably caused them yourself. Studies show that damaging roots increases sucker formation. This began to dawn on me when I dug up a bed surrounding my venerable crape myrtle. The tree, which had been perfectly well behaved up to that time, immediately started putting out a forest of suckers. And two years later it is still doing it. Sucker formation is not confined to small trees and shrubs (although some species are more prone to it than others). I discovered I had caused the same problem by running the lawn mower over the huge surface root of an oak tree. This root now spends its time putting out horrible gnarled suckers. And the moral of this is—surround your trees with a bed of something that doesn't need serious digging to keep it relatively free of weeds. And when you plant the bed, don't disturb the soil too much.

This can be achieved by the mulch method. If you have a tree in the middle of a lawn, surround it by a generous ring of as much compost, leaf mold, and other organic matter as you can come up with. You could even underlay the mulch with a thick layer of newspaper to really keep the grass in its place. Don't let the mulch pile up against the tree trunk or you may girdle the tree by a new and different system—providing a happy home for fungi and insects that destroy the bark. If you are a really excellent gardener, convinced that your compost and mulch are free of weed seeds, you can plant the ground cover in your bed immediately. If you are like me and know that your organic matter is liberally laced with weeds, leave the bed alone for a while, weeding occasionally, until it is fairly free of weeds. Then plant. Ivy, pachysandra, and periwinkle (*Vinca*) are the classic ground covers under trees.

There are few finer sights than an old tree alone in the middle of a velvety lawn and surrounded by a bed of ivy that spreads to the very tips of the branches. This is not achieved in an instant. Ground covers take a while to cover the ground. And you will have to weed occasionally while the ground cover gets there. But once it does, you have a beautiful picture that takes almost no maintenance—except to trim the ivy from the tree trunk occasionally. (Pachysandra won't even need this care.) You don't actually need miles of lawn and ancestral oaks to create this serene picture. I have seen lovely front doors flanked by small trees in twin beds of ivy.

SHADE TREES

The tree you plant to shade the patio or door depends on where you live and how big your house and property are. The ideal tree is native, or very well adapted to your area, and will grow to an appropriate size: big enough to walk under comfortably, but not so large that its roots threaten the foundations. Some trees should be struck off your list of candidates no matter what their size. You don't want slippery fruit or prickly nuts all over an area where people walk. Unless you are prepared to do a lot of sweeping up, exclude messy trees from your list. Plant flowering cherries, loquats, apples, franklinias, and dogwoods at the edge of a large patio or further away where you can enjoy the sight of them but where they won't drop debris on the paving.

Consider how much shade you really need. If you live in a cool area where it is seldom too hot to sit in the sun, the best bet is probably a deciduous tree with feathery foliage that casts a light shade. High-headed *Sophora japonica*, Russian olives, acacias, or thornless honey locusts (*Gleditsia triacanthos*) fill the bill. They are fast-growing, easy to prune to any shape you like, and their leaves cast dappled shade. They even tolerate salt, alkaline soil, and drought.

FLOWERING TREES

My idea of a pleasing, low-care garden is one with maximum flower power for minimum work, and this means planting flowering trees and shrubs as well as annuals and perennials. Why grow a hedge of evergreen shrubs that are the same all year round if you can instead have one of camellias, which brighten the gloom of a January morning? Purists will argue that planting them as a hedge does not bring out the brightest and best in camellias and this is doubtless true if you insist on a tightly clipped hedge. But why not leave the hedge loose and informal and encourage the flowers?

Some fool of a landscaper installed pittosporum and aucuba against a shady red brick wall that I can see from my desk. How much better to have used gardenias, hollies, Oregon grape holly, camellias, abelia, calycanthus, or mountain laurel, all of which would have gladdened me with their flowers or berries at least once a year.

The same principle holds for trees, especially small trees. Most large trees are pollinated by wind and don't have very showy flowers, although I admit to a weakness for the glowing burgundy of red maple flowers in spring. There are a few exceptions: large trees with impressive flowers, such as horse chestnuts, tulip trees (*Liriodendron tulipifera*), Southern magnolias, basswood (*Tilia*), or teak. Yes, the tree they use for garden furniture (*Tectona grandis*). This deciduous Indian native has very large leaves with a touch of orange and is covered in summer with enormous panicles of feathery cream flowers. I had always assumed teak was restricted to the true tropics until I drove past a healthy little specimen flowering in a Georgia garden one day and nearly caused a traffic accident. The book says teak is hardy only to Zone 10 and naturalized in many parts of the tropics and subtropics, but Georgia is in Zones 8, so teak will clearly stand occasional temperatures below 10 °F.

These big flowering trees all have the virtue of interesting leaves and attractive shapes as well as fine flowers. But the aristocrats among flowering trees are found among cultivated descendants of the small trees that flourish on the edges of forests. And this is how many of them look best in the garden—seen against a backdrop of forest trees, where they will flower early in the spring before the larger deciduous trees leaf out. Hawthorns, plums, cherries, crabapples, magnolias, dogwood, desert olive, mesquite, redbuds, and dozens more I cannot think of at the moment, give you plenty of scope for brightening up the garden with many color schemes and minimal care.

Weeping trees undoubtedly give you a lot of flower power for your money because they are often clothed in flowers right down to the ground. They are, however, difficult to place appropriately in the garden and often look odd. You are on your own if you want a weeping cherry or pear. I have always avoided them because I don't think I am a good enough designer to place a weeping tree where it would look right.

COMMUNITY FORESTRY

The push is on to do something for our environment that extends beyond our own garden walls. Why not get together a gang of neighbors to plant and maintain trees in the streets and public places where you live? I'll tell you why not. Before you can say "xylem and phloem," you're known far and wide as Dr. Community Forestry, and every lumber company with a guilty conscience, and every government agency or landscaper that overestimated the demand, will be on your back to accept 200, if not 2000, tree seedlings that they know you are dying to break your back planting. My overtaxed home nursery has, in the last few months, acquired from these sources 50 sawtooth oaks, several dogwoods, and 100 loblolly pines. I mean, how can you say "no" to a bunch of homeless trees when the local library sits surrounded by the parking lot from hell? You have to pot up most of the seedlings, depleting your precious stock of soil, and then you have to water them for nine months until fall planting season comes—because planting a tree in spring in a public place where it won't get watered dooms it to slow death. In contrast, and rather to my amazement, planted in the right places in autumn, every one of the 350 trees and shrubs our "Wilmington '96" volunteers planted last fall has come through the winter in glowing health without attention.

The idea behind community forestry is that, although most local governments are too broke to perform this service, there is nothing like the right trees and shrubs to improve the looks of a shopping mall, town center, or highway, and that these trees are most likely to survive with a bit of tender loving care. This is especially true in harsh climates where young trees need water. Los Angeles planted more than a million trees in honor of the Olympics, but three years later more than half of them were dead, unable to survive southern Californian summers without assistance in their early years. Young trees are also unlikely to survive children running over them, casual vandalism, or the county maintenance squad carelessly wielding a brush cutter. The vigilance of their human neighbors can go a long way to preventing unnecessary deaths.

There are grants available if you want to undertake a bit of neighborhood beautification and your local county council, forestry commission, or whoever looks after these things, will probably greet your enquiries with whoops of joy.

Street Trees
There is more to urban reforestation than just gathering up your neighbors and some money and plunging in with a spade. The choice of trees is crucial. Many trees will not survive the heat and pollution of a parking lot or city street and you need professional advice to find those that will. And there are several other things to consider when you undertake public plantings.

A stroll round most towns will show you trees with concrete or paving only a few feet from their trunks on all sides. It is no good expecting a tree to thrive with its trunk in a ten foot square patch of earth in the middle of an acre of concrete (but it's amazing how many struggling trees you can find in such situations). In Savannah, workers are busy digging up paving around juvenile street trees and replacing it by bricks bedded in sand. This surface will take pedestrian traffic but it is porous so that water drains through to the tree roots.

Then there is traffic safety. Most of us know of corners made dangerous by trees and shrubs that have grown until they block the view of a motorist trying to make a turn. Anything planted on a sharp corner should be low enough so that a motorist can see over it even when it is full grown, which means that it can be little more than ground cover. If a car swerves off the road, its occupants are more likely to survive a collision with a hawthorn than with a palm tree, so there are rules that say things like no tree with a trunk diameter of more than four inches can be planted less than eight feet from the road where the speed limit is more than 40 miles an hour unless the tree is protected by a guard rail to slow down errant vehicles. Call your friendly local bureaucrat for the relevant rules and regulations before proceeding.

But do proceed if you can possibly find the time and energy because there are few more rewarding sights than your hideous local shopping center made even mildly attractive by the energy of the local residents and shopkeepers.

Some Good Deciduous Shade Trees

You will notice that the Deep South, southwestern U.S., and northern U.K. are not well represented on this list because many of the best shade trees in these areas are evergreen, not deciduous.

Botanical Name Common Name	Origin Family Adaptation	Advantages	Disadvantages
Acer platanoides Norway maple	Europe to Iran Aceraceae Zones 3-8 Most of U.K. and eastern two-thirds of U.S. and southern Canada	Rapid growth when young; probably the most popular maple; pale yellow autumn color in colder areas; many lovely varieties are available	Many old specimens in New England have outgrown their sites in less than 100 years; be prepared to remove it when it gets large
Acer pseudoplatanus Sycamore Great maple False plane tree	Europe and western Asia Aceraceae Zones 4-8 or 9	Pyramidal shape; tolerates salt spray in coastal areas; leaves yellowish between veins; lovely silvery exfoliating bark on older specimens	Weak wood; older specimens drop branches; winged seeds produced in large numbers can be messy
Acer rubrum Red maple Swamp maple	Eastern N. America Aceraceae Zones 2-9 Grows well in U.K. and in most of U.S. except dry West and Southwest	Fairly fast growth; the best tree for red autumn color in New England; handsome rounded shape and spreading branches	Starts dying and dropping limbs after about 100 years: consider replacing an old specimen; autumn color poor except in northern part of its range
Acer saccharinum Silver maple White maple River maple	Quebec to Florida, west to Minnesota Aceraceae Zones 2-9 Most of U.K. and all of U.S. except dry West and Southwest although it is often planted in Texas	Fairly fast-growing; yellow and red autumn color even in low-chill areas	Rather messy; in dry areas aggressive roots cause damage to sewers and concrete

Sugar maple

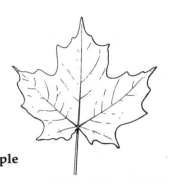

Hornbeam

Acer saccharum Sugar maple Rock maple Hard maple	Quebec to Florida and Texas Aceraceae Zones 2-9 U.S. and southern Canada except dry South and West; most of U.K.	The maple sugar maple; has the most spectacular yellow autumn color among northeastern trees	Intolerant of air pollution so don't plant it if your rainfall has a pH of less than 6.0
Aesculus Hippocastanum Horse chestnut	E. Europe, Asia Hippocastanaceae U.K., northern U.S. including northern California; and Canada Zones 4-8	Medium growth; graceful spreading branches; handsome 5-part leaves; huge spikes of white or red flowers; glossy brown chestnuts; brown leaves in fall	A bit messy: sticky leaf bud scales, large spiky nuts
Carpinus Betulus Hornbeam	Europe Betulaceae Zones 3-8	To 70 feet in damp soil or clay, less in dry sandy soil; yellow autumn color even in warm areas	
Fagus grandiflora American beech	North America Fagaceae Zones 3-9	Prefers moist well-drained soil; rounded shape; yellow fall color even in low-chill areas; nuts attract wildlife	Branches low so little will grow under it; nuts messy; retains leaves into winter
Fagus sylvatica European beech	Europe Fagaceae Zones 4-7	To 100 feet with rounded shape; small nuts provide food for many animals; fine orange-brown autumn leaves which stay on the tree for most of the winter in mild areas	Very dense shade; prefers alkaline soil but tolerant of acid soil
Gingko biloba Gingko Maidenhair tree	SE China Gingkoaceae (a rare, broad-leaved deciduous gymnosperm) Most of U.S. and U.K. Zones 3-9	Upright shape, fast-growing; easy to grow in almost any soil except very sandy; fan-shaped leaves; yellow autumn color; resistant to pollution; good street tree	Females are messy and smelly so plant only males
Juglans nigra Black walnut (*J. cinerea* is a good substitute in mountainous areas)	Ontario to Florida and Texas Juglandaceae Zones 4-9	Probably North America's most valuable hardwood; handsome pinnate leaves; hardier than English walnut; nuts good eating for people and wildlife	Secretes juglone, a chemical that prevents many plants from growing beneath it; catkins and nuts a bit messy

Deciduous shade trees, contd.

Liriodendron tulipifera Tulip tree	N. America Magnoliaceae Zones 4-9, Southern U.K.	Moderate growth to over 150 feet. Large, tulip-shaped leaves; white teacup-shaped flowers in summer; yellow autumn color even in warmer areas	Upright tendency not ideal in a shade tree
Platanus x *acerifolia* London plane	A hybrid of unknown origin Platanaceae Zones 5-10	To 90 feet; good street tree; tolerant of dirt and pollution; handsome vase shape; long-lived; silvery exfoliating bark	Fruits rather messy
Platanus wrightii Sycamore Buttonwood	Arizona, New Mexico, Mexico. Platanaceae Well-drained moist areas along riverbeds	To 80 feet; the giant of desert-adapted trees; wide-spreading and graceful with maple-like leaves	Needs space to spread to its mature 80 foot width; not salt-tolerant; needs moist soil in desert areas
Populus fremontii Cottonwood	Dry western U.S. from Idaho to New Mexico Salicaceae River edges with damp soil	Fast growth to 100 feet; large leaves with silvery tint dance in wind; fairly salt-tolerant	Messy cottony seeds; weak wood so tends to drop twigs
Prunus serotina Black cherry	Nova Scotia to N. Dakota, to Florida and Texas Rosaceae Zones 3-9	Valuable timber tree (cherry furniture); tolerant of salt air and sandy soil; fruit loved by wildlife.	Tends to rather upright growth and straight, uninteresting trunk; cherries messy
Quercus macrocarpa Bur oak	Southern N. America Fagaceae Zones 2-8	To 60 feet; rounded shape; large leaves and rough bark; salt tolerant; dry alkaline soil, but tolerates acid soil and urban conditions	Acorns large; difficult to transplant
Quercus robur English oak	U.K. Fagaceae Zones 4-8	To 80+ feet when grown in the open so that its vast branches can spread; very long-lived; in U.K. is food for many insects so it attracts insect-eating birds	
Tilia americana Basswood	New Brunswick to Virginia and Texas Tiliaceae Zones 2-8 or 9	Handsome spreading tree; tolerant of most soils and conditions; bees love the nectar	Flowers and fruits messy; little autumn color
Tilia cordata Lime, linden	European Tiliaceae Zones 3-7 or 8	Popular street tree with small leaves that move in the wind; strong wood	
Tilia platyphyllos Lime, linden,	Temperate Europe Tiliaceae Zones 4-7	To 90 feet, long-lived, tolerates pollution; leaves dance in a breeze; tall vase shape	

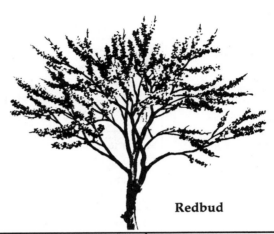

Redbud

Small Trees that Flower in Spring (seldom more than 25 feet high in cultivation)

Don't forget ordinary old fruit trees, which have pink or white flowers in spring and produce fruit as well (see Chapter 11).

Botanical Name Common Name Varieties	Origin Adaptation	Description	Culture
Cercis canadensis Eastern redbud 'Forest Pansy' (purple leaves), 'Silver Cloud' (variegated leaves) 'Alba' (white flowers)	Eastern and central U.S.; northern Mexico; edges of slightly acid woodland. Zones 4-9 Not very hardy in Britain or Pacific Northwest as it prefers summer heat	Largest redbud; dark pink or white flowers appear on branches in early spring before leaves; autumn color of leaves ranges from pale green to yellow	Hard to transplant. Not fussy about soil although it does best in deep loam with good drainage and moisture, of about pH 6.5
Cercis chinensis Chinese redbud 'Avondale' (vast numbers of dark flowers)	Much of China Zones 6-8	Usually a shrub with several stems	'Avondale' does well in Eastern U.S. and Pacific Northwest
Cercis mexicana Mexican redbud	Mexico Zones 6-10 Not very hardy in Britain or Pacific Northwest as it prefers summer heat	Shrubby, fine-textured	Same as for other redbuds
Cercis occidentalis Western redbud	Arizona to Oregon Zones 7-9 Not well adapted to Eastern U.S. or Britain	Usually grown as a multi-stemmed shrub	Drier, more alkaline soil than eastern redbud
Cercis racemosa Chain-flowered redbud	Central China Zones 7 or 8-10 New to western horticulture. Will probably do best in Northwest U.S. (and Britain?) and coastal Atlantic and Gulf areas	Pendulous 3 inch panicles of flowers	Same as for other redbuds
Cercis reniformis Texas redbud 'Oklahoma' (glossy leaves and redder flowers than eastern redbud, but hard to propagate) 'Texas White' (white flowers)	Texas, Oklahoma, Mexico Zones 6-10 Not very hardy in Britain or Pacific Northwest as it prefers summer heat	Very similar to western redbud	Same as for other redbuds

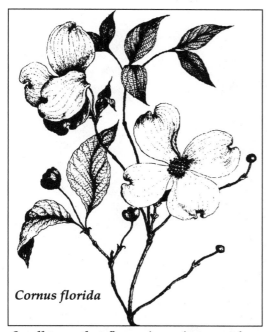

Cornus florida

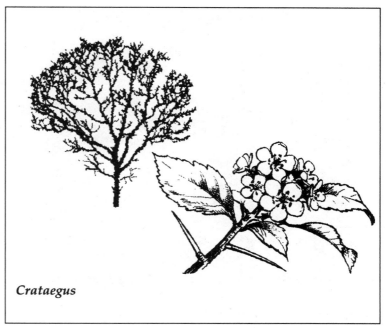

Crataegus

Small trees that flower in spring, contd.

Cercis siliquastrum Mediterranean redbud	Spain to Israel Zones 6-9 Is the best redbud for Britain and probably for Southwest U.S. and Pacific Northwest	Tree or shrub	Same as for other redbuds
Cornus florida American dogwood 'Rubra' and 'Cherokee Chief' have pink bracts	Maine to Florida and west to Kansas and Texas Zones 5-10 Adapted to the edge of acid woodland	Tree with horizontal trend to leaves and branches; tiny flowers, surrounded by large 4-part showy white bracts are produced in spring; leaves turn to red or rusty in autumn	Must have shade in the south although it will take full sun in the north as long as you keep it well-mulched. Keep well watered for the first year. Pink-flowered varieties are less vigorous than white-flowered and harder to establish
Cornus mas Cornellian cherry	Europe, Asia Zones 4-8	One of the first signs of spring in northern U.S. and Midwest; yellow flowers followed by fruit for birds	Prefers rich, well-drained soil but not particularly fussy
Cornus Kousa Kousa dogwood 'Rubra' (pink bracts 'Variegata' (variegated leaves)	Japan and Korea Zones 4-7 (and northern part of 8?)	Drooping horizontal branches and showy white bracts. Resistant to dogwood anthracnose. Hybrids between *C. florida* and *C. Kousa* are also resistant	Same as American dogwood
Crataegus spp. Hawthorn	Northern hemisphere Zones 3-9	Thorny small trees and shrubs, useful as hedges or specimens; pink or white flowers in spring followed by berries and good fall color	Very tough; tolerant of salt air, sand, and neglect

Star magnolia

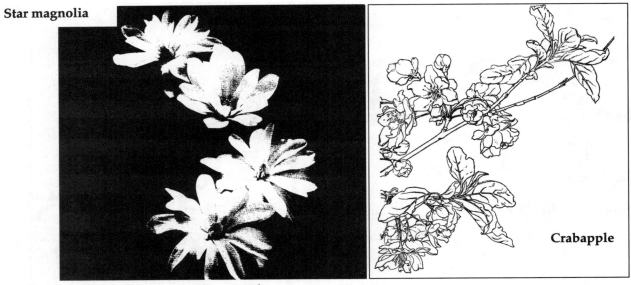

Crabapple

Small trees that flower in spring, contd.

Magnolia hybrid 'Ann'	Recommended for Midwest U.S. Zones 5-7	Compact tree with bright red flowers	Not fussy about soil; water well for first few years
Magnolia hybrid 'Galaxy'	Recommended for U.K., Northeast U.S., California, and Pacific Northwest. Zones 4-9 or 10	Large rose-magenta flowers somewhat later than the saucer magnolia and so less liable to frost damage	Not fussy about soil; water well for first few years
Magnolia hybrid 'Paul Cook'	Recommended for Deep South Zones 7-9	Vigorous grower with bright pink flowers up to 12 inches across; large medium green leaves attractive all summer	Not fussy about soil; water well for first few years
Magnolia salicifolia Anise magnolia	Japan Zones 5-8 (or 9?)	Narrow tree with narrow, willow-like leaves. Star-like flowers in late spring. The leaves smell slightly of anise (or licorice)	Magnolias require warm microclimates in the colder part of their range, and may do better in towns than in the surrounding country
Magnolia sieboldii Oyama magnolia	Japan and Korea Zones 5-9 Does well in U.K., Northeast, Pacific Northwest and California	Blooms after the leaves have emerged in late spring. The flowers are small and white with red stamens, followed by yellow seed pods in August	Same as for anise magnolia
Magnolia stellata Star magnolia *M. x loebneri* 'Leonard Messel' is a pink flowered star magnolia hybrid	Japan Zones 5-8 Does well in most of U.K., northeast U.S., and Midwest	Most people's favorite magnolia. Slow growing; fat gray furry buds in winter open to large white star-shaped trembling flowers before leaves open in spring	Same as for anise magnolia. (*M. kobus* is similar but hardier so you might want to try this is you live in a chilly area.)

Small trees that flower in spring, contd.

Magnolia x *Soulangiana* Tulip magnolia Saucer magnolia	Hybrid of *M. quincapeta* and *M. heptapeta* Zones 5-9 Slightly less hardy than star magnolia	Large purple to pink flowers; trees flower when they are very young and are basically globe-shaped but develop interesting shapes as they age and can be pruned in many ways	Flowers best in sun. Water in dry spells for the first few years ; liable to bloom so early that the flowers are damaged by frost; likely to be replaced in popularity by other hybrid magnolias for this reason
Malus baccata Siberian crabapple	Europe, Asia Zones 2-7	Fragrant white flowers; orange fruit; early	Hardiest of the crabs; easy
Malus floribunda Japanese flowering crabapple	Asia Zones 4-7	Flowers more reliably than most crabs and cherries; spreading shape with flowers that are dark pink in bud, fading to white as they open; yellow fruit in fall	Likes some soil moisture and sun
Prunus 'Okame'	Japan Zones 4 or 5-9	Fine cultivar that flowers early in spring	Easy; tolerates salt, sand, and dry soil
Prunus cerasifera Flowering plum 'Krauter Vesuvius'	Asia to Balkans; naturalized in Europe and N. America Zones 8-10	One of the best plums for California; new foliage purple; flowers pink, double	
Prunus Maackii Amur cherry	E. Asia Zones 2-6	Slow-growing, with white flowers, followed by black berries; gorgeous red exfoliating bark	Likes moist soil
Prunus mume Flowering apricot	China, Japan Zones 6-10	Earliest cherry to flower, with pink flowers in January in Zone 8	Prefers moist soil; grows more slowly but survives in dry sand
Prunus Sargentii Sargent cherry	Japan, Korea Zones 5-8	Largest flowering cherry with upright spreading branches; sometimes used as shade tree; good fall color	Sun to part shade; moist soil for at least much of the year
Prunus serrulata Japanese flowering cherry 'Kwanzan' (pink), 'Shirotae' (= 'Mt. Fuji') (white)	Japan Zones 5-8 or 9	Double blossoms and a horizontal trend to the branches make these cultivars the most spectacular of the cherries	Sun to part shade; moist soil for at least much of the year

Small Trees that Flower in Summer

Botanical Name Common Name Varieties	Origin Adaptation	Description	Culture
Albizia Julibrissin Silk tree Mimosa	Iran to Japan Naturalized in southeast U.S. Zones 7-10	Fast-growing tree with divided leaves. Pale pink, powder puff flowers in early summer	Well-drained soil. Tolerates several months of drought. Flowers best in sun
Aralia elata Japanese angelica tree	Japan Zones 4-8 or 9	Single or multi-stemmed tree with shapely dark trunk(s) and pinnate leaves; small creamy flowers in large clusters appear in August	Not fussy about soil. Survives drought. Flowers best in full sun
Franklinia Alatamaha Franklin tree	Known only in cultivation. Zones 5-8	Multi-stemmed shrub or tree with open branching habit. Teacup-like white flowers in late summer. Lovely autumn color even in the South	Susceptible to a root rot spread by cotton in the South. In the North, it likes well-drained acid soil. Sun (part shade in the South
Hibiscus syriacus Rose of Sharon Althaea	E. Asia Zones 4-9	Upright slow-growing shrub or multi-stemmed tree. White, pink, or purple flowers rather like those of hollyhocks are produced in late spring and early summer	Needs well-drained soil. Survives several months without water. Give it sun in the north. It flowers even in shade in the South
Koelreuteria paniculata Golden rain tree 'Fastigiata' (upright, columnar growth)	China, Korea Zones 5-10	Crooked trunk and branches. Pinnate leaves. Yellow flowers in long panicles in July to August, followed by brown fruit	Not fussy about soil. Tolerates drought
Lagerstroemia indica Crape myrtle New varieties flower longer and are more mildew-resistant than older varieties	Asia In Zone 6 severe winters kill the tops but the roots survive and new shoots appear in the spring. These usually flower Zones 7-10	Tropical tree common in South and California. White, pink, magenta, or purple flowers in panicles. Handsome bark	Survives drought. Not fussy about soil. Appreciates a good mulch. Requires full sun if it is to flower well
Oxydendrum arboreum Sourwood Sorrel tree	Eastern U.S. Pennsylvania to Louisiana and Florida. Zones 4-9	Slow-growing tree or shrub. Many panicles of small white flowers appear in summer. Scarlet autumn color	Moist, well-drained soil. Mulch heavily. Flowers best in full sun but will tolerate partial shade; propagated by seeds
Vitex Agnus-castus Chaste tree Hemp tree Monk's pepper tree	Southern Europe; naturalized in southern U.S. Zones 6-10	An aromatically scented tree or shrub with small lavender flowers borne on branching spikes July to September	Needs well-drained poor soil with good drainage
Cotinus Coggyria Smoke tree	Southern Europe to Asia Zones 5-10	Multi-stemmed tree or shrub to 20 feet with pink-gray flowers in summer and orange fall foliage	Drought-tolerant; sun

CHAPTER 6

Shrubs and Vines

Shrubs and vines are the workhorses of the garden. They provide shade, privacy, shape, and flowers, and once you have planted them they need very little care. If your garden is small, there may be no room for trees and you will use shrubs instead to provide shade, shape, and wildlife habitat. In a small area, choosing the right shrubs becomes crucial because they will become the focal points of the garden. But shrubs are very forgiving. They are cheaper than trees to buy in the first place, smaller so they are less trouble to prune, and easier to rip out if you find you have made a mistake.

Many neighborhoods contain a dull and limited selection of shrubs and it is easy to brighten up your property. My driveway lined with hydrangeas draws raves from passersby when it bursts into flower in June although it is only two years old and needs little care. A clump of shrubs that flower in autumn, or that flaunt orange berries or fascinating bark in winter, might be equally stunning in your neighborhood.

PRIVACY AND POLLUTANTS

The very first shrubs to plant in a new garden are the ones you need for privacy. I say this with feeling, having neglected privacy hedges for more interesting projects for several years. The new garden seemed so peaceful that I didn't feel encircling hedges were a high priority. But now the road is busier, the neighbors' bonfires more repellent, the teenagers in the softball field across the road noisier, and I am planting hedges as fast as I can go, cursing that I didn't do it sooner.

There are many choices to be made. You can use individual shrubs, strategically placed to block a view without giving a walled-in feeling, or you can use a solid hedge to block out the rest of the world. The hedge can be formal or informal, tall or short. Of these choices, a formal hedge takes up the least space since you can keep it pruned into a narrow wall. Informal hedges of flowering shrubs are very attractive, but they take up a lot of space if you choose shrubs with graceful spreading branches.

Kerria japonica

Variegated Leaves

Another trick for dispelling gloom, particularly in a shady place, is to plant shrubs with variegated leaves. These are leaves with stripes that lack green chlorophyll so that they appear white or yellow. Variegated Chinese privet (*Ligustrum sinense*) contains so little chlorophyll that it is a wonder it survives at all. Its tiny cream-colored leaves are a bright spot in a dark corner. More dramatic are shrubs with large leaves edged in white for a horizontal zigzag effect. I have a variegated lacecap hydrangea. The flowers are very pretty but they last only for a few weeks and I was on the verge of replacing the shrub when I noticed that it keeps its leaves all winter—unusual in a hydrangea and a real gem in a shady spot.

Variegated shrubs sometimes put out branches with solid green leaves and these must be pruned out as soon as you notice them. Otherwise, they will end up taking over, because they are more vigorous than their non-variegated relatives.

SHRUBS FOR SPRING FLOWERS

Few gardens are complete without shrubs for color in spring. The choice is so great that the usual problems are deciding what to omit and how to create a harmonious color scheme. Unless you are of the persuasion that flower colors never clash, there are some horrible color schemes to be seen in our suburb each spring as yellow forsythia and kerria compete with coral flowering quince, while salmon and purple azaleas swear at each other. Defeated by the color problems, I started to plant only shrubs with white flowers. That is the coward's way out and you will have to make your own decisions. But it is hard to go wrong planting some of the many white-flowered viburnums, even if you aren't struggling with a color scheme. Spiraeas are another good choice for white flowers in spring. Common old bridal wreath spiraea (*Spiraea* x *Vanhouttei*) is hard to beat. Spiraeas do best in full sun and they love moist soil although they'll survive in dry.

As well as choices about color, you have to make choices about shapes. Each shrub has a definite natural shape that has to be considered when you are after a particular effect. I once planted a group of flowering quince (*Chaenomeles speciosa*) in search of the upright shape characteristic of these spring beauties and discovered that I had something more like a ground cover. It turns out that the growth habit of this shrub varies with the variety.

An excellent spring flowering evergreen is Indian hawthorn (*Raphiolepis*). This is not a hawthorn (*Crataegus*), but a broad-leaved evergreen that comes in pink and white-flowered species. It grows to about five feet if left to its own devices (the pink variety is taller and coarser), but you can shear it after it flowers to keep it tidy so it is very useful as a foundation plant that will not outgrow its site. This is the southern equivalent of the much more beautiful moun-

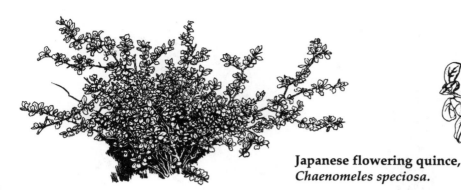

Japanese flowering quince,
Chaenomeles speciosa.

tain laurel (*Kalmia latifolia*), which is also now available in a wide
range of shapes, sizes, and colors. Because it is native and slow-
growing, Americans tend to ignore *Kalmia*. But it is well worth the
wait. If I had to choose the most beautiful flower I know, this would
be it. The delicately colored petals that look as if they have holes in
them are exquisite. If mountain laurel were suddenly discovered on
a South Sea island, gardeners would kill for it and build greenhouses to carry it through the winter.

Northerners have long envied Southerners a range of broad-
leaved evergreens, but many of these shrubs are also well adapted
to the North. *Pieris* is a charming evergreen for the North, with its
drooping clusters of flowers in white and burgundy in spring, and
many new varieties. Another smasher is Oregon grape holly
(*Mahonia*), which has the inestimable advantage of blooming in dry
shade—which indeed it needs in the South—and which comes in
several species and varieties. My *Mahonia bealei*, with yellow pendu-
lous flowers followed by blue berries that the birds devour, has shot
up at an alarming rate since I moved it into the shade because I kept
bumping into its prickly leaves and couldn't find anywhere else to
put it. Its branches are sternly upright, which makes a nice contrast
to the droopy pittosporum it sits beside.

Various species of California lilac (*Ceanothus*) are among the
few blue-flowered shrubs that bloom in spring. They are utterly
spectacular planted about with orange California poppies and they
also look good with the yellow flowers of Scotch broom (*Cytisus*).

SUMMER-FLOWERING SHRUBS

It is a pity most people give up on flowering shrubs after the spring
burst, because there are plenty of shrubs that flower in summer and
even in autumn; and it is a lot easier to produce a burst of color
with a shrub than with the same area of perennials and annuals.

My summer favorites are hydrangeas, from the oakleaf
hydrangea's white flowers in spring, through the summer-flowering blue, pink, and red varieties of *Hydrangea macrophylla* to the
'Savannah Blue' that graces the Christmas dinner table. 'Savannah
Blue' is a good example of the way plant names get messed up.

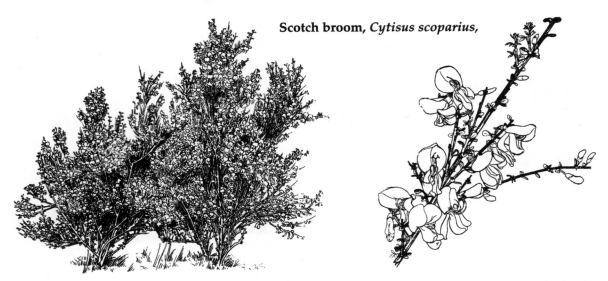

Scotch broom, *Cytisus scoparius,*

When we moved to our present house, a large hortensia hydrangea was growing on a sandbank in much more sun than most hydrangeas tolerate in this climate. This plant flowers from spring to fall with the biggest flower trusses I have ever seen on a hydrangea—up to 18 inches across—even though the plant was suffering from severe chlorosis when I inherited it (and still is, for that matter; *mea culpa*). I have spread this plant around the neighborhood and my own garden by way of cuttings. It flowers in sun or deep shade, needs no watering, and is altogether an admirable plant; but its name is lost with its previous owner's records so we christened it 'Savannah Blue.'

Blueness in most hydrangeas depends on available aluminum in the soil, which depends on pH. pH 5 to 5.5 gives you blue flowers; pH 6 to 6.5 gives you pink. It's amusing to sprinkle lime or aluminum sulphate on your hydrangeas and produce a multicolored row. There are now also varieties that are red even at high pH. The white-flowered tree-like peegee (*Hydrangea paniculata*) and the lovely hills-of-snow (*H. arborescens*) are hardy to Zone 4 and oakleaf hydrangeas to Zone 5. The regular florist's hydrangea (*H. macrophylla*), including both lacecap and hortensia varieties, is hardy only to Zone 6. I wish I could grow the climbing hydrangea, *H. anomala petiolaris*, with lovely lacecap flowers, but it doesn't like our hot summers.

In Zones 6-9, butterfly bush (*Buddleia davidii*) flowers for most of the summer in shades of purple and white. Further north, you can treat it as an annual, since it flowers rapidly from seed. Prune it almost to the ground every spring to increasing flowering, which occurs on new wood. Buddleia is mildly fragrant and attractive to butterflies. I am also looking forward to finding a spot for several shrub buckeyes (*Aesculus*), with rather similar flower panicles. These American relatives of the European horse chestnut look amazing as specimen plants grown by Larry Lowman in Arkansas and there are species for almost every part of the United States, from Zones 3 to 8. The flowers are typical horse chestnut-like affairs in red or white.

Best of the small summer-flowering shrubs for Zones 2 to 7 or 8 are probably the potentillas and hypericums. These flower all summer although they are usually not exactly covered with flowers. *Hypericum prolificum* and *Potentilla fruticosa* are yellow, but red and very pale cultivars of several species are now with us.

I have mixed feelings about hibiscus. There are three main species for garden use: the Chinese hibiscus (*Hibiscus rosa-sinensis*), hybrids of the southern swamp hibiscus (*H. Moscheutos*), and the shrub althaea or rose of Sharon (*H. syriacus*). Chinese hibiscus is tropical and has to be brought indoors for the winter as if it were a pelargonium, but it grows rapidly in full sun in summer and comes in a vast array of cultivars. There are also many great cultivars of althaea, including a lovely thing I covet that blooms for a long time in a shady spot under pine trees on a neighboring island. Since they are hardy to at least Zone 5, the althaeas are worth investigating. What I am not so keen on is the various moscheutos hybrids and selections. They are easy to grow from seed and you will see them in seed catalogues. Their trouble is that they are slow to get going in the spring and the branches are not particularly graceful, so you have an ungainly shrub for months, which then produces flowers in ones and twos, usually hanging them among the foliage where you can't see them—although they are spectacularly large. I know some people swear by hedges of these beasties and I have never seen such a hedge so I don't know how their owners manage the slow-start-in-spring problem.

Another fine shrub for the South is oleander *(Nerium oleander)*, hardy in Zones 8 to 10 with white or pink flowers for several

Oleander

Spiraea Douglasii, native from British Columbia to northern California and hardy to Zone 5, produces rose-colored flowers in late spring.

months in summer. Oleander may be badly damaged by a hard freeze but it flowers on new wood so you can cut a damaged specimen to the ground and it will flower within months. The fringe tree (*Chionanthus*) is an attractive, pollution-tolerant shrub that blooms white in early summer as does the sourwood (*Oxydendrum arboreum*). If you live far enough south, *Lantana camara* is covered in multicolored flowers from midsummer to frost. It is a fairly untidy plant. Perhaps it could be civilized by pruning; I haven't tried.

SHRUBS FOR WINTER COLOR

Shrubs that actually flower in winter in mild climates are jewels beyond price. Camellias bear away the crown, but I am also very fond of winter jasmine, (*Jasminum nudiflorum*), gorgeous as it tumbles over a wall or down a slope and covered with yellow flowers as early as January. Then come *Viburnum tinus*, wintersweet (*Chimonanthus praecox*), the daphnes and flowering apricot (*Prunus mume*).

The shrubs that keep colored berries into winter are also highly desirable, especially if they can be viewed against a snowy background. Pyracantha, ardisia, cotoneaster, mountain ash, ardisia, chokeberry (*Aronia arbutifolia*), and nandina are among the best. Autumn color is not easy to achieve except in the North, but there are a few plants that will give you the yellow and red foliage without which fall is not fall. *Nandina domestica* takes some years to develop into a good-looking shrub, but when it does you get value for money in the form of red leaves and berries which last for most of the winter on a graceful bush. Nandina does not spread sideways at an irritating rate as so many shrubs do, but it does have one vice: it is a leggy beast, losing all its lower branches with age; hence its common name, heavenly bamboo. You may like it this way, perhaps at the back of a border, but if you want it to fill in down to the ground this too can be achieved. Cut off one or two branches every year at whatever height pleases you and each will soon be topped by a horizontal spray of leaves. There is also a dwarf variety that you could put in front of the large one to achieve the same effect.

FRAGRANT SHRUBS

When flower fragrance stops you in your tracks, you realize that highly scented flowers are rare. This happened to me when I walked into a town courtyard flooded with the scent of Confederate jasmine (*Trachelospermum jasminoides*). I returned home determined to track down fragrant flowers wherever I could find them. In a large garden, a faint scent that you have to get your nose into is not really adequate. I want the heady, spread-far-and-wide scent of night-blooming epiphyllums or ginger lilies.

First of the fragrant shrubs in my garden each year is winter daphne, *Daphne odora*, flowering in January. Most of the daphnes are

White buckeye, *Aesculus parviflora.*

fragrant but this one is a knockout, with waxy white and pink flowers on a rounded evergreen shrub that grows slowly to about six feet. Many people find daphnes difficult to establish, but you are equally likely to have beginner's luck. Just plant them in fall or winter and let them go. I have never even watered mine—not once, and it is in a dry shady spot under a sassafras tree. I think perhaps daphnes like dry soil because many of them are happy in California and a neighbor, who has had three daphnes die on her, waters her garden mightily.

Dreamiest of the scented spring shrubs are lilacs and viburnums. Unhappily, modern breeding has bred the scent right out of many originally fragrant plants and you cannot assume that the lilac you order from a catalogue will be fragrant. Check out varieties with your own nose, preferably somewhere full of lilacs, such as the Arnold Arboretum or Kew Gardens, before you buy.

Next in the flowering order come roses, very few of which meet my standards of fragrance. Don't trust catalogues. Jackson and Perkins says 'Queen Elizabeth' is fragrant, for heaven's sake. That's not fragrant. The Gallica rose 'Hippolyte' is fragrant, like many old roses. Find room in your garden for a few of these lovelies.

Topping the list of fragrant summer-flowering shrubs are gardenias. The white waxy flowers over shiny evergreen leaves are one of the few consolations for hot humid summers because gardenias don't grow well in many parts of the world. (And forget about growing them as house plants; unless you have a greenhouse, it's almost impossible to give them the humidity they need.) While reveling in six foot shrubs of *Gardenia jasminoides*, don't forget the dwarf *G. jasminoides radicans*, a delightful ground cover gardenia that is a miniature version of its big cousin, spreads rapidly, and is easy from cuttings. You could also try the white flowered sweet pepperbush (*Clethra alnifolia*). Tea olives (*Osmanthus fragrans* and *O. fortunei)* have amazingly fragrant flowers from October well into the winter. But the flowers are small and unimpressive so I am growing mine as a hedge, hoping that the necessary pruning will not remove all the flowers.

COLORFUL FOLIAGE

Even if you don't like the island beds of dwarf conifers and heathers so popular in England, the idea of many different colors and textures of foliage that remain interesting all winter, is a useful one. Foliage colors range from the red of Japanese maples and sumac through hundreds of different yellow-leaved conifers and broad-leaved evergreens to the blue tinge of Colorado blue spruce. Then there are odd shrubs whose new growth is colored, such as redtips (*Photinia*). A sheared redtip hedge as the new growth starts in spring is a lovely sight.

Hollies

Holly (*Ilex*) is a large genus containing evergreen and deciduous species, with large and small leaves, with and without spines, that range in size from dwarf plants ideal for foundation plantings to largish trees. In nearly all species, the female produces red berries that ripen rather slowly during the winter, providing later-winter food for wildlife. The foliage ranges from shiny leaves with a decidedly blue tint, through plain old green to yellow variegated. Note that only female hollies produce berries and that you need both male and female if you want berries, although there are a few self-fertile hollies around.

In general, evergreen hollies do well in Britain and eastern North America. Where evergreen holly grows well, small-leaved Japanese holly (*Ilex crenata*) Chinese holly (*I. cornuta*), or dwarf yaupon holly (*I. vomitoria*) are common substitutes for slower growing boxwood for low hedges or accent plants.

Among the larger hollies, nothing beats the native English holly (*Ilex aquifolium*), with shiny prickly leaves and big waxy red berries to pile on the mantle at Christmas. In the States, English holly thrives only from Zone 6 through the cooler half of Zone 8. But there are many acceptable substitutes for other climates. For the Northeast and sheltered spots in southern Canada, my favorites are the "blue" hybrids sold as 'Blue Prince,' 'Blue Girl' and the like. (The ones with female names are female and vice versa; get it?) These are very like English holly.

For the Deep South, the best choice for berries is the hybrid 'Savannah.' This is a rapid grower but it goes up not out so it needn't take much space in the garden. In fact you can easily high-head it to produce a not-so-small tree. 'Savannah' produces prolific red berries and has almost spineless leaves—which would be more beautiful if they were a bit less yellow and more blue. The native yaupon holly (*Ilex vomitoria*) has fascinating translucent berries and small leaves but its natural growth is irregular and untidy. It needs to be shaped to earn a spot except in a wild garden.

Watch how birds treat a holly once it has produced berries. In England a pair of mistle thrushes will defend a holly overwinter, saving the berries for food when they nest in the spring. An undefended plant loses all its berries much earlier in the winter.

Hollies produce most berries in sun, which is a sadness to those of us with much shade. You could collect hollies for ever and never run out of varieties to try. Prominent among breeders is Kathleen Meserve who created the 'Blue' series. By crossing the beautiful (mainly *I. aquifolium*) with the hardy, she has created dozens of fine hollies for most climate zones. Any of her *Ilex x Meserveae* hollies are likely to please.

PLANTING AND CARING FOR SHRUBS

Shrubs, like trees, are usually sold in containers, balled and burlapped, or bare root. Plant most of them as you would trees. However, some shrubs are exceptions to the rule that you shouldn't amend the soil in a planting hole. The obvious examples are rhododendrons, azaleas, heaths, heathers, and anything else that likes a really organic soil.

These acid-loving plants have shallow roots, which grow out sideways. You will get them off to a good start if you place very acid soil around them. If you do not, their roots will ignore the soil altogether and grow only in the mulch you spread around them. When planting a lot of acid lovers in a bed, the easiest approach is to dig as much organic matter as you can into the whole bed, although the bed does not have to be dug very deep.

If you are planting azaleas and rhododendrons in isolated planting holes around the shrubbery, dig a shallow hole that is, ideally, four times as wide as the shrub's root ball. Place the soil you have removed in a wheelbarrow or on a tarpaulin and mix it with leaves, pine bark, compost, or whatever organic matter is available, and use it to backfill the hole. Surround the plant with a wide ring of mulch to suppress weeds because you cannot cultivate among these shallow roots and will have to pull weeds by hand.

All shrubs will appreciate a mulch—which may be of stone if you are gardening in a desert landscape. If you can remember to give your shrubs a shovelful of compost twice a year they will also appreciate it. Shrubs are tolerant of neglect and tend to be missed when it is feeding time in the garden.

PRUNING

There is almost no limit to the number of different ways in which you can prune a shrub. Most can even be shaped into small trees and pollarded! However, most pruning methods can be divided into natural pruning and shearing.

Natural pruning emphasizes the shape that the shrub adopts in nature while keeping its size under control. Newly planted shrubs should not be pruned. Let them grow freely while you discover their natural shape. Viburnums form horizontal layers, forsythia

ATTRACTING BIRDS

A garden containing a variety of native plants, fresh water, and nesting sites, and tended by a gardener who doesn't use pesticides, will attract plenty of birds. Your compost pile and the rich organic soil you are building in the garden will attract even more. A mockingbird follows my progress through the garden, sometimes perching on my fork like an English robin, ready to pounce on grubs and worms I unearth.

A variety of birds is desirable to help you keep weeds and other garden pests under control. Most common garden birds eat either insects or seeds (and fruit). Seed-eaters will eat your weed seeds but can also be a nuisance because some will prefer the seeds you plant in the garden. Surveying the single aster that had survived from a large planting of seeds in an Idaho garden, Bruce Bowler said resignedly, "I think we support 300 head of quail on this hillside."

Insectivorous and carnivorous birds are particularly desirable in the garden because they keep insect and rodent pests under control. These are also the birds most likely to be killed by pesticides.

Feeders Put out a variety of feeders containing several kinds of food and keep them supplied year round, or at least

throughout the winter. In the spring, reduce the amount of food slowly. Feeders can be as fancy or simple as you choose. Corn or sunflower seeds thrown on the ground will attract ground feeding pheasants, grouse, quails, mourning doves, and sparrows. To save money on bird seed, which can become quite an expensive item, you can grow your own sunflowers, thistles, and grains.

Hanging feeders full of suet or peanut butter will provide protein for insectivorous birds such as wrens, woodpeckers, and nuthatches, although I don't recommend suet for warm parts of the world. You can prevent the depradations of mammals by hanging these feeders at least four feet from the ground from a branch too light to support a squirrel or raccoon. Small seed-eaters such as warblers and finches will flock to hanging feeders containing thistle or other small seeds. These come through our part of the world mainly on migration and in flocks. It is a lovely sight to wake one winter morning and find the thistle feeder noisy with the cries of goldfinches and pine siskins fighting for space on the perches.

Platform feeders can be as simple as a shelf tacked outside the kitchen window. Seeds, fruit, meat scraps, and almost any other kind of food can go on a shelf and will attract a variety of birds.

Shelter It may take a surprisingly long time for birds to find your feeders. It was

and some spiraeas put out long thin branches that droop toward the ground in a fountain, bamboo is straight and upright. When the shrub starts to outgrow its space and needs to be cut back, this natural shape should remain after pruning. If you shear the top off bamboo or forsythia to reduce its height, what you usually have left is an ugly mess.

Retain the natural shape of a multi-stemmed shrub by pruning it from the base. If a shrub has a dozen stems emerging from the ground, cut half of them off at ground level to thin the shrub and let light and air into the interior. This is not an easy job, since it involves groveling around under the shrub trying to reach stems in the middle of the plant. It can be a real chore even with a nice upright lilac. With a prickly specimen like a Father Hugo's rose, it is almost enough to make you give up gardening. The advantage of making your

more than a year after we moved to our present house before we had even half the number of species that flocked to our previous garden only a few miles away. You can speed up this process by placing your feeders near shrubbery in which birds can hide while deciding to make a dash for the feeder, although eventually birds will come even to feeders out in the open.

Nest sites One morning I found a chewed up fish on my car and discovered a green heron nest in the oak overhead. That was a thrill. But if your garden contains even young shrubs and trees, you will soon be host to a number of nesting birds. It takes careful observation to find most of them. You cannot usually hope to see adults teaching their offspring to fly. In fact, you may only know you have families when you find old nests or see juvenile birds on feeders. Wrens, for instance, may leave the nest and be on their own in less than an hour.

Birds are very fussy about where they nest and this has led to the decline of species that can seldom find precisely the type of hole, flat branch, or pile of rocks they require in our vanishing habitats. It is well worth contacting a local ornithology group or extension service to find out how to provide nest sites for birds that are now rare in your area for lack of nest sites. For instance, householders have increased the populations of rare wood ducks and eastern bluebirds by providing and maintaining the right kinds of nest boxes in appropriate habitats on their properties. These are both species that nest naturally in the hollows in old trees that are becoming increasingly rare.

Water The more different sources of water you can provide, the more birds you will attract. Ponds, shallow birdbaths, dripping fountains, and streams will attract various species. Provide as many of these as you can and keep them filled, especially in hot or freezing weather.

Enjoying birds Now that you have slaved for your bird population, get yourself a field guide to birds in your area and a pair of binoculars and provide yourself with a comfortable seat from which to watch. Except for birds that visit you only on migration, you will find that the same species are nearly always to be found in your garden so you don't have to identify very many species before you know nearly all of them.

People with good ears learn to identify birds by their calls. This is a mystery to me. I can hum tunes but never remember their names. Thom Smith, on the other hand, identifies nearly all birds by their song and even knows the woodpeckers apart by the sound of their tree-tapping.

You might like to join ornithologists doing research on bird populations. You can do this by joining something like Cornell Lab of Ornithology's "Feeder Watch." Feeder Watch members count the birds that come to their feeders during several days of the year and send the results in for analysis. Birds that are becoming more or less common are recorded and reasons for the changes explored. In the Feeder Watch newsletter, you read about new feeders and about hawks swooping to snatch a starling from a feeder. You really feel you have become part of the vast army of amateurs who are fighting to preserve at least some of our wildlife.

pruning cuts in the center of the bush and as near the ground as possible is that the pruning cuts don't show and the shrub looks as good as new when you have finished.

Many conifers, such as yews, cypresses, and junipers, have one main trunk so that you cannot prune them by removing stems at ground level. But the principle of natural pruning remains: cut branches off close to the trunk or at any rate well inside the plant so that the cut ends don't show. It is difficult to prune back an overgrown juniper so that it does not look as if it walked into a buzz saw, but it can be done if you are careful where you cut.

When a shrub ceases to flower as well as it once did, removing the tangle of stems in its center may help. This is especially true with roses, which sometimes get a bit jungly in the middle. However, the usual reason that shrubs flower poorly is either that they are dying of old age or that nearby trees have grown while you weren't watching and a

GREEN THUMB TIPS
ANTI-TRANSPIRANTS

In the snake oil department, you will sometimes see "anti-transpirants" advertised as winter protection for shrubs and some nurseries swear by them for needle-leaved evergreens. These are coatings sprayed on the leaves, designed to close the stomata in the leaf so that the plant cannot lose water while the ground is frozen and its roots cannot absorb water. Work at the Connecticut Agricultural Research Station shows that they don't work. Even if anti-transpirants are applied thickly to all leaf surfaces, they fall off within a few days, meaning they are absolutely no use for protecting a shrub for the winter.

shrub that needs sun to flower is now in the shade. No amount of pruning will help here.

Natural Shearing

Natural shearing may sound like an oxymoron because there is nothing natural about running hedge clippers over a shrub to prune it. But some shrubs can be treated in this way and still retain their natural grace. These are the shrubs that have a naturally curvaceous shape. Given enough space, box, pittosporum, and many azaleas naturally grow in attractive curving billows with leaves all the way to the ground. But they also put out long straight stems that stick out from the shrub and spoil its shape. There is nothing wrong with shearing these shrubs into what is really a tidification of their natural shape.

Shrubs look subtly wrong when sheared into unnatural stiffness with no sort of rhyme or reason. These are the shrubs that gardeners disparage as "evergreen mothballs." One garden in Savannah contains azaleas, dotted randomly around the lawn and each carefully sheared into a sphere on a stem. They look awful. In contrast, camellias pruned as mophead trees placed symmetrically to line the front path are attractive, because the setting and plantings are formal, even though camellias are not natural mopheads.

HEDGES, FORMAL AND INFORMAL

It may seem obvious, but when you plan a hedge, make sure that the shrubs you buy have been grown so that they fit your purposes. If you are going to grow a cherry laurel into a small tree, buy a plant with a single stem in the first place. I made this mistake with a stilt hedge of redtips (a hedge with naked trunks at the bottom). When I bought the plants, I was planning a solid hedge so I bought baby plants with two or three stems apiece which had been pruned low to make them branch. When I later decided on the stilt bottom, I had to remove extra stems and side branches. As a result, the hedge will always be standing on crooked stems instead of nice straight stilts. I suppose I should rip it out and start again, but I know that I shan't.

If you find yourself presiding over an informal hedge that has outgrown its allotted space, cut the whole thing down to about eight inches from the ground. Most shrubs will survive this drastic surgery if you perform it in late fall or early spring. Or you could prune a few shrubs each year, making the massacre less noticeable. New stems will grow rapidly from the stubs because they have a huge root system to draw on, and the new plants will have their normal graceful shape.

While you have the hedge cut down, you may want to get at its base and dig up stems on the outer edges with their roots. If you plant these amputees in the home nursery, you will soon have plenty of new shrubs for elsewhere in the garden or to replace any plants in the old hedge that do not survive.

Sheared Hedges

It seems that in every part of the world two groups of shrubs are used for sheared hedges: those that are usually grown and the aristocrats that make better hedges. The plants that are usually grown include privet *(Ligustrum)* in most of the United Kingdom and the northern United States, redtip and wax myrtle *(Myrica cerifera)* in the South, and New Mexican privet *(Forestieria neomexicana)* in the dry West. These are common because they grow fairly rapidly, providing privacy fast. Because they are fast-growing, they need to be sheared almost every day, it sometimes seems, and often reward the exhausted gardener by developing large holes and thin spots. They also have larger leaves than the aristocrats so that they are inevitably rather coarse in texture.

If you can bear to wait for the final effect, there are small-leaved shrubs adapted to all areas that need to be sheared only once a year, grow thick and dense, and make much more beautiful hedges. In England, the aristocrats are yews and boxwoods. In the northern United States, Canadian hemlock *(Tsuga canadensis)* is probably the first choice, but yews also make wonderful hedges. For the West, western red cedar *(Thuja plicata),* Italian cypress *(Cupressus sempervirens)* and alkali-tolerant Texas mountain laurel *(Sophora secundiflora)* are hard to beat or, if your soil has a little more moisture, small-needled evergreens such as Lawson's false cypress *(Chamaecyparis lawsoniana)* or sawaro *(C. pisifera).* In the Midwest and Middle Atlantic States, yew, chamaecyparis, and boxwood get the nod, and in the Deep South small-leaved box, hollies, and cherry laurel *(Prunus caroliniana)* make the finest hedges.

If you shear your hedge properly, you may despair during the early years because you keep cutting the plants back into foot-high bushes in an attempt to make them develop branches all the way to the ground. But remember that while you are chopping them back, they are developing big root systems. As soon as the base is filled in to your satisfaction, you can let them grow upward much more rapidly. By the time they are twenty, or even ten, years old, you will have a hedge that anyone might think had been there for centuries. The secret is to cut back viciously whenever a bare spot starts to develop. The idea is to admit light and water and to cut the tips off all stems in the area so that they will develop multiple branches. The labor involved in creating a picture-book hedge with these fine plants is much less than that needed to keep a more plebeian hedge from getting out of hand.

Since your formal hedge is there for the duration, it is worth giving it a good start in life. Dig a trench and mix the soil with compost, manure, leaf mold and lime (if your soil is very acid). Buy tiny hedging sized bare-root plants, which are cheapest from a large nursery that specializes in hedge plants. It is a waste of money to start with foot high plants that have been grown in containers in the nursery. These have usually already lost branches near the base and need to be cut down almost to the ground as soon as you have planted them.

If you want rapid good looks from your hedge, plant in a double staggered row with the plants as little as 18 inches apart. A single row looks just as good in the end but takes longer to fill the gaps between the plants. If the baby plants have pointy tops, as Canadian hemlocks do, cut the top inch off each plant. Now surround the plants with a few inches of mulch and keep them watered. After six months, or whenever you can see that the plants have started to grow, cut an inch off the top of each plant. This encourages new branches to grow sideways, which is what you want.

Your plants will put on most of their growth when leaf buds open in spring. In early summer, when you can see the new growth clearly, prune and mulch. The first step in pruning is to take about half the new growth from the top of the plants, giving the hedge a flat top. Then look at the sides. Since a thick base is your main concern at this point, shear the sides of the hedge so that they slope inward toward the top so that light and water reach the bottom branches. Now look at the space between the plants. This is probably filling in nicely with horizontal branches that do not need pruning, but if you think the lower branches are a bit thin, cut out some of the hedge above them to give them more light. If the plants get enough warmth and water during the summer, they may put on quite a bit of growth and respond well to a repeat pruning in the fall.

As a general rule, hedges fill in faster if they are pruned little and often, so any juvenile hedge should be pruned as often as you can bear to do it. Once your hedge is a few years old and filling in

Training a stilt hedge.
Tie the trunks to stakes and side branches to bamboos attached to neighboring bushes. Thicken the hedge by cutting out the tip of each branch frequently to induce branching. Once the hedge has reached the size you want, all it needs is to be sheared once or twice a year.

nicely at the base, however, it will not need pruning except once a year in early summer, although if you are really fussing over the hedge a late-summer pruning as well won't hurt. Once the base is as thick as you want it, you can prune the sides vertically if that is the final shape you want. I have grown plenty of beautiful hedges with vertical sides, but it may well be that a slightly sloping hedge has less chance of developing bare spots.

There are few satisfactions in life that compare with contemplating a thick, full hedge of perfectly sheared hemlock, holly, or yew that you have grown with your own fair hands.

Once you have mastered the art of the sheared hedge, the opportunities are endless. You can plant walls around garden rooms, privacy hedges, backgrounds for flowers, arches over gateways. But try not to get carried away as I have. While one 30 foot hedge behind your main flower bed will not take long to prune each year, miles and miles of formal hedges most definitely will.

Formal hedges made of fast-growing plants create many problems. For one thing, they easily get too tall. The world is full of hedges that were supposed to stop at eight feet high and got carried away. You must be able to reach the middle of the top of your hedge comfortably from a stable stepladder. Mature hedges can easily grow more than 18 inches a year. There are few tasks more awkward than trying to take a couple of feet off the top of a fifteen foot privet hedge. And the hedge doesn't look too good when you have finished, either. So if you aim for an eight foot height in a fast-growing hedge, make sure your spring shearing takes the hedge down to at least seven feet.

Small birds with retiring dispositions will find your formal hedge the ideal nesting spot. You will seldom see any sign of their presence until a family of wrens staggers from the hedge one day and takes to the air. Meanwhile they have been busy feeding on insects in the hedge and dropping a little natural fertilizer around its roots.

TOPIARY

Topiary is the art of pruning trees and shrubs into architectural or fanciful shapes. For my money, the term should not be used for the practice of building animals of chicken wire and growing ivy over the resulting structure: an abominable practice that is perhaps a logical outcome of the modern desire for instant everything.

You can buy container-grown instant topiaries that only need to be kept in shape thereafter, but these are an expensive substitute for the fun of growing your own, which is not at all difficult to do. As with formal hedges, the secret of successful topiary is to use appropriate plants and to prune them little and often. Any small-leaved evergreen can be used for topiary and you are most likely to

Beginning topiary.
To convert a mophead into a double ball, let a few shoots grow out of the top of the mop. Select the strongest and let it grow until it is tall enough to form the nucleus of the second ball. Then remove its growing tip so that branches form and shear frequently until the top is bushy.

find plants adapted to your area in a local nursery that grows its own plants.

In South Carolina, Pearl Fryar had an urge to make a splash in his garden and began to create magnificent topiaries without even knowing the word. Since he had not read the books, he developed cultural practices that worked for him and ended up with one of the most interesting topiary gardens in the United States in little more than a decade. The garden is interesting because he learned how to create new shapes as he went along. These include hearts, made by tying two vigorous shoots together, and fan shapes in which leaves are stripped from the bases of branches to reveal the branch shape.

Fryar obtains his evergreens from a local nursery, so that they are well adapted to the soil and climate, and he gets them cheap because he will take any distorted or half dead specimen the nursery wants to get rid of. He plants them in unimproved soil, waters them for only a couple of weeks, keeps them heavily mulched with pine straw, and never fertilizes. To the surprise of the experts, the lack of water and fertilizer in the sandy soil and hot humid summers of South Carolina don't seem to bother the plants at all, which only shows what beginners may have to teach the rest of us.

PROPAGATING SHRUBS

For instant shrubbery, you can divide many established shrubs. Most shrubs have multiple stems emerging from the soil and most of these stems have roots attached. All you have to do is separate the bush into clumps of, say, three stems each and plant them as separate shrubs. You can do this at any time of year, even in summer if you keep your new shrubs well-watered until they have had a chance to grow more roots.

Shrubs such as indica azaleas and winter jasmine have drooping branches that root where they touch the ground. These can be separated from the parent plant and grown as new shrubs.

The simplest method is first to cut the branch between the new roots and the parent plant and leave the baby shrub for a few months before transplanting it to its new home. If you move the juvenile immediately after cutting the stem it will need tender loving care for a few months while it grows the extra roots it will need. As usual, the necessary aftercare is greatest if you transplant the new shrub in spring or summer.

Cuttings

Many shrubs are absurdly easy to propagate from cuttings. If you are pruning a hydrangea, viburnum, or fatsia in the autumn, chop a branch into pieces about ten inches long, stick the pieces into sandy soil in the shade, and about half of them will be rooted shrubs by spring. I planted my hundred feet of hydrangea hedge by this simple system one fall—and it bloomed the following summer!

If you can root a shrub by simply sticking cuttings in the ground, there is no point in doing anything more complicated. But many plants do not root well with this treatment and you will get a much higher success rate by going to a little more trouble. Professionals propagate shrubs from small cuttings which are potted up in containers to be grown on for sale when they have formed nice little shrubs. There is a lot to be said for following a similar regime in the home garden.

First, make sure that your cutting has at least two nodes (buds) on it. Cut the stem just below the node that will go into the soil because roots form most readily at nodes. The other node sticks up into the air to produce the cutting's new leaves. If you are taking the cuttings in summer, the equivalent is to remove the leaves from the part of the stem that will go underground and leave just two or three leaves above ground. Your object is to leave the cutting with some leaf surface for photosynthesis, but not with so much leaf area that it loses water too rapidly by transpiration.

Many people let cuttings rest in a damp place for several days before planting them so that they form a callus over the cut surface. The roots will grow from the callus. Before planting your cutting, dip its end in rooting hormone, obtainable from any garden center, and you may speed up root growth.

Now, place the cuttings in a medium with very good drainage so that the new roots will get lots of air. Sand, perlite, and vermiculite are all good choices. Put the cuttings in a shady place, water them, and most of them will root. You'll know they are rooted when they start to produce new leaves. Then harden them off as you would seedlings (Chapter 10) before planting them in the ground.

Many books tell you to place cuttings in pots and cover the pots with plastic bags to keep them moist. Perhaps the air at my house is more full of fungus spores that most but I find most of my cuttings rot under these conditions. It may work for you. Many

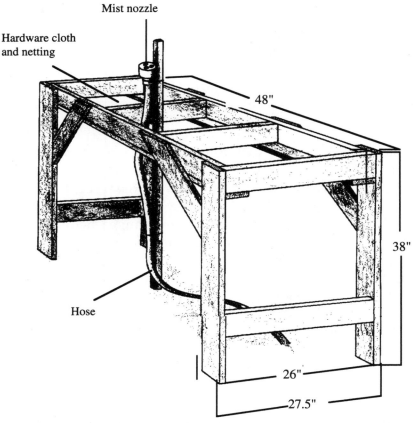

A misting table for rooting cuttings.

Most of the table is made of treated 1 x 4 lumber. Line the table with strong wire netting (such as dog fencing) for support. Over the wire netting lay fine, permeable netting. Window screening works well. Then fill the table with vermiculite, sand, or perlite and it is ready for your cuttings.

plants, such as sedums, pachysandra, ivy, and aucuba, will root from cuttings placed in water. The problem with this system is that you still have to go to the trouble of planting the rooted cuttings in soil and keeping them very well watered for a period before you plant them in the ground. I think it is easier to root the cuttings in sand in the first place.

BUILDING A MISTING TABLE

If you are an impecunious gardener planting an estate on a shoestring, there is no substitute for building yourself a misting table. With this, and a bag of vermiculite, you can root even the slow specimens, such as hollies, azaleas, rhododendrons, and junipers, without using rooting hormone and without even reading the instructions about "root from semi-hardwood cuttings taken in midsummer." Almost anything will root on a misting table in summer without any attention at all.

The misting table shown in the figure is made from treated lumber, chicken wire, and hardware cloth (or window screening). Its only specialist equipment is the misting nozzle which you can buy at your garden center or through most gardening catalogues. The misting tables of my youth lived in shaded greenhouses, so I was skeptical when told by a Georgia gardener to place the thing in full sun. The idea is that cuttings taken in summer root faster when they get as much light as possible for photosynthesis. It works like a charm.

The misting nozzle produces such a fine spray that it uses only a trickle of water so we leave it on 24 hours a day. To save water, you could put a timer on it so that it comes on every ten minutes for a minute or two, which is what they do in commercial greenhouses.

Take your cuttings and make sure you have at least one leafless node beneath the surface of the vermiculite. You can leave quite a lot of leafage on the top because in the constant mist cuttings seldom wilt except in a high wind. Then do as I say not as I do and label the cuttings. I have many mystery cuttings growing into little shrubs in my nursery and I don't know what they are because I omitted to label cuttings from friends, certain that I should recognize them later, which I don't. I even showed some of the shrubs to Simone van Stolk, who gave me the cuttings, and she didn't recognize them. Not until I had ordered *Viburnum tinus* from a mail order place and planted it, did the penny drop and I realize what the dozen baby shrubs in my nursery were.

Pull the cuttings up occasionally to see if they have rooted. Things like geraniums, gardenias, and hydrangeas root in about a month in summer and are then ready to be planted in containers full of compost. Tough customers, such as azaleas and most evergreens, may take most of the summer to root. When you have potted up the cuttings, leave the pots in the shade of the misting table for a week or two so that they get plenty of water while their roots settle into the soil and then move them to a drier part of the garden for a month or two before planting them in the ground.

Birds love the misting table and never seem to dig up the cuttings when they come to take a bath. You might think it would be worth integrating the misting table into the general garden waterworks, for instance by directing runoff from the table into your stream or pond, but I am not sure this is really worth doing because there is so little runoff. It is more convenient to have the table near nursery, pots, and compost to save toing and froing.

VINES FOR ALL PURPOSES

The world is full of beautiful vines, plants that grow long and thin, twining and twisting around and through anything they come in contact with. And there are few prettier sights than an arbor or tool shed covered with the flowers of a clematis, rose, or silver lace vine. Vines give you a lot of flowers for their size and are well worth incorporating into a garden.

Some vines, like ivy and Virginia creeper, have sucker-like attachments that will grip almost anything. Others, like grapes, wisteria, and beans, hold on by twisting as they grow so that they twine round anything they encounter. Still others, like climbing roses and kudzu, have no means of attaching themselves but a

Clematis viticella

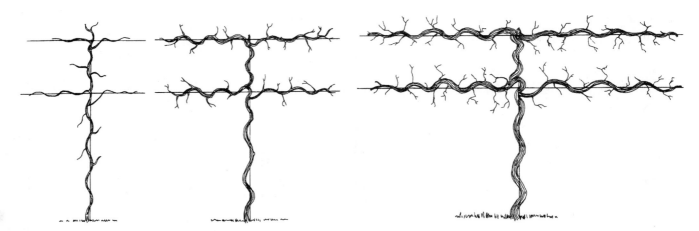

Pruning a wisteria as an espalier.

Use stakes or strong wires to support the vine. If you purchased the vine while it was flowering, it should continue to flower every year while you are training it. Let the plant grow to its final height without pruning and then select four strong side shoots to act as the side arms. Remove all other shoots. Let the side arms grow to their final length, shortening any branches they put out almost back to the side arm.

Wisteria blooms on new wood so it can be pruned heavily until it loses its leaves in autumn without reducing the following year's bloom. Heavy pruning is needed to keep the plant under control and to ensure lots of flowers. For maximum flower power, do not water or fertilize a wisteria.

strong tendency to grow upward so that they can easily be trained to cover tall structures.

It is a sad fact that one person's decorative vine is another's noxious weed. I first met Virginia creeper (*Parthenocissus virginiana*) when it covered a brick house in England. It was pretty all year, turned a wonderful red in autumn, and was well-behaved, needing to be trimmed back from windows and doors only once a year. Now I live in its native habitat, Virginia creeper is a complete pest, combining with other native vines, such as grapes, trumpet vine (*Campsis radicans*) and honeysuckle to smother hedges and destroy clapboard in a single season. Even wisteria, that beautiful spring bloomer, is a weed here, growing 70 feet up into pine trees and threatening fruit trees and lawns with its huge curling tendrils. Which only goes to prove that if you live in a mild moist climate, such as most vines love, it pays to be careful what you plant.

When choosing a vine to hide a pole, cover a wall, or hang over an archway, consider the effect you are after and how much effort you are prepared to devote to training the vine. Annual vines and some perennials, such as sweet peas, castor beans, black-eyed susan (*Thunbergia*), and morning glories are grown from seed and provide a rapid display of flowers and foliage. But the effect does not last long and you have to plant them again next year.

In complete contrast, it is many years' work to train a wisteria or rose against the side of a building, but once you have finished the vine will need pruning only once or twice a year to give you a lovely floral display for many years. In between the two come things like clematis, which are perennials but relatively slow-growing and not a big nuisance to prune. Some of the hybrid clematis are lovely, but I should really like to be able to grow some of the species that don't like my climate. Among the few that do tolerate the Deep South are Japanese clematis (*Clematis diosoreifolia*) with fragrant white flowers, and *C. Armandii* but I am also about to try *C. maximowicziana*, despite the negligible chance of ever pronouncing its name, because it flowers in autumn when flowers are so welcome. I hope

Northwesterners enjoy *C. viticella* and gorgeous *C. montana* 'Grandiflora,' which grows so well in that area and in Britain and is even hardy north of Boston.

The virtue and vice of most vines is the speed with which they cover the ground. If you have an ugly fence between your house and the road, you can beautify it in a few months by vines along and through it. Or you can make it a permanent feature of the landscape by covering it with climbing roses Carolina jasmine (*Gelsemium sempervirens*), or cup-and-saucer vine (*Cobaea scandens*).

An old wisteria trained against a building and kept well pruned is a lovely sight and will eventually develop a trunk as thick as that of a small tree.

PRUNING AND TRAINING VINES

Pruning grape vines for maximum fruit production is a science, and the subject of heated arguments, so better consult your local experts. But the principles of pruning most vines are relatively simple. You cut out the growing tip of a vine if you want it to branch and then prune out branches as necessary to keep the vine within the bounds you have allotted it. Thicken it up by cutting a branch or two near the base. It is also worth remembering that many woody plants flower more profusely if you pull the branches down until they are more or less horizontal. (This is not magic; it is a result of the way flowering hormones travel around the plant.) This is one reason fruit trees are often espaliered so that their branches are horizontal and that gardeners train climbing roses horizontally along fences and trellises.

ARBORS AND ARCHES

If you live on a hillside, you probably have plenty of surfaces on which to grow vines. But if your country is flat, you may be, like me, always in need of more fences and trellises for new and interesting vines.

Trellises can be built against the sides of buildings. If the vine is something fast-growing, you can even get away with something tacky like chicken wire because it will soon be invisible beneath leaves and branches. Chicken wire wrapped around a lamp post is not very visible and makes one of the best supports for things like clematis that climb by tendrils. You can also use pillars covered with vines as accents, perhaps spaced along a garden path with ropes or chains slung between the pillars. But one of the best ways to use vines is to cover arches that mark the entrances to garden rooms. A rose-covered arch over the front gate is a traditional treat in a cottage garden. Perhaps an arch can span the gap between house and garage, inviting you to the path that leads to the back garden.

Arbors are structures with tops but no sides that provide a shady spot to sit or to shelter house plants for the summer as well as a horizontal surface for vines. The most elaborate arbors are huge tunnels covered with plants that lead from one part of the garden to another. Californian Thomas Church played a large part in making arbors part of the home landscape. He built simple box-like arbors of metal or wood to provide shelter for a sitting area. Then he trained vines, and even trees, in geometric shapes over the arbor to provide leafy shade in summer and handsome woody shapes in winter.

Consult pictures of gardens ancient and modern for shapes of arbors and arches that appeal to you. You can buy metal rose arches, plastic and wood clematis trellises from garden supply stores, but most of these are much too small. What is the use of a three-foot wide rose arch? By the time it is covered with roses, there won't be room for you to pass through without getting scratched to pieces, let alone you, a friend, and the garden cart. It is much better to build your own structures and make them a decent size and reasonably strong—because a healthy vine is a lot heavier than it looks and can soon demolish a fragile trellis. It is also worth remembering that the appearance of a structure will change as the vine grows up it. We built some sturdy, but rather ugly, square rose arches one year because I knew that the Lady Banks roses destined to cover them would soon give a pleasantly rounded shape to the top of each arch. By the same token, a sturdy vine may be just what you need to disguise the appearance of a functional, but ugly, tool shed.

Cobaea scandens.

The cheap lattice or trellis that you can buy from home supply stores in large sheets is a boon when it comes to building structures for vines to scramble over. Arbors, rose arches, cucumber trellis, privacy fence, and lots more can be constructed from this material. Cheap lattice is very fragile and must be framed if it is to stand up for any length of time. If you build your frame of pressure treated lumber and nail the lattice to the frame, you will have a sturdy structure that will last.

Do not skimp on installing the arch or arbor. If you live where the soil seldom freezes in winter, you can get away with digging two-foot holes for the feet of the structure, adding concrete at the bottom of the hole for extra support. If you live with cold winters, you need to be much more thorough than this if your arch or arbor is not to heave part way out of the ground after a few years. Your posts must reach to below the frost line and rest on sturdy foundations. Consult a book on building garden structures, and don't rely on one written for California if you live in New England.

ROSES

The wild roses of a country hedge or Chinese hillside have been bred over the centuries into a bewildering array of modern roses. In general, wild roses form large bushes and flower only once a year. Breeding has aimed at producing plants that flower throughout the summer, have larger flowers and a variety of plant shapes, including climbers, small bushes, and miniatures (in which both the plant and the flowers are small).

If you plan a large collection of modern hybrid tea roses, you need the advice of a good rose book or your local rose society. Many roses are difficult to grow well, being susceptible to mold, rot, blight, bugs, and just about anything else that can attack a plant. Rose lovers go to endless trouble with sprays and fertilizer to produce prize blooms and attractive foliage.

But even if you are not a true rose grower, or if you refuse to use fungicides and insecticides in the garden, there is no reason why you cannot have a few easy-care roses that will give you great pleasure. Roses have an intimidating reputation, but in every part of the world there are dozens of species and varieties that behave beautifully with absolutely no care. You just have to find them—which is not always easy. Many of these roses are not modern varieties but old roses known to gardeners for a century or more, and species roses, roses that are little changed from their wild ancestors.

Old Roses for All Areas

In all parts of the world, gardeners have been rescuing old roses from obscurity. Read one of the delightful books about the Texan "rose rustlers" who scour cemeteries and country properties for roses imported by settlers that are no longer offered commercially.

Unlike most modern roses, which are grafted onto foreign rootstock, old roses can usually be propagated by cuttings and several nurseries now have stocks of old roses for sale.

In the northern and midwestern United States, hardiness is the main barrier to rose-growing. When experimenting with hardiness, it is worth remembering that yellow roses, for some unknown reason, are generally less hardy than pink ones. But at least one yellow species rose flourishes in cold areas: Father Hugo's rose (*Rosa hugonis*), a Chinese rose that forms a huge bush about ten feet high and the same across, absolutely covered with gorgeous single flowers in early summer. This is a dense prickly affair and might be just what you need to keep deer or cows out of the garden. One of the few roses that will take really boggy conditions is *Rosa palustris*, native to the eastern United States. *R. palustris scandens* was in the Empress Josephine's collection at Malmaison and was painted by Redoute as *R. hudsoniana scandens*. That information courtesy of Bill Welch; I like a little history and romance with my plants.

Among other roses that are easy in the North 'The Fairy' (a polyantha) forms a bush about four feet in diameter and will give you sprays of small pink roses from July until well after the first freeze. You will nearly always be able to pick a bunch for the Thanksgiving dinner table. 'Betty Prior' is a single floribunda that is similarly easy if you like its rather hard pink color, which I don't.

In the Deep South, humid summers guarantee fungus infections for most roses. Worst of these is black spot, which looks just as it sounds. The leaves develop black spots, turn yellow, and fall off. Some books advise picking off all diseased leaves and burning them to reduce the number of fungus spores, but this is the sort of impractical advice you get from books. Research at Cornell University shows that a spray of 5% baking soda in water, applied to both sides of the leaves every ten days, prevents black spot by raising the pH on the leaf surface so that fungus spores will not germinate. This is good advice for organic rose growers but again sounds like an awful lot of work. Much more to the point is to plant roses that are immune to black spot—and there are plenty of these.

Start with two lovely climbers from China that flower only once a year: then go on to what is probably a hybrid between them, 'Fortuniana.' The first of the species is the Cherokee rose (*Rosa laevigata*), which arrived in the Southeast in the eighteenth century aboard tea clippers. It was planted as a hedge to keep animals in, and a very effective large hedge it would make, with its vicious thorns and rapid growth to 30 feet and more. In spring, the Cherokee rose is covered with huge single white flowers with yellow stamens that darken with age. Plant it on a bank as a ground cover or where it can climb into a tree. A dark pine tree or an old pear with a Cherokee rose cascading through its branches is a glorious sight. The other species is Lady Banks Rose (*Rosa banksiae*)

Rosa 'Fortuniana' is believed to have inherited its thorns from the Cherokee rose and its double flowers from Lady Banks.

another climber, with tiny leaves, almost no thorns, and small double yellow or white flowers that last for three weeks and more in late spring. Unhappily, it doesn't seem to like the British climate and is hardy only to Zone 7 (as is the Cherokee rose). Also a rampant grower, Lady Banks looks at her best hanging over a tall wall or spreading through a tree or informal hedge. You can train it over a rose arch or arbor as I have done, but it will drive you mad trying to keep it down to size unless your arch is bigger than mine.

Among the most fragrant of all roses is Shakespeare's musk rose, "with sweet musk roses and with eglantine." Once thought extinct, the musk rose (*Rosa moschata*), which reached England from Asia in 1521, was rediscovered in this century in both England and South Carolina and is now available again. It needs a humid climate.

Oddly enough, 'The Fairy' is also happy in the South, although it does not flower as abundantly as in the north. And there are several hybrid teas, such as 'Tiffany,' 'Peace,' 'America', 'Garden Party,' 'Touch of Class,' 'Chicago Peace,' 'Mr. Lincoln,' and 'Angel Wings' that are also fairly resistant to disease and reasonably well-suited to life in the South. To my sorrow, the beautiful new David Austen roses suffer badly from black spot and so do such lovelies as 'Constance Spry' and 'Iceberg' (among the best of white roses for California where it grows into a large shrub). Many of the old roses are tougher. In my garden, the nineteenth century Gallica rose 'Hippolyte' produces a wonderfully fragrant display of cabbage-like maroon flowers even in part shade, and is followed by a mass of pale pink smaller flowers from the Damask rose 'Ispahan', which forms a spreading bush about four feet high. Noisettes are a group of old roses that were actually developed in the South, and sound as if they should be well adapted to the area—but most of them get black spot rather badly and are, anyway, exceedingly hard to find.

SHRUB ROSES

Most of these old roses fall into the general category of shrub roses, meaning that they form naturally graceful shrubs that don't need much pruning. 'Bonica' is a justly popular modern shrub rose. After years of neglect in favor of hybrid teas, with their fussy habits and huge flowers, shrub roses are coming back into favor. The Meilland family of France has devoted itself to breeding many lovely shrub roses that can be treated exactly like any other shrub. Instead of being planted in separate beds because they need special care, shrub roses can be used as hedging plants, placed in the shrubbery, or used as specimens in the middle of the lawn or drooping over a pond.

Plant shrub roses in big holes with lots of humus. I never spray them (although some of them could do with it), and feed them only compost. They need six hours sun a day, but if you plant them on

A hybrid tea rose

the shady side of a fence the taller ones will grow up to the sun and flower beautifully along the top of the fence.

Old roses that flower only once a year bloom on old wood so they should be pruned only after they have flowered. Thin out the jungle that may develop in the center by cutting some old canes off at ground level. And you may want to cut vigorous canes back by about a third to improve the shape of the bush.

Modern Roses

I am no expert on hybrid tea roses but our local expert, Patty Thigpen, has explained a few mysteries. First she says that you cannot count on a hybrid tea to do its best for more than about five years in the South. Plan on replacing them after this time. Have you ever wondered whether you should buy a rose in a container or bare-rooted? It turns out there is no difference between the two, except that you have better control over the bare-root plant. The reason is that most rose growers are in the North. They dig the plants as soon as they lose their leaves in autumn and keep them in cold storage. Then they ship them bare-root from January on—to retailers as well as to you and me. They arrive very dehydrated which is why you are told to soak a bare root rose overnight before planting or potting it. You know when you have done this properly, but you don't know if the garden center down the street has, so it is safer to take possession of bare-root plants.

Patty also debunked some myths about watering and fungicides. We had been taught not to water roses from above as it encouraged fungus. Patty says it doesn't make much, if any, difference. I also thought you had to cover every leaf surface with your chosen fungicide, which is the main reason I never bother to spray roses at all. Patty says you can make quite a dent in the fungus problem by spraying the lower half of the plant and even the ground beneath the plant. I don't mind slopping a little sodium bicarb over the mulch so I guess I'll even try that this year. I am always happy to pass on the wise remarks of gardening experts.

Prune hybrid teas in spring so that you leave only three or four canes. Then prune these canes back to three or four buds—usually determined by where you can find an outward-facing bud which you cut above so that the bush will open up as it grows.

CAMELLIAS

Popular theories notwithstanding, a Southern Belle is not born with a camellia (pronounced "camaylia") between her teeth; she is born with a trowel between her teeth and dirt under her fingernails (and she never wears white shoes after Labor Day or puts dark meat in chicken salad). Nevertheless, for winter flower in the garden, there is absolutely nothing to beat camellias if you are lucky enough to be able to grow them. Camellias will not stand heavy freezes and are best adapted to Zones 7-10, although many gardeners in more northerly areas have considerable success growing the hardier varieties in warm microclimates. And breeders are, as ever, working hard to extend the northern range of these lovely plants.

There are some 45 species in the genus *Camellia*, most of them small trees or large shrubs from open woodland in Asia. The three species usually found in cultivation in the west are *C. japonica*, *C. reticulata*, and *C. sasanqua*, as well as hybrids between them. The x *williamsii* camellias popular in England are hybrids between *C. japonica* and *C. saluenensis*. The huge decorative camellias associated with gracious living in the Deep South are varieties of *C. japonica* which bloom from December to March. *C. sasanqua* has less dramatic flowers and flowers earlier.

A camellia of the 'Perfection' series.

Camellias are preeminently flowers to cut and enjoy in the house. Although the leathery evergreen leaves are attractive year round, most varieties are not particularly impressive when in bloom. The plant is dotted with flowers rather than covered with them.

We seldom see 40 foot camellias like those that grace gardens in New Zealand. This is because every now and then most of the Northern Hemisphere gets a hard freeze that kills the tops of many camellias. Rapid thawing after a freeze is the usual reason that a plant is damaged by unusual cold so protect your plants by placing them where they are not exposed to the first sun of a winter's morning.

Camellias need good drainage and air circulation. An ideal position is under high shade from pine trees. If you plant them under maples, oaks, or other trees that produce a lot of surface roots, give your camellias extra fertilizer and root prune them because these trees steal a lot of nutrients. Though why I say that I don't know. Most of mine are perfectly happy, neglected in dry soil under oak trees.

Camellia Care

I consulted our local camellia judge, Jean Driscoll, on the care of camellias. Hers are the most gorgeous things. She says as follows. Camellias put a lot of energy into prolific bloom and should be fertilized twice a year. Fertilize in February and June.

There are two schools of thought on mulching camellias. One says to remove all mulch in spring and then put down fresh mulch. This has the advantage of getting rid of any fallen petals, which may transmit a fungus disease called petal blight. Many growers, however, merely add more mulch each year and avoid petal blight by picking up fallen petals.

Old-timers say that you should prune a camellia so that you can throw a cat through it. The idea is to keep the bush fairly open to improve air circulation and minimize infections. Prune between

March and July, after the plant has flowered and before it sets next year's flower buds.

The main diseases of camellias are camellia dieback, scale, and petal blight. Treatment for camellia dieback is simple: if a branch dies, prune it back to healthy wood. Petal blight is a fungus that turns your best flowers to mush. Cleanliness is the only defense, which means picking up fallen petals. To make this easier, Jean will not keep a camellia variety that "shatters," dropping its petals separately.

Scale is a tiny insect. It looks like a white fuzz on the backs of leaves and flowers. Spraying with horticultural oil (also known as dormant oil) will control it. Spray when the new growth is half grown in summer and again in the fall. Spray only when the temperature is between 40 and 80 °F because the oil can damage foliage at higher and lower temperatures. Add a drop of detergent to the spray mixture to help it stick to the leaves. You have to spray the undersides of the leaves to get at the scale. And don't spill the oil as I once did. It is disgusting stuff to clean up.

Spraying for scale is a time-consuming task. If you have more than a few camellias, you will want to look for other solutions. Scale seldom kills a plant but it is very unsightly, turning the leaves a horrid brown color. One alternative to spraying is heavy pruning. Scale takes several years to disfigure a plant. If you prune hard after the plant has flowered, you can improve the appearance of the foliage without spraying.

For big flowers that hold up their heads, remove most of the flower buds on each plant, starting in July as they begin to form. A plant three feet high should be left with only about five flower buds.

Someone discovered that applying the growth hormone gibberellic acid gave you bigger, earlier camellia flowers. You apply gibberellic acid in September, in several sessions, to no more than one-fifth of the plant. Find a likely looking flower bud (round) and the leaf bud next to it (pointed). Twist off the leaf bud and a little cup will be left. Squeeze one drop of gibberellic acid into this cup with an eye dropper. The flower will appear in about six weeks after gibbing and will be of a slightly different color from an ungibbed flower.

Camellias are easily propagated from cuttings taken in June. And this is a practical way to increase your stock of favorite varieties because camellias flower when they are very small so you don't have long to wait. Grafting is for the times when you have a camellia you don't want to keep. Instead of uprooting it, cut it down and graft a desirable variety into the rootstock to produce a large new plant rapidly.

Varieties

The best protection against scale, and most other camellia problems, is to choose the right varieties. Many varieties are completely immune to scale, hold up their flowers instead of drooping, and have flowers that do not shatter. If you plan a large collection of camellias, throw out all plants that do not meet these criteria.

'Mine-no-uki' (white) and 'Cleopatra' (pink) are free-flowering varieties of *Camellia sasanqua*. *C. japonica* varieties with desirable characteristics include 'Omega' (white with blush edging), 'Ville de Nantes', 'Carter's Sunburst', 'Giullio Nuccio', 'Daikagura' (early), and 'Dixie Night Supreme' (all variegated red and white). Pink and red varieties include 'Betty Sheffield Supreme', 'Drama Girl' (single, coral), 'Mark Allen', 'Elsie Ruth Marshall', 'Francie L.' (a hybrid of *C. japonica x C. reticulata*), and 'Kramer's Supreme' (fragrant).

White camellia flowers are easily spoiled by air pollution so don't plant them if your air is bad. Good white-flowered varieties include 'Snow Man' and 'Charlie Bettes'. I am also devoted to the 'Perfection' series. These are old varieties with small, exquisitely formal flowers in a number of colors.

Camellia blossoms are best enjoyed close up, singly or in small groups on the coffee table. Cut the flowers with short stems and float them in a bowl or huge brandy snifter. The cooler they are kept, the longer the flowers last, so I sometimes prolong their stay in the house by putting them in ice water and storing them in the refrigerator at night.

AZALEAS AND RHODODENDRONS

As camellias start to fade, azaleas take their place. The thousands of species and varieties of azaleas and rhododendrons all belong to the genus *Rhododendron* and the distinction between the two is fuzzy. In general, rhododendrons have leathery evergreen leaves whereas azaleas, even when they are evergreen, have the thinner leaves usually found on deciduous shrubs.

Most rhododendrons are native to temperate parts of Asia, although there are a number of species from the Americas. Thanks to the efforts of breeders, there are now azalea and rhododendron varieties for nearly all parts of North America and Europe, although most are not easy to grow well in arid regions. Start your search for locally adapted varieties in a nearby nursery. If you become addicted to this lovely genus, you can then branch out in search of native species and the more exotic varieties, which will be harder to find.

The cultural requirements of rhododendrons and azaleas are the same as for camellias—somewhat acid soil and a heavy mulch. They are less susceptible to disease than camellias but they do need to be watered and mulched, at least until well-established.

A rhododendron flower.

Rhododendrons grow fairly slowly, but the larger varieties eventually reach enormous size. England and Wales contain many driveways that are now almost impassable from the growth of rhododendrons planted in abundance on every fashionable estate when they were introduced from China and the Himalayas at the beginning of the twentieth century. If you are gardening in a small space, consider pruning your rhododendrons into trees as they age or stick to the many small and even miniature varieties.

Perhaps because they grow poorly in the Deep South, my favorite members of the genus are the dozens of rhododendron varieties with huge globular waxy flower trusses, which thrive in most of Britain, in Zones 5 to 7 of the eastern United States, and in western mountain areas and the Pacific Northwest. Breeder David Leach is extending the range of these beauties farther and farther north. In the north, many rhododendrons curl their leaves in very cold weather and some people consider this unsightly. I think it is well worth putting up with for the sake of the wonderful flowers and the summer foliage.

The biggest evergreen azaleas (Zones 7 to 9) are the Southern Indicas, which will form a ten foot hedge in time. Kurume and Satsuki varieties seldom get over four foot tall and can be kept pruned almost to ground cover size. They have rather horrid little tight opaque flowers; to my eye, rhododendron flowers should be open and translucent, like those of the indicas and "real" rhododendrons. It all depends what you were raised with. Among the deciduous azaleas (Zones 4 or 5 to 8), the Mollis, Knap Hill, and Exbury hybrids are the best known. Most of these are hybrids of oriental azaleas with North American species such as *R. calendulaceum*, *R. viscosum*, and *R. arborescens* and they come in many colors and sizes. One advantage of these hybrids is that they are not particularly fussy about pH and can be grown in neutral, although not in alkaline, soil.

Since rhododendrons and azaleas are shallow rooted, they can be moved at any time of year and can be purchased when they are in flower so that you can see precisely what you are getting. The flowering season can be extended over a four-month period by choosing varieties that flower at different times. It is also convenient to be able to move azaleas in order to reorganize color schemes— which easily get out of hand when you have orange, purple, coral, and pink azaleas in flower at the same time!

CHAPTER 7

Lawns, Grasses, and Ground Covers

I agree with Russell Webber, a Texas gardener who wrote, "On the whole, I don't much cotton to grass. Even northern grass, some of which, at least, is worth growing. All southern lawn grasses are awful." But despite the contempt in which many gardeners hold the grasses that usually cover most of their property, it is very difficult to live without a lawn of some sort, unless you are lucky enough to be gardening in open woodland.

Perhaps one of these days we shall abandon the struggle to keep our lawns green and lush without using fertilizers, pesticides, and enough water to keep the Third World in wheat. Lawns are a relatively new invention. They were so expensive to plant and maintain that in the eighteenth century only the wealthy possessed them. The rest of us peasants planted our land with vegetables, herbs, and flowers with paths between. Southerners might have "swept yards" of sand surrounded by flower beds. Those living in desert or forest left the countryside as they found it around their front doors.

But we have now become accustomed to a smooth floor of green as a setting for our houses and plants, and lawns are not going to disappear from the home landscape in the foreseeable future. We also have to admit that lawns have their virtues. If the garden looks a mess and guests are expected, the fastest way to improve a horrible situation is to mow the lawn and tidy its edges in a few prominent spots. And, as the kids point out when I threaten to plow the whole lot up, everyone needs somewhere to play frisbee.

In some privileged areas, "lawns" can be made of ground covers that take somewhat less maintenance than grass. California's decorative dichondra lawns spring to mind. But this is the exception. On the whole lawns are made of turf grasses and most turf grasses are demanding, invasive, and prone to more diseases and pests than most other plants put together. Plant breeders are working on the problem. Within a few decades, we should have turf grasses for most parts of the country that require mowing only a few times a year, survive dry spells, and are more resistant to pests.

CHOOSE THE RIGHT GRASS

Turf grasses are locally adapted and if you are starting a lawn in an area that is new to you, your first stop should be the garden center to find out what local lawns are made of. Then do a little investigation into whether there are useful alternatives to the local standbys. For instance, Midwesterners are turning to native buffalograss (*Buchloe dactyloides*), a short grass that evolved on the western Great Plains. Completely drought-resistant, buffalograss grows to only about five inches high so it needs little mowing. It turns a rather yellowy color in summer which some people dislike, but then warm-season grasses are brown rather than green for six months of the year in my part of the world.

Grasses are usually divided into warm-season grasses, grown in the South, and cool-season grasses, grown in the North. Warm-season grasses green up only during hot weather. Cool-season grasses are green in cool weather. When choosing grass seed or plugs at the garden center, remember that many grasses do poorly in shade and that particular types of grass may be recommended for shady areas in your part of the world.

Whatever type of grass you are going to plant, it is well worth preparing the ground thoroughly. You will have years to regret the low spots you omitted to fill and the shady spots you neglected to prepare properly. Make sure that the shape of the lawn is appropriate to your lawn mower. If you have a large ride-on mower, you need wide curves at the corners if you don't want to spend your life trimming corners the mower could not reach. Till the soil thoroughly, incorporating organic matter as you go, get rid of any weeds, and then make sure that you have leveled out bumps and hollows.

If you are sowing seed, for instance of fescue or ryegrass, try sowing it less thickly than the package recommends. This is a modern move to reduce maintenance. Plants further apart compete with each other less and use less moisture. You mow these lawns rather high, which disguises the fact that the plants are rather far apart. (This system does not work with sod-forming grasses, such as centipede, bluegrass, or St. Augustine, which expand to fill the available space.)

Keep a new lawn watered until it is established and mow it only to three or four inches in length until the plants are well grown. There is a lot to be said for planting lawns in the fall so that they have the winter to become established. A fall-planted lawn may have some bare spots that need repair next spring, but you will have saved yourself a lot of water and trouble trying to get a new lawn through its infancy in hot weather.

RENOVATING A LAWN

It was a dictum of James Crockett that lawn does not need serious renovation until it is less than 25% grass. If you are dealing with a warm-season creeping grass like centipede or St. Augustine, even a couple of hundred square feet of lawn destroyed in repairing the septic system will fill itself in in a month or two if you keep it watered.

However, perhaps you have a bit of lawn that is mainly weeds, or mainly bare ground, and that really does need renovation. The first job is to decide what killed the lawn in the first place. The usual causes are excess shade and compaction of the grass and soil. Neither of these can be solved just by reseeding the lawn. If foot traffic is compacting and killing the grass in one part of the garden, the only solution is to replace the grass with a path or to devise some system to direct the traffic to other areas. If grass keeps dying in the shade under a tree, have you merely planted the wrong species of grass, or should you replace the grass with a shade-tolerant ground cover? If you have bare ground where there should be lawn, even the local weeds are not growing there and the soil, if any, must be incredibly poor—or else you have a patch like mine where a gushing downspout washes away every plant whenever it rains. Directing the water to some other part of the world is the only way to solve this one.

Renovating a patch of lawn is much like starting a new one. You have to get rid of the weeds and improve the texture and nutrient content of the soil. If you are using sod to fill a bare spot, you will have to cut into the existing lawn in straight lines. If you plan to use seed, continue your soil preparation into the remaining lawn as necessary, avoiding straight edges between old and new lawn. When you plant lawn seed in an old or new lawn, you will lose a lot of the seed to birds unless you rig up a system of sticks and string over the seeded area until most of the seed has germinated or cover the area with cheesecloth, which will protect the seed, reduce erosion, and rot away in a year or two.

LAWN MAINTENANCE

I think the first thing to decide about a lawn is how much perfection you demand. The less you demand, the less work your lawn will be. Although the British are known for perfect lawns, it is my experience that they are more tolerant of imperfection than Americans. In hot dry summers, my British friends heave sighs of relief that the lawn needs mowing less often than usual, ignore the brown patches, and save the water for their flowers.

Even if the finest lawn in the neighborhood has you gnashing your teeth with envy, remember the human and financial cost of that perfection. Perhaps your own gardening time has been better spent. Another advantage of a less-than-perfect lawn is that interesting wild flowers will appear. Our lawn harbors a rare native orchid that appeared one spring.

The first rule of maintenance is that a healthy lawn is more resistant to weeds than one that is dying by inches. In an old lawn, dead grass stems build up at soil level, forming a layer of thatch that rain has difficulty penetrating. It is well worth spending a cool day in fall or spring giving the lawn a thorough raking that removes the thatch. (There are also gadgets for removing thatch that attach to tillers and lawn mowers.) You can increase the lawn's ability to absorb moisture by poking holes in it. You can buy exotic looking "aerators" for this purpose, but I doubt whether they work any better than just stabbing the lawn with a garden fork—a boring but useful activity. The dogs will help by excavating frequent holes in search of moles.

Keeping the lawn well fertilized is the next step to minimizing weeds. It is quite amazing what a difference this makes. Whether you believe in using inorganic fertilizers or not, after raking the lawn in spring fertilize it with sifted compost. This is a big help in controlling pests, particularly the fungus infections that mess up lawns in so many areas. It is also a good idea to adjust the pH at this time, usually by liming. If you rake, aerate, and fertilize for a couple of years, the weed population in the lawn will fall dramatically.

I used to think lawns should be thoroughly weeded—but I don't like to use herbicides and hand-weeding is impossible in any but a small lawn. However, lawns look better when they are green and, with a warm-season lawn, the only way to have a green lawn in winter is by leaving the weeds alone. I see two main disadvantages to not weeding the lawn. One is that some plants grow a lot faster than others. In summer, the plants that invade if we don't weed our lawn grow faster than the grass and make the lawn look

UNDERSTANDING THE ENVIRONMENT
GRASSES AND COW PASTURE

One of the reasons I am not fond of grasses—except in a wheat field or prairie, where they belong—is that they symbolize the destruction of so many habitats. When tropical forest is cleared by settlers, the soil quickly becomes too poor to grow crops and is turned into cattle range—by planting rampant and invasive grasses, such as Johnson grass (Sorghum halapense). Johnson grass was imported to the southern United States from the Mediterranean in 1880 as a forage crop and then planted in Central America.

This horrible stuff exemplifies just about everything that is wrong with importing plants that you don't know enough about. In Texas, it is still used for hay, but gardeners know it as a pernicious weed. In Central America its invasive habit has caused the extinction of hundreds of native species.

On the banks of the Tempisque River in Costa Rica's Palo Verde National Park a dense growth of Johnson grass has prevented the river from overflowing its banks in the normal spring floods for the last few years. Without the floods, the wetlands where migrating water fowl used to feed by their millions are drying up. Park rangers have introduced some cattle into the park to try and control the grass, and this is an act of desperation since cattle are terribly destructive to the native vegetation.

In centuries to come, this may be our epitaph: "They turned the world's loveliest ecosystems into cattle pasture."

less than smooth unless we mow it very often. The other problem is that all the flowers in a weedy lawn may detract from the appearance of flowers in your borders. I remember the disappointment of waking up one spring morning in New York to find that my carefully planted daffodils had burst into flower over night and that they made no sort of color splash at all beside the millions of dandelions flowering merrily in the lawn. Of course the solution to this would be to take the dandelions into account and plant only white or pink-flowered daffodils or to throw the money into blue-flowered hyacinths, scillas, and the like that would complement the dandelions. But it is hard to remember this in autumn when you are ordering bulbs and the dandelion flowers are long gone.

Mowing

Since I consider lawn maintenance a waste of time that would be better used for other things, the largest lawn mower you can afford comes high on my list of priorities. I know it uses a lot of energy and pollutes the air, but I console myself that I save even more energy and air pollution by staying home at weekends to tend the garden instead of taking to the road in an even more polluting car.

By increasing the cutting width of a mower from 18 inches to 24 inches, you about halve the time needed to mow an acre of lawn. This is the argument for a big mower. On the other hand, power mowers demand maintenance time and if you have a small lawn, you will undoubtedly save time by using one of the excellent modern reel-type mowers that takes nothing but muscle power.

It is not necessary to catch and remove the clippings every time you mow unless the lawn is very long when you start. There used to be a theory that leaving clippings on the lawn caused thatch buildup but it is now clear that this is not so. Thatch forms whether you remove clippings of not. You probably want to collect clippings in fall when the lawn is covered with leaves, and in the spring to remove winter debris. For many gardeners, whatever collects in the lawn mower bag is the main supply of organic matter for the garden.

But in summer, when the lawn is mowed regularly, it is better to leave the clippings on the lawn. They will decompose quickly and return nutrients to the grass. Investigate mulching lawn mowers, which chop the clippings finely and push them down into the grass. Mowers that aren't specifically designed as mulching mowers tend to toss clippings to one side to form windrows, which are not particularly sightly but won't do the lawn any harm. You may be able to buy a mulching blade to replace the present blade on your lawn mower.

Don't mow the lawn too short. Longer grass is more drought-resistant and also looks greener than very short grass so set the mower on the high side and mow little and often for the best effect.

Taraxacum officinale, **the common or garden dandelion, a European native.**

A handy tool for edging the lawn—particularly if you sharpen it occasionally.

Keeping a Lawn in Place

The edges of lawns are always a nuisance, especially if you are afflicted with creeping grasses. Faster than you can say "weed," Bermudagrass can invade a flower bed and set up shop for life. And every possible solution to the problem causes problems of its own.

An excellent-sounding solution is to edge your driveway and flower beds with something solid that will slow the grass down: bricks, paving stones, railroad ties, or plastic or metal strips. Many of these certainly look nice, but they do not solve the edging problem, although they may make it more manageable. Grass grows over, under, and through any combination of edging that I have ever encountered and then you are left with the task of weeding grass out of the edging as well as the flower bed or drive.

Edging also requires maintenance of its own. Bricks and wood strips move during the winter, or you catch them with the mower and knock them out of place. A single brick is little trouble to replace, but a long plastic edging strip can take all afternoon to replace and you could have edged most of the lawn in that time.

Although I do have edging strips in parts of the garden—partly because they look attractive—I am not sure that it is not easier just to clip the edges of the lawn, after every mowing if possible. A power edger can make this job much easier but every now and then you are going to have to repair a badly decayed edge by hand.

This is quite a rewarding activity because it looks so good when you have finished. The most important tool is a sharp semicircular edger, or nursery spade if you prefer. I find the easiest way is to go right along the edge with the edger and then to crawl along, tossing the individual clumps of turf into the wheelbarrow. A word of warning: if you are a compulsive edger of lawns, don't remove any more lawn than you have to each time you do the edges. I have a friend whose beds have edged further and further into the lawn every weekend for years until she now has about double the intended area of flower bed to maintain.

ROADSIDES AND ROUGH LAWNS

The verges of roads have long been habitats where many wild flowers flourished. During the pesticide-happy 1960s, maintenance departments almost wiped out this artificial habitat by spraying herbicides that saved them from having to mow the verges. Luckily, rising herbicide costs and public outcry has put paid to this dreadful practice in most parts of the world and our roadsides are once again valuable and interesting habitat for wildlife. It is well worth strolling your local roads and identifying the flowers you find. Anything that thrives in that polluted and exposed environment is a low-maintenance candidate for your own wild garden.

In addition to the flowers that flourish in the roughly mown grass of most roadsides and roadside ditches are the "wild flowers" planted by highway departments in ever-increasing swaths. Many of these plantings are still in the experimental stage and many of the flowers are not really wild or even native. The idea is not to make a showcase of native meadow flowers but to find flowers that make as colorful a show as possible with little maintenance. Suitable plants depend upon the climate, the type of soil, drainage, and the level of the water table. Patches of flowers by the roadside can save a lot of money in the long run because they need mowing only once or twice a year. They can provide us with many ideas for our own wild gardens.

The easiest type of wild garden to start and maintain is merely an area of lawn that you mow infrequently. These "rough mown" areas are common on large estates and are easily adapted to the smaller garden. Here you plant spring bulbs that will naturalize. Since the bulb foliage must be allowed to ripen and die after flowering ceases, lawns containing bulbs cannot be mowed for the first time until early summer. Then the lawn is mowed to about six inches and wild flowers that bloom in midsummer start to send up flower spikes. Sometimes the area is mowed again at the beginning of August. This shears the plants that will bloom in the autumn, producing multiple stems and more flowers. The area is usually mowed again in late fall.

If you develop such a wild garden, you will probably want to plant spring bulbs. But there is no need to plant anything else. It may be more interesting just to wait and see what wild flowers invade the area. This strategy works best, of course, if you live in fairly rural parts where wild flower seeds blow into your garden repeatedly. In only two years, our rough lawn has filled up with goldenrod, perennial ageratum (*Eupatorium*), *Verbena tenuisecta*, wild poinsettia (*Euphorbia cyathophora*), morning glory, and several other attractive wildlings.

If you live in California, open woodland is probably your model for meadow. You might imitate oak woodland, with small trees scattered through a pasture bright with California poppies.

Unless you have a large garden, finding a happy home for this garden can be a problem. Orchards are traditional sites for rough lawns, but in a small garden, your fruit trees are probably scattered around and not grouped in an orchard. One solution is to borrow an idea from the highway department and locate your garden in the middle of a neatly mowed area of lawn. You could make this look even more intentional by placing a tall "architectural" plant, as the landscaping people say, in the middle. An ornamental grass is the obvious choice, preferably something that doesn't grow so tall that it dwarfs your wild flowers. Give your wild meadow a symmetrical shape—circular or oval so that it is easy to mow around—and you

Eupatorium coelestinum

will have a wild meadow that looks perfectly at home in the formal setting of a suburban front lawn.

Prairie Gardens

Prairie gardens are more complicated than simple rough lawns. They aim to reproduce specific ecosystems so you cannot just leave them full of imported lawn grasses. You have to get rid of the lawn and start over.

While you want to improve the texture of the soil by digging and weeding it, you may not need to increase the fertility. The American prairies once contained the most fertile soil in the world—up to six feet deep. If you are repairing degraded prairie, do a little digging. If the soil is a good dark color as far down as you can see, it is probably fertile enough. If not, give it a good start by digging in lots of organic matter.

Prairie is about a 70:30 mixture of grasses and forbs (which means all herbaceous flowering plants except the grass family). If you live in a prairie state, you are probably trying to recreate the biome of your home before it was turned into agricultural land. This is a noble undertaking and the subject of intense research. The American prairie was so thoroughly destroyed before it was studied by biologists that in many cases we do not even know what plants it contained. It is also difficult to reproduce the fires and grazing by animals that was responsible for maintaining the prairie ecosystem. You have to imitate these by judicious mowing, perhaps supplemented by occasional burning if your local authority permits it.

Your starting point must be a local university, arboretum, or library where you can get the latest information on plants believed to be native to your county. It is essential to do this on a local level because "prairie" is actually a large number of different grassland ecosystems, each with it characteristic flora, with many local differences. Some of the plants you identify will be readily available from seed companies. Others you will have to track down.

GROUND COVERS

Ground covers always seem to me like excellent ideas that seldom live up to expectation. The expectation is that you can plant a ground cover that spreads by itself for purposes such as landscaping a slope, replacing lawn, landscaping difficult ground under a tree, keeping the weeds under control in a shrubbery, and providing a pleasing contrast to taller plants. But it seldom seems to work out like that.

Our front door was landscaped with a few well-chosen shrubs surrounding a small lawn that was made more interesting by islands of low-growing juniper. The trouble is that the blue-green of the juniper is spoiled by weeds: grass in summer and artichoke weed in winter. When I pull the weeds out, I always manage to damage a branch of the ridiculously fragile juniper, which turns brown over the ensuing weeks and leaves an ugly hole when removed. It is an unsatisfactory planting and I shall have to remove it when I decide what to put in its place, but it seems a pity it doesn't work, because the idea was a good one.

The groundcover planting that does work is a pair of beds full of ivy flanking shallow steps in deep shade under an oak. It is hard to think of anything else that would thrive in this situation. The ivy has to be pruned fairly often to keep it in its beds, and oak seedlings have to be plucked from the ivy at intervals, but the ivy doesn't mind being trodden on when I do this and the beds are always attractive.

Probably the main reason groundcover plantings don't always live up to their billing is that we choose the wrong plants. Most of us can think of settings in which ground covers work very well. There is a shop in the village with an island bed containing a crape myrtle and several different colors of low-growing junipers in a gravel mulch. The bed is very attractive and the junipers don't get many weeds, probably because they are surrounded by the asphalt jungle rather than the planted spaces of my garden. The classic under-planting of an old tree with a huge circle of pachysandra or ivy is also always a lovely sight.

Planting a large groundcover bed is an expensive and time-consuming operation and a big disappointment if it doesn't work out. Not only do you have to acquire the plants, but you also have to weed the bed for several years while the ground cover fills in. Good ground covers take at least three years to give the area a finished look, even if you plant closely. As a result, I tend to be very conservative in my groundcover choices.

Most ground covers come in variegated as well as ordinary varieties. The variegated forms may be very pretty, but they are a lot less vigorous. We have both types of liriope. The common or garden variety has spread into a band three feet wide in six years, while the variegated is still in individual clumps which have not even fully grown together. If you want swift ground cover under a tree, the variegated form would be much too slow, whereas if you want an edging for a border, the variegated form would be ideal and the common form too invasive.

It saves a lot of time in the long run if you prepare the ground properly before planting. You are hoping that these plants will look after themselves, so give them homes they like and as little competition with weeds as possible to get them off to a good start. I like to till the soil with organic matter, add lime as necessary, and weed for at least a couple of months before planting. (The delay in planting also gives me time to grow at least most of the plants I am going to use.)

Some people rake the leaves out of ground cover beds in the fall, but this is a mistake, even though ground cover full of leaves does look untidy until the leaves sink down through the ground cover, which they will. You are presumably not planning to mulch or fertilize your ground cover, so it is a good idea to let nature supply a bit of nourishment in this way.

The Big Five Ground Covers

Some people count things like ferns and low-growing roses as ground covers, and they can certainly be used as such, as can things like trailing lantana, crown vetch, and cotoneaster. But to me, a ground cover has to be evergreen, or at least green for most of the year, and it has to spread by way of its roots. That is the trouble with junipers. Even though some of the spreading branches root where they touch the ground, a juniper has one main stem and root ball so that weeds and grass growing through the branches have little competition. In contrast, the roots of liriope and periwinkle spread through the surface of the soil, allowing weeds very few crevices in which to germinate. Here, then are what I think of as the great ground covers.

UNDERSTANDING THE ENVIRONMENT
OZONE DEPLETION

One of the things that is probably going to affect the plants that we (and, more important, farmers) grow in the near future is the thinning of the ozone layer in the atmosphere.

Ozone is a form of oxygen, but it contains three atoms of oxygen (O_3) instead of the two found in ordinary oxygen gas (O_2). Radiation from the sun causes ozone to form from oxygen high in the atmosphere. Once formed, the ozone layer in the atmosphere is a good absorber of high energy ultraviolet radiation (UV) and prevents a lot of this radiation from the sun reaching the earth. UV radiation damages genetic material, causing skin cancer in humans and killing many smaller organisms outright. UV does not penetrate far into biological tissues, which is why it causes only skin cancer in humans. It also causes genetic damage to the outer layers of other land animals without fur or feathers to protect them and to land plants. Aquatic organisms are generally safe from it, since water rapidly absorbs UV.

In the 1980s, a large and growing hole in the ozone layer over the Antarctic was discovered.

Since that time the number of holes and their size has increased rapidly. As the holes increase, so does the amount of UV radiation that reaches the earth.

We are destroying the ozone layer, mainly by using chlorofluorocarbons (CFCs). These gases are used in aerosol sprays, refrigerators, and air conditioners, among other things. CFCs are ideal aerosol propellants because they do not react chemically with whatever is being sprayed. But this same lack of chemical reactivity means that they are not broken down in the air. They make their way to the stratosphere where they are broken down by radiation from the sun, releasing free chlorine atoms that react with ozone and break it down.

It appears that the danger to life on earth from ozone depletion is so great that we must stop using these compounds almost immediately. Despite the expense involved in switching to alternatives to CFCs, the alternatives are probably much worse.

Gardeners can obviously protect themselves from rising levels of UV by protecting their skin from sunlight at all times. Already, sailors and gardeners, who spend a lot of time outdoors, have high, and rising, rates of skin cancer.

Ivy (*Hedera* spp.)

Ivy is cherished for its shiny foliage and its tolerance of shade and drought, although in most areas it also does fine in sun. Ivy has two forms, juvenile and adult. The foliage in a groundcover bed is all juvenile, but if ivy is allowed to grow up a support, it will eventually mature, producing green flowers followed by black fruits on the tips of stems. An ancient ivy-covered wall is invariably full of birds' nests and a noisy place in spring.

English ivy, *Hedera helix.*

The classic ivy is English ivy (*Hedera helix*, Zones 5-9) which comes in variegated forms and various leaf colors. 'Wilson' is hardy to Zone 4 and is also safer in Zone 5, where the wild type sometimes gets chewed up by a hard winter. If you plant ivy in the spring, you usually have to water for a few months, but planted in autumn it is completely carefree, except for a little weeding while it covers the ground.

Periwinkle (*Vinca* spp.)

Periwinkle is not as formal as ivy and it may need a little more encouragement to completely cover an area. It bulges and billows, throwing up pretty blue or white flowers in spring, which I find a real bonus. It is best suited to informal areas, rather further from the house than your clipped beds of ivy. Vinca likes soil containing a lot of organic matter and it likes quite a lot of water, at least for its first year. It is slightly less of a shade plant than ivy, thriving under deciduous trees as well as on sunny banks.

The best species for the North is *Vinca minor* (Zones 4 or 5-8), and the best for the West Coast and South is the larger-leaved *Vinca major* (Zones 7-9). Both species come in various varieties, with variegated or ordinary leaves and blue or white flowers.

Vinca minor, periwinkle, or myrtle, is a European native with blue (or white) flowers in spring, which makes a good ground cover in informal areas.

Lily Turf (*Liriope* spp.)

Liriope and monkey grass (*Ophiopogon japonicus*) form the evergreen foot-high grass-like edgings often seen in the South (Zones 6-10). They are certainly easy-care, drought resistant ground covers, thriving in sun or shade and covering the ground quickly as their roots spread. Liriope puts up not-very-interesting flowers that look rather like grape hyacinths and come in several colors. Even if you like the flowers, no one could enjoy the large black seeds that follow, which are rapidly stripped off by the wildlife, leaving bare stalks that die back fairly rapidly. If the flowers or stalks offend you, monkey grass is better; I think the varieties generally sold must be sterile because I have never seen it flower.

Monkey grass is particularly invasive and has just about taken over a flower bed at the local library which we mistakenly edged with it two short years ago (although, admittedly, this bed gets extra water). Some experts say that monkey grass needs afternoon shade in the South, but our bed at the library is in full sun. It might perhaps be better to use liriope instead to cover an area that really bakes in summer. The University of Florida even recommends *L. platyphylla* as the best turf substitute for southern Florida, so you know this will stand full sun.

These turf substitutes need almost no care. Every other year or so they start to get brown tips to the leaves. Then you just mow them in winter with the blades set to about four inches and new growth covers up the mess at high speed. These ground covers take a bit of getting used to if you're not familiar with them because they look like very coarse unmown grass. This doesn't look particularly good when used, as it often is, between lawn and path. This planting just looks as if the lawn mower has fallen down on the job. In fact it is really better to use these species purely as sheets of ground cover, however tempting their neat appearance makes it to use them for edging. Take care where you put them, however, because once you've got them it's almost impossible to get rid of them.

Pachysandra (*Pachysandra* spp.)

Pachysandra is one of the most elegant ground covers because its foliage grows in rosettes of pointy-tipped leaves which form an attractive pattern. It grows to a maximum of twelve inches high and can be used only in shade because the foliage turns yellow in the sun. It is particularly good in rather moist areas under trees, although it is quite drought-tolerant. The species to use in the South is the native *P. procumbens*. In the north, use Japanese pachysandra (*P. terminalis*). Pachysandra expands outward as a clump around the parent plant and doesn't go off in random directions as ivy and periwinkle do so it is fairly easy to keep in place although you have to start the plants close together for it to cover the ground rapidly.

Pachysandra likes fairly rich soil so it is important not to remove leaves that fall on it in autumn.

Plants to Combine with Ground Covers

I am not mad about mixed plantings that combine masses of other plants with ground cover because ground covers are, by definition, invasive, and you spend your life having to arbitrate disputes, by disentangling the roses from the ivy and tearing straying liriope out of the shrubbery. However, in areas like our front entrance, the planting would be pretty dull if all you had was a sheet of ground cover. The answer seems to be to include a few other plants that have a chance of fighting off the ground cover and can add a bit of color and height to the planting. Ornamental grasses or dwarf conifers are likely candidates.

If you want flowers to bloom through your sheet of ground cover, you have to choose the ground cover with care because almost nothing can compete, for instance, with the matted roots of liriope. Ivy, periwinkle, and pachysandra, however, leave a bit more soil space and are more compatible with other plants.

Tall bulbs are an excellent choice to combine with ground covers. When they emerge, they grow fast enough to push through the foliage above and when they die back, the ground cover disguises the messy bulb foliage. A lovely combination in light shade is lilies and ground cover. In Zones 7 southward, Guernsey lilies (*Lycoris* spp.) are a good choice, blooming without foliage in the fall. The leaves then emerge, dying back in spring so that the groundcover stands alone during the summer. Under deciduous trees, daffodils grow happily through ground cover and, in the South, so do ordinary lilies. This combination would also work in the North, as long as the ground cover is not in shade so deep that the lilies will not bloom.

Zephyranthes atamasco, **the eastern rain lily or Easter lily.** Bulbs combine well with ground covers because they are dormant and invisible for much of the year and their foliage and flowers rise above the ground cover when they are actively growing.

ORNAMENTAL GRASSES

I am no expert on ornamental grasses, having once fallen afoul of a large pampas grass, which put me off the whole business. Clumps of this grass doubled in size every year in the damp soil of our previous garden and its razor-sharp leaves made cutting back the ugly dead leaves an agonizing experience. In my jaundiced view most home landscaping with grasses just looks messy. I am not, of course, talking about grasses in the prairie garden, the wild meadow, or seashore plantings. Here they are entirely appropriate and, indeed, essential. I am talking about those beds in suburban gardens, where too-large grasses flop over the path and cut your legs. The pretty blue spiky clump that you often see in desert gardens is *Festuca glauca*, which would be much more appropriate for most of these pathside situations.

On the other hand, you do sometimes see grasses used well and many of them produce seed heads that are your birds' favorite foods. Grasses are nothing new in the garden. They were popular with Victorians, when they were generally used as specimen plants, isolated in the middle of a lawn or at the edge of a pool where, it must be confessed, many of them look quite spectacular.

Grasses differ from most garden plants in their vertical lines. Large grasses also move very gracefully in the wind. Late in the season, many grass flower stalks and heads turn translucent, creating magical effects when the sun is behind them. Even the dreaded pampas grass (*Cortaderia selloana*) I confess looks fine in autumn with the evening sun behind it. (But get the variety 'Pumila' which is not such a people-eater.) I know of plenty of clumps of pampas grass in Zone 5, by the way, although the books all seem to say it is hardy only to Zone 8.

I am sure that the place to start is with your native grasses—best for wildlife and least likely to be invasive. If you see a handsome-looking clump on a local road verge, it is easy enough to gather a few seeds and grow your own. Little bluestem (*Schizachyrium scoparium*) is one of my favorite American natives, for its striking blue color in late summer, followed by reddish brown winter color. Lemongrass (*Cympogon citratus*) is a handsome introduced species that I would grow if it didn't look so much like the Johnson grass I loathe.

An advantage of grasses is that many of them will grow in shade. They can look very impressive in containers flanking a doorway, even in deep shade. I don't know why we seem to have given up growing tall plants in containers. It is true that containers are one of the best ways to show off plants that hang and droop, but a six-foot bell flower (*Campanula pyramidalis*) towering over a twelve-inch pot is also a lovely sight, as is a four-foot fountain grass (*Pennisetum setaceum*) with its slender leaves and late-summer flowers.

Culture

Ornamental grasses are not necessarily a low-maintenance alternative to perennials as their advocates would sometimes have you believe. Many of them are aggressive growers that can easily turn a border into a hay field. Even tidy slow-growers like silver spike (*Spodiopogon sibiricus*) or *Carex conica* tend to die out in the center as they spread and need regular division and replanting. So choose your grasses with care and place them where they have room to spread. You can tell when to divide a grass by examining it. If it is getting bare in the center and the stems are getting floppier as the years go buy, it is time to divide. Divide grasses during vegetative growth. For cool weather grasses such as the fescues and feather-reeds this means fall or spring. For warm weather grasses such as miscanthus, divide in spring.

Several grass species have loose seed heads that blow off in autumn winds creating something of a snowstorm effect in your garden or the street—which may or may not be socially acceptable.

Many grasses do thrive in soil, such as heavy clay, that would choke most perennials. Also, most grasses tolerate drought, common in their native prairies. As a general guideline, the wider the leaf, the more shade and the more water a grass needs.

Never fertilize grasses. And if you plant them in the fall, you never have to water them after you have given them a good soak on planting. Grasses shouldn't be mulched either—or at least not with organic mulches against the stems. This treatment will kill grasses, such as the fescues, that are adapted to dry environments.

Bamboos

Bamboos are another of those love-hate groups of plants. Although we tend to think of them as tropical, many species are adapted to temperate areas and Vermonters can have stands of bamboo as easily as Texans.

The advantages of bamboos are the graceful appearance of many species and the fun of growing your own canes (culms, actually), which can be used to build fences, bean trellises, sweet pea fences, and dozens of other structures. The disadvantage is that most species are quite horribly invasive.

We inherited a garden in which the owners had planted a bamboo hedge. The bamboo had been selected by the local university extension service and was guaranteed to be perfect for its site. Which is when you learn to distrust experts, because this bamboo spread by underground runners, into the lawn, into my best azaleas, into the lily bed and everywhere else it was not wanted. I finally resorted to all-purpose herbicides in an attempt to control the monster. The bamboo loved the herbicides and merely branched more aggressively when treated. I really got worried when it started to spread into the garden next door. Then I read of a householder who had sued for vast sums in compensation for a bamboo that had spread from a neighbor's garden and invaded his own valuable plantings. At that point we moved and I have never dared to plant a bamboo since. (Even paranoids have real enemies.)

Never plant a bamboo that spreads by underground runners. Even if you plant only clump-forming bamboos, I think it is safest to plant your bamboo in the middle of a lawn where continual mowing around the edges may keep it under control. Another safeguard is to plant bamboos that are only marginally hardy in your area. If the clump is cut down to the roots by a hard freeze every few years it is much less likely to get out of hand than one that loves your climate. Do not believe what you read about planting bamboos in concrete

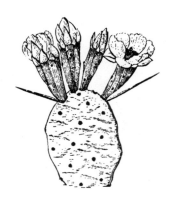

Opuntias have attractive flowers and bloom fairly freely in the garden.

Opuntia salmiana, **a tropical species from Brazil.**

pipes sunk in the ground or similar containers in order to keep it in place. Even this type of planting requires constant vigilance to prevent the bamboo escaping and bamboo has gimlet-like bud tips that will eventually penetrate anything in which you try to contain it.

All of that said, there is no escaping the fact that bamboos are beautiful and useful and many of us want to grow them. Unfortunately the most beautiful ones, to my eye, are the ones with huge culms such as those used for scaffolding and buildings in tropical countries. Most of these are not hardy in temperate areas. The biggest bamboos that are hardy to about Zone 6 are *Phyllostachys vivax* and *P. viridis* but these, unfortunately, spread by underground runners. The hardiest bamboo usually grown in the United States is umbrella bamboo, *Thamnocalamus spathaceus,* which is a clump-former and the main food of the giant panda. Even if you don't have a panda, this attractive plant might be nice to grow for its zoological associations.

One of the cleverest uses I have ever seen made of bamboo was to add bright green foliage to a desert garden in the Southwest. In fact, the garden looked positively lush, with ocotillo (*Fouquieria splendens*) flowering happily in front of the bamboo. It seems to me a brilliant idea to use bamboo in a desert garden because no matter how aggressive it may feel, no bamboo is going to travel far or fast in a garden that gets less than ten inches of rain a year.

Cactuses and Euphorbs

Like bamboos, cactuses (cacti?) and euphorbs are plants that most Northerners assume they cannot grow, although many are much hardier than is generally believed. The cholla or prickly pear cactus (*Opuntia humifusa*) is native from Florida to Montana and southern Ontario. And very out of place it looks too, flowering in a pine forest! It is happier in sandy soil in the sun, where it forms a large handsome clump, covered with clear yellow flowers in summer, to be followed by purple, edible fruit—a good choice to deter children from a short cut across the front lawn since the spines are vicious, penetrating even thick leather gloves. It doesn't work with dogs and cats, however. I once planted it to deter the animals from excavating a bed of lilies and it had absolutely no effect.

Cacti and euphorbs are frequently confused because they have evolved parallel adaptations to resisting drought and many of them look very similar. Cacti are members of the family Cactaceae, native to the Americas from Alaska to Patagonia. Euphorbs are members of the Euphorbiaceae, native to the Old World, from Europe through Africa and Asia. To add to the semantic confusion, both are frequently called "succulents," an unscientific name for any drought-resistant plant that stores water in swollen stems and leaves—which many cacti and euphorbs do.

The genus *Euphorbia* itself is a huge one with some members that don't look like xerophytes at all. But most (all?) have bracts with inconspicuous flowers, which gives them an interesting and unusual appearance.

All Western gardeners are probably familiar with the dictum that one must never plant cacti collected in the wild. I encountered a Californian once who was proud of a garden that he never watered. It was full of cacti collected from the wild. It's enough to make you weep. Our deserts have been raped by thoughtless and unscrupulous landscapers and homeowners and they will never recover. Now, even the remaining saguaros (*Carnegiea gigantea*) are beginning to suffer damage from air pollution and it is not clear that even those in nature preserves will survive. But the conservation problem does not mean you cannot have cacti in the garden. Although most of them are slow-growing, they are not difficult to propagate from cuttings and many are easy from seed. If you want to try cactus from seed, start with the vast genus *Opuntia,* which also produces many hybrids, or with the charming barrel cactuses (*Echinocactus*). Another favorite of mine is the gorgeous desert spoon (*Dasylirion Wheeleri*) which looks like a sea urchin on a stalk and makes the most amazing formal accent in a border.

I am also fond of century plants (*Agave americana*), even though such stiff plants are not easy to position in the landscape. In a nearby suburb, a handsome variegated variety is often to be found planted beside front walks. Century plants don't really take a century to bloom. They may bloom when as few as ten years old, producing a vast spire of yellowish flower clusters. Then the parent plant dies and offsets spring up around its base.

FERNS AND HOSTAS

Ferns and hostas are the traditional plants to grow in shade, where the large horizontal leaves of hostas are an attractive foil for the vertical divided foliage of ferns. I don't think it is really fair to count them as ground covers because they don't spread much and they are not particularly low-growing, although they can, of course, be used to carpet the ground. Both groups contain members that will take more sun than one usually imagines. I inherited a lovely stand of holly fern in a Savannah garden and started dividing it to spread around the garden. "Only in deep shade,"warned my neighbors, but it was too late because I had already planted a dozen clumps under a crape myrtle, where they are in part shade in the summer and full sun in winter. And to everyone's surprise, they are doing well. Which just goes to show, but it is obviously safer to start your fern and hosta collection in the shade garden.

California lace fern, *Aspidotis californica.*

Hostas are too slow-growing for my impatient taste—and as a consequence, they are too expensive for my frugal purse. You have to be quite a fanatic to pay $20 for a plant that is going to take most of the rest of your life to grow to a couple of feet across and doesn't even put out a leaf until spring is half over. But a genus that is expensive, slow-growing, attacked by slugs in the North and heat-stroke in the South has to have something going for it or it would have been lost to horticulture years ago. And if you are feeling rich, there is no question that hostas are very handsome plants. I like the way they are often used in New England to disguise the decaying foliage of bulbs. The timing is just right, because the hosta leaves begin to spread as the tulips die. A clump of variegated hostas with red tulips and pale blue forget-me-nots beside a semi-shady path or under a deciduous tree is a lovely combination.

I am fond of ferns, although I confess I have trouble telling one from another, which probably means I am not as fond of them as I think. Unless they are as different as maidenhair fern (*Adiantum pedatum*) and holly fern (*Cyrtomium falcatum*), they all tend to look like ferns to me, although I do know that some are evergreen and some deciduous.

Ferns evolved early, before gymnosperms and flowering plants, and they reproduce by spores, not seeds. The sporangia that produce the spores appear on the underside of the fronds, usually as brown spots that are sometimes mistaken for disease. Although the ferns in temperate regions today are all small, the tropics still contain some minor members of the once-mighty tree ferns that formed forests through which dinosaurs roamed and which, when they died, formed coal. Just for their romantic associations, I would love to grow a tree fern and I envy mightily those in frost-free areas who can. Perhaps I will cherish one in a container and lug it indoors for the winter—although that would be a sorry substitute for a ground-growing tree fern, so graceful as you look up through its branches into the forest canopy overhead and wait for monkeys and pterosaurs to glide through the branches—not at the same time, of course; many millions of years apart.

CHAPTER 8

Perennials

Nothing in my new garden gives more pleasure than the not-very-large, border of perennials, small shrubs, bulbs, and annuals. It will be years before the fascinating trees and shrubs I have planted around the place come into their own, but the border is instant pleasure. The six foot hedge of sheared yaupon holly, that will one day provide a backdrop, is still little more than a row of cuttings from the beautiful berried holly near the marsh. The border itself is two years old and I have begun to weed out early mistakes and even to pull together some sort of color scheme. The perennials flower generously even in the summer heat, when I neglect them shamefully. On any day of the year I can step out to the border and pick at least a small bunch of "posies" (our librarian's lovely word), even if it is only a few confused sedums that have decided to bloom in January.

Herbaceous perennials are flowering plants without wood that live for more than one year. This gives them properties that appeal to every gardener. Unlike annuals, perennials give you a second chance. If a perennial behaves miserably this year, you may be able to resuscitate it by dividing it and giving it a liberal helping of compost in the fall. If you hate the color scheme you've created, you can dig up perennials and move them around until you get it right. You can move plants from shade to sun, from wet to dry, until you find the spot that makes them happy (or until you decide they just don't like your garden and chuck them on the compost pile).

Perennials are always surprising you by their adaptations. The general hardiness zones listed in catalogues usually apply no doubt, but beyond that anything goes. Who would have predicted that the European mullein, completely happy in a moist mild English flower bed, would

GREEN THUMBS TIPS
DWARF VARIETIES
FOR THE SOUTH
If you garden in the soggy south, many plants that are well-behaved elsewhere, grow tall and untidy and fall over in the border. Look for dwarf varieties that will perform better. For instance, dwarf *Gaillardia* 'Goblin' and 'Baby Cole' grow as tall in my Savannah border as full-sized *Gaillardia grandiflora* in Beth Bowler's desert bed in Boise.

feel at home naturalized in American semidesert, with its bone dry summers and long cold winters? It seems that mullein (*Verbascum Thapsus*), which has a rosette of hairy gray leaves and tall spikes of yellow flowers, doesn't care where it is as long as it has well-drained soil. Just because a particular perennial has never been grown in your area does not mean that it will not grow there. Americans usually list garden phlox as a plant for the sunny border. The British often grow it in considerable shade. If a plant is not happy in one situation, try it in another. Experiment!

If you are new to perennial gardening, a word of caution is in order. Many choice perennials are slow to get going after you have planted them. Do not assume that a plant that does absolutely nothing for the first year, or even two, is dying; it may just be getting its roots dug in. Don't start your first perennial bed with nothing but expensive (which usually means they are slow) species and varieties. Throw in some quick and easy things to keep you going as well as lots of annuals.

DESIGNING A BORDER

The most important function of a flower bed is to supply a splash of color in the landscape. But before you lay out a huge flower bed, herbaceous border, perennial bed, or whatever it is called in your part of the world, it is worth considering other functions the bed is to serve and how you propose to tend it. For me, flower beds have to supply flowers for the house, food for birds and butterflies, and experimental areas to try out new plants. No matter how you plan, however, something always happens that changes things. My informal borders turned formal one winter when a neighbor decided to get rid of dozens of dwarf hollies. I couldn't bear to see the lovely little things thrown away and had neither the time nor inclination to clear ground for a parterre so I spaced them along the fronts of several flower beds where they have added a note of formality ever since.

Borders have more character throughout the year when they have a few strong textures in them as well as masses of flowers. My dwarf hollies are one way to achieve this. Another is to include plants with vertical lines such as ornamental grasses or yuccas. These can be spaced along the border or set asymmetrically in clumps. Plants with big leaves, such as elephant ears, caladiums, gunneras, or bergenias can also be used as accents.

Any border looks better when the plants are of varying heights. Include a few monsters at the back of the border for drama and some low creeping things to spill over the front of the bed and soften its edges. Some plants with tall narrow flower spikes also look good at the front of the border, especially in front of something that flowers at a different time. After studying a formal border edged with knee-high box, I also realized you can save yourself some weeding by edging the border and planting things close together, both of which ensure that most weeds will be choked or hidden from view.

Preparing a New Border

Gardeners with established borders that are not quite satisfactory tell you that they would love to start over, installing drainage tiles in a wet area, raising the bed, or whatever they have concluded the solution to their problem may be. It is certainly worth doing a thorough job of preparing the soil before you plant perennials that may stay in one place for many years. This involves the stern discipline of sticking all the plants you are collecting into your nursery bed for six months or more while you work on the border—which you never get time to do because the nursery is now so crowded it takes up all your time, but that is the way things go.

If you are killing lawn to create your border, you can use newspaper, compost, leaf mold, black plastic or whatever to kill the grass. (Even the colored inks in newspapers are now biodegradable and won't harm plants, but don't use glossy newspaper supplements, it says here.) Better still, till the soil and plant a cover crop Let it grow for a few months and then dig or till it in. Repeat the cover crop. The cover crop will add organic matter to the soil and also kill perennial weeds and grasses. If all this is too much like hard work, at least add large amounts of coarse organic matter to the soil and leave it over winter to settle in. Then weed and plant in the spring.

Start with Natives

A good approach to starting a border is to select native perennials that will give a good show and tolerate neglect. If these form the background of the border, you will have an attractive display while you experiment with other plants that may or may not please you. This chapter contains suggestions for natives that will probably be happy in borders in various parts of the world, chosen without regard for color scheme. I have assumed that the border is reasonably well-drained. If it is not, you should be collecting plants that like or tolerate wet feet.

Spacing

A vexed question in perennial borders is how widely to space the plants since many perennials take a few years to reach their full glory and you have to give them space to expand. One solution is annuals, which can fill part of the border while your perennials expand. Another is fast-growing perennials, such as coreopsis, salvias, and gaillardias, which flower the first year from seed. Fill empty spaces with these in the early years and then remove them later as slower growing plants expand. If it breaks your heart to remove a perfectly good coreopsis (not to mention the seedlings it has probably sown), pot them up to give to friends or sell at the your spring plant sale.

Some people like their flowers, at least at midsummer, so close together that no earth shows. Close planting also has the advantage of choking out, or at least hiding, most weeds. Other people prefer their plants well spaced so that each can form its characteristic clump and a neat band of mulch or groomed soil lies around the clump. If you are planting in a dry part of the world, you must leave considerable space between plants. Plants in a desert are naturally a long way apart because each needs to spread its roots over a considerable area to collect the water it needs.

Caring for Perennials

Perennials are easy-care plants, but they do need to be weeded, deadheaded, fed, and divided. After a plant has flowered, cut off the dead flower heads and any dead foliage. This makes the border look a lot better and provides extra space where a neighbor that will flower later can expand. You really need to remove dead heads every week or so, but if you get behind with this chore console yourself with the knowledge that many perennials will sow their own seeds if you leave the seed heads to ripen. In fact, some perennials are short-lived and will disappear from the border in a year or two unless you leave at least some seed heads to produce seedlings.

Native Plants to Start a Border

Note: I may have stretched the definition of "native" in places. For instance, several species of *Verbena* and *Lantana* originated in Central America and are now found on roadsides, naturalized in the southern United States. Whether they got there under their own steam or escaped from gardens, I do not know; but I have counted them as southern natives. The same goes for Europe: people started moving plants in Europe and Asia long before records were kept and it is difficult to know where many species originated.

Natives for a Mainly Sunny Border in the Northern Prairie Biome (into Canada)

Asclepias syriaca (Common milkweed)
Asclepias tuberosa (Butterfly milkweed)
Aster novae-angliae (Michaelmas daisy)
Aster oblongifolius
Aster praealtus

Echinacea purpurea (Purple coneflower)
Erigeron annuus (White-flowered fleabane)
Filipendula rubra (Queen of the Prairie)
Geum triflorum (Prairie smoke)
Liatris spicata. L. squarrosa (Blazing star)
Monarda fistulosa (Pale bergamot)
Ratibida pinnata (Prairie coneflower)
Rudbeckia hirta (Black-eyed susan)
Salvia azurea (Blue sage)
Solidago canadensis (Canada goldenrod)
Verbena stricta (Hoary vervain)
Vernonia altissima (Ironweed)
Artemisia spp.
Schizachyrium scoparium (little bluestem)
Yucca glauca (Great plains yucca)
Anemone occidentalis (Pasque flower)
Anemone patens (pasque flower)
Clematis virginiana (Virgin's Bower)
Helianthus annuus (Sunflower)
Lilium philadelphicum (Prairie lily)

Echinacea purpurea

Most perennials eventually form clumps in which the center is deprived of light and water and stops flowering. Then the clump needs to be divided in spring or fall. In some ways, it is easier to divide in spring when the plant is beginning to put out new shoots because then you can see which roots have healthy shoots attached and should be replanted and which should be thrown away. But it is usually better for the plant to do this work in autumn.

There are several ways to divide clumps. Start by finding out if you can divide the plant without digging it up—which will save strain on the plant and your back. Do this by thrusting a sharp spade down into the middle of the clump and jumping on it if necessary. Some plants will obligingly come in half when you do this and you can dig up one half and replant it. On others, a sharp spade makes little impression, and you wonder if it can really be true that perennials are non-woody. Then you have to dig the whole thing up. You may then be able to tear it apart with your hands or a couple of forks back to back. Some clumps present you with a solid mass of plant parts on which hands and forks make little impression. Then you have to take an axe to the root system, shuddering as you cut through perfectly healthy roots and shoots. Even small

Natives for a Sunny Border in the Southern Prairie Biome

Antennaria rosea (Pink pussy-toes)
Asclepias tuberosa (Butterfly milkweed)
Asclepias viridifolia (Green milkweed)
Aster oblongifolius (Aster)
Baptisia australis (Blue baptisia)
Callirhoe involucrata (Poppy mallow)
Dalea aurea (Indigo bush)
Echinacea angustifolia (Purple coneflower)
Gaura Lindheimeri
Liatris punctata, L. pycnostachya, L. squarrosa (Blazing star)
Monarda Russelliana
Oenothera missourensis (Missouri evening primrose)
Penstemon Cobaea, P. grandiflorus, P. secundiflorus (Penstemon)
Ratibida pinnata (Prairie coneflower)
Salvia azurea (Blue sage)
Salvia coccinea (Red Texas sage)
Solidago mollis (Goldenrod)
Spaeralcea coccinea (Scarlet mallow)
Echinocereus Reichenbachii (Hedgehog cactus)
Schizachyrium scoparium (Little bluestem)
Yucca glauca (Great Plains yucca)

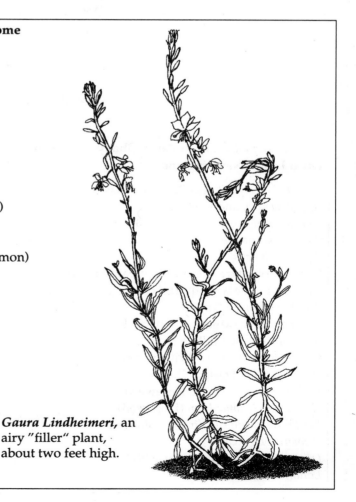

Gaura Lindheimeri, an airy "filler" plant, about two feet high.

divisions will survive but if your object is rejuvenation not propagation there is no need to divide a clump into more than two or three parts. Before you replant your newly divided plants, renovate the soil completely. Get all the weeds out and dig in lots of compost. After replanting, water thoroughly.

Most established perennials need to be divided every two or three years. Since I can never remember what likes to be divided and what doesn't, I take my cue from the plants and divide only when they seem to be flowering less vigorously than before or when the clump is so large it is taking up too much space in the border.

The care of a perennial border develops an annual routine. I think the most important part of this is the trouble you take to put the border to bed in the autumn. Cut down all dead stalks, weed thoroughly, and cover the border with a thick layer of compost. If you are not going to bother with the compost or some other form of mulch, don't deadhead and weed at this time of year since the border's own decaying vegetation will provide protection for the plants during the winter. But I prefer to do this work in autumn because, except in very cold areas, autumn is the best time to plant perennials. In the Deep South, in fact, autumn planting is essential. Dozens of species will thrive if planted in the fall and plain old die if you plant them in spring. Water the bed after this procedure, particularly in colder areas, so that the roots are in good contact with the soil before winter's freezes and thaws set in.

Some perennials, such as lilies and delphiniums, must either be staked or they will fall over. I am hopeless at staking. I usually

Natives for a Sunny to Partly Shady Border in Great Lakes, New England

Anaphalis margaritacea (Pearly everlasting)
Aquilegia spp. and hybrids
Arabis Drummondii (Rock cress)
Aster novae-angliae
Aruncus dioicus
Castilleja septentrionalis (Yellow paintbrush)
Dicentra canadensis (Squirrel corn)
Dicentra eximia (Turkey corn)
Iliamna remota (Moutain hollyhock)
Baptisia tinctoria (Yellow baptisia)
Geranium maculatum (Wild geranium)
Heliopsis helianthoides (Oxeye)
Helenium autumnale (Sneezeweed)
Heracleum Sphondylium (Hogweed)
Mertensia virginica (Virginia bluebells)
Clematis virginiana
Lilium philadelphicum (Prairie lily)
Lilium canadense

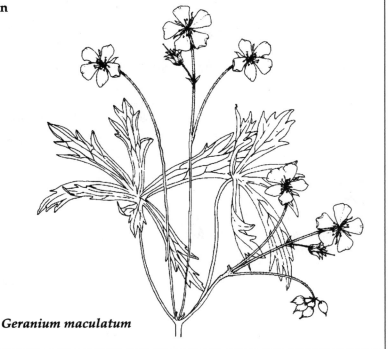

Geranium maculatum

forget it until the flower falls over and gets a right angled crick in its stem. Sometimes this doesn't matter: you just get a short flower instead of a tall one. But usually it is more sensible to put stakes in place when the flower spike starts to shoot up. I favor bamboo stakes and raffia ties because they are not very noticeable in the border. But some of the metal hooks and frames you can buy are also inconspicuous and save the trouble of tying stem to stake.

PROPAGATING PERENNIALS

I seldom buy more than one or two of a new plant that I want to try. Perennials are fairly expensive when you buy plants and most are easy to propagate when you decide that the plant is happy in your border and you would like to have more of it. Division works with plants that form clumps—meaning that the roots get bigger and produce additional stems. But there are some plants that have only a single main stem or root, no matter how large they become. These plants have to be propagated from cuttings or seed.

Cuttings can come from either roots or stems. Things that form big knobbly roots, such as cannas, baptisias, and ginger lilies, can usually be grown from root cuttings. Cut off a hunk of root in autumn, replant it, and it will produce a new plant next spring. Stem cuttings are made just like those from shrubs—cut off a length of stem bearing a few leaves, treat it with rooting hormone if you have any, stick it in the ground and keep it moist until new leaves show that it has rooted. Cuttings are usually taken in late summer. Almost anything with fleshy stems, such as balsam and begonias, roots easily from a cutting.

Natives for a Sunny Border in Midatlantic States (Zones 5-7)

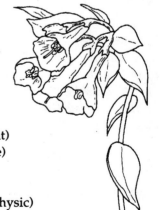

Andropogon scoparius (Little bluestem)
Andropogon virginicus (Broom sedge)
Arabis Drummondii (Rock cress)
Aster carolinianus (climbing aster)
Baptisia australis (Blue baptisia)
Baptisia tinctoria (Yellow baptisia)
Baptisia villosa
Bouteloua cirtipendula (Side-oats grama)
Chelone glabra (Turtlehead)
Cimicifuga racemosa (Black snakeroot)
Clematis virginiana
Collinsia verna (Blue-eyed Mary)
Coreopsis auriculata, C. verticillata
Fothergilla Gardenii
Heracleum Sphondylium (Hogweed)
Koeleria cristata (Junegrass)
Kosteletzkya virginica (Seashore mallow)

Lobelia cardinalis
Mertensia virginica (Virginia bluebell)
Penstemon canescens
Phlox divaricata
Phlox maculata
Physostegia virginiana (Obedient plant)
Oenothera speciosa (Evening primrose)
Tiarella cordifolia (Foamflower)
Verbena stricta (Hoary vervain)
Veronicastrum virginicum (Culver's physic)

Mertensia virginica

Experiments with seeds are cheap and easy and many perennials are as easy as annuals from seed, although they take longer to flower. Americans will probably want to cultivate a Canadian or British seed company because United States companies seem depressingly conventional in their perennial offerings. I enjoy Chiltern Seeds in Cumberland, which offers seeds of lilies, palm trees, and proteas along with their shasta daisies and arabis. Start seeds of perennials just as you would annuals (Chapter 10). The only perennials that you absolutely cannot start from seed are named varieties that have been vegetatively propagated. In this case, a particularly meritorious seedling was pounced on and named and will not come true from seed.

Here are a few favorite perennials for different times of year.

SPRING FLOWERS

Peonies (*Paeonia* spp. and hybrids)

Peonies are arguably *the* most magnificent cold-hardy perennials, producing huge flowers in all shades of white through red and purple at about the time that cherries flower in the spring. They have the added virtues of being long-lived and requiring little care. Peonies flourish from Zone 2 to Zone 6 (and are worth trying in Zones 1 to 8). As long as they get a cold spell in winter, peonies have been known to thrive in neglected gardens for more than 50 years. If your peonies don't thrive and you are in a cold part of the world, it is almost certainly because you have planted them too deep or fertilized them too much.

Natives for a Sunny to Partly Shady Border in the High Plains/Mountains

Allium drummondii (Wild onion)
Anemone patens (Pasque flower)
Balsamorhiza sagittata (Balsamroot)
Baptisia australis (Blue baptisia)
Bouteloua curtipendula (Sideoats grama)
Castilleja miniata (Paintbrush)
Callirhoe involucrata (Buffalo poppy)
Collinsia Torreyi
Dicentra uniflora (Steer's head)
Epilobium glaberrimum (Willow herb)
Erythronium grandiflorum (Avalanche lily)
Euphorbia marginata (Snow on the mountain)
Helianthus anuus (Sunflower)
Lewisia rediviva (Bitterroot)
Lilium philadelphicum (Prairie lily)
Mertensia ciliata (Moutain bluebell)
Oenothera missourensis (Missouri evening primrose)

Penstemon angustifolius (Penstemon)
Ratibida columnifera (Coneflower)
Zauschneria californica latifolia (California fuschia)

Lewisia rediviva

Peonies need a fair bit of sun. In northern areas, they thrive in east-facing beds. Further south, a little more shade won't do any harm. If your peonies stop flowering, the two most likely causes are increasing shade from an expanding tree and plants that have sunk too deep in the soil.

When you buy a peony, you get a rooted crown with several dark red "eyes" or buds on top. They should go almost four feet apart in soil enriched with compost, leaf mold, bone meal, and any other organic goodies you can find. Make sure the eyes are at soil level. The plant will sink somewhat and if the eyes end up more than an inch or two below ground level, the plant will not flower. Don't mulch peonies for the winter. They don't care how cold it gets and soggy mulch might cause rot.

Most peonies flower the year after they are planted but they will not come into their full glory until several years later. The plants grow from about fifteen inches to three feet high, depending on the cultivar, and the foliage is attractive throughout the summer. Peonies need water when they are in active growth, but they don't like to stand in a puddle. And although they don't really need it, you may speed up a newly planted clump by giving it a few shovels full of compost every spring.

Peonies

Natives for a Sunny Border in Lower South: Gulf Coast, Zones 8 to 10

Amsonia Tabernaemontana (Blue star)
Adropogon littoralis (Bluestem)
Andropogon virginicus (Broomsedge)
Asclepias spp.
Baptisia alba
Boltonia asteroides
Callirhoe Papaver (Poppy mallow)
Cassia corymbosa
Coreopsis auriculata, C. lanceolata
Echinacea purpurea
Gaillardia pulchella (Blanketflower)
Gaura Lindheimeri
Hamelia patens (Firebush)
Hibiscus Moscheutos
Hymenocallis latifolia (Spider lily)
Ilex vomitoria (Yaupon holly)
Lantana camara, L. montevidensis
Liatris spicata (Blazing-star)

Oenothera speciosa (Evening primrose)
Phlox carolina
Rhexia mariana (Maryland meadow beauty)
Solidago spp.
Stokesia laevis
Tradescantia virginiana
Verbena rigida
Verbena tenuisecta
Yucca flaccida

Tradescantia virginiana

Helleborus niger, **Christmas rose.**

The one snag with peonies is that they tend to flop over, particularly in a wet spring. Staking is difficult and not particularly attractive for these basically informal plants. I think it is better to let them flop. The problem of flopping flowers is even worse with the peony's regal relative the tree peony—a Japanese import that grows to about five feet high and is hardy from about Zones 5 to 7 as well as in Britain.

Hellebores (*Helleborus* spp.)

Hellebores are often the earliest flowers of spring. The Christmas rose (*H. niger*), may flower through the snow. Hellebores are natives of limestone regions in Europe and Asia and indispensible if you have moist alkaline soil. The large, nodding rose-shaped flowers are not to everyone's taste because of their odd green through pale purple colors. One answer is to combine them with clear-colored neighbors, such as forget-me-nots.

Rock cress (*Arabis spp.*)

Many of the most useful perennials for spring are low-growing things that can be used to underplant spring-flowering bulbs. Arabis, with soft gray foliage covered with open white flowers in later spring is one of the best of these for Britain and most of North America. Try it with red tulips or irises of any color. In my Zone 5 garden, arabis was slowly but definitely invasive, taking over part

---

Natives for a Sunny Border in Desert/Semidesert Northwest U.S.

Anaphalis margaritacea (Pearly ever-lasting)

Anemone occidentalis (Pasque flower)`

Aster spp. (Aster)

Balsamorhiza sagittata (Arrowleaf balsamroot)

Calochortus Nutalii (Sego lily)

Castilleja spp. (Paintbrush)

Chrysothamnus nauseosus (Rabbit brush)

Cryptantha torreyana (Cryptantha)

Erigeron compositus (Fernleaf fleabane)

Eriogonum ovalifolium (Dwarf buck-wheat), and other *Eriogonum* spp.

Gaultheria procumbens (Creeping wintergreen)

Geum triflorum (Prairie smoke)

Gilia aggregata (Scarlet gilia)

Lewisia rediviva (Bitterroot), *L. Tweedyi*

Linum lewisii (Wild flax)

Lomatium spp. (Desert parsley)

Lupinus spp. (Lupine)

Mentzelia laevicaulis (Blazing star)

Oenothera caespitosa, O. heterantha (Evening primrose)

Paeonia brownii (Wild peony)

Phacelia hastata (Scorpionweed)

Phlox spp. (Phlox)

Ratibida columnifera (Coneflower)

Solidago spp. (Goldenrod)

Sphaeralcea munroana (Orange globe mallow)

Viola beckwithii (Violet)

Wyethia amplexicaulis (Mule-ears)

Xerophyllum tenax (Bear grass)

Lupinus

of the lawn after five years or so, which was no hardship since I am not fond of lawn. You can get arabis in double as well as single forms and there is a pink cultivar that looks marvellous with tulips in the dark rose-lavender-purple color range.

Arabis is easy from seed, fairly long-lived, and reasonably drought-tolerant.

Primulas *(Primula)*
There are primulas suited to every situation, from a shady bog to a sunny border—where hybrid primulas can produce displays in almost every color. Many primulas, like *Primula juliae* and *P. vulgaris* that grace a shady rock garden, are small, but there are also larger species, such as the dramatic *P. florindae*, the giant cowslip, which can reach three feet in height and *P. japonica*, a large mauve candelabra for damp places. Primulas need cool soil so there is no point even trying them in the warmer half of the country and even in New England most do better in at least part shade.

Primula bulleyana

Aubretia *(Aubretia)*
I cannot imagine spring in Britain without purple aubretia tumbling over stone walls at the feet of King Alfred daffodils. If you can grow it, do. It is easy from seed and long-lived. It is hardy to at least Zone 6 but does not like the heat of North American summers.

Primula juliae

Phlox *(Phlox* spp.)
Phlox is an American native with species that flower in spring and summer in colors ranging from purest white through pink, lavender, and purple. The spring-flowering species are low creepers, used for

---

Natives for a Sunny Border in Pacific Northwest

Anaphalis margaritacea (Pearly everlasting)
Amelanchier alnifolia (Saskatoon berry)
Angelica Hendersonii (Angelica)
Arctostaphylos columbiana (Hairy manzanita)
Balsamorhiza sagittata (Balsam root)
Camassia quamash (Blue camass)
Ceanothus velutinus (Snowbrush)
Clematis hirsutissima (Sugarbowl)
Dryas drummondii (Yellow dryad)
Gaillardia aristata (Brown-eyed susan)
Heuchera spp. (Alumroot)
Heracleum lanatum (Cow parsnip)
Iliamna rivularis (Mountain hollyhock)
Iris missouriensis
Epilobium angustifolium (Fireweed)
Mertensia ciliata (Mountain bluebell)
Pedicularis groenlandica (Elephanthead)
Philadelphus lewisii (Mockorange)

Penstemon speciosus (Penstemon)
Plectritis congesta (Sea blush)
Sidalcea Hendersonii (Checker)
Wyethia helianthoides (White mule-ears)
Zigadenus elegans (Mountain death camass)

Angelica Hendersonii

the same purposes as aubretia. *Phlox subulata* is moss phlox, native to the eastern United States with many named varieties in all colors. A virtue of moss phlox is that the foliage is attractive for most of the year, a mat of dark green spikes that stays compact and tidy if the plant is in a fairly sunny location. Wild sweet william (*Phlox divaricata*) is a must for woodland gardens in the northeastern United States Its deep violet-blue flowers in May are followed by smooth green foliage that looks good all summer.

The best known phlox is a giant of summer borders, the clump-forming *Phlox paniculata*, with many fine cultivars. Garden phlox does have its problems, however. If it gets too much water, it tends to flop or need staking and it is prone to mildew. More resistant to fungus and flop is the slightly shorter *P. carolina* (usually sold as *P. maculata*).

Salvia (*Salvia* spp.)

The salvias, or sages, belong to a huge genus with representatives native to all parts of the world. Those that are not hardy in the

---

Natives for a Sunny Border in Coastal California

Abronia latifolia, A. maritima, A. umbellata (Sand verbena)
Aconitum columbianum (Mokshood)
Agave spp.
Antennaria rosea (Pink pussy-toes)
Arctostaphylos uva-ursi (Bearberry)
Armeria maritima californica (Thrift)
Camassia Leichtlinii, C. Quamash (Camass)
Calochortus luteus (Yellow Mariposa lily)
Castelleja foliosa, C. latifolia (Paintbrush)
Ceanothus spp. (California lilac)
Cirsium spp (Thistle)
Cistus x hybridus (Rock rose)
Clarkia amoena, C. rubicunda (Farewell-to-spring)
Coreopsis gigantea (Sea dahlia)
Dudleya virens (Live-forever)
Delphinium nudicaule, D. cardinale (Scarlet larkspur)
Epilobium angustifolium (Fireweed)
Erigeron glaucus (Seaside daisy)
Eriogonum giganteum (St. Catherine's lace)
Eriogonum parviflorum (California buckwheat)
Eriogonum umbellatum (Sulphur flower)
Eriophyllum staechadifolium (Yellow yarrow)
Erisimum suffrutescens (Wallflowers)
Erythronium grandiflorum (Avalanche lily)

Eschscholzia californica (California poppy)
Gaultheria Shallon (Salal)
Geranium viscossimum (Sticky geranium)
Heliotropium curassavicum (Heliotrope)
Holodiscus discolor (Ocean spray)
Lantana montevidensis (Trailing lantana)
Lasthenia glabrata (Lasthenia)
Layia platyglossa (Tidy tips)
Mentzelia laevicaulis (Blazing star)
Oenothera Hookeri (Evening primrose)
Opuntia spp. (Prickly pear)
Paeonia californica (Wild peony)
Penstemon Eatonii, P. barbatus, P. Palmeri
Polypodium Scouleri (Polypody)
Solidago canadensis (Goldenrod)
Wyethia angustifolia, W. glabra (Mule ears)
Zauschneria cana (California fuschia)

Eriogonum parviflorum, buckwheat, has white flowers tinged with pink in most months of the year.

North are often grown as annuals since most salvias flower within a few months from seed. Although many of them flower in summer, I list them among spring flowers because various blue cultivars of *S. farinacea*, mealy-cup sage, are an invaluable addition to the spring border in the American South and in Britain. If you keep the dead heads sheared they will rebloom several times during the summer.

Most of the blue-flowered sages also come as white varieties which are not nearly as vigorous. *S. azurea* is another good blue-flowered species, taller than *S. farinacea* and naturalized over much of the warmer half of North America.

A favorite of mine is *Salvia coccinea*, Texas sage, which blooms in summer. This is one of those drought-resistant toughs, essential to all dry gardens. It may form a gangly shrub in the South, but is better kept cut back so that it forms a bushy plant. The flowers, which look like miniature snapdragons, are of the loveliest clear red. *S. elegans*, pineapple sage, is similar with scented foliage.

Poppies (*Papaver* spp.)
Oriental poppies, *Papaver orientale*, are the jewels among perennial poppies. With big, silky flowers in many colors from white through red and purple with various markings, they do well in cooler parts of the world. Fond of dry soil and sun, oriental poppies are usually propagated by division and are best left alone, when they are long-lived and form quite large clumps in the garden.

Columbine (*Aquilegia* spp.)
The delicate nodding flowers of columbines make a fine contrast to the rather solid flowers of many spring bulbs. This a big genus, with species native to most parts of the Northern Hemisphere and the species hybridize readily so there are also dozens of garden cultivars with bigger flowers, but lacking the airy delicacy of the species. Most of these cultivars have *A. canadensis* in their ancestry but the red-flowered species itself is also charming. Most columbines have multi-colored flowers in a wide range of colors which make the single-colored species the more desirable. That best adapted to the Deep South is *A. Hinckleyana*, a bright yellow columbine discovered beside a Texas stream. The mountain columbine, *A. caerulea*, state flower of Colorado, is a lovely clear blue that no mountain garden should be without. The main European species is *A. vulgaris*. It is important to find columbines that like your part of the world because they will self-seed where they are happy, a real bonus in the woodland garden. Although most of them are woodland plants, plenty of columbines will also stand full sun in cooler parts of the world.

Phlox carolina

SUMMER

Many spring-flowering species are adapted to the shade of deciduous trees, flowering before the trees leaf out. In contrast, most summer-flowering plants are adapted to the wide open spaces of grassland, desert, or ditch, and prefer full sun. Only in the Deep South are there many species that flower in shade in summer. For the best flower power, your summer border should get at least six hours of sun a day, and preferably more.

A friend wandered round my garden one July day looking for novelties and remarked, "Mainly daisies, I see," in disparaging tones. I was crushed, but there is no question that one of the challenges of the perennial border is to vary the constant procession of daisy-flowered species, which are easy to grow and which flower in summer. All these are composites, members of the large family, Asteraceae. They include erigeron, echinacea, asters, stokesias, coreopsis, gaillardia, heliopsis, helianthus, rudbeckia, asters, and chrysanthemums. Yellows and purples are their dominant colors. It is reassuring to learn that the composites evolved from the rose family relatively recently (probably some 35 million years ago) and have coevolved with sophisticated insects, which are particular about the species they pollinate. So a wide range of native composites in your garden ensures a diversity of indigenous insects to feed your native insect-eating birds and amphibians.

Blanket flower (*Gaillardia* spp.)

As I write this in January, *Gaillardia pulchella* is flowering reproachfully on my compost heap. I ripped the poor things out of the holly border where they had given me bouquets of red daisies with a wide yellow fringe for the Christmas dinner table. Not that I am trying to rid the bed of gaillardias. Dozens of self-sown seedlings will be in flower there within a month or two. But the old plants do get brown, bent, and scraggly around the base, so out they come. The legginess is worse in our soggy part of the world and I should probably stick to dwarf varieties such as 'Goblin.' But I can't resist the new double all-red varieties such as 'Red Plume,' which I think comes only in the full-sized variety.

Gaillardias started out as several wild species native to Nebraska and points south, but I rather think the species' gene pools are getting mixed up now that the plant breeders are at work. Gaillardias are short-lived perennials that act as annuals in many places, but they self-sow readily.

Coreopsis (*Coreopsis* spp.)

I am beginning to tire of the eternal yellowy yellow of coreopsis so it is a pleasure to read that European breeders will soon be offering many new varieties of this indestructible beauty. They have already given us a lime yellow starry affair, *C. verticillata* 'Zagreb' that is lovely in the front of the border or as edging for a path in areas where the coveted lady's mantle, *Alchemilla mollis*, isn't hardy.

Fleabane *(Erigeron* hybrids)

Fleabane is not a very nice name for this aster-lookalike that flowers in summer. The best ones for the garden are hybrids of *E. speciosus*, native to western North America. It does not do well in the southeastern states and likes full sun and moist soil elsewhere.

Coneflower *(Echinacea* spp.)

I don't really warm to the purple coneflower, *E. purpurea*, or its western relative, *E. angustifolia*. This is churlish of me because the brown-eyed flowers with drooping purple petals are reliable and long-lived in any type of soil from Zone 4 to Zone 8, even if they don't flower as generously as coreopsis at any one time. I think my problem is the slightly prickly stems. I don't like a plant to reach out and grab me as I pass, even if it doesn't draw blood. But there is no denying that a mass of echinacea in the midsummer garden can take your breath away.

Penstemon Cobaea

Rattleweed, False indigo (*Baptisia* spp.)

Baptisias belong to a rather neglected genus of central and eastern American legumes that add height to the border in spring and early summer with pea-like flowers in blue, yellow, or white. In appearance, the plants remind me of acanthus, justly popular with English and Californian gardeners for their handsome foliage and tall spires of flowers. The flowers of baptisia are, perhaps, best described as "interesting." They are certainly not exactly beautiful, but the very dark stems are unusual and make a smashing contrast to the flowers. Propagate from root cuttings, watering furiously for the first months after transplanting.

Penstemon (*Penstemon* spp.)

The genus *Penstemon* is to the western United States what baptisias are to the East—a neglected group of native plants with lots of unrealized potential as garden flowers. There are more penstemons than there are baptisias but perhaps they are even more neglected because many are difficult to propagate from seed, which makes the development of cultivars difficult. Penstemons, however, are easily propagated from cuttings and they should be offered by more nurseries. Most penstemons like dry soil and must have perfect drainage.

Lupines (*Lupinus* spp.)

The tall spires of lupines can make a striking display in the summer border. Best-known are the Russell hybrids, cultivars developed in England from a genus that is native mainly to the western United States. Russell lupines grow well in much of the United States and when happy will self-seed themselves. In the dry west and the humid south, however, they are better replaced by native species such as *Lupinus perennis* in the East (blue flowers), Texas bluebonnet (*L. subcarnosus*) in its native biome, and perhaps *L. sparsiflorus* in the dry west. (The flowers aren't really as sparse as the name suggests.) I think my favorite wild lupine from the west coast is the pink and white form of the bush lupine, *L. arboreus*, which is a pleasant change from the many blues in this genus. Although garden lupines need plenty of nutrients and water to produce at their best, the wild species can survive neglect, although they produce better displays in decent garden soil than they do in the wild.

Delphinium (*Delphinium* hybrids)

There are few finer sights than a planting of well grown delphiniums with their towering, if disaster-prone, blue or white spires. For the casual gardener who loves the colors and the flowers but cannot stand the spraying and staking that such a display entails, there are several alternatives. If you treat delphiniums with less than tender loving care, and particularly if you deprive them of water, they develop shorter, wiry stems that don't need staking. The flowers are less spectacular, of course, but the colors are just as fine. After their first display, cut the dead heads off promptly and you will usually be rewarded by a crop of smaller flowers later in the summer.

Verbena (*Verbena* spp.)

I am rather proud of the perennial verbenas, feeling that I single-handedly reintroduced them to southern gardens—which I didn't and anyway it was a complete accident. Searching seed catalogues geared to Britain and the Northeast for perennials that might survive southern summers, I purchased *Verbena rigida* and *V. rigida polaris* from Parks Seed. Five months after sowing, they were in flower, and by the second year had formed a twelve inch border of purple and pale blue along the front of a sunny border, where they bloomed from spring to frost without deadheading. There turned out to be a snag, as there are to so many good things. The species was highly invasive and the third year I had to weed it out of the border and relegate it to a sunny spot where the roots of a crape myrtle would compete with it. Nevertheless, I had discovered a new genus that I can imagine no southern gardener doing without.

Native to the Americas, perennial verbenas are not terribly easy to find. They are not hardy north of Zone 6 and most of the cultivars are therefore bred as annuals for the north which is not what the southern gardener needs. There is also a certain amount of confusion about the species names and I am not sure I have them right even now. To the best of my knowledge and belief, as we lawyers say, *Verbena tenuisecta* is the one with ferny foliage and globular flower heads in bluish purple (occasionally white) that flowers by southern roadsides in spring and doesn't mind being mowed. *V. rigida* is upright and hairy with lance-shaped leaves and purple flowers. The variety *polaris* is not white but pale blue and much less vigorous than the species. The one with ferny foliage and virulent pink or pinky purple flowers is *V. tenera* and you can rapidly tire of the color. Its main virtue appears to be that it sometimes flowers right through a mild winter. *V. halei* looks as if it might be interesting, but I have not tried it. The perennial, but not the annual, verbenas are drought-tolerant and bug-free, demanding only well-drained soil and full sun to give of their best. In even partial shade, they get leggy and do not flower well.

Lantana (*Lantana* spp.)

Lantana is another southern and western standby and breeders are finally discovering the potential of this genus. Lantanas have rather woody, gangly stems, which are the better for frequent and severe pruning—although it is hard to make yourself do the necessary pruning when the plant is still flowering madly. Lantanas have rounded or flattened heads of small rather phlox-like flowers. An intriguing feature is that the flowers in one flower-head are often of

Verbena **hybrid.**

several colors. The two main species are *Lantana Camara* and *L. montevidensis*, both natives of South and Central America and naturalized in southern North America. *L. Camara* flowers for a long time and forms quite a large shrub. It has become a serious weed in Hawaii, where it is not cut back by frost.

The species with most garden potential appears to be *Lantana montevidensis*, which is naturally low and trailing and purple. This flowers for longer than *L. Camara*, even after considerable frost in autumn. Yellow and white varieties are now available. If only the breeders would produce a cultivar with a slightly less prostrate habit and slightly less enthusiastic growth, they would have a winner because lantanas don't seem to care whether the soil is bone dry or sopping wet, the bed sunny or partly shady. They are easy from seed, but if you want to propagate a desirable variety, stem cuttings in summer are the way to go.

Yarrow (*Achillea* spp.)

It is a sadness to me that this lovely European native doesn't really like the sunny South. The ferny foliage, flat-top flower sprays and wide variety of colors makes it an awfully useful plant if you can grow it—which you can wherever summers are reasonably dry. The only variety that might do for you in a southern garden is *Achillea* x 'Coronation Gold,' with stout stems and golden heads that last forever in arrangements. Common yarrow, *A. millefolium*, has naturalized in areas of the west with less than ten inches of rain a year so I suppose it is no wonder it doesn't like sog. This species has been cultivated in Europe since at least the fifteenth century. Achilles is supposed to have used it to staunch bleeding, which I suppose is where it got its name.

AUTUMN

There are plenty of plants that flower after the summer show has faded, but the two that seem indispensible are asters and chrysanthemums. Many people would add sedums to that list, but I have to confess that I don't like sedums much because they don't like me, so I have not had much experience with them—besides which, nearly all the sedums that have survived in my garden arrived as nameless cuttings wrapped in damp paper towel; they have never been identified, which makes them hard to write about.

If you have moist heavy soil, the cardinal flower, *Lobelia cardinalis*, is a lovely autumn bloomer, to be replaced in dry soil by the California tree poppy, *Romneya coulteri*. I am also devoted to hardy ageratum, *Eupatorium coelestinum*, a tall affair with fluffy blue flowers heads that doesn't seem fussy about soil. It tends to sow itself around, so if it really likes your garden, you may want to relegate it to the rough meadow or even woodland, because it flowers in considerable shade.

Achillea, **yarrow.**

Aster (*Aster* spp.)

There are about six hundred species of aster and many of them are scraggly affairs, so it is worth trying the many good cultivars that have been introduced of recent years. If you live in the South, it is also worth noting that hybrids of *A. novae-angliae* are more fungus-resistant than those of *A. novi-belgii*. In the dry west, stems do not grow as long, but in damp areas it is a good idea to treat asters as we do garden chrysanthemums, shearing them (or pinching them if you're feeling energetic) once when they start to grow in the spring and again about 100 days before first frost. This will make them a lot more compact and floriferous than if you had left them alone.

Chrysanthemum

Even in Zone 5, I found that some chrysanthemums acted as perennials, returning year after year. The trouble was that there was no predicting which would behave in this way. You certainly couldn't tell from the catalogue descriptions. (And, come to think of it, they are pretty unpredictable in the South as well.) The trouble with this unpredictability is that when chrysanthemums emerge in the spring, you don't know what you have got unless you had the forethought to plant them a long way apart and to write all this down in your notebook. You end up saying to little shoots, "If you're that gangly yellow jobby, I don't want you, but if you're that white spider one you can stay." At this point, the truly organized would uproot and divide the lot, replanting them in the nursery until they bloom in fall and you find out what you have got. (The answer is that the least desirable varieties are still with you; the prize specimens are gone.) The less energetic remind themselves to dig out any chrysanthemums that they do not want the following year while the plants are in flower. The rest of us happy-go-lucky souls just live with whatever shows up.

Chrysanthemums are so easy from slips that you don't really need to gamble like this. A specialist catalogue will reveal dozens of desirable varieties that you can treat as annuals, buying the slips in the spring and bringing them to maturity in the fall, then discarding them if you don't like them and hoping they will come back if you do. This is one group of perennials where planting in spring is perfectly acceptable, even in the South.

However laissez-faire your attitude, it is well worth doing the pinching or shearing necessary to turn the tiny spring shoots into a hefty clump by autumn. (This does not apply if you are trying to grow huge blooms for the flower show, but if you are, you doubtless know more about it than I do, anyway.) The first round of pinching comes when the shoots are about four inches high. The second is more critical and difficult to judge. The rule of thumb is 100 days before first frost in the South and about two weeks earlier in areas with cooler summers.

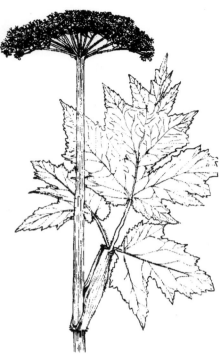

Heracleum Sphondylium may grow to more than six feet tall.

BIG PLANTS FOR BACKGROUND

There is nothing like really gigantic perennials (or even annuals) for adding a feeling of drama to a garden. Presumably people with small gardens turn the page when they read that a plant reaches six foot or more, not realizing that the plant may be only a foot or two wide—of course it may not, and you may have a disaster on your hands. But since many of these big plants are easily grown and very decorative, I think we should be a bit more adventurous with them. Snakeroot *(Cimicifuga)*, cow parsnip *(Heracleum Sphondylium)*, Blue star *(Amsonia Tabernaemontana)* and goatsbeard *(Aruncus dioicus)* are all American natives that usually exceed four feet in height. From Europe and Asia come things like bear breeches *(Acanthus)*, Italian bugloss *(Anchusa azurea)*, *Ligularia japonica*, and giant hogweed *(Heracleum mantegazzianum)*.

If you live in Britain or the Deep South, the plume poppy *(Macleaya cordata)* is one Asian native that may love you not wisely but too well. It is grown for its large palmate gray-green creamy leaves rather than its tall panicles of off-white flowers. All it seems to demand is dry soil. Apart from that, it will take rain or drought, humidity and cold. I don't know how it would cope with colder winters but it is such a dramatic plant that it might be worth a try. Easy from seed. If it is too aggressive in the border, try replanting a seedling as a specimen, say at a corner of the house. Mine lives on a windy corner. It doesn't collapse under the strain and looks most dramatic from a distance.

If you have damp, heavy soil, the meadow rues *(Thalictrum)* may be your tall plant of choice. They are covered with pink or white flowers in midsummer.

PERENNIALS THAT TOLERATE DROUGHT

When you start looking for plants to try in a dry garden, certain plants are more likely to work than others. Most plants with gray or hairy leaves are adapted to long dry spells and indeed many of them will die in an irrigated bed. This was brought home to me when I installed a soaker hose in a bed with a lush edging of woolly gray lamb's ears *(Stachys byzantina)*. During its first summer in moist soil the stachys slowly faded away to a few tattered remnants. Another general rule is that dry-garden plants need well-drained soil. This usually means soil that contains a lot of sand and gravel, whether or not it also contains much organic matter: many dryland plants are not heavy feeders.

GRAY PLANTS AND WHITE GARDENS

The idea of creating a garden where one color predominates appeals to many gardeners. The most famous single-color garden is Vita Sackville-West's White Garden at Sissinghurst, which is still delighting visitors forty years after it was started. At its inception,

Sackville-West described the garden thus, "I am trying to make a gray-and-white garden...I cannot help hoping that the great ghostly barn-owl will sweep silently across a pale garden, next summer, in the twilight." She never claimed more for the white garden than that gardens showcasing a single color scheme are "amusing." If successfully worked out, however (no easy undertaking), they are also exceedingly attractive.

The ideal location for a white garden is behind walls or tall hedges. The impact of a white spring garden is diluted if you can see a neighbor's pink and purple azaleas through your white tulips and dogwoods. Another place for white flowers is wherever you sit in the evening. In subdued light, colors disappear, but white stands out. If you can also choose fragrant flowers, a white garden by the terrace can make warm summer evenings a deep delight.

Although I have designed them in my head, I have never created a white garden. I am afraid the choices would be too difficult. I am sure that foliage with a lot of yellow in it must be excluded, but would a touch of yellow in the flowers be too much? Sackville-West admitted very pale yellow flowers to her garden. Must I leave out shasta daisies because of their yellow centers and eschew my favorite white iris, because of its yellow heart? If yellow must go, how about pink? Obviously 'Miss Lingard' phlox belongs in the garden, but must my roses be as white as 'Iceberg'? Could I get away with a blush camellia like 'Omega'? Somehow I feel sure that a touch of palest blue would not muddle the color scheme because there is blue in the leaves of the gray foliage plants I am going to use.

When I first thought about it, I was sure a white garden would be effective only in places like Britain, New England, and the Pacific Northwest where the environment gives an impression of lush greenery, and whites and grays are a soothing refreshment. Surely in semi-desert biomes there is too much silver and white about already? But last summer I was stunned by artemisia 'Silver King' in Beth Bowler's western desert garden. The four-foot mound of glittering silver looked like a fairy castle under the afternoon sun. Of course part of its impact may have resulted from the purple coneflowers and gomphrenas that grew nearby, but my faith was shaken.

FLOWER COLORS

The name of Gertrude Jekyll is inextricably associated with any discussion of color in the garden, and if you haven't read her *Colour Schemes in the Flower Garden*, I recommend it. Her American equivalent is Louise Beebe Wilder, whose 1918 book, *Color in My Garden* should be required reading for gardeners in the eastern United States. She grew an amazing selection of plants in her garden at the colder end of Zone 6. Modern editions of both these books illustrated in color are particularly useful to the imagination-impaired.

ATTRACTING BUTTERFLIES

Butterflies come to our plants in search of food, for themselves and their offspring. Many adult butterflies feed on nectar from flowers, using their long tubular probosces, which have surprising sucking power as you know if a moth or butterfly has ever landed on your arm and sucked your sweat (which is attractive because it contains salts).

Nectar contains sugars and amino acids and it is no evolutionary accident that flowers that rely on butterflies for pollination produce nectar. The nectaries in a flower have evolved so that when the butterfly feeds on nectar, it brushes against the plant's stamens so that pollen sticks to its hairy body. When the butterfly moves on to the next plant, some of the pollen brushes off on the second plant's anthers and pollinates it.

The other occasion on which a butterfly approaches a plant is to lay eggs on it. The eggs hatch into caterpillars which eat the plant's leaves. Eventually, the caterpillar will be large enough to turn into a pupa (chrysalis) which may remain on the plant or drop down to the ground while the larva metamorphoses into an adult butterfly.

Butterflies find their food plants by both sight and smell, using chemoreceptors on their legs and probosces to confirm that they are on the right plant. Although butterflies will take nectar from many different flower species, they are much more fussy about the plants where they lay their eggs. The caterpillar has to eat the leaves of this plant and plants produce defensive chemicals that deter insects from eating them and may kill the caterpillars. Caterpillars can survive only when they have the enzymes needed to detoxify the defensive chemicals of the plant they are eating. For instance, caterpillars of the cabbage white butterfly can detoxify the mustard oils that crucifers use for defense, so cabbage whites lay their eggs on any member of the crucifer family—cabbage, broccoli, Brussels sprouts, mustard greens, and their relatives. Many caterpillars feed on grasses, which is another reason not to use pesticides on your lawn and

You have to consider the light in which colors will be viewed. In muted light, in the shady garden or under overcast skies, cool, pastel colors pack much more punch than they do in glaring sunlight. Especially with a beige and gray background of desert colors, flowers can never be too bright. The most virulent purples, scarlets, and yellows are delightful in a gravelly desert garden or a southern border in midsummer, where they might be merely glaring in a New England or English border.

After you have grown a lot of flowers, you tend to think of colors as either saturated or transparent. Sometimes petals are really transparent, or at least translucent, as in the case of many campanulas and anemones. The same color effect comes from plants with many tiny flowers separated by space, such as alyssum, *Eremurus* (foxtail lilies), and Michaelmas daisies. In other cases, the colors seem transparent because they contain a lot of white or pale green, as is the case with hellebores, baptisia, pale pink roses, and dianthus. Saturated colors look more solid and are, I think, more common. They are found in dahlias, coreopsis, chrysanthemums,

to encourage native grasses to take up residence in your wild meadow.

If you just want to see the butterflies and not encourage the caterpillars to eat your plants, plant mainly nectar flowers, such as lantana, butterfly bush (*Buddleia davidii*), impatiens, cosmos, heliotrope, marigold, Swan River daisy (*Brachycome*), asclepias, *Verbena lacianata*, California buckeye (*Aesculus californica*), rabbit brush (*Chrysothamnus*) and dame's rocket (*Hesperis*).

Caterpillar food plants for many species include *Asclepias tuberosa*, cassia, aristolochia, *Passiflora*, pentas, *Carya* (hickory), walnut (*Juglans*), sweetgum (*Liquidambar*), persimmon (*Diospyros*), birch (*Betula*), red and silver maples, spicebush (*Lindera benzoin*), black cherry (*Prunus serotina*), sassafras (*Sassafras albidum*), tulip tree (*Liriodendron tulipifera*), cottonwoods (Salicaceae), and birches. That should keep you busy for a while.

Food plants of rare and endangered butterflies in Britain include violets (*Viola canna, V. odorata*), primroses (*Primula vulgaris*), honeysuckles, Devil's bit scabious (*Succisa pratensis*), plantains (*Plantago maritima, P. lanceolata*), stinging nettles (*Urtica dioica*), ivy (*Hedera helix*), holly (*Ilex aquifolium*), alder (*Frangula lanus*), horseshoe vetch (*Hippocrepis comosa*), clovers (*Trifolium*) and bird's foot trefoil

The large blue, which is on the verge of extinction, feeds on wild thyme (*Thymus drucei*) as a young larva and later on the larvae of *Myrmica* ants. The need to find two larval foods is probably the reason for the demise of this species.

The endangered swallowtail, *Papilio machaon* of the East Coast of Britain feeds, like many American swallowtails, on Umbelliferae, members of the carrot family, in particular on milk parsley (*Peucedanum palustre*), fennel (*Foeniculum vulgare*), wild carrot (*Daucus carota*), and angelica (*Angelica sylvestris*). Another endangered species, the chequered skipper (*Carterocephalus palaemon*), still found in Scotland, needs wood false brome (*Brachypodium sylvaticum*) and other brome species and purple moor grass (*Molinia aeruleas*)

If you are serious about butterflies, your goal will be to provide habitat where rare and endangered species can breed. The first step is to discover your locally endangered species and their food plants (which, in a butterfly book, means the plant the caterpillars eat). Many butterflies are rare or endangered because they are extreme specialists feeding on only one or two species of plants. If the plants become rare, so do the butterflies.

daylilies, peonies, oriental poppies, phlox, and the flowers of many bulbs. Saturated colors tend to overwhelm transparent colors. It seems to be true that delicate colors are best with other delicate colors where they don't face too much color competition.

One of the most difficult parts of composing color schemes in the garden is that things don't flower when you think they will. Deciding on a purple and white cascade down a wall, you plant aubretia and arabis, which then don't flower at the same time next spring. The best solution to this is to compose your pictures by moving things that are already in the garden. You can pick a bunch of one of the flowers you are thinking of moving and stick it alongside the plant you hope it will complement. If it looks good, note the plan in your garden book for execution later.

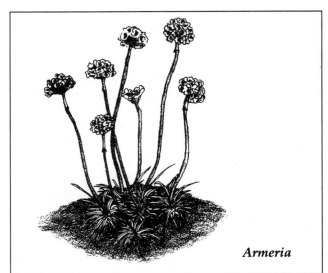

Armeria

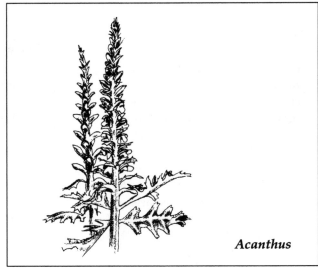

Acanthus

Some More Good Perennials

Botanical name Common name Desirable varieties	Native to Adaptation	Description	Culture
Acanthus spp. Bear breeches	Mediterranean native Zones 8-10	Spires of pea-like flowers tower to 4' above decorative leaves. *A. mollis* has purple or white spiky flowers. *A. perringii* is dwarf, to about 12" with rose flowers.	Long-lived; tolerate light shade in hot areas; propagate by division in autumn; slow from seed.
Aconitum napellus Monkshood	North European native Zones 3-7 or 8	Delphinium-like plants to about 3'. *A. autumnale* blooms in autumn; *A. fischeri* has dark blue flowers.	Sun or part shade; moist soil. Well-suited to the wild garden as they do not like to be moved. Do not need staking despite their height. Propagate by division.
Alchemilla mollis Lady's mantle	European native Zones 3-7	Yellowish decorative foliage and sprays of small chartreuse yellow flowers are a classic edging for paths. *A. alpina* has gray leaves and yellow flowers.	
Anchusa azurea Italian bugloss 'Dropmore'	Mediterranean native Zones 3-8 or 9	To 5' with coarse foliage. Masses of tiny forget-me-not-like blue flowers in early summer. *A. capensis* is dwarf, blooms all summer and tolerates quite a lot of shade.	Needs excellent drainage and sun; drought-tolerant. Short lived.
Amsonia Tabernaemontana Blue star	Southeastern U.S. native Zones 3-8 or 9	To 4' with light blue flowers in early summer over willow-like leaves that turn yellow in autumn. *A. ciliata* is smaller and has darker flowers but is hardy only to Zone 6.	Full sun, well-drained, fairly moist soil.
Armeria maritima Thrift Sea pink	Native to Europe and Asia Zones 3-10 *A. gigantea* : Zone 5 and south	Dwarf plants with grass-like foliage and rather chive-like spherical flowers held well above the foliage.	Adapted to dry sandy soil in full sun. Good varieties propagated by division.

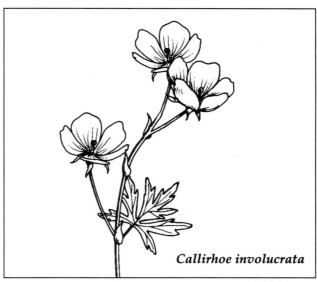

Callirhoe involucrata

Perennials, continued

Artemisia spp. Mugwort Dusty miller Southernwood 'Powis Castle'	N. America and Europe Zones 3-10 for various species	Silver-gray foliage is the main reason to grow artemisias. *A. lactiflora* to 5' has fragrant creamy flowers in tall panicles in late summer. *A. stellerana* is a creeping form widely used in seashore plantings; *A.* 'Silver King' reaches 5'; *A. schmidtiana* is smaller.	Full sun; ordinary soil; drought-resistant. Shear occasionally to keep them tidy. *A. lactiflora* may need staking; dry for winter bouquets.
Aruncus dioicus Goatsbeard	Eastern U.S. native Zones 4 (5?)-7	To 7' and rather weedy with snowy feathery flower spikes; excellent for the wild garden.	Moist soil; shade and lots of water in the South.
Asclepias spp. Milkweed	N. America to Mexico Zones 4-10	To about 3' with aster-like foliage and flattened heads of orange, red, and pink flowers.	Late to get going in spring so it is easy to dig them up by mistake. *A. incarnata* likes boggy soil. The other species are not fussy. Difficult to transplant so best started from seed.
Begonia grandis (also found as *B. evansia*) Hardy begonia	Japanese native Zones 8-10	Very like angel-wing begonia, with bell-like purple and red flowers curving over the purple and green foliage in late summer.	Like most begonias, these do best in shade. Drought-tolerant.
Bellis perennis English daisy Double daisy	European native; naturalized in San Francisco. Zones 5-8	Big pink and white double daisy flowers about 6" tall rise above basal foliage. In cool areas, the plants flower for most of the summer.	Sun or part shade, moisture. Suitable for a rock garden or the edge of a bed. They naturalize in grass if happy; prefer cool summers.
Boltonia asteroides 'Snowbank'	Eastern and central U.S. native Zones 4-9	Boltonias (to 4') look like scruffy asters; most have white flowers. Their main virtue is that they can tolerate more heat than most asters so they are useful in the South.	Not fussy about soil; prefer full sun.
Callirhoe involucrata Buffalo poppy Poppy mallow	Midwestern U.S. Zones 4-9	Large crimson flowers are produced in summer on 8" plants with feathery foliage. There are also varieties with white and pink flowers.	Dry soil, drought-tolerant. Short-lived although they may self-seed. Difficult to transplant, so grow them from seed.

Perennials, continued

Cassia spp.	Most are native to tropical America; *C. marilandica* is hardy to New England	Sennas are really small leguminous trees with yellow pea-like flowers in autumn. They make a pretty accent at the back of a border.	Cassias are said to prefer rich moist soil and sun but my *C. corymbosa* is doing nicely in dry sand and part shade; drought-tolerant. Propagate from fresh seed.
Cerastium tomentosum Snow in summer	Mediterranean native; does well in arid West Zones 4-8	Low-growing; gray foliage, with white flowers in early summer. Suited to underplanting shrubs or edging paths.	Not fussy as to soil; cannot stand much moisture so it may die in an irrigated bed.
Chrysanthemum Parthenium Feverfew	Zones 4-7 or 8	Small, daisy-like white flowers cover upright plants to about 2' tall in midsummer.	Ordinary garden soil; sun.
Chrysanthemum x *superbum* Shasta daisy	Zones 3-9	Large, white daisy-like flowers in early summer.	Easy; ordinary garden soil; sun.
Cimicifuga racemosa Snakeroot	Native to northeastern U.S. west to northern Arizona. Zones 4 -7 or 8	Large plant with ferny leaves; White frothy flowering spikes to 8' in midsummer. *C. simplex* is smaller, blooms later, and is not as hardy.	Lots of moisture and part shade. Difficult to propagate by either seed or division which is why these plants are difficult to find.
Clematis hirsutissima Sugarbowl	Native to western Canada to Wyoming	Not a vine but a herbaceous perennial with nodding bell-like purple/blue flowers in late spring: very gorgeous.	Ordinary garden soil; sun, part shade.
Clematis recta Bush clematis	East Asia Probably Zones 5-8	Another herbaceous clematis with starry white flowers for most of the summer.	Cool loamy, slightly acid soil; seem to do best if shaded in the afternoon, so try them on an east wall or in the shady garden.
Corydalis bulbosa (often listed as *C. solida*) Purple fumewort	European-Asian native Zones 6-8 or 9	Dicentra relative to about 12" with lavender flowers in spring. Other corydalis species have blue or yellow flowers.	Woodland shade. Carefree; do not fertilize.
Corydalis lutea Yellow corydalis	European Zones 5 or 6-8	To about 12"; ferny foliage with yellow flowers in late spring.	Needs good drainage; moderate moisture; happy in woodland soil in part shade.
Dianthus spp. Pinks Carnations	European Hardy to Zone 8; grown as annuals elsewhere	Single and double flowers in shades of white, red, and pink on mat-forming plants.	Rich soil with good drainage and flower best in full sun. Shear back after flowering. Propagate by division or seed.
Dicentra spp. and hybrids Bleeding-heart	Species native throughout Northern Hemisphere Zones 3-8	Arching stems bear heart-shaped drooping flowers in early summer over attractive foliage. *D. eximia* is dwarf with pink flowers. *D. canadensis* is dwarf.	Deep rich moist soil in shade, although they will tolerate morning sunshine in the North.
Filipendula rubra Queen-of-the-prairie	North American Zones 3-7	Pinkish flowers on 5-6' stems in later summer. Spectacular!	Ordinary soil; drought-resistant.

Helenium autumnals

Geum **hybrid**

Geum rivale Water avens	European native Zones 6-8	Reddish, nodding flowers on hairy stems to about 12".	Moist, even soggy, soil. Easy from seed.
Helenium autumnale Sneezeweed 'Butterpat', 'Crimson Beauty', 'Riverton Gem'	Native to much of N. America Zones 3 to 9	Late summer, yellow, mahogany, and gold daisy-like flowers; excellent fall flower for the Deep South.	Prefers moist soil, but tolerates dry.
Heuchera sanguinea and hybrids Coral bells	Arid western U.S. Zones 4-7 or 8	Red and pink bell-like flowers to 12".	Drought-tolerant.
Kosteletzkya virginica Seashore mallow	Eastern U.S. native Zones 6-10	Large pyramidal plant to 5' tall by 4' across with maple-shaped leaves. Profusion of bright pink flowers like single roses in late summer or autumn.	Native to brackish and freshwater marshes but drought resistant when established. Easy from seed. Doesn't like to be moved.
Lavandula spp. Lavender	Mediterranean native. Does well in arid western U.S. Zones 4-7 or 8	Gray, scented foliage with long-lasting lavender flowers in midsummer. Eventually forms a shrubby plant up to 18" in diameter.	Dry sandy soil is ideal, but lavender is not very fussy. Some varieties cannot tolerate Deep South humidity. Shear in spring to make the plant more bushy.
Ligularia spp. Senecio Golden-ray	Asian native Zones 7-10	To 5' with yellow, daisy-like flowers, often in spires, and good foliage. *Ligularia tussilaginea* 'Aureo-maculata' and 'Argentea' have variegated leaves.	Damp; even standing water.
Malva spp. Mallow	Species native to Europe and N. America Zones 3-10, depending on species	Flowers like single roses in pastel shades. *M.Alcea fastigiata* is a big mallow with tall lilac flowers in summer.	Partial shade in South; sun in North.

Paeonia brownii Wild peony	N. America Zones 4-7	Unusual green/yellow and pink flowers above grayish divided foliage.	Ordinary soil.
Pedicularis groenlandica Elephanthead	Labrador to British Columbia, New Mexico Zones 3-8	Tall peduncles of dark pink flowers in midsummer.	Moist soil.
Phacelia hastata Scorpionweed	Western N. America Zones 5-9	Pinkish, rather azalea-like flowers over grayish leaves in early summer.	Dry soil.
Phlox divaricata Blue phlox	Eastern N. America Zones 4-9	Low, plant with notched blue flowers in spring. *Laphammi* is a subspecies with larger bluish flowers without the notch.	Shade, woodland soil, acid may make flowers bluer; 'Chatahoochee' has a maroon eye and is long-flowering in full sun, sandy soil.
Rodgersia	Europe and Asia Zones 5-8	Huge leaves to 5'; tall panicles of creamy flowers.	Damp.
Salvia coccinea Texas sage	Native to Texas and Plains Zones 5-10	Delicate clear red flowers on a shrubby plant for most of the summer.	Very tolerant, although it prefers moist soil. Flowers first year from seed: easy.
Salvia greggii Autumn sage	Native to Texas and Mexico Zones 7-10	To 3' with scarlet or lavender flowers in autumn.	Flowers first year from seed: easy.
Sedum hybrids and cultivars	Asian Zones 3-7 or 8	'Autumn Joy' has maroon flowers and gray leaves; good seed heads. 'Honeysong' is *S. maximum atropurpureum*.	Drought-resistant; ordinary soil.
Solidago Goldenrod	North American Zones 3-10	Gold-yelllow flowers in later summer. Most are tall; 'Cloth of Gold' is only about 8" high.	Happy in terrible soil; drought resistant.
Stokesia laevis (also *S. cyanea*) Stoke's aster 'Alba', 'Blue Danube'	Eastern N. America Zones 5-9	Blue fluffy flowers for much of the summer; rather untidy.	Tolerates shade, though flowers better in sun.
Lupinus texensis Texas Bluebonnet	Texas native and state flower. Popular roadside flower.	A lupine with lovely clear blue flowers.	Sow seeds in fall. Soak in warm water for 3 days, changing water every day or put seed in freezer 24 hours before planting.
Thalictrum spp. Meadow rue	Species native to much of the Northern Hemisphere. Zones 5-8	*T. rochebrunianum* grows to 6' with ferny foliage and fluffy pink/lavender flowers in midsummer; *T. kiusianum* is dwarf to 9"	Prefer moist soil and sun or part shade.
Viola beckwithii Violet	Western N. American native	A violet with charming white, burgundy and red flowers.	Desert conditions.

CHAPTER 9

Bulbs, Corms, Tubers, and Rhizomes

The average garden contains dozens of trees, shrubs, and annuals, but rather few of the large group of plants covered in this chapter—perennials that store food in underground structures that botanists call bulbs, corms, rhizomes, or tubers. Many of these are among the easiest of plants and some of them produce what, to my eye, are the loveliest flowers in the plant kingdom.

Most of these plants are monocots, members of the large class of flowering plants with flower parts in threes and only one seed leaf. Grasses are also monocots and so are orchids, which make up the largest plant family of all. Monocots can usually be distinguished by their elongated leaves with parallel veins, which provide interesting vertical notes in the garden. In fact lots of monocots, like grasses, bamboos, yuccas, and papyrus, are grown almost exclusively for their dramatic foliage.

MONOCOT ADAPTATIONS
Unlike dicots, which make up the majority of flowering plants, monocots never evolved the ability to make true wood. Palms are the only real monocot trees. If you were to dig up a palm tree, you would find that the root system consists mainly of a large bulb, which doesn't look nearly big enough to supply a tree with water and nutrients. The existence of this storage organ is the reason landscapers can treat palms in a cavalier fashion, sometimes leaving them by the roadside with their roots exposed to air, treatment that would kill any self-respecting dicot—and indeed sometimes kills the palms.

Waterlilies are the dicots most similar to monocots, so botanists speculate that monocots and waterlilies evolved from a common ancestor, some 100 million years ago. This ancestry probably explains why so many monocots are happiest when they are in or near water and is why ponds and bogs are in this chapter. I was amazed to discover that daffodils, which I think of as hillside-bred, were happy in a bed that was waterlogged for months every spring. Of course many modern monocots are perfectly happy on dry land. Most of the popular spring bulbs, such as daffodils, tulips, and crocuses originated in the

Daffodils

mountains of southern Europe, North Africa, the Middle East and the Himalayas where they usually get plenty of rain during the bulbs' growing season, but survive dry summers by losing their leaves and becoming dormant.

Perhaps monocots are underused in the garden because many look so terrible when you acquire them. Mary Helen Ray gave me a long-coveted division of her queen lily (*Curcuma petiolata*) the other day—a bundle of long, dying leaves with a rhizome like a misshapen potato at the end. It stretches the imagination to envision the clump of tropical-looking foliage with rosy pink flowers that this rhizome will produce in about six months.

Storing food in an underground organ permits a plant to survive from one year to the next, so all the plants in this chapter are perennial by nature and are often planted in the perennial border. Indeed I sometimes wonder why gardeners usually think of them separately from dicot perennials. Maybe the only reason is that they are usually offered for sale in autumn and not in spring!

Because of its stored food, a bulb will survive, and usually flower once, in an area to which it is poorly adapted. This amounts to treating the bulb as an annual. Southerners often plant bulbs that will not survive hot southern summers for the show they will produce the first spring after they are planted. In February, when little else is stirring in the garden, tulips, anemones, and hyacinths are blooming cheerfully in the rain outside my front door. Only the hyacinths will return next year, but I think the modest sum I spent for the bulbs last fall well spent (although the two months the tulips spent in the refrigerator as a substitute for cold weather rather disrupted the domestic economy).

CHOOSING BULBS FOR YOUR AREA

When they think of bulbs, most people think immediately of the spring bulbs grown in the Netherlands, the snowdrops, daffodils, crocuses, and tulips that herald spring after a cold winter. And indeed it is a sadness to live in an area where these traditional favorites do not do well. But it is more satisfying to search out the bulbs that do well in your area than to plant sad imitations of the flower displays of other climates. Don't forget your natives, or species that are so well naturalized they seem native: bluebells and snowdrops in parts of Britain and various species of wild onion, trillium, iris, and fritillary in most parts of the United States.

Here is a short list of bulbs that do so well in particular areas that they will act as perennials and not need to be replanted each year. I have not included daylilies in the regional lists since they do well in most areas.

Pacific Northwest and Britain

All the Dutch bulbs do well in this mild, damp climate. For spring bloom: daffodil, tulip, hyacinth, crocus, grape hyacinth, snowdrop, winter aconite, scillas, ranunculus, anemones, native starflowers, crown imperial, Dutch iris, and dogtooth violets (including the Oregon natives, *Erythronium oregonum* and *E. montanum*). Snowdrops and daffodils will naturalize. Crown imperial will give you a dramatic touch if you can find a corner where the two or three foot stems will not be knocked over by spring winds.

Summer flower may be had from many iris, foxtail lilies *(Eremurus)*, most true lilies *(Lilium)*, dahlias, red hot poker *(Kniphofia)* and cammasses *(Cammassia)*.

Chionodoxa, **Glory of the snow**

Coastal California, Desert Idaho, Washington, and Nevada (Dry part of Zones 5-9)

The Dutch spring bulbs listed above do well in these areas where they get winter rain and cool temperatures, and the summer is not humid. For the woodland garden, *Erythronium californicum, E. tuolumnense, E. revolutum,* and *E. citrinum* are lovely natives.

Coastal natives for summer bloom include species of *Calochortus* and fairy bells *(Disporum Smithii)*. Don't omit the Pacific hybrid irises, among the most attractive of their genus, and, in southern California, *Hymenocallis latifolia*. Bearded irises like the desert, with a little rain in spring and dry conditions during their summer dormant period. Cyclamen are Mediterranean natives and most hardy species are happy near the coast.

Rocky Mountains and Plains (Western third of Zones 3-5)

Spring favorites are squill, crocus, grape hyacinth, glory-of-the-snow, winter aconite, kaufmanniana and clusiana tulips, followed by daffodils and the hybrid tulips. For the woodland garden, try avalanche lily *(Erythronium grandiflorum)*, which is difficult to grow at lower elevations. In moist areas, try buttercups, Siberian iris, and Mariposa lilies.

For summer bloom, bearded iris will do well in most areas, and native *Iris missouriensis* appreciates damp shade. Natives for sun include *Allium drummondii, Anemone patens,* sand lily *(Leucocrinum montanum)*, and prairie lily *(Lilium philadelphicum)*.

Ranunculus

Great Lakes (Damper parts of Zones 3-5)

The year starts with species crocuses, winter aconite, glory-of-the-snow, species tulips, *Iris cristata*, and miniature daffodils. It is generally too cold for snowdrops and hyacinths, but many tulips and daffodils will settle in happily even in northern Ontario. So too will native white dogtooth violet *(Erythronium albidum)* or *E. americanum*, lovely with trilliums, showy lady's slipper *(Cypripedium reginae)*, and *Phlox divaricata* in the woodland garden. Red Darwin

Gladiolus

tulips underplanted with white anemones are a lovely, if trite, combination, but mulch the anemones well for winter if you hope to have them return. Crown imperial does well in sandy soil as far north as mid-Michigan, but it needs protection from wind.

Bearded iris are the obvious summer choice. I would also include *Kniphofia*, dahlias, Siberian iris, and hybrid lilies, as well as native *Lilium canadense* and tiger lily (*L. tigrinum*).

Middle Atlantic (Eastern part of Zones 6 and 7)

This may be the best place in the world to grow bulbs since the northern European species do well and many Mediterranean and Central American bulbs will also survive the winter.

Crocus and daffodils are most at home in Zone 6, where your rough meadow should be "a crowd, a host, of golden daffodils," not to mention white and pink daffodils, crocuses, snowdrops, ornithogallum, dogtooth violets, and winter aconites. Anemones flourish here so you can use them to underplant bulbs. And don't forget Japanese anemone (*Anemone huphensis*), with colchicums and autumn crocuses for a delicate autumn display.

Just about all the irises will grow for you. In dry parts of the garden or sandy soil, German bearded iris will be spectacular. Alliums, gladiolus, and cannas will enjoy the same conditions, as will huge foxtail lilies and tiny blackberry lilies (*Belamcanda*).

In damper areas (even in partial shade), native lilies and most hybrid lilies will flourish, as will natives such as *Iris virginica, I. verna*, and *Canna flaccida*.

Dry Southwest

South African natives do well here. For spring bloom, try oxalis, starflowers, amaryllis, Dutch iris, freesia, and ixia; in partial shade, baboon flower, and harlequin flower (*Sparaxis*). Ordinary grape hyacinths cannot stand the heat, but try the starch hyacinth (*Muscari racemosum*), which has naturalized in parts of Texas.

In summer, crinums come in a wide variety of species and hybrids. Lily of the Nile (*Agapanthus*) likes dry soil and may like your garden, although it is prone to die of unknown causes. Cannas, montbretia (*Crocosmia*), and gladiolus will also do well.

Try 'cemetery white' iris (*Iris* x *albicans*), spuria irises (which like alkaline soil) and Italian iris (*Iris kochii*). Lilies that can stand the heat of summer include some Aurelian hybrids, Madonna lily (*Lilium candidum*), and tiger lily (*L. tigrinum*).

For autumn bloom, experiment with members of the exotic ginger family, cyclamens, and *Lycoris*.

Humid Gulf Coast and Deep South (Zones 8-10)

Gladden the spring garden with amaryllis (*Hippeastrum*), Dutch iris, starflowers, Easter lilies, and snowflakes. A few of the tazetta narcissus do well. Try 'Fortune' and paperwhites, which flower in December or even late November if they settle in. Freesias, agapanthus, *Alstroemeria*, and ixia may may do well for you, although I have found them all a bit temperamental. Where summers are humid and soil damp, Louisiana iris, Siberian iris, yellow flag (*Iris pseudacorus*), summer snowflake (*Leucojum aestivum*) elephant ears, caladiums, and callas (*Zantedeschia aethiopica*) will flourish in damp soil. In dry shade, try hardy cyclamen.

Most ordinary perennials and annuals flourish in spring and autumn, but fade in the heat of summer. This is when the summer bulbs come into their own, reviving the spirits with glamorous flowers just when the flower bed and its owner are feeling most wilted. For summer bloom, cannas, *Pancratium*, *Habranthus*, *Zephyranthes*, *Lycoris*, crinums, Aurelian hybrid lilies, *Crocosmia*, *Lilium speciosum*, tuberoses, blackberry lily. For flowers late in the season, try the schoolhouse lily (*Hippeastrum bifidum*), many of the gingers, and spider lilies (*Lycoris*).

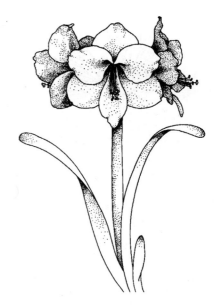

Amaryllis, *Hippeastrum*

PLANTING AND CARING FOR BULBS

It is rarely worth buying cut-price bulbs, unless you plan to treat them as annuals when a bargain bundle is often a good buy. Even if you look at them before you buy, it is difficult to tell whether a bulb has been incorrectly stored or has internal damage. You avoid disappointment by buying from a reputable supply house whose bulbs will be in good condition and produce satisfying results.

It is important to plant bulbs and many rhizomes at the correct depth. There is usually no difficulty about this because the information will come with any bulb you purchase. If you are given plants, the general rule is to plant about three times as deep as the bulb is high. This means digging a hole six inches deep for a two-inch bulb. There are exceptions to this rule, however. Bearded iris and amaryllis should be planted so that they protrude slightly above the surface. Cannas and callas don't much care about depth. I plant cannas rather deep to give the long stem some support. Tulips too seem to do better when planted rather deeper than usual.

The traditional recipe for fertilizing bulbs is to sprinkle bone meal in the planting hole. But modern bone meal, produced by sterilizing bones before grinding them, produces a much less nutritious fertilizer than the ground up bones our ancestors used. Modern bone meal is considered little use as a bulb fertilizer. Instead, prepare the soil by digging in a large quantity of compost, leaf mold, or composted manure. If you are still not sure the soil is rich enough, you could add some of the specially formulated bulb fertilizer sold by garden centers and bulb companies. Most bulbs like soil with a slightly acid pH of between 6 and 7, so add lime if your soil is very acid.

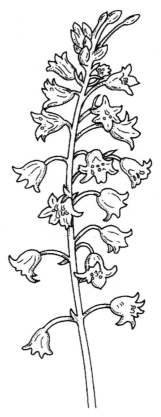

Scilla

Dahlia hybrid

An obvious problem is how to fertilize bulbs in the years after you planted them. I usually fertilize when the leaves are visible. Even if the experts are right and this does not do much good, I feel it must be better than never fertilizing at all. Even species that normally do not need fertilizer will be the better for it if they are planted so as to naturalize in grass. Grass competes heavily with plants for nutrients and you don't want your precious bulbs to lose the competition.

When leaves and flowers are growing, the plants need as much light and water as possible for photosynthesis. This means leaving most of the foliage when you cut flowers for the house and not knotting daffodil leaves in an attempt to tidy them.

Winter Storage

Bulbs often grow best where they are not hardy. In the North, cannas, gladiolus, and dahlias produce fine displays but must be dug up, dried, and stored indoors in a cool place over the winter. When stored bulbs up and die, it is usually because the environment is not cool enough. Nearly all bulbs will stand a little frost, so an unheated garage is usually a better place for them than the spare bedroom. Net bags or old stockings that you can hang from hooks are useful for holding the bulbs because they permit air circulation. I recycle those net bags potatoes come in.

An old wives' trick that seems to increase the survival of stored bulbs is to store bulbs and rhizomes upside down. Botanists suggest that this helps growth hormone to move toward the growing tip.

Propagating Bulbous Plants

Bulbs that have performed well but eventually stop flowering may be signalling that they need to be divided. Sisyrinchium and irises, for example, seem to need dividing every few years to keep them flowering.

It is obvious when amaryllis and daffodils have produced babies: you can see the infant bulb and its leaves. Dahlias, daylilies, and iris rhizomes, however, just form bigger and bigger clumps each year and it is not as obvious how they should be divided. Each bulbous division of a daylily root will eventually form a flowering plant, but the general rule is that the larger the root clump, the bigger the plant next year, so do not divide the roots into really small pieces. The same goes for things like ginger lilies and cannas. Chop the rhizomes only into about six-inch pieces when dividing them.

Many bulbs are easy from seed, and the seed companies add new species to the list every year. Some bulbs take years, but others flower within a few months. Try some of the new cannas, such as 'Tropical Rose' (a dwarf, at about 30 inches high), that flower within four months from seed. Every spring, the ground beneath my sassafras tree is bright with Asian *Lilium formosanum*, that I raised from seed. I take much more pride in this tough little clump (a sassafras is all roots and suckers) than in the hybrid lilies that I bought as bulbs.

Blackberry lilies (*Belamcanda)* are easy from seed and may even sow themselves, as may gladiolus and amaryllis. We have a feral gladiolus that has become something of a weed around the place. It has ugly yellow and rust flowers, but I nevertheless feel guilty as I weed out the vast crop of seedlings from the bed where I thought I'd eradicated it. Who am I to make war on this determined little plant? I am happy to see that it now seems to have spread itself to the woodland garden, where it looks incongruously formal but can stay.

After many false starts with plants and corms, I have also decided that the only way I seem able to grow hardy cyclamen is to start them from seed. Cyclamen take forever to germinate and rodents find the corms and leaves delicious so you have to be dedicated or nuts to take this route, but if you are in love with cyclamen, what else can you do? Try and find a local nursery (Montrose is mine) where the owners have experimented to find where cyclamen grow best in your area and whose plants and seed will be fresh, fresh, fresh.

Winter aconites are another favorite that I find difficult to get started. The corms you buy always seem dried out and seldom grow. The very best way to acquire them, as well as cyclamen and lily-of-the-valley, is to beg part of a clump from a friend who has a healthy planting. Use a large spade, disturb the roots as little as possible, and plant in a similar area of your garden at high speed. With a bit of luck and a lot of water, you will soon have a spreading clump.

Some of the bulbs you treat as annuals may also be easy from seed and this is much cheaper than buying bulbs. Most years I grow miniature dahlias from seed planted in December or January. They flower in spring and die of heat stroke in June, but the spring display is spectacular and they are as easy as marigolds. I am especially fond of the 'Rigoletto' series. Another genus that is easy is the ginger lilies (*Hedychium*). These beautiful, fragrant monsters positively pop up from seed and seem to tolerate any sort of abuse as long as they get plenty of moisture.

Seed is an excellent way to get started with protected or endangered native bulbs. It is a shame to install a precious rare plant in your garden if you don't know if or where it will grow well. Better by far to obtain seed from a reputable nursery that produces its own seed so that you will have a number of seedlings to try out in shady, sunny, dry, and moist parts of the garden. There's no telling where a plant may prove happy. The plant your garden book says needs

Blackberry lily, *Belamcanda*

Iris missouriensis.
Native iris will naturalize for you
only if you can give them
precisely the conditions they
need.

damp shade may prefer dry sun in your garden. There's usually a reason for these divergences from form, even if you can't always figure out what it is. One winter I feared I had lost my precious callas (*Zantedeschia aethiopica*) to a hard freeze. Not until the following fall did they leaf out again. (Luckily I'm no obsessive weeder, or I'd doubtless have winkled them out during the summer.) Then I wondered if perhaps it was dry weather rather than cold that had killed the foliage so I moved them to my soggy bed, planted them a little deeper for luck and they survived 18 °F for several days the following winter without a sign of damage. The moral is that you never know, and plenty of seedlings is an excellent way to find out.

Forcing Bulbs
Nothing cheers a January day like a bowl of white hyacinths or paperwhite narcissus enlivening a dark corner of the house with light and fragrance. However I almost gave up growing bulbs for the house because I had such difficulty getting all the bulbs in a bowl to flower at once. There is nothing at all attractive about two hyacinths finally lumbering into flower after the other four in the bowl have gone over. When you think of the time and money you have expended to produce this disappointment it is enough to make you weep.

It turns out that there are solutions to this, as to most gardening problems. One is to plant only one bulb. This might be a hyacinth in a specially designed hyacinth glass or a single crocus in a Delft windmill, or a single paperwhite in the shoe that remained when the dog ate the other one. The other solution is to force the bulbs in some ordinary plant pot and transplant them before putting them on display. Depending on how they developed, a dozen hyacinths might give you two bowls of six or four bowls of three for the house, but each bowl would contain bulbs with perfectly synchronized flowers.

Bulbs need special treatment to burst into flower in the house in midwinter, long before their natural flowering season. You can treat the bulbs yourself, but these technological days you can also buy bulbs already treated that only need to be potted up and given light and water to flower in winter.

USING BULBS IN THE GARDEN
One difficulty with placing bulbs in the garden is how to disguise the moth-eaten foliage that usually remains when the flowers have gone and that always gets much taller than you expect. One solution is to place bulbs some distance from the house, where they will simple be overlooked after they have flowered. Bulbs combine well with shrubs that flower at the same time—white hyacinths or bluebells under a dogwood, daffodils in front of white azaleas. That part

of the garden is a focal point when bulbs and shrubs are in flower, but inconspicuous later in the year. I achieved a symphony in pink by lining a (very short) driveway with flowering almond (*Prunus triloba*) and pink lily-flowered tulips. To my amazement, they flowered at the same time and the purply pink of the tulips was spectacular with the whitish pink of the flowering almond. Equally to my amazement, the tulips decided to settle in, and the picture was repeated year after year until the family built a woodpile over two of the almonds and the others shaded out their tulips. Such triumphs are rare and never to be forgotten!

A second solution is to place bulbs in beds that you plant with annuals every spring. Even if the annuals are not particularly large by the time the bulbs stop flowering, their flowers, not the dying bulb foliage, will be the obvious feature of the bed.

The only really satisfactory place for bulbous plants that love water is a bog garden. I say this with feeling, having tried vainly to imitate Mary Stoller's summer display of *Colocasia antiquorum esculenta*. (The usual common name is elephant ears, but I prefer to think of it as dasheen or taro, the stuff of delicious dishes indigenous to romantic, tropical places.) *Then* she tells me hers are in standing water most of the time and no wonder they don't like life on my sand dune. Perhaps taro is too big for this idea, but people have kept water-lovers happy even in dry gardens in mini-bogs created by burying an old sink, bucket, paddling pool, or similar container in the ground. It is worth considering, if you are not yet ready to embark on artificial pool and bog gardens.

NATURALIZING BULBS

Where they are well adapted, dozens of bulbs and rhizomes will naturalize in the garden, multiplying each year to give you a finer and finer show. When trying out a bulb that is new to me, I usually put it in the perennial border near the house, where I keep an eye on it and occasionally weed, rather than in the rough meadow or woodland garden where plants have to fend for themselves. If the plant is happy, it is ready to be moved out to a wild area where conditions are similar and, with any luck, becomes a permanent part of the garden. Of course my "perennial" border gives tidy gardeners nervous breakdowns because it is always full of a jumble of plants on trial, but that's the way it goes.

One group of plants that is moving in the opposite direction is the hippeastrums, crinums, and similar large bulbs. These are naturalized hereabouts and I obtained most of my Brand X varieties from neighbors who were grubbing them out. I planted them initially at the edge of woodland, in shrub borders, and anywhere they would get a little sun. But they look wrong. The formal, waxy flowers look incongruous in an informal area or under a tree and by midsummer the foliage is so untidy it looks as if the plant is dying. I can think of

UNDERSTANDING THE ENVIRONMENT FRAGRANT FLOWERS

Butterfly ginger is probably pollinated by a moth or similar insect in its native habitat. (I am not suggesting nobody knows, but I don't). This seems the most likely reason for its powerful fragrance, which is strongest after dark. Moths fly mainly at night, an adaptation that permits them to avoid competing with their close relatives, the butterflies, which fly during the day. The excellent eyesight of a butterfly is little use at night so moths use their sense of smell for things, like finding mates, where butterflies would use their eyes. Moths have amazingly sensitive olfactory organs, and can undoubtedly smell a ginger lily from, literally, miles away. The same reasoning applies to night blooming cereus (*Epiphyllum* spp.) which opens huge highly-scented flowers for just one night.

no solution except to put them in a bed among perennials with boisterous foliage that stays attractive all summer. The crinum foliage will be somewhat hidden and the formal flowers will help out the "all daisy" look of the midsummer border.

FLOWERS FOR SPRING

In upstate New York, the first flowers of the year were always species crocuses poking from a snowdrift near a heating vent on the Cornell campus in the middle of February. These dainty yellow and blue cups appeared before the winter aconites, before the snowdrops, and many weeks before the larger hybrid crocuses. In this list, I have divided bulbs into those that flower in spring, summer, and autumn. This is a trifle arbitrary because things bloom at different times in different areas and many genera contain species that bloom both early and late. We usually think of irises as flowers of early summer and this is where I have listed them, but a few species are among the earliest flowers of spring.

Anemone

E.g. *Anemone apennina* (Apennine anemone, Zones 5-8), *A. blanda* (Greek anemone, Zones 5-8), *A. coronaria* (poppy-flowered anemone, Zones 7-10), *A. sylvestris*.

Red, blue, and white-flowered anemones with their fern-like foliage are among the best bulbs to plant in clumps beneath deciduous trees. Where they are not hardy, they are often treated as annuals. They may also be dug in late summer for winter storage and replanted in very early spring. *A. coronaria* comes from the Middle East and is probably the biblical "lily of the field." Not surprisingly, it likes well-drained sandy soil and dry summers and does best in the western United States.

Brodiaea (Starflower)

The genus *Brodiaea*, sometimes sold as *Triteleia* or *Ipheion*, is native to the western United States, and contains several species that are lovely in the garden. Clusters of starry blue, red, yellow, or white flowers are borne on stalks up to 18 inches long, surrounded by delicate grass-like foliage. Most are hardy from Zones 5 to 10 and prefer full sun and excellent drainage. Left undisturbed, they will often form large clumps. Because they are not very large, they look best planted in groups of a dozen or more.

Chionodoxa (Glory-of-the-snow)

E.g., *Chionodoxa gigantea*, *C. luciliae*, and *C. sardensis*.

Chionodoxas are Asian natives which are happy in Zones 3-10, blooming shortly after the first crocuses. The plants reach only about nine inches and the blue and white flowers are small and starry. They look lovely in masses under deciduous trees or on

Anemone coronaria

banks. This is one bulb that doesn't need fertilizer and often sows its own seeds. Although they really prefer cooler areas, you sometimes see them naturalized in lawns in the Deep South.

Crocus

Crocuses are native to southern Europe and Asia, with species that flower in earliest spring and latest autumn. Best known are the Dutch hybrids, largest of the group, with bell-shaped flowers on stalks up to about 6 inches tall, and available in a wide range of colors from white to yellow and purple with many bicolored varieties. The species crocuses are smaller, with shorter stems. Crocuses do best from Zones 3 to 6 where the earliest spring flowers will often be *C. biflorus*, *C. chrysanthus*, *C. susianus* (my own favorite), *C. imperatii*, or *C. sieberii* planted in sunshine in the warmest microclimate in the garden. The hybrids flower later and the crocus season can be extended by planting some of these in partial shade. Crocuses will multiply rapidly into large clumps if you give them rich soil. Crocuses are traditionally planted to naturalize in grass but they also look well in the border, planted in clumps near the front where perennials will later hide the foliage.

Autumn flowering species include *Crocus cancellatus*, *C. medius*, *C. speciosus*, and *C. zonatus*. Grow these like the spring-flowering crocuses. I prefer to plant them under deciduous shrubs or elsewhere away from the border where their foliage is not as liable to be shaded by chrysanthemums and other autumn perennials for which I have, as usual, not allowed enough room.

Species crocuses

Eranthis (Aconite)

The common winter aconite is *Eranthis hyemalis*, which vies with snowdrops and species crocuses to produce the first flowers of spring. Each short stem bears a small globe-shaped golden flower above a ruff of leaves. The first sign of spring on our hillside in upstate New York was always a glowing patch of yellow where winter aconites had escaped from the border beside the house and spread into the lawn. (They are so short that they will naturalize even in a mowed lawn.) Winter aconites are hardy from Zones 3 to 8 but it is my experience that they are next-to-impossible to start from bulbs purchased even from a reputable supply house. They can be started from seed (taking 2 or 3 years to flower) or better still by begging a clump from someone who has lots of them.

Erythronium (Dogtooth violet, trout lily)

Erythronium is an almost entirely North American genus with many species adapted to deciduous forests, where they flower before the trees leaf out in spring. Obviously, they do best in light shade in the woodland garden. They are often called trout lilies because of the brown speckles on their leaves. The one European species common

Freesia
Freesias are known for their fragrance but I have two clumps of hybrid freesias that smell vaguely of pepper—and nothing else, so you cannot count on fragrance from modern hybrids.

in cultivation is the dogtooth violet, *E. dens-canis.* Trout lilies grow to about eight inches tall with dainty spreading bell-like flowers that hang their heads. Start with species native to your part of the world and beware of wild-collected plants, because trout lilies are vanishing from their native habitats.

Erythronium bulbs die rapidly if they dry out so the surest way to acquire plants is to buy seeds or container-grown plants or to beg a clump from a friend.

Freesia
Several species of this popular cut flower are hardy in Zones 8-10. Even there they are difficult to establish in the garden and, like ornithogallum, irritatingly erratic, so that your Texas neighbor may have large clumps of these delicate beauties while you struggle in vain. I do not know the secret, except that they are supposed to like lots of sun and very fertile soil. In recent years, the Dutch bulb industry has started selling freesias treated so that they flower in summer. Where summer evenings are cool, you can plant the bulbs in spring for summer flower and then pot them up in autumn for winter blooms indoors. I have never attempted this, but it sounds well worth a try because the heavily scented flowers are wonderful indoors.

Fritillaria (Fritillaries)
Fritillaria imperialis (crown imperial, Zones 4-8), *F. lanceolata* (riceroot fritillary), and *F. meleagris* (checkered fritillary, Zones 2-8 or 9) are widely grown. The three foot stems of crown imperial pop up in very early spring. With its crown of leaves overhanging bell-shaped red and orange flowers, crown imperial has a stately appearance that makes it the cool-climate equivalent of hippeastrum, which is equally stiff and incongruous in a spring garden full of chionodoxa. Crown imperial does well in sandy soil as far north as mid-Michigan and Minnesota, but it needs protection from wind.

Galanthus (Snowdrop)
The hanging white heads of *Galanthus nivalis* (snowdrop) and *G. elwesii* (giant snowdrop) appear early in spring in Zones 3 to 7 or 8. They grow best in light shade where summers are not too hot and they do not need to be fertilized. Where they are happy, they will self-seed freely and form large clumps over the years.

Hippeastrum (Amaryllis)
Hippeastrum hybrids are hardy in Zones 8-10. Even further north, they are relatively easy to grow by a mixture of indoor and outdoor culture. They produce tall stalks, each with two or three spectacular lily-like flowers that last for up to 2 weeks in a cool spring. You can extend the season by planting some in the sun and some in shade, where they will flower later. Amaryllis don't seem to mind drought,

but the flowers will be fewer and smaller each year unless you feed them during the summer when the leaves are storing food. You can tell how you are doing by the size of the bulb, which is planted so it is partly above the surface. If your compost is going where it will do most good, the bulb will reach humungous size by the end of summer and probably produce offsets. You can be sure such a mother bulb will produce a fine display the following spring and the offset may flower the following year. Amaryllis produce seeds freely so it is fun to grow your own hybrids as Simone Van Stolk does, developing flower types and colors that are not commercially available. The seedlings take three or four years to reach flowering size. Various smaller hippeastrum species produce attractive spots of color later in the year.

Hyacinthus (Hyacinth)

There are several species of hyacinth which will probably naturalize in your garden, although we tend to think of these fragrant flowers as the stiff stars of bedding displays. The large-flowered hyacinth usually used for this purpose is *Hyacinthus orientalis* which, however, will often naturalize if given the chance, coming back with smaller flowers in following years.

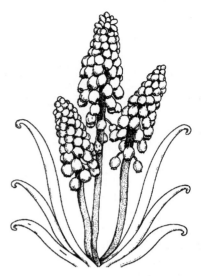

Muscari, **grape hyacinth**

Ixia (Corn lilies)

Ixia hybrids are among the loveliest spring bulbs for the dry garden in Zones 7-10 of the western states. The bulbs need dry soil to mature in summer so they will not naturalize in areas with summer rain (or irrigation). Corn lilies look a bit like freesias, with many starry flowers in all colors borne on tall, wiry stems. The stiff stems make them perfect cut flowers and they last for ages in the house, making a fine show when mixed with Dutch irises. Fertilize them in fall and late winter. If they naturalize for you, you will get years of pleasure from them.

Muscari (Grape hyacinth)

Muscari botryoides (common grape hyacinth), *M. armeniacum* (Armenian grape hyacinth) and several other species are the odd-looking miniatures with flowers like upright clusters of blue grapes. They do best from Zones 2 to 8, although the starch hyacinth *(M. racemosum)* has naturalized in parts of Texas. The foliage tends to get horribly messy in warmer areas and detracts from the flowers. Grape hyacinths add a useful note of blue to the early spring garden. (There are also white cultivars.) The look good in masses combined with the yellow flowers of early daffodils in the rough meadow and will often naturalize and spread by self-seeding. They are also appealing in the rock garden where the flowers can be admired in closeup—although why I say "admired" I don't know

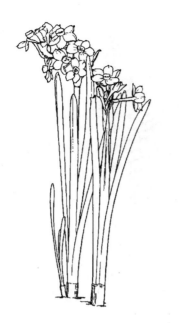

Narcissus come in all shapes and sizes and some are better adapted to some parts of the country than others, so it pays to experiment.

because I don't think much of the flowers; it's their color that makes grape hyacinths worth growing.

Narcissus (Daffodils, narcissus, and jonquils)

Narcissus species, hybrids, and cultivars are an essential part of the spring garden, at least where winters are reasonably cold, said she with a sigh. Most are hardy from Zones 4 to 10, but only a few are worth growing in states south of Zone 7 if you have ever experienced the glory of naturalized daffodils further north or in Europe.

There are dozens of groups of narcissus. If you get hooked, join the Narcissus Society and learn all about them. The shows of new varieties each year are something to behold. But if you are merely an ordinary gardener, choose anything you like the look of from the catalogue and plunge in. In my experience, the early varieties and species, such as 'February Gold' and 'February Silver' are the most difficult to establish. This may be because I tend to forget where they are and dig them up. Many of the early types are miniatures so you cannot just naturalize them in the rough meadow. They need to be in the rock garden or somewhere that they won't get lost.

If your soil is reasonably heavy and fertile, daffodils will not need fertilizer, but if it is very sandy, annual fertilizer will keep the flowers big and beautiful and keep the plants multiplying.

Tulipa (Tulip)

The best known tulips are the Darwin, cottage, Mendel, and lily-flowered tulips which open large cups in a wide range of colors in late spring. However, with a bit of ingenuity you could have tulips in flower for four months or more by planting different species and cultivars. Among the earliest, are *Tulipa kaufmannia* and *T. fosteriana*. The species tulips mostly have fairly small flowers and are particularly at home in the rock garden because tulips do best where the bulbs get a chance to dry out in summer. When they get this, they will naturalize from Zones 3-7 and occasionally a little further south where the large-flowered kinds do not get enough cold in winter to naturalize.

The large-flowered tulips tend to produce smaller flowers after the first year, since they seldom get the care in a garden that they get in the bulb fields of Holland. As a result, there is a lot to be said for buying new tulips every year and moving them, after they have flowered, to an informal border in a less conspicuous part of the garden. I remember a bed beside a garage casually planted with hostas, daylilies, and the previous years' tulips. The tulips produced a multi-colored display for a long while in the spring, followed by the daylilies, and then the hostas (some of which are quite sun-tolerant) spread their enormous leaves over the bed for the rest of the year. The whole was most attractive.

Tulips are at their best in a mass—preferably of a single color. They come in various sizes and shapes, including the wrinkled parrot-flowered tulip shown on the right.

FLOWERS FOR SUMMER

Allium (Flowering onions)

The flowering onions are a decorative and neglected genus, possibly because people think they will smell of onion. They don't; indeed many of them have fragrant flowers. The Texas native rose leek (*A. canadense)* smells like a carnation (and why is it called a Canadian onion in Latin?).

Most alliums are not widely adapted and plant distributors, understandably, prefer plants that do well almost anywhere. If you plant onions that are not locally adapted, they can be awfully temperamental, flowering one year and not the next. There are few parts of the world without indigenous onions of one type of another, so consult your local wild flower book for species almost bound to do well in your area and then experiment with exotics with huge flowers, such as *A. albopilosum* and *A. giganteum*.

Begonia (Tuberous begonia)

Tuberous begonias are Andean natives with wondrous flowers. In areas where summers are not too hot, I cannot imagine a summer terrace without baskets of tuberous begonias and fuschias weeping luxuriant flowers from the branches of a shade tree overhead. Or

Calochortus

you can grow the upright kinds in a shaded bed or container under the tree. (Don't bother with either of these beauties in the Deep South where they cannot take the hot summer nights. It is a sadness.)

Modern tuberous begonia cultivars are basically greenhouse plants with a long growing season. Plant them indoors as much as two months before the date of last frost on top of very fertile soil with an initial soaking. (You can add a little soil over the corms after the shoots have appeared.) Keep the corms warm until shoots appear. (Plant three or four corms in each hanging basket.) When the shoots appear, give them as much light as possible and keep them lightly watered until the great outdoors is reliably frost-free. Then put the baskets outside in the shade or plant the small plants in fertile shaded soil. Garden plants need little care except for a drop of water in dry periods but you will get more and larger flowers if you keep the plants well fertilized. Growers advise using very dilute houseplant fertilizer every time you water.

Calochortus

These western North American natives include the Mariposa lily (*C. venustus)*, the only member of the genus not hardy north of Zone 7 and preferring sun to shade. All of them need dry summers and well-drained soil so they are ideally suited to a gravel bank along a driveway or path in hilly country. The bulbs need to dry out after the foliage dies in the autumn, so anyone trying to grow calochortus in an area that is really too damp for them has to dig up the bulb in midsummer, dry it and store it, and replant before the ground freezes.

Cammassia (Cammasses)

Especially if you live in the West, this native genus is a must for summer flowers. Camasses produce spikes of starry blue, violet, or white flowers in early to midsummer and produce absolutely enormous bulbs if left alone, which they should be. American Indians cooked these for food, although they are reportedly very poisonous when raw. Hardy to Zone 3, camasses like normal to wet soil. The favorite garden species are *C. leichtlinii, C. cusickii,* and *C. quamash,* all of which would be happy in that boggy area by your pond.

Canna

I can't think where cannas have been all my life until I discovered them during the last few years. At least, perhaps I do know where they have been—growing in six foot scarlet spires in stultified beds in front of the town hall—a sight not destined to win admiration from an avant gardener. For summer-long color in hot areas, I am convinced there is no more carefree plant.

Cannas are native to the tropics and subtropics from India to the American Southeast and the species have become hybridized beyond hope of sorting out. They are hardy to Zones 6 or 7 but are easily lifted and stored for the winter in more northern parts. The main colors are red and yellow and the species grow to about six feet, but hybridizers have now produced varieties only about two feet tall and in a wide range of colors. The bright lemony yellow flowers of the southeastern native, *C. flaccida*, take a lot a beating although they are smaller than the flowers of the new hybrids. Cannas usually flower the first year from a rhizome planted in spring. Chop them to the ground when the foliage gets ratty-looking in autumn.

Cannas spread most rapidly in moist rich soil but I think they flower for longer in dry sandy soil. In fact, it doesn't much matter where you put them as long as they get some sun. They are subject to one irritating pest, a leaf-roller caterpillar, which shreds the otherwise handsome foliage. However, we learn that some varieties are more resistant than others and any day now I am going to harden my heart and start tearing out those cannas that suffer badly from the caterpillar.

Crinum

Crinum is another tropical and subtropical genus with species from Asia to southern North America, not hardy north of Zone 7. Like cannas, crinums have hybridized and naturalized extensively in the Deep South. Bill Welch has tracked down heirloom varieties in Texas gardens, including gardens started by former slaves and unchanged since the nineteenth century. He reports that the common 'milk and wine lilies,' with white petals streaked with pink, are old hybrids of *C. scabrum* and *C. bulbispernum*.

There are species and varieties of crinum that bloom from early to late summer, so if you have space for these rather large plants, they can keep a flower bed going through even the August doldrums. The lily-like flowers are most appealing; the untidy yellowing foliage is not. You can either learn to love it or find ways to disguise it with other plants—which is possible because the flowers are held well up above the foliage.

A few species, such as the Brazilian native, *Crinum erubescens*, and the Texan *C. americanum* live in bogs or even ponds but most other crinums, as far as I can tell, prefer near-desert conditions, since they grow happily on coastal sand banks in the South. Crinums reproduce by seed and offsets from the bulb and most reproduce freely if you leave them alone.

Crinum, a milk and wine lily; their main disadvantage is messy foliage.

Crocosmia (**Monbretia**)

Crocosmia potsii, which often travels under its old name, montbretia, is one of a number of gladiolus relatives from South Africa. It is a big plant, to about four feet, with foliage rather like that of a gladiolus but with smaller, looser red or orange flowers borne in abundance on tall wiry stems. Flowers and foliage contrast delightfully with other perennials that flower at the same time, such as mealycup sage, coreopsis, stokesia, and white daisies. No southern gardener should be without them. Crocosmias are hardy to Zone 7 and flower best in fairly dry, not-too-fertile soil. Happy in an ordinary flower bed, crocosmia is probably better off elsewhere, especially if the flower bed is small, because it spreads rapidly and looks better if left undisturbed. The foliage tends to be floppy if its gets too much water and good drainage seems essential. Crocosmias will also take considerable shade; in fact this is the year to test part of a clump in the toughest place in my garden: under a huge live oak, which steals all moisture from the soil and casts dense shade. We shall see.

Dahlia

Modern dahlias are descended from several species native to the mountains of Mexico. It is a sadness to live in an area where they can't stand the summer heat. Except in the southern third of North America there are few more generous plants, producing masses of luscious long-stemmed flowers for garden and house from midsummer to frost. The variety of flower types is stunning, from single to double, pompom to cactus-flowered, in a color range of everything except blue.

Dahlias are easy to grow although the more fertile the soil, the more generous the bloom. Tall varieties, to seven feet, are gorgeous, but do need big strong stakes, which should be put in at planting time. If you are anti-staking, grow shorter varieties or pinch out growing tips to keep the plants shorter. As soon as the foliage is cut down by the first frost, dig up the plants, allow them to dry for an hour or two, and store them in dry vermiculite, styrofoam peanuts, or something of the sort. The storage challenge is to keep them cool enough so that they don't sprout. If you have an unheated garage with one wall attached to the house, that wall is probably the best place because it will be frost-free, but only just. In spring, divide the clumps if you like, but remember that the larger the root clump, the larger the plant, so I like to keep the big clumps of favorite varieties and give smaller bits that fall off the roots to friends.

Gladiolus

The garden gladiolus is a breeder's mishmash of species from South Africa. They are invaluable in the summer garden as cut flowers, even if you find them too prone to collapse for the border. They are hardy only to Zone 8 and even south of this they seem to do better if dug up every winter, probably because the bulb may rot in wet soil in winter. They are often treated as annuals, planted every couple of weeks from last frost to autumn.

Gladiolus need good drainage, but the main thing they are fussy about is pH, which needs to be between 6.5 and 6.8. Above pH 7.5, they suffer from chlorosis. The corms need to be covered by two or three inches of soil and produce lots of little cormlets which take about a year to grow to flowering size. Glads are not difficult to grow, but they are difficult to place in the garden unless you are deeply into staking because the flower heads are too heavy for their stalks. For this reason, many people grow them in a vegetable or cutting garden and use them only as cut flowers.

Hemerocallis (Daylily)

My favorite daylilies are the old-fashioned ones, including the tawny daylily *(H. fulva)* which is the common beasty that has naturalized on roadsides throughout much of the United States and which looks lovely in rough meadows or on roadside banks. *H. flava*, the lemon daylily is also an old fashioned lovely and I like to think of it in ancient Chinese gardens where it was grown for food and medicine—the flower buds are delicious dipped in batter and lightly fried.

Varieties developed by the thousands since the 1930s have achieved great popularity because they are undeniably beautiful, easy, and unaggressive. They ask only reasonably fertile, well-drained soil and plenty of sun, and flower for up to a month in early summer. In very hot areas, the high dappled shade of pine trees helps the appearance especially of dark-colored varieties. The flowers come in all colors except blue and hundreds of new varieties are developed every year so the choice is endless.

I think I dislike the plastic fantastic flowers that hybridizers have inflicted on modern daylilies and that look so horrid when they go over, which they do every day, since a daylily flower lasts, as its name implies, for only a day. Of course breeders are working on flowers that last for more than one day and they will doubtless succeed. And equally of course, aficionados go round the garden every day deadheading their daylilies to avoid that morning-after look. But a plant that needs deadheading every day is not a happy camper in an easy-care border, so I am steadily moving my hybrid daylilies to distant corners of the garden where the ghastly remains will be less obtrusive.

I am at one with Frederick McGourty that a bed full of daylilies is about as interesting as a TV dinner, but daylilies are useful in a mixed border, although you have to put up with a lot of foliage for a fairly short season of flowers. I also like them in a band along the

Hemerocallis, **daylily**

Hymenocallis narcissiflora,
Peruvian daffodil

edge of a path or lawn, where the foliage is an attractive edging when the flowers are gone.

Hymenocallis (Spider lily)

Assorted hybrids of the spider lily or Peruvian daffodil look much like crinums but prefer wetter soil. (And why they are called 'Peruvian,' I don't know. Several are North American natives.) Spider lilies have the advantage over crinums that the foliage is much less messy. The yellow or white flowers are fragrant and intricate, borne on nice upright stalks. If you can grow crinums, you should grow spider lilies too. Most are hardy to Zone 7, but if I had a pond in Zone 6, I would see if *H. liriosme* would enjoy life in either pond or bog. I think it might.

Iris

There are iris species and hybrids that flourish in almost any climate and any conditions. Check your wild flower guide to find if you have native irises. These are fun to grow if you can give them the conditions they prefer. Irises hybridize easily, however, so I sometimes wonder if there are really any pure natives left in most parts of the world, since the locals have hybridized with garden introductions in many areas.

On a rocky New York hillside, one gardener has built a terrace of local stone looking out from the old farmhouse over a wide valley. At the edge of the terrace, and in spaces between the stones, bearded iris of every hue flourish in the well-drained soil, with arabis at their feet. Cold salmon with dill sauce at lunch on this terrace in June was an unforgettable feast for the soul, not to mention the stomach.

Bearded iris are happy wherever they have sunshine and reasonably dry feet in summer. They flourish in an Idaho desert garden and in sandy soil. In the damper east, plant them very high, with most of the rhizome on top of the soil. The other major group of irises that prefers dry summer weather is the 'Pacificas' (*I. tenax* hybrids) grown on the West coast and well adapted to a Mediterranean climate, although they are grown as far north as Maine. These are beardless irises that come in shocking color combinations and have a pleasantly short stout shape.

Plant all these drought-loving irises about 18 inches apart because otherwise they will need frequent dividing. Divide them after they have flowered and when you replant remember that they grow from the rhizome toward the leaves. If you put them in backwards, they grow into each other.

There are at least a kerzillion iris species and varieties and it all gets quite confusing when you try to sort them out. Even the bearded iris (formerly known as "German" which they are not) come in at least 15,000 varieties in every imaginable color combination except real red. Summers in the Deep South are too wet for most bearded iris, where the only ones that usually do well are 'cemetery whites,' *Iris x albicans*. At least, that's probably not true. Among 15,000 varieties there *must* be some that can cope with the Deep South, but finding out which doesn't sound like a time- or cost-effective experiment.

The biggest group of irises for the South are the Louisianas, bred from a melange of southern species but not at all restricted to the South, since they are hardy to at least Zone 4. They like soggy, fertile, acid soil and come in a wide range of modern varieties. They share a bed happily with *Iris tectorum*, the roof iris, grown in China on thatched roofs, the European yellow flag, *I. pseudacorus*, and even with Japanese iris, the exotic hybrids derived from *I. ensata*, which are equally at home farther north, as are Siberian hybrids. The Siberians actually prefer cooler weather and are a striking sight in a New England border with their tall slim foliage. There is a myth that Siberians need lots of water, but they are perfectly happy in an ordinary mixed border. For dry, alkaline soil in the South, spuria hybrids with their grass-like foliage are the answer. Japanese iris are not only lovely with their large flat flowers, but have the advantage of blooming later than most iris and extending the season. They need positively swampy, acid soil during their spring growing season but can stand drier conditions for the rest of the year. Their major disadvantage is that they tend to be short-lived in the garden.

While enjoying all these rhizomatous irises, do not neglect the many lovely bulbous species, some of which flower in early spring. Dutch iris are among the best in the South, preferring dry sandy soil. If they get this, they will naturalize and may join daffodils in the wild meadow.

Bearded iris.
Plant with the top of the rhizome above soil level if you live where it rains much during the summer.

Lilium (Lily)

Lilies are gorgeous and carefree. Since most parts of the world have at least a few species of native lilies, there's probably something for your area. Of the exotics, I can never predict which will and which will not naturalize so I like to grow plenty from seed to experiment cheaply.

Lily bulbs will not take the dehydration that daffodils and tulips tolerate, so it is best to buy and plant them in the autumn when they will be freshly dug, rather than in the spring when they will have been stored over winter. Keep the bulbs moist and plant as soon as you receive them. Set them at the usual bulb depth except for madonna lilies *(L. candidum)* which should be covered with only an inch of soil.

Most lilies like fairly fertile soil, whether sand or clay, and they don't like to have their feet in water although they need moisture while actively growing. The general rule seems to be that they tolerate drought after they have flowered, rather like bearded iris.

Many varieties also flower cheerfully in considerable shade, so this is one place to look if you need flowers for a woodland garden. In sun, shade the roots with perennials or groundcover plants. A happy lily will multiply, but there is usually no need to divide the clump as long as you give them a good layer of compost every spring and fall.

Of the modern Asiatic and Aurelian hybrids, I think the Aurelians tolerate southern heat better than the Asiatics. Lilies also come in varying heights so look out for short ones if you hate staking or live in a windy area. Another tip that reduces the need for stakes is to hill earth up around the stem as it grows in spring as you do with sweet corn. Among the species, some favorites are *L. formosanum* (a parent of the florist's Easter lily), *L. regale* (a parent of the Aurelians from limestone areas in China), the dear old tiger lily, (*L. tigrinum*, as happy under a southern live oak as under a Canadian hemlock) and one that does very well for me, *L. speciosum rubrum*. You have many more choices north of Zone 8.

FLOWERS FOR AUTUMN

In autumn, one of the best plants for damp shade is the hardy begonia, *Begonia grandis*. It really is hardy too, to at least Zone 5. This is a fairly large plant, looking like an angel wings begonia, which flowers in a glorious cascade of pink and purple. I don't know how much drought it can stand, although many begonias are surprisingly tolerant of dry soil. The problem you may have is finding it; few nurseries seem to carry it. For dry shade, I have developed an

Lilies.
Left: *Lilium canadense*. Right: *Lilium speciosum rubrum*.

affection for the strange little toad lilies *(Tricyrtis* spp.), Asian natives with arching leafy stems bearing little purple flowers in the leaf axils. They would win few plaudits in the spring, but in dry shade in October they are not to be despised.

Colchicum

Although I value the crocus-like colchicums for their autumn flowers, like autumn-flowering crocuses, I find them difficult to place in the garden. What do you do with a thing that produces leaves in spring, loses them in summer, and then puts up flowers in autumn? At least, what do you do if you don't have a rock garden, which is the ideal location for these delicate beauties. Among the bigger species, which have a fighting chance in a mixed border, is *C. speciosum*, which grows up to 12 inches high and has large flowers looking more like tulips than crocuses.

Cyclamen

Hardy cyclamen, like miniature versions of the florist's cyclamen, are a delight in autumn in Zones 4 or 5 to 9, although there are also species that flower in spring and summer. Best known is *C. hederifolium* (formerly *C. neapolitanum*), which blooms any time after August before the leaves appear, which they do in autumn. Other hardy species for dry shady areas are *C. coum* and *C. purpurascens. C. Cilicium* and *C. intimatum* seem to prefer some sun. Cyclamens are long-lived and will form sheets of flowers where they are happy. They are best planted where they can be seen close up, in a shady rock garden or under a favorite tree whose leaves will produce the humusy bedding cyclamen love. Whatever else you give them, they must have perfect drainage.

Gingers

Gingers are several tropical genera (including *Hedychium, Cautleya, Costus, Alpinia,* and *Roscoea)* that flower over a long period in late summer and autumn. Like bananas and cannas, they are members of the large family, Zingiberaceae, and they have canna-like foliage and rhizomes. Gingers are adapted to life in the shade of a moist forest and they are hardy only through Zone 8.

Queen of the bunch is butterfly ginger (*Hedychium coronarium*), native to India. It will grow in full sun in a bog but will take much drier soil in the shade. The flowers look like white cannas with droopy petals and they have such a powerful fragrance that a single long-lived stem in a vase perfumes a room. *H. coccineum* is slightly smaller and red. The rhizomes grow swiftly as long as they get lots of water and the small slice of rhizome that you buy or get from a friend will be a large clump in a year or two.

Tulbaghia (Society garlic)

I first grew society garlic (*T. violacea*) because of its charming common name which, I like to think, means that this is a garlic fit to go into society. (It is not really a garlic.) But it also produces lilac harebell-like flowers on eight inch stems for a long time in summer into autumn and the rest of the time has low foliage which competes with liriope for good looks as a ground cover. It is hardy only to Zone 8.

BUILDING A GARDEN POOL

The ideal garden pool sits in a sunny area at the edge of shrubbery where animals can hide. Garden waterworks tend to expand as time goes by so it is worth considering how the pool can later be joined to such features as a bog garden, a fountain, the drainage from the roof or driveway, and a natural or artificial stream, perhaps with a bridge over it to carry a path. Or is there a network of canals in your future? Canals are worth pondering before you plunge for a circular or rectangular pool. In a formal area, H-shaped or I-shaped canals, with lawn or orchard beyond them can be very effective. Have a look at some of Russell Page's designs, which bring the ideas of great eighteenth century European stately gardens down to a scale suitable for the home garden.

In the event that you have a good layer of clay near the surface, you may need little more than a bulldozer (or shovel, depending on the scale) to excavate the pond. In this case, the edge of the pond will be permanently damp and your bog garden is ready made, just waiting for you to install gunneras, iris, primulas, callas, ginger lilies, elephant ears and all the lovely things that enjoy soggy ground. If you do not have the clay, the pond will have to be lined with a PVC or butyl liner, concrete, or whatever, to keep the water in place. Then where do you put your bog plants? One possibility is to have the bottom of the pond at two levels; a deep part for fish and water lilies on one side and a shallow area for bog plants on the other. If you go this route, build a ledge to hold soil in the shallow part. You also need a ramp where wildlife in search of a drink can get right down to the water. Few animals can reach the water in a pond if it is far below the rim, so a ramp will increase the variety of wildlife the pond attracts.

Yet another method of providing animal access and a bog is to add a stream. If you have a naturalistic pond, one way to do this is to find somewhere uphill from the pond from which a stream might, realistically, emerge. This could be a hillside, where there might be a spring, or merely a shrubbery on the border of the property where the stream might be flowing from next door or from the roadside ditch. Then dig your stream, line it, and install one of those clever recirculating pumps to take water from the pond to the top of the stream, whence it can trickle down through your cunningly land-

A pond with canals.
You could keep the water moving
gently in a system like this with a
recirculating pump and some pipes.

scaped stream bed on whose banks water-loving plants will
flourish.

When it comes to setting the pump to control the stream's
rate of flow, note that most artificial streams look odd because
they flow too fast. Especially if you live in flat country, the
stream should barely move or it will look most peculiar. Even on
a reasonable slope, a stream galloping along at ten knots looks
phony on a hot July day.

"Naturalistic" ponds, and streams that don't look as if
nature made them, are pet peeves of mine. I am not enticed by
irregular pools, surrounded by artfully artless slabs of stone
sitting in the middle of suburban lawns. If your pool is in the
middle of a level lawn, it will look much more at home if it is
formal in nature and regular in shape. Make it circular, rectangular, or square, and surround it with brick or concrete, not
irregular stones, and make the stream that runs to it a canal
without any wiggles in it. Then put statuesque clumps of
papyrus, gunnera, and rodgersia beside the canal, or grecian

urns full of something elegant. Now you have a gorgeous work of art, not a poor imitation of nature, and the wildlife will like it just as well.

If the little stream trickling down the hillside is out of the question in your city backyard, the answer for bog plants and wildlife is probably a fountain. A lion's head built into a wall or a *mannequin pis* standing on a slab can drip a little trickle of water onto a stone that funnels it partly into the pond below and partly into the bog garden on either side. A recirculating pump, with the mechanism hidden by the wall or underground, completes the water circuit (although in hot weather, you have to add more water surprisingly often, even to a small enclosed setup like this).

If fountains and recirculating pumps are beyond your means, it's amazing what can be done with a garden hose that snakes through the shrubbery and disgorges onto a stone slab, where the water is again directed partly into the pond and partly into the bog garden. Or, in this case, you can just take the hose straight to the pond and let the pond's overflow create the bog. A hose left on slow trickle for the summer uses surprisingly little water. If you live where it rains occasionally in summer, you will probably be able to supply this setup from a rain barrel set under a downspout and equipped with a hose outlet. (Look for them in catalogues.) A black hose is much easier to disguise than a green or yellow one.

If you have just won the lottery, by all means bring in a landscape firm with garden pool experience and sit back while minions install the pool you have designed. If not, I think the first step is to lay hands on all the water garden catalogues you can find and study the wide range of do-it-yourself pool supplies that are available. If there are any freshwater ponds or streams near you, however, or even if you are well supplied with roadside ditches, you will find it much more satisfactory to go and collect your own, locally adapted aquatic plants. If you are lucky, you may even collect a few snails and aquatic insects on your plants and your little ecosystem will be well on its way.

A pond doesn't seem like a pond without fish, but it is not entirely easy to decide what type of fish. Goldfish are traditional, and certainly showy, but, like most members of the carp family, they are aggressive omnivores, eating anything in sight, including amphibians and invertebrates who may take up residence. If you want the local wildlife to enjoy the pond, you can't have goldfish. Some kind of local minnow is a better idea. No matter what kind of fish you install, herons will probably find the pond and go fishing. A heron fishing in your pool surely completes the picture. Nevertheless, many people object. (Perhaps they've become personally attached to the goldfish?) Then the only solution may be to keep a cat, or a dog that is more of a mighty hunter than most dogs I've known. That may keep the heron away—although any cat fierce or

Butomus umbellatus, **an attractive plant for pond or bog.**

energetic enough to see off a heron will probably lay the corpses of painted buntings and squirrels on your doorstep every morning. I feel that expendable fish is the lesser of these two evils, but you will have to make your own compromises.

It says here that ponds look better if you can restrain yourself from planting too many different things. There is no doubt that some of the loveliest ponds are decorated with nothing more than a clump of a decorative grass or a sheaf of irises, but the temptation to try out more and more water-lovers is impossible for this addicted collector to resist.

Pond Maintenance

You can buy dozens of chemicals and supplies for getting rid of the algae that develop on the pool's surface and wall, for feeding the fish, feeding the snails, killing the mosquitoes, and on and on. But I liked the advice of a Washington pond expert, whose name I unfor-

---

A FEW PLANTS FOR THE BOG GARDEN

Banana
Caladium
Geum rivale (Water avens) European native Zones 6-8; Reddish, nodding flowers on hairy stems to about 12"; easy from seed
Zantedeschia (Calla lilies)
Canna
Chelone lyonii (Pink turtlehead)
Colocasia antiquorum, C. antiquorum esculenta (Taro, elephant ear)
Cyperus alternifolius (Umbrella grass)
Darmera peltata (formerly *Peltiphyllum peltatum*); native to Oregon and California; Zones 5-10; to 5 feet with pink-purplish flowers
Gunnera manicata
Ginger lilies: *Hedychium coronarium, H. coccinea*
Helenium autumnale (Sneezeweed) Native to much of North America Zones 3 to 9; yellow, mahogany, and gold small daisy-like flowers; excellent fall flower in South
Ligularia Asian native. Zones 7-10 To 5' with huge, yellow, daisy-like

flowers. *Ligularia tussilaginea* 'Aureo-maculata' and 'Argentea' have variegated leaves
Hibiscus Moscheutos (swamp rose mallow) Southeastern native, but hardy to Ohio; to 8 feet, but usually more like 3 feet; cream or white flowers in midsummer.
Irises: Japanese and Louisiana varieties, *Iris pseudacorus* (yellow flag)
Pontederia cordata (Pickerel rush); native to Virginia, with arrow-shaped leaves and small blue flowers.
Primula japonica, P. florindae
Rodgersia podophylla
Sagittaria japonica (Arrowhead) Arrow-shaped leaves and white and purple flowers; often grown in small ponds because it does not take over or hide the pond.
Typha (Cat tail). These bulrush lookalikes have spread around the world and while pretty, tend to be aggressive (like many water-lovers). *T. angustifolia* grows to 4 feet; *T. minima* to 20 inches
Sarracenia (Pitcher plant)

Sagittaria, **arrowhead.**

tunately cannot remember, which was: don't. Leave the pond alone and let the ecosystem develop naturally. The pond may go through some disquieting evolutions on the way. Our water contains a lot of iron, and after a week or two a new pond was covered by a bright orange scum which was no thing of beauty. But eventually, as we environmental types would have predicted, whatever eats the orange scum showed up and removed it or at least reduced the population of whatever it was to a tolerable level.

Most ponds will take a while to turn into balanced ecosystems. After all, its inhabitants have to find their way to your pond from elsewhere. But they will find your pond eventually, unless you are living in the middle of the Sahara. Once arrived, they have to fight it out for rights to their particular niches in the pond and that may lead to messes like the orange scum. But all will settle down eventually. Don't expect crystal-clear water in a pond where nature takes its course, but it won't be a muddy mess either.

The one bit of maintenance you undoubtedly will have to perform is occasionally shoveling out some of the debris that accumulates on the bottom. Succession goes on and, left to its own devices, any pond will eventually eutrophy and turn into dry land. So every few years, or more often if you have put the pond too close to a tree, take a large bucket on a warm day, wade in and remove a few bucketfuls of bottom mud, taken great care not to puncture the plastic liner.

It doesn't do the ecosystem any good to have to keep adding water to replace any that leaks out, so drain the pond and look for leaks if you think you have one. Pond supply companies sell repair kits that are not difficult to use, although emptying the pond so that you can get at the leak is an undoubted pain.

What about ponds that freeze in winter? The old-fashioned treatment was to rescue the fish, drain the pond and start again in spring. But technology has leapt to the rescue with de-icers and agitators. For the price of one of these gadgets and a little electricity, you can keep at least part of the pond ice-free all winter for which the wildlife will thank you. If the pond is big enough, water birds may even take up residence or visit as they pass through on migration.

CHAPTER 10

Annuals

nnuals are the garden's quick shot of color. When the perennial border looks like last night's dinner party or you can't stand your boring front door a moment longer, annuals are the fastest solution. Botanically speaking, annuals are plants that grow from seed, set flower, and die, all in one growing season. But gardeners also use the term to describe perennials that they throw away after one year, usually because they will not survive the winter.

Unlike annuals, biennials spend their first year of life growing foliage and roots, postponing flowers until the second year, when they die. This rather slow lifestyle and subsequent death is not what a gardener really wants and biennials might have been banished from most gardens before now if they did not include some of the most useful and long-lasting of flowers. Pansies, wallflowers, foxgloves, and sweet williams have such fine flowers that we put up with their dilatory habits. In addition, many biennials self-seed freely so that once you have a stand of sweet

william or foxglove established, you can almost forget that they are not perennials.

Annuals have got themselves a bad reputation, as the villains of Victorian bedding displays and the mainstay of gardeners who have not learned to grow perennials. But in truth, annuals are as necessary to the well-clothed garden as shrubs and perennials. Ryan Gainey holds that annuals are part of creating a romantic garden— which I take to mean a garden exuberantly clothed in a mass of flowers and foliage. And so they are.

DESIGNING WITH ANNUALS

I am beginning to think that I have spent too much time experimenting with annuals that are new to me (although I shall be unable to resist growing a few new ones each year). If you agree with Louise Beebe Wilder that the highest aim of a gardener is "to fashion, from the myriad shades and diverse forms laid to our hand, a series of lovely pictures to rejoice the eye," then annuals are your most important tools. To compose

Larkspur
In good soil, the plants grow to six feet if you thin the seedlings. Each plant produces up to a dozen flower spikes, in colors from royal blue to white and hot pink, that last well as cut flowers. The plants self-seed readily.

garden pictures, you need to know your plants well—their color, how big they get, what the foliage looks like, and when they flower. I shall never reach that point with perennials. My borders will always contain newly discovered natives, donations from friends, and new varieties that will take years to show what they can do. And by the time my latest lily, baptisia, or sarracenia has strutted its stuff (if it hasn't died), it has turned into a large handsome clump that flowers better if left undisturbed. So I shall leave it undisturbed and shall have to compose my picture around it with flowers I know well—the annuals.

If your cherished perennial is an indian paintbrush or penstemon with gay red flowers, might it not look fine set in a sea of white alyssum? If it leaves a collection of tattered leaves after it has flowered, a swift infusion of impatiens, in colors chosen to harmonize with whatever flowers next, may be in order. If a pergola is covered by an old rose that flowers in spring and tends to lose its leaves to black spot later in the year, why not plant clematis or a gloriosa lily at its feet to scramble up the branches and flower in early summer, at the same time planting annual 'Heavenly Blue' morning glories, which will scramble up rose and clematis and open sky blue flowers in midsummer? A footing of pink or pinky purple petunias would enhance all of these flowers and help to keep the roots of the clematis cool. You see the idea?

Most choice perennials come in the colors God gave them, but with annuals you call the shots and can carry out any color scheme that occurs to you. If you are suddenly smitten by the notion that pale violet might sit well with the scarlet of a prized oriental poppy, you can find pansies in that, or most any other, color and try it out next spring. Plants of the color and form you need for your scheme are not difficult to find since many seed companies now put out catalogues with lots of color photographs to help you choose.

Once you start thinking along these lines, the only problem is growing enough annuals to compose your pictures. And here, self-seeding annuals are enormously useful. I always have all the white zinnias and purple *Viola* 'Black Prince' I need if I can just remember not to do too thorough a job of tidying up the corner of the herb garden where they propagate themselves.

Heirloom Annuals and Seed Saving
The heavy hand of plant breeding has fallen on annuals with disheartening results. If you want to know how petunias lost their throne as most popular plant in North America, try growing some of the latest varieties. It's like the green revolution in agriculture, when plant breeders produced grain varieties of amazing productivity—as long as they were pampered within an inch of their lives with pesticides, water, and fertilizer. But try to grow miracle rice in your peasant paddy and you were likely to starve. In an attempt to

produce bigger and varicolored flowers, breeders have given us amazing varieties that die with the speed of light if you omit to pull the first weed that shows its head. I live in tobacco-growing country so I fondly imagined that modern nicotianas as well as new varieties of our native verbena would be great additions to my repertoire of annuals. What a bust! The plants I grew in unimproved soil produced a few miserable flowers and succumbed to pests after a month in the garden.

This makes me a diehard reactionary, but if you want to use annuals to paint garden pictures rather than push your horticultural skills to the limit, I am convinced that you are better off begging the seeds of your neighbors' heirloom marigolds and sweet williams than experimenting with the latest award-winning pink ageratum or double petunia. And don't omit to save your own seed. With marigolds and dianthus, this is easy because the seedheads dry out on the plant without spilling many seeds. Pick the seedheads, shake the seeds out onto a bit of paper and store them in a closed plastic bag or small glass bottle in the refrigerator until you are ready to plant them. Things like pansies are a bit more difficult because seeds are shed as they ripen so you have to pick the seed heads before they are fully ripe. Let them ripen and dry on a sheet of newspaper in an airy place and collect the seeds when the pods open.

Some of the older varieties stay in the main seed catalogues but you should also try seed exchanges and some of the smaller companies that specialize in old varieties. In an attempt to save garden cultivars from extinction, the National Council for the Conservation of Plants and Gardens in the United Kingdom has put together a network of collectors, each of whom acts as custodian of a particular genus. Formed in 1982, the Council now has more than 5000 members who care for 400 collections of plants. In the United States, a start has been made in this direction by the Thomas Jefferson Center for Historic Plants at Monticello, which preserves heirloom varieties as it finds them and disseminates the plants through its seed catalogue.

GROWING PLANTS FROM SEED

When you want a spot of color in a hurry, a few flats of annuals from the garden center are the answer, but if you find yourself using more and more annuals, you will want to grow your own from seed that you order from a catalogue. Growing your own is the only way you can get precisely the species, varieties, and colors that you want. It also sounds as if it would save you money when you compare the price of a flat of pansies with the price of a packet of seeds. But any money you save has a tendency to slip away on the latest seed-starting device or on hundreds of packets of seeds, so don't count on it.

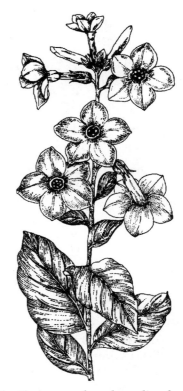

Nicotianas produce long-lived tubular flowers on handsome plants that range from about one to four feet tall, depending on the variety.

Zinnia
There are several different flower forms in various heights from about 6 to 30 inches and in all colors except blue. Zinnias flower rapidly from seed and make the best show if you plant them at intervals throughout the summer. This permits you to rip out old plants as soon as they become disfigured by mildew and still have a good display.

Seeds can be sown directly in the garden and indeed some seedlings dislike being disturbed so much that this is the best way to grow them. Sowing in the ground only works where there is a reasonable chance that the seeds will germinate undisturbed by the birds and rodents waiting to eat them, or by you washing them away and digging up the seedlings while planting bulbs. In practice, this means that the best seeds for sowing outdoors are those that germinate rapidly, like marigolds, zinnias, and poppies, or those that you can bury quite deeply, like sweet peas. Some people are more adventurous, but I find that if I sow slow-growing things like begonias, ageratum, and petunias in the ground, I get very few plants from a packet of seed.

If you are already growing seeds successfully, you undoubtedly have a system that works for you; and there are as many systems as there are gardeners. The main thing is to understand the needs of germinating seeds and baby plants and to find the easiest way to supply these needs. Many a sturdy seedling has been raised on the kitchen windowsill (a good spot, since it tends to be cool, moist, and light) so do not be deterred if you don't have ideal conditions indoors. Plenty of seeds can also be started outdoors in containers raised above the ground to reduce the depradations of birds and squirrels.

A HOME LIGHT TABLE

Seedlings need a lot of light and supplying this light is difficult in the average home. You may think your living room is full of sunlight for most of the day, but your house plants probably bend toward the window, showing that they would be happier if they had even more light. And most seedlings require a lot more light than do house plants, which have been selected as house plants precisely because they can survive low light levels.

After growing seedlings on crowded windowsills with lights clamped to the curtain rods for many years, my life changed when my husband built me an A-frame light table from a design he found in *Fine Gardening* magazine. The essence of this design is room for at least six flats of plants in minimal space. The lights hang by hooks from chains so that they can be raised or lowered. A timer, such as you can buy in any lighting department, turns the lights on automatically for 16 hours a day, and the whole A-frame can be folded up and stored in a closet when not in use.

The lights in this structure are workshop holders containing the cheapest fluorescent bulbs. You can buy fluorescent bulbs called grow-lights or something similar, which give out light of the ideal wavelength for plant growth. But these are expensive and in my experience not worth the money. Your seedlings are not going to spend their entire lives under lights and it is more important that they should have lots of light than special wavelengths. So it is

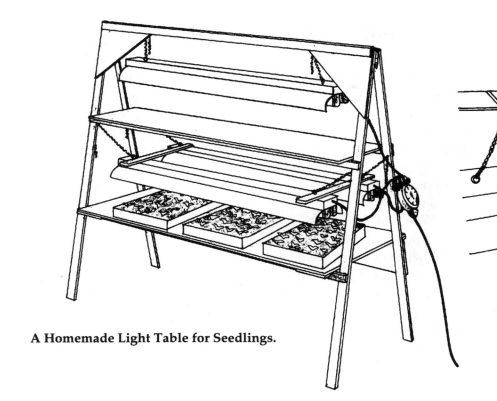

A Homemade Light Table for Seedlings.

The table is made from 1x2 lumber and 3/8" plywood sheathing. The top shelf is 16" x 56". The bottom shelf if 24" x 56". The electric cords from the lights (with 48" tubes) plug into a gang plug attached to a timer and an extension cord. 4" strap hinges hold the uprights together. The light fixtures are suspended from the frame by cup hooks so that the height of the lights can be adjusted.

better to buy cheap bulbs and replace them as soon as they start to get dim at the ends—which is the way fluorescents show they are dying.

Germination

Although seedlings grow best at low temperatures, many seeds germinate faster at much higher temperatures. It is amazing how fast most seeds germinate if you give them "bottom heat" by setting them on something warm such as the top of the refrigerator, a not-too-hot radiator, or a commercial heating pad. I use a warming plate from a now-defunct restaurant. I have no idea what the temperature of the plate is (it is too hot to leave your hand on), but seeds love it.

The main disease of young seedlings is "damping off," caused by a fungus. You know your seedlings have it if their stems wither and the plant falls over. It is easy to avoid if you germinate seeds rapidly and then transplant them into flats that go on the light table.

You can use small pots for germination if you transplant the crowded seedlings soon after they have germinated. You need a sterile medium to protect your seedlings from disease. A large bag of something like Pro-Mix is an easy way to buy this, but there are dozens of possibilities. Simone Van Stolk makes her mix from cheap cat litter, sterile sand, and sterilized compost. (The smell of trays of compost sterilizing in the oven is enough to drive the family into leaving town—which may or may not be a good thing, depending

Nasturtiums

upon how you are feeling about the family.) Three hours in the oven at 300 °F will sterilize a layer of compost about an inch deep.

Soak the potting mix in water and fill your pot almost to the brim. Now insert a plant label with at least the name of the seeds and the date of planting on it. Sprinkle the seeds on the surface of the mix. If the packet says that the seeds need light to germinate, leave them uncovered. But most seeds will germinate in the dark and I cover them with a pinch of dry sphagnum moss. This may be pure snake oil, but I read somewhere that it tends to prevent damping off and I have so far avoided damping off so who am I to question superstition?

Now put the whole pot into a lightweight plastic bag, which saves you having to water. The ones you buy to store food in work well. Twist the bag closed, pop the twisted end under the pot, and place the whole lot in your chosen warm spot.

Check these pots every day because things like zinnias and marigolds germinate in 24 hours if your bottom heat is pretty fierce and as soon as the seedlings germinate they need light. Take the pot out of its plastic bag and put it in a waterproof tray on the light table, as close to the light as you can. The waterproof tray is so that you can water your seedlings from the bottom by pouring water into the tray. Seedlings get mashed if you try to water them by pouring from the top—not to mention the mess you will make spraying water all over the spare bedroom or kitchen floor.

If some of your pots of seeds don't germinate, try just leaving them alone. You may find that slow-starters, such as cyclamen, shoot up months later. Sometimes you have obviously got the conditions wrong. This is unlikely to happen with annuals, but once you get good at starting seeds you'll find yourself trying tricky perennials and even shrubs and trees.

The problem may be too much heat. Some seeds, such as spinach, will not germinate except in the cold. Of course the seed packet should have told you this in the first place, but lots of seed packets do not have enough information on them. You can sometimes rescue pots of seeds that haven't germinated by putting them

UNDERSTANDING THE ENVIRONMENT
SEEDS THAT NEED LIGHT TO GERMINATE
These seeds belong to "fugitive species," opportunists that take advantage of disturbances in an ecosystem. In nature, pin cherries, oriental poppies, achillea, arabis, gaillardia, and many others, shed seeds that become buried under falling leaves and similar debris. Here the seeds remain, usually for many years. Then the soil is disturbed, perhaps when a tree blows down in a gale or a rock rolls down a hillside, opening up a light gap in the forest. The seeds are exposed to light and germinate,

flowering and setting seed before the light gap is closed up again by the succession of perennials, shrubs, and climax trees that will eventually fill the gap. You notice this happening in the garden when you cultivate a bed that is infested with weeds. After your efforts, the weeds are gone, but several new species of weed spring up. You have induced them to germinate by turning the soil and exposing them to light. If you can kill them off before they flower and set seed, you will get fewer weeds in this bed in future years.

in the refrigerator for two months or even in the freezer, to imitate a northern winter. (It might be easier just to put them outdoors.)

Another possible germination problem is seeds that need scarification, which means they have hard seed coats, which need to be damaged before they will germinate. To scarify seeds, rub them between two pieces of sandpaper and soak them in warm water for 24 hours before planting.

TEMPERATURE AND LIGHT

The higher the temperature, the more light plants need. Plants grow faster in the warmth and must photosynthesize faster if they are not to get yellow and sickly. (High temperature, especially at night, is the main reason so many northern natives "grow themselves to death" when planted in the South.) Seedlings that don't get enough light also get tall and thin—"etiolated." Etiolation is produced by plant hormones that make light-starved plants grow upward rapidly in an attempt to reach more light.

In winter, it is almost impossible to give plants as much light as they would get in a sunny spot in summer. Even the sunlight falling on a greenhouse in winter is much weaker than it would be in summer. And a light table does not produce as much light as the sun. The result of all this light starvation is that you must grow seedlings at low temperatures if you hope for healthy plants with large root systems that will burst into life when you put them in the garden.

Place your light table in the coolest spot you can find that still stays well above freezing. Perhaps you have a cellar that would do, a garage, utility room, or a spare bedroom where the heat is turned off. If every part of the house is heated in winter, put the table near the coolest window you can find. Finding a cool spot for the light table is even more of a problem in midsummer when you are starting seedlings to plant out in autumn.

To increase the light supply to seedlings on the light table, put seedlings of the same height together. Then lower the lights until they are less than an inch from the tops of the seedlings.

When a seedling germinates, the first leaves that show are seed leaves, the cotyledons in ones and twos that give monocots and dicots their names. The first true leaves appear next and are the sign that the seedling can be transplanted into more spacious quarters. Tiny seedlings, such as those of lobelia, sweet alyssum, begonias, and ageratum can be left a bit longer, until they are large enough to handle, but they too must be pricked out before they become too crowded.

I like to prick out seedlings into waterproof flats containing plastic cell-packs. Use the largest cells for your largest seedlings. Fill the cells loosely with sterilized potting mix and then turn the pot of seedlings, soil and all, out onto the counter. Break the ball of soil

UNDERSTANDING THE ENVIRONMENT SCARIFYING SEEDS
On the island of Madagascar off the coast of Africa lives a tree found nowhere else. Some years ago, biologists realized that all members of this species on the island were very old. No new trees seemed to have grown in more than two hundred years and efforts to make the large seeds germinate failed. One day some bright biologist remembered that Madagascar had been the home of a large bird, the dodo, which was hunted to extinction in the eighteenth century. Perhaps the tree's seeds needed to pass through the gut of a large bird to germinate? A conservation program of force-feeding turkeys with the seeds was started. And it worked! The turkey-scarified seeds germinated and seedlings are now being transplanted into the wild to repatriate a tree that missed extinction by a turkey's whisker.

Sweet william, *Dianthus barbatus.*
The hybridizers have not messed with this sweet-scented biennial, which lasts for a long time in the house,, so you can save seed from plants of your favorite color and have more of it next year.

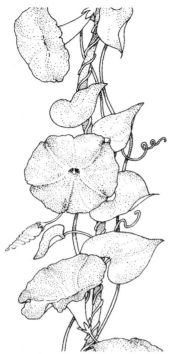

Morning glory
This annual vine will cover a structure or shrub with red, white, or blue flowers in a couple of months. Before sowing, the seeds should be scarified by soaking them in water overnight or rubbing them between two pieces of sandpaper.

gently into a few pieces to separate the roots. Handling tiny seedlings can be nerve-wracking at first, but seedlings are tougher than they look. Handle seedlings by the leaves rather than the stem because a plant can grow new leaves but not a new stem.

Transplant two or three times as many seedlings as you need, to allow for losses, but even so, you will probably have more seedlings than you can accommodate or need so choose the larger seedlings to pot up first. Pick up a seedling by its leaves and pull its roots gently out of the soil ball, breaking the soil ball up further if necessary. Push the roots down into the soil in a cell with your finger and sprinkle a little extra soil on top to make sure all the roots are covered. Seedlings are tough at this time of life and don't much care how deeply you plant them so I usually plant them a little deep to cover up some of that gangly stem. Don't forget to move the label from the germination pot to the flat when you have finished transplanting.

Once the seedlings are pricked out into cells, they will grow rapidly and need more nutrients than most potting mixes provide. Give them their first serving of water and fertilizer before you put the flat back under the lights.

You can use soluble houseplant fertilizer or compost or manure tea. To save trying to remember when you last fertilized, it is easier to use a very dilute fertilizer solution every time you water. There is no need to be precise about quantities of fertilizer. The seedlings will slowly turn yellow if they are not getting enough fertilizer and you can increase the dose. It is more important not to overfertilize because fertilizer burn will kill plants rapidly. If the plants shrivel up or turn yellow rapidly when they have plenty of water, they are probably suffering from an overdose of fertilizer and will die. If green algae start growing on the surface of the potting mix, you are watering too often or using too much fertilizer.

GREEN THUMBS TIP
STARTER MIX

Much of the soil substitute sold as "seedling starter mix" or "potting mix" in discount stores, and even garden centers, is useless. I have no idea what is in it but if it dries out it has a consistency like cement and few seedlings can push their roots through it. Make sure when you buy commercial compost for starting seeds that it bears the name of a reputable firm.

Why can't you just grow seedlings in soil you dig out of the garden? Sometimes you can, if the soil is exceedingly good, but garden soil used in a container generally does not contain enough air. Seedlings and container plants need to be watered frequently and this further compacts the soil. Root cells must respire just like other cells and for this they need to be able to absorb oxygen from the air.

Good commercial potting mixes usually contain quite a lot of peat moss and vermiculite, which is visible as gray particles in the mix. Vermiculite is a mineral made by heating mica ore and contains millions of tiny air spaces, which hold air and water. Vermiculite is also an excellent medium in which to start cuttings. It holds many times its weight in water, but even when soaking wet it contains a lot of air.

HARDENING OFF

Hardening off means moving a plant into a different microclimate by degrees so that it can acclimatize gradually to the harsh world outside after the cushioned comfort of the light table. If they are not hardened off, most seedlings will die when transferred to the bright light and damaging wind in the garden. Hardening off permits them to develop more chlorophyll and stems that can stand the strain. Plant stems grow stronger when exposed to wind, which leads one to wonder whether it might be helpful to turn a fan on seedlings while they are still indoors. I have never tried this, but it would not do away with the need to acclimatize the seedlings to sunlight.

If the weather is warm, start to harden your seedlings by moving them outdoors to a shady spot sheltered from the wind. Before you do this, however, transfer the cell-packs from their waterproof flats into flats with holes in the bottom. You will be watering from overhead from now on and the seedlings need good drainage. Leave the seedlings in the shade for a few days and then, if they are destined for a sunny spot in the garden, move them into more and more sun for a few days. The whole hardening off process takes about a week. This can be an exhausting business in spring when you have hundreds of tender seedlings and there is still a danger of frost at night. Gardeners can be seen carrying dozens of flats out every morning and into the front hall for people to trip over at night. Many annuals can take quite a bit of frost so unless you expect a heavy frost (below about 25 °F) don't bother to bring in lobelia, pelargoniums, alyssum, dianthus, snapdragons, sweet williams, pansies, and a dozen more I cannot think of at the moment. All are quite frost-tolerant.

Garden centers want plants to flower while they are in flats because people are more likely to buy plants that are in flower. But when you are growing your own seedlings, it is a mistake to let them flower before they are planted in the ground. When a plant puts its energy into making flowers, its leaves grow more slowly. You will get a large flowering plant sooner if you pinch off all flower buds while the plants are in flats.

BUILDING A COLD FRAME

Once you start moving seedlings into the garden, a cold frame is a very useful gadget to possess, particularly in colder climes. This is merely a frame covered with a hinged glass lid. The figure shows a simple frame built from scrap lumber and an old window. The frame is usually placed facing south so as to admit as much sunlight as possible. The cold frame increases the temperature around your plants, making it possible to put even tender annuals outdoors when there is still a chance of frost or when the weather is simply too cold for plants to grow rapidly. It is particularly useful in areas with long, cool springs and autumns.

GREEN THUMBS TIP

USING PEAT POTS

If sowing seeds in the garden produces few plants, even plants that dislike being disturbed can be started indoors if you grow them in peat pots, which can be planted in the garden pot and all. The secret is to tear off the rim of the pot when you plant it and make sure the pot is covered by at least half an inch of soil. If any part of the pot is exposed to the air, it acts as a wick from which water evaporates, drying out the roots and killing the plant. If you plant tiny seeds, such as poppies, in peat pots, thin the seedlings to one plant per pot by cutting off the extra plants with scissors so as not to disturb the roots.

A cold frame to make.
The lid is a standard 32" x 42" window. The outside dimensions of the base are 34" x 45".

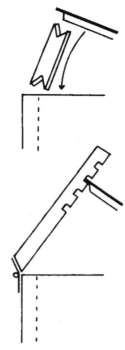

Venting the cold frame
Top: you can make a vent prop from any piece of wood. Bottom: For a sturdy prop in windy areas, notch a 2x2 and attach it to the frame by a hinge.

You can grow plants in the cold frame either in pots or planted in the ground. Many people in cold areas grow crops such as salad greens in a frame all winter. These are plants that grow well in cold weather but would be killed by heavy frost. To use the cold frame for this purpose, insulate it by piling bales of hay or other insulation against the sides and throw a couple of quilts over the top on cold nights. With this system, you can grow some vegetables all winter in areas as cold as Zone 4.

Gardeners through the centuries used the heat from a layer of decomposing manure or compost at the bottom of the frame to make it into a "hot bed," where seeds could be germinated and growth speeded in cold weather. You can imitate the same system today with a commercially available electric hot pad in the bottom of the cold frame if you find yourself wanting to hurry seedlings on their way.

Transplants

Small plants that you buy or raise from seed deserve the best possible start in life when you put them in the ground. Your aim is to have them grow new feeder roots, to anchor the plant and absorb water, as soon as possible. Dig a planting hole and add a cupful of compost or a handful of leaves or grass clippings. If the plant will need staking, now is the time to pound in the stake so that you don't disturb the roots by doing it later. Then remove your transplant from its pot and examine the root system. If you see fine white roots among the soil, all is well and the plant can just be popped in the hole. If the roots almost hide the soil, and especially if the roots have grown in circles round the inside of the pot, pull some of them away from the root ball before you plant.

Your next goal is to make sure that soil comes in contact with all the roots. Fill the planting hole with soil and press it down gently around the plant leaving a little depression in the soil. Water the plant in by filling this depression with water a couple of times. This will wash soil down around the roots and fill up any air spaces. For the first week after planting keep the plant watered but leave it alone. If it looks happy after a week or two, give it a feeding of weak liquid fertilizer to encourage it.

Most annuals appreciate rich organic soil full of moisture and nutrients, but a few are contrary and produce many leaves and few flowers if you make them too comfortable. This is particularly true of nasturtiums, which won't flower at all if the soil is too rich. I usually don't fertilize annuals at all unless they start looking a bit yellow around the gills—which they never will if you have planted them in fertile soil to begin with. But yellowing leaves sometimes do indicate nutrient deficiency and then a little fertilizer is indicated. The safest way to do this is to use a dilute solution of compost or manure tea. This is so dilute than it will not harm the plants and indeed can be used every time you water.

Similarly, most annuals flower best with as much sun as you can give them. Few annuals do well in the shade, although plant breeders are working on this problem. Impatiens, lobelia, and begonias appreciate some shade. Remember, however, that this may depend on where you live. In the South, petunias, marigolds, sweet alyssum, and lobelia all flower well in considerable shade even in winter, and geraniums do best in almost complete shade year round.

It is seldom worth bothering with pest control on annuals. A few chewed leaves will not harm a fast-growing plant and when your zinnias develop unsightly mildew it is time to pull them out and consign them to the compost heap.

It is, however, worth pruning some annuals. Things like impatiens, petunias, lobelia, and sweet alyssum tend to get rather gangly in their old age, with large expanses of stem between the flowers. You can often give them a new lease on life by shearing them back.

Self-seeding
In a formal bed of annuals, you have to cut off dead flowers for appearance's sake. But if you have annuals in a less formal setting, such as the vegetable garden or mixed border, many of them will sow their own seed and reappear the following year if you leave the seed heads to ripen. Sometimes the self-seeded plants are sturdier than their parents. I plant California poppies for their lovely splash of orange. But they are not really happy in our humid climate and die out rapidly in spring. I had just about decided not to grow them again when one winter I realized that the gray leaves that were

Pinks, carnations, *Dianthus*
Most dianthus are really perennials but many are grown as annuals because they flower rapidly from seed and can be removed when they start to look messy in hot summer weather.

Ivy-leaved pelargonium, widely used in hanging baskets
Pelargoniums are easily propagated by cuttings and do poorly from seed so this is the way to multiply them.

taking over one corner of the vegetable garden were a huge clump of two or three California poppies. These produced an amazing display, flowering for a full three months from February to May with at least 50 flowers on the clump at all times. Obviously at least one of the original poppies I planted had genes that permit it to thrive in the humid south and it has multiplied rapidly—evolution in action!

ANNUALS FROM CUTTINGS

Many annuals are easy to grow from cuttings and indeed this is the best way to propagate them. Most pelargoniums do not come true from seed and have to be grown from cuttings.

Taking a cutting from an annual—or a perennial—is just like taking one from a shrub. Cut off a stem with at least two leaf nodes and remove all but two or three leaves. Dip the cut end in rooting hormone if you are feeling energetic and stick it in moist well-drained soil so that at least one node is covered. You can go to the trouble of putting the cuttings in a pot of sand and covering the whole thing with a plastic bag, but this is not really necessary. I take cuttings of geraniums throughout the year and just stick them in the soil in the shade of the parent plants. Geranium cuttings survive better if you let the cut ends dry out for a day or two before planting them but when I do this I often forget to plant them so I prefer to plant them right away and lose a few.

In a month or two your cuttings will have grown roots and more leaves. In the autumn, I pinch off any flower buds that have formed and transplant the cuttings into a pot, crowding many of them into the same pot. The cuttings are then moved into a frost-free area, such as the garage, for the winter. If they are cool enough, they will need little water and light. I water them only when they wilt, which is seldom more than twice during the winter. In the spring, you can either wait until the weather warms and plant the cuttings straight in the garden or you can give them a head start by potting them up indoors. Separate the cuttings into pots, and give them light, water, and fertilizer. They will grow rapidly into flowering plants ready to go in the garden. Pelargoniums, like many annuals, will survive light frosts so you might like to experiment by putting some of them outdoors a bit earlier than you think is really safe. Impatiens can also be grown from cuttings in this way, as can wax begonias and ageratum.

ANNUALS FOR AUTUMN SOWING

I am particularly fond of the seeds, seedlings, and bulbs that we plant in autumn and forget over the winter. In spring, up they pop to delight us with what almost seem like flowers that arrived by themselves. Among the plants for autumn planting are biennials, which don't flower until their second year. Another is cool-weather annuals that usually germinate in the autumn and grow slowly through the winter, flowering in the spring. Larkspur, cornflowers (*Centaurea*), pot marigolds (*Calendula*), nasturtiums, sweet peas, annual poppies, and stocks (*Matthiola*), all fall into this category. They are especially valuable for warm-winter areas where most spring bulbs do not do well. If you live in the Deep South, California, or the almost frost-free parts of the British Isles, you will get more spring satisfaction from planting these seeds than from spending a lot more money on a disappointing display of daffodils.

Some of these plants will flower during any warm spell in winter, at least south of about Zone 6, but to do this, most of them need all the winter sun you can give them; which may not be the same as full sun in summer. Make sure you know where house and trees cast their shade in winter before you plant pansies where they will be shaded in December. I speak with feeling after some disappointing mistakes.

Biennials

Grow biennials from seed just as you would annuals, but start the seed in June to August so that you have sturdy little seedlings to plant out in the garden in autumn. In southern England and the Deep South, biennials such as pansies and double daisies (*Bellis perennis*) will flower for most of the winter. With petunias, *Dianthus* (pinks), and snapdragons they will stand quite a few degrees of frost and burst into renewed flower whenever the temperature rises.

Antirrhinum (Snapdragon)

Snapdragons don't bloom right through the winter as pansies do, but they do burst into flower in the South as the temperature begins to rise in February. They come in a staggering array of sizes and colors. I especially like the tall varieties, popped into the perennial border in fall to give the border a fully clothed look as early as February when perennials are still slumbering. Start them from seed in summer for fall planting and December or January for spring.

Consolida ambigua (Larkspur, often sold as *Delphinium ajacis*)

This less-grand member of the delphinium family is easy as pie from seed sown in the ground in later summer. Tall spikes of pink, white, blue, or purple flowers appear above feathery foliage in spring. Pick flowers for the house and side branches will then develop smaller flowers so the display goes on for several months. Thin the seedlings to give the plants a chance to reach a reasonable size. The larger plants flower much better and the seeds are so small that it is difficult to sow them as far apart as they should be—which is about 12 inches.

Dianthus (Pinks, carnations, sweet williams)

The genus *Dianthus* contains annual and perennial members, and the smaller species (pinks) rank second only to pansies as winter

Antirrhinum majus, **snapdragon**

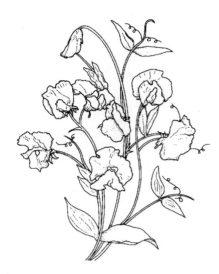

Sweet peas are among the best of annuals for cut flowers.

flowers for mild-winter areas. Treat them like pansies, planting them in a sunny area in late summer and give them a little more room than pansies because they put on rather more growth in cold weather. Like pansies, dianthus tend to fade away during hot weather so Southerners treat them as winter annuals, although many of them will behave as perennials in cooler areas, flowering through the summer.

Luckily the plant breeders haven't messed too horribly with sweet williams *(Dianthus barbatus)*, biennials that produce a fine display in the border and make great cut flowers. Buy a mixture of old-fashioned varieties with bicolored flowers and save your own seed from the flowers you like the best.

Eschscholzia (California poppy)
Sow the seeds of California poppies where they are to grow in autumn. Bright, opaque orange sounds as if it should be a "difficult" color in the garden but for some reason it is not. Plant breeders being what they are, California poppies now come in various rather dull yellow, red, and white varieties which old prune-face here thinks is a mistake because a California poppy to me is, by definition, orange.

Lathyrus odoratus (Sweet pea)
There is surely no lovelier annual than the sweet pea, with its pest-free growth, haunting scent, and armfuls of flowers for many weeks in spring. Sweet peas make wonderful cut flowers and the more you cut them the more they bloom so cut an armful for the house every day as soon as they start to flower. The modern hybrids have long strong stems and come in a multitude of colors. The older varieties are often more fragrant, but all sweet peas smell wonderful. Sweet peas come in a variety of colors that blend together beautifully so a packet of mixed seeds is quite acceptable although you can also buy single colors.

There are bush varieties, just as there are with garden peas, but the full glory of sweet peas is a long row of six foot climbers clothed from top to toe in translucent lavender, red, pink and white. You are on your own as far as supports go. It is not easy to provide one that looks good and that sweet peas like, especially since it has to be out in the open to give the plants enough winter sun. Perhaps you have two rose posts fairly close together, between which you can stretch black nylon netting of the kind sold for peas. Traditional pea brush is a possible solution. This is merely branches pruned from trees or shrubs, with the side branches left on for extra support and poked into the ground near the seeds.

Both sweet and garden peas climb by rather small tendrils and are not very good at starting up their supports. It is worth giving the small plants a helping hand by pulling them gently in the direction of the supports when you find them lying in a tangle on the ground.

Plant sweet pea seeds in early autumn against their trellis. They appreciate *very* rich, moist soil so lay on the compost or manure and dig it in deeply. Unless you have grown peas on the same site within the last two years, roll the seeds in legume inoculant before you plant. Plant the seeds in a trench about two inches deep in the South to about six inches in the north. Plant fairly thickly, in a double row with the seeds about an inch apart. Don't worry if the peas germinate in the autumn and even get slightly frost-bitten. (I think they are a little less hardy than garden peas.) The plants will recover and spring into life in the spring.

Lobularia maritima (Sweet alyssum)

Alyssum flowers so rapidly from seed that it can be planted where it will flower. Since it is quite hardy, I plant it in the edge of the border and in containers of pelargoniums in autumn. It is at its best where it can fall over the edge of something. By spring, it has formed a cascade of tiny white flowers. Since it is fairly hardy, Northerners may want to start seedlings indoors and plant them outside amid hyacinths or tulips a month or two before the date of last frost.

Nasturtium

Nasturtiums germinate rapidly and dislike disturbance so sow seed where they are to grow—preferably where they can ramble over a path or the edge of a border. Nasturtiums are supposed to do best in poor soil, but the fancy new varieties that abound seem to me to like rather richer bedding than their peasant ancestors. In northern

---

GREEN THUMBS TIP

MAKING CUT FLOWERS LAST

Does cutting stems under water preserves the life of cut flowers? Should I add preservatives to the water? Yes and yes, but it helps if you understand why.

Plants draw water up into shoots from their roots through xylem tubes. Dissolved food travels round the plant in similar tubes called phloem (a bit like our blood vessels). Water evaporating from leaves pulls water up through the xylem under tension. When you cut a stem, you break the water columns in the xylem. The plant continues to pull water up the tube, leaving an air bubble at the cut end. If you later put the stem in water, air bubbles in most of the tubes prevent water from being taken into the xylem. If, however, you cut off an inch or two of the stem under water, you prevent many air bubbles forming. Then move the stem as swiftly as possible from the container in which you cut the stem to the final vase for arrangement and most of the xylem tubes will be clear of air bubbles and can draw water up into the stem.

Floral preservatives usually contain sugar, chlorine, and acid. The sugar provides food and the chlorine sterilizes the water, preventing the growth of algae and bacteria which will block the tiny xylem and phloem tubes. The acid is though to prevent chemicals from blocking the xylem. Lemon soft drinks make good floral preservatives, since they contain acid (lemon) and sugar (don't use diet soda). You can buy floral preservative or you can dissolve a tablespoon of chlorine bleach, a teaspoon of table sugar and a tablespoon of vinegar or fresh lemon juice in a gallon of water. (The quantities are not critical.)

The plant hormone ethylene is a gas that speeds ripening of fruit and it also causes rapid senescence (aging) in cut flowers. So do not place cut flowers near fruits such as apples that produce ethylene. Silver ions block the effect of ethylene on flowers and the life of cut carnations can be more than doubled by placing the stems in a solution of silver thiosulfate. Look for silver-treated flowers when you are buying cut flowers.

areas, sow seeds as early in spring as you can. At Giverney, Monet's country farmhouse, the wide front walk is often planted with the nasturtiums he loved. By later summer, the plants have covered half the path in a stunning streak of gold and orange. Nasturtiums are also fine when they trail from window boxes, if you have one in full sun in a northern summer.

Pelargonium (Geranium)

Pelargoniums are usually grown in set pieces in the sunny border in summer. But in the South, modern varieties die of heat stroke in the sun in summer, which is how I discovered that they flower all year in the shade. Indeed they are the only annual I know of that flowers in shade in midwinter.

You often see seed for pelargoniums advertised nowadays, but in my experience, this is a tough way to acquire a new plant unless you are a real addict. Germination is poor, growth slow, and the seedlings tend to keel over from unidentified diseases. I usually end up with only one or two plants from a packet of seeds. Propagate them from cuttings.

Petunia

If, like me, you had rather given up on petunias as untidy and not very flowerful, help is at hand. Abandon those huge multicolored grandiflora varieties that have been so popular with garden centers for the last decade or more and go back to the old-fashioned multi-floras—which are harder to find. (Try the Stokes catalogue.) With good, fertile soil, a little manure tea, and occasional pinching, they will bloom for you all summer in the north and most of the winter in the south. Multifloras are smaller plants than grandifloras, with smaller flowers. Their big advantage is that they branch more than grandifloras so you don't get those long stringy stems with one flower on the tip. All types of double petunia are fussier and less free-flowering than the singles.

Petunias will take several degrees of frost, although they may stop flowering for a while. Take advantage of this to pinch them back, and they will come bursting back to life in short order.

Another grudge of mine against petunias is that open-polli-nated varieties are almost extinct and all you can usually find is the scentless sterile hybrids. Susan McClure says that Seeds Blum may be the last place on earth that you can buy open-pollinated petunias. We need to save some heirloom varieties if any are still lurking out there.

Viola hybrids (Pansies)

Pansies are highly bred biennial members of the genus *Viola*, which also includes all the lovely species of violets as well as johnny-jump-ups, those small, persistent occupants of many an unweeded corner of the garden. Thanks to the efforts of breeders, pansies come in

Zonal pelargoniums, so-called because of the zones of different color on their leaves.

most colors and various patterns and will flower in the autumn from seed planted in May in warmer parts of the world. For areas with mild winters, Thompson and Morgan has seed of pansies bred especially to flower all winter. Other varieties tend to stop flowering when the temperature falls much below freezing. Most pansies need to be deadheaded frequently for maximum flower power.

Pansies

DROUGHT-TOLERANT ANNUALS

The drought-tolerance of annuals depends on your climate and the time of year. In most places, annual and biennial seedlings planted in autumn need no water once they are established. The plants grow slowly in the cool weather and even dry parts of the world like California get enough winter rain to keep them going.

Finding drought-tolerant annuals for summer gardens is more difficult. Among drought-tolerant annuals:

Abronia (Sand verbena)

Amaranthus (Love lies bleeding)

Ammobium (Winged everlasting)

Brachycome (Swan River daisy)

Calandrinia (Rock purslane)

Calendula (Pot marigold) A cool weather annual, for winter use in the South.

Catharanthus roseus (Vinca, Madagascar periwinkle) Vinca is one of the success stories: a drug saved for modern medicine from a trop-

---

A SOUTHERN GARDENER'S JANUARY

Why the year starts with January, I don't know. It certainly isn't the beginning of the gardening year—which usually starts in October for me. But we are slaves to convention. And so are the mail order gardening outfits. They send out their seductive catalogues in January, February, or March when it is months too late to plant trees, shrubs, or perennials with a reasonable hope of success. And months too late for all the winter annual and vegetable seeds you wanted.

This situation makes for another characteristic feature of southern and British gardeners: they hardly ever plant fresh seed. Knowing they will have lost the catalogue by fall when they need the seed, they order seeds of anything that might come in handy in spring. This doesn't work because September reveals a dozen needs you didn't anticipate, but it does ensure a vast supply of aging seeds. My first laugh of the New Year came from the Smith and Hawken catalogue, which offered a dainty file box, about three inches deep, for storing unused seeds. My seeds occupy an entire vegetable drawer in the refrigerator.

You do learn some things from being out of whack with the rest of the world, however. One is that old leek and onion seed won't germinate. And it is even possible to keep sweet alyssum seed so long that it won't germinate.

In January when the catalogues have not come, you consider ordering from last year's catalogue. Sometimes you even do it, but you live to rue the day because all the prices and ordering instructions have changed in the meantime. If you are lucky, your plants and seeds will arrive, along with some random-looking charge to your credit card, and a sharp or kindly note pointing out the minimum order for one variety of canna and please bear this in mind in future. If you are unlucky, your order will be shuffled to the bottom of the pile and your seeds and plants will arrive in July when you are on vacation in some lovely mountainous area where it snows in the summer. Even if you were at home, you couldn't or wouldn't plant anything in July.

Oenothera biennis
Here is a biennial for the adventurous. A British company sent me the seed as a substitute. The first year, it formed a decorative rosette of leaves about 18" across. The following spring, it went berserk, each plant sending out half a dozen four-foot spikes and obliterating the amaryllis and lavatera in the same bed. It wasn't exactly covered in flowers, but they were a wonderful clear yellow. I tore it out thankfully when it had flowered, but I have scattered the seed in the rough meadow, where I think it will naturalize since the field guide says it is native.

ical ecosystem that is rapidly disappearing. The white- or purple-flowered plant produces vincristine, a chemical that has saved the lives of thousands of children who now survive childhood leukemia. It is also a tough little annual that survives drought and seeds itself in my hot summer garden and poor soil. Older varieties had a high leaf to flower ratio, but newer varieties have more flowers and more colors. Slow from seed, so start it early.

Celosia (Cockscomb) These strange-looking flowers are easy to grow in dry summer conditions unless they are randomly attacked by pests, which they sometimes are.

Centaurea (Cornflower, Bachelor's button) Not as tolerant of poor soil as the books suggest, but tolerant of drought and may act as perennials in the South.

Clarkia (sometimes sold as godetia) Lovely western U.S. natives that thrive in cool, dry summers in poor soil.

Datura (Trumpet flower) Several spectacular species that are most effective in containers in hot areas. Chop them down in autumn and overwinter indoors and they will return year after year. Slow from seed—allow 3 months.

Dianthus (Sweet william, pinks, carnations) We don't usually think of dianthus as drought-resistant but they are quite tough, especially in cooler weather.

Gazania Fascinating striped daisies, which act as perennials in the Southwest.

Gomphrena (Globe amaranth) Neat mounds of spherical flowers, to about 18 inches if you keep them dry, with fascinating color from white through a fine range of lavenders and violet.

Helianthus annuus (Sunflower) A pestilential weed in much farm country but there are some fine cultivars.

Lantana montevidensis (Trailing lantana) Really a perennial but fast from seed so perfectly acceptable when used as an annual. Comes in some pretty grim shades of lilac and yellow as a rule, so watch out for better colors and grab the seed if you find them.

Lasthenia glabrata (Lasthenia) A salt-tolerant annual with yellow flowers.

Layia campestris (Tidy tips) A western wild flower popular as an annual in England. It produces an attractive mound of yellow flowers with white tips to the petals.

Melampodium A Southwestern native and the latest in a long string of annuals that horticulturists are trying to convince themselves grow well in the impossible summers of the Deep South. I don't know why I dislike its starry golden-orange flowers, while enjoying the very similar flowers of *Zinnia angustifolia*.

Mesembryanthemum (Ice plant) Thousands of hybrids and species of South African succulents are grouped under this name. Many of them are ground-hugging and fine for edges, cracks in stonework, and as ground covers in dry parts of the world.

Nemophila (Baby blue eyes)

Nigella damascena (Love-in-a-mist) A feathery Mediterranean native that you might mistake for a cornflower, for dry areas where summer nights are not too humid.

Phlox Drummondii (Annual phlox) A Texas native, in cultivars of many colors, that is very useful where summers are long and hot. and comes in lovely colors.

Salvia Dozens of species and colors of this tough genus have brought this flower back from its despised position as the centerpiece of Victorian bedding displays. Plant breeders have done a good job. All that remains is for us to try all the hundreds of varieties available in our own gardens—an impossible task, but there is nothing wrong with settling for almost any variety of the blue sage, *S. farinacea,* or some of the newer variations on red sage, *S. splendens.*

Tithonia rotundifolia (Mexican sunflower) A monster, with flaming orange flowers with white centers that grows to six feet and falls over. "Interesting" is the word, but it is better behaved in a dry climate and makes a striking accent in a desert garden. Easy and quick from seed.

Verbena Attractive flowers in many colors. The annuals are less tolerant of drought and neglect than the perennial species.

Zinnia Sow seed where they are to grow and keep reseeding every month or so to replace mildewed old plants.

ANNUALS FOR SHADE

Ageratum You can now buy ageratum in wishy washy shades of pink and white as well as all the lovely shades of blue and purple. I suppose the white does show up better than the blue in shade, of which ageratum can tolerate a surprising amount. Slow from seed so start it early.

Begonia (Wax begonia) Surprisingly drought-resistant in the shade.

Digitalis (Foxglove) The Foxy strain of *D. purpurea* blooms both the first and second years from seed; up to three feet tall.

Impatiens. Besides regular impatiens *(I. Wallerana)* and balsam *(I Balsamina),* several other species are now being offered by seed companies and sound as if they might be worth trying. Carefree in the north, where they also tolerate sun, it takes too much water to keep *I. Wallerana* going where summers are long and hot. The finest display of impatiens I have ever seen was on the shady side of a funeral home with a white pillared porch and foundation planting of clipped yew. Every summer, the owner planted wine-colored impatiens (for a funereal effect?) in front of the yews. I don't know what the secret was, whether lots of pinching or little-and-often fertilizer,

Clarkia
Justly popular in England, clarkia hybrids should be more widely grown in the United States. They are drought-tolerant and floriferous.

Gerbera.
Being South African, you would expect these large daisies to like dry soil and sun but mine do best on an old compost heap in deep shade.

but by midsummer the impatiens had formed a wall of color two feet high that stretched in an unbroken curve down from the yews and over the edge of the lawn. Impatiens stay much more compact when grown in sun. My favorite is the appropriately named 'Blitz Violet,' a color to knock your socks off even in bright sun.

Myosotis sylvatica (Forget-me-not) A charming annual for shade in cool-summer areas.

Nicotiana (Flowering tobacco) We don't usually think of nicotiana as a shade plant but in most areas it flowers well on a north wall, though it has a bit of a tendency to lean out from the wall toward the light. A dwarf variety might stay in shape better in such a situation.

TALL ANNUALS

We usually think of annuals as fairly small, but there are a number that reach four feet or more at high speed and are useful when you want a little instant action in the garden. They can, for instance, give a settled look to a bed you have just planted with perennials which will take at least a year to grow to their full glory.

Many of these tall beauties are best enjoyed from a distance. Especially in windy areas, they have a tendency to flop around and many have rather coarse untidy foliage. The back of the border may hide some of their deficiencies and permit them to show off their flowers.

Althaea rosea (Hollyhock)

Amaranthus (Love-lies-bleeding) Among my favorite tall annuals are the amaranths. I stumbled on this large genus when I bought a packet of amaranth 'Illumination' one year. The seedlings sulked for a while in the cool spring weather but then they took off like rockets to almost six feet, spreading huge yellow and red leaves to the sun. I had stuck them near the street for want of other space and they stopped traffic. I felt I should have put up a notice saying, "Amaranth 'Illumination.' You can get the seed from Burpee." It would have saved me many repetitive conversations.

Amaranth has a romantic history. Its seeds were used by the Aztecs to make flour. Tropical experiment stations are now working with this genus, trying to find substitutes for grains such as wheat and oats. Grains are the most important human food plants and most of them cannot be grown in the tropics. Tropical countries, with their exploding populations, have to import grains and would be much more self-sufficient if they could grow their own substitutes to use for making bread and other flour products.

Antirrhinum (Snapdragon) Tall varieties.

Cleome spinosa (Spider flower) Cleome grows rapidly to up to five feet and produces big airy flower clusters up to eight inches across. Cleome is native to tropical America and comes in pink, lavender, and white and also has decorative seed pods. (*Cleome lutea*, a smaller species native to western North America, has yellow flowers.)

Consolida ambigua (Larkspur)

Hesperis matronalis (Dame's rocket)

Nicotiana, tall hybrids

Tithonia

Verbascum (Mullein) Gray-leaved plants that send up tall flower spikes. *V. bombyciferum* 'Arctic Summer' is a fine variety which may self-seed.

AN ANNUAL MEADOW

The idea of an annual meadow, I take it, is to remind the viewer of the prairie in spring as our ancestors must have seen it, of a California pasture bright with orange poppies, or of vacations in Europe before the advent of agricultural herbicides, when one would round a curve and open up a vista of scarlet Flanders poppies in a wheat field. Corners such as these are still to be seen, along the edge of a plowed field, in rescued corners of prairie, in a mountain meadow, or even in the roadside plantings of wild flowers that are partly the result of Lady Bird Johnson's hard work.

The difference between a rough lawn or prairie garden and an annual meadow is that the rough lawn is permanent. The annual meadow, in contrast, needs to be renovated every year. Succession being what it is, even mowing will not prevent perennials from eventually overwhelming annuals in a meadow. Look on an annual meadow as an experiment in producing a sheet of flowers, to be repeated or modified next year if you like the look of it. I have seen meadows effectively used in rectangular beds in the middle of lawns in a housing development as well as in less formal settings.

You can buy all sorts of aids to producing your meadow, from seed mixes to seedlings ready to plant. You can even buy seed or seedlings in sheets of landscape fabric which you merely roll out on top of prepared soil and water. It is no good thinking that you can just sprinkle a wildflower seed mixture on a corner of the lawn and stand back. Lawn grasses and the local weeds will rapidly overwhelm most seedlings that are lucky enough to germinate. You have to start by removing any turf, cultivating the soil, and weeding thoroughly. Don't enrich the soil, since the plants in your meadow are wild flowers, not adapted to rich garden soil. Then sprinkle your seeds over the area as thinly as possible, cover with a thin layer of grass clippings or hay, or rake the seed in lightly, water, and wait. If you notice aggressive local weeds rearing their ugly heads before the meadow seedlings have got a good start, a weeding now will improve the look of the meadow later on.

Of course it is essential to plant the right seeds. A good (and expensive) commercial wildflower mix is probably the way to go for

Layia, tidy tips.
Another western U.S. native popular in Britain and not widely grown in the United States. The (usually) yellow flowers make a decorative mound.

Shirley poppy, *Papaver rhoeas*
Favorite flowers for the meadow
garden, many annual poppies will
settle in and seed themselves. They
seem to do best in a moderately
fertile soil and are quite drought-
resistant.

your first meadow. The plants have been chosen for their wide
adaptability in your area and to be as tough and fast-growing as
possible. Many of these mixtures also contain perennials and annual
grasses that don't grow too tall and provide a bonus of interesting
seed heads in autumn and winter.

If you enjoy your first annual meadow, you can keep it going
from year to year with a little attention. First mow it in late autumn
or early spring with the mower on a high setting. Then weed it as
early in spring as possible to get rid of perennials before the
meadow seeds germinate. (Some will have germinated over winter
so you have to learn to recognize them.) You will probably find that
some local wild flowers, which would be weeds if they showed up
in the border, have seeded themselves in your meadow. If your
meadow is some distance from formal plantings, it is a nice idea to
encourage these locals and to covert your meadow gradually from
the plants chosen by the seed company to the plants of your local
biome. You can speed this process by collecting the seeds of attractive local wild flowers from road verges and hedgerows. Weedy
locals, however, are not a good idea if your meadow is upwind from
the vegetable garden or you will merely exacerbate what you probably already consider a weed problem.

One of the most effective places I have seen mixed perennial
and annual meadows is in suburban or countrified areas of
semidesert in the American west. Here, there is usually an irrigated
area around the house and, in summer, dried up grass on the road
verges and surrounding hillsides. By planting lupines, yarrow,
mullein, poppies, buckwheat, paintbrush and a few grasses in the
area between watered lawn and road, a colorful and natural-looking
transition between the garden and its dry surroundings is achieved.
Such a planting is really a concentrated version of the plants that
grow on the surrounding hills, with a little more attention to color
than nature pays. For instance, spots of red are very effective in
contrast to the prevailing gray, white, and ochre, so the meadow's
owner makes sure that something red is in flower all summer. If you
have a formal front garden, cut off from an informal road by a wall
or hedge, a meadow in this location is a delight to visitors and
passersby.

CHAPTER 11

Herbs and Fruit

Vegetable gardens have come and gone in my life, depending on the quality and distance of the nearest farmers' market or greengrocer, but I cannot imagine having a garden without some fruit and herbs. Even now, when stores contain a much better variety of fresh herbs than heretofore, it takes more planning than I am capable of to decide in the morning whether basil or marjoram is the herb for tonight's meal. How much more pleasant to step out of the door at mealtime in search of a handful of sage or a bay leaf, as the culinary fancy strikes. Even the most citybound can have a small herb garden in a container on the balcony or in a window box, to gladden the senses and the palate. If you really become interested in herbs, you will find yourself tempted beyond their use in cooking, and investigating recipes for pot pourri, pomanders, and holiday decorations, all of which give great delight to the maker and the user.

A fruit garden is a little more complicated because fruit trees take space and they also take time to bear fruit. At one peripatetic period of my life I calculated that I had planted 96 fruit trees and never tasted the fruit from any of them because we moved before they were old enough to bear. It was a pleasure to visit the same houses in later years and find that my neglected apples and grapes sometimes really were the hardy, tasty varieties I had hoped when I planted them.

EDIBLE LANDSCAPES
Rosemary Creasy made edible landscapes popular by pointing out that you can have a most attractive garden around the house even though almost everything you plant is edible. This, of course, was well known to our ancestors who, unless they were born with silver spoons in their mouths, made food the focus of the garden. An English cottage garden was, and still is, made up largely of rows of cabbages and potatoes, with

fruit trees, herbs, and flowers planted round the edges. A settler's garden in Texas or California often consisted of a fenced vegetable garden, with a few flowers and herbs. The flowers were for decoration; the herbs had many uses besides cooking. Lavender blossoms scented linens; artemisias were used as an insect repellent, to flavor vermouth, and as vermifuges; madder (*Rubia tinctorum)* and woad might have been grown to produce dyes, and dozens of herbs were grown for their medicinal properties.

Planted outside the fence, where they would not shade the vegetables, were fruit trees, such as mulberry, persimmon, and fig. An orchard might also be a fenced paddock, where chickens, geese, cows, or horses grazed on grass and fallen apples. A porch or arbor would usually be home to a grape or hop vine.

It was, after all, downright extravagant to plant a shade tree or vine that was merely decorative. And that is doubtless the reason that Victorian bedding plants and flowering shrubs became so popular: their presence in the garden showed that you were wealthy enough to grow things purely for decoration, a cachet that later attached to tanned bodies, to a man who could afford a nonworking wife, and to a woman with fingernails so long she was clearly incapable of manual labor. If we have now put aside at least this particular pretension, perhaps it is time to consider where we might use edible plants in our own landscapes. If you want a small (or even a large) tree to shade a terrace, what is wrong with an apple or a cherry tree? One of the things that's wrong with it is the fruit that it drops on the ground or on your head, but many homeowners put up with similar irritations from sweetgums or horse chestnuts without overmuch grumbling. The other common objection is that fruit trees take too much work. And indeed, if you read an article on the subject in a gardening magazine, you might be pardoned for thinking that your apple tree will die on the spot if you don't spray it twenty times a year and cosset it within an inch of its life. But these articles are directed at the grower who wants the highest possible yield from an orchard. Even neglected trees produce fruit, as the orchards near abandoned farms bear witness. And if this year the apples are full of worm holes, you can make cider from them or leave them for the wildlife instead of displaying them in your fruit bowl.

I find it one of the great pleasures of having a garden that it produces so many things that add to the quality of life. In a world that, for most of us, is all too full of long commutes, dirty clothes, and toddlers underfoot, it lifts the spirits at the end of a long day to nip into the garden and pick a sprig of parsley for the potatoes, a lemon for the gin and tonic, and a rose for the dinner table—instant gracious living for the downtrodden workers of the world.

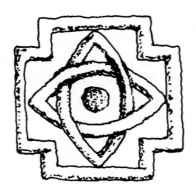

A small knot garden.

KNOT GARDENS AND PARTERRES

Of course herbs can be grown anywhere in the garden. Many are very decorative and are often used, like angelica, fennel, and lavender, in the flower garden. But if you plan to use your herbs, rather than just admire them, it is more convenient to have them segregated near the kitchen door than in some distant flower bed. There is a move afoot today to make our herb gardens formal and decorative. Perhaps this is part of the urge for gracious living. Perhaps it is nostalgia for what we imagine of domestic life in the seventeenth century: women in gardens and stillrooms, tending and processing herbs for medicine, dyes, and food. This image may well be the reason that the chosen style for a decorative herb garden is often a knot or parterre.

A knot is a garden made of low hedges entwined so that they look like patterns made from rope. Plans for enormously complicated knots can be found in seventeenth century books. Often, the spaces between the ropes of the knot appear to have been filled with colored gravels, not with plants. Rosemary Verey has created a lovely, simple, gravel-filled knot garden at Barnsley House. The term "knot" is sometimes used for any garden containing symmetrical, curved hedges. Strictly speaking, however, I think a true knot should give the impression that strands of the "rope" pass over and under one another. Otherwise, the garden belongs in the larger group of formal gardens known as parterres. "Parterre" is French for "on the ground" and can be used for any formal garden designed to be viewed from above, when the formal design is seen to best effect. Unlike a knot, a parterre need not include miniature hedges. The design can be outlined in bricks, gravel, liriope, tall privet or holly hedges, or anything else that grabs your fancy. The one constant is that the garden includes some kind of geometric, repeating pattern, whether of straight lines or curved.

GREEN THUMBS TIP SHADE FOR SOUTHERN HERBS

If you live in the Deep South, you will be able to grow a wide range of herbs if at least part of the garden is in the shade. The ideal spot for the garden is half under a deciduous tree, where the leaves will shade about half the garden in summer, but leave it sunny in winter. This will permit you to decorate the winter garden with sun-loving flowers such as nasturtiums and alyssum and will also speed the growth of winter parsley and sorrel while slowing its demise from heat stroke in summer.

Alternatively, put the garden against the north wall of the house. This will cramp your style in winter, when the garden will be in almost total shade, but it will yield more herbs in summer than would a garden entirely in the sun. Perennials such as lavender, rosemary, marjoram, and bay grow well in complete shade year round.

A herb garden laid out as a parterre made of stone or concrete slabs.

A herb garden laid out as a parterre with a sheared bay tree standard in a pot for a centerpiece.

It is possible to create a lovely herb garden in a knot. The snag is that you tend to trip over the hedges when tending the garden or picking herbs—especially in the dark. (In an ideal world, vegetable and herb gardens would have lights that can be turned on when you find yourself harvesting in the dark, which the disorganized among us often do.) Even if your herb garden is merely edged with a low box hedge the tripping-over-the hedge problem remains. For which reason, I think the most practical herb garden is one with an even more ancient history, stretching back to the Persian gardens of three thousand years ago: a parterre built of brick, paving stones, or gravel. This might be a circular affair with a sundial or bird bath in the middle and the beds and paths radiating out like spokes. Or it might be a checkerboard, squares of paving alternating with beds, with your precious bay tree or a dwarf banana in the center in an Italianate pot that can, if you are strong and live where bay and bananas are not hardy, be brought indoors for the winter. Herb beds need to be small, so that you can reach from the path into the center of the bed to weed or pick. And, unless the garden is tiny, remember the rule about making paths wide enough so that you can get at least your small garden cart along to deliver compost or seedlings.

STANDARDS

The bay tree or sundial in the center is designed to add height and elegance to what might otherwise be a rather flat, uninteresting area. Many herbs are woody shrubs or herbaceous perennials with tough stalks that lend themselves well to being trained as standards or other topiary shapes, permitting you to achieve height in the herb garden even without statuary or expensive pots. A standard is merely a ball on top of a straight stalk, grown like a mophead tree.

The classic standard for a herb garden is bay, *Laurus nobilis*, which grows into quite a large tree if you don't stop it. Bay, or sweet laurel, is a Mediterranean native, and an ancient symbol of peace and victory. Hence its use to make the laurel wreaths that were used to crown Roman generals, emperors, and poets. Aromatic bay leaves have long been used in cooking and are a necessary ingredient of *bouquet garni*. Unless you live in Zones 8 to 10, where it is hardy, grow bay in a pot and give it a warm sunny spot in the garden in summer.

Lugging large pots in and out is not for the weak and feeble, so if you live where bay is not hardy, you would probably prefer to make a standard out of something else. You might try sea buckthorn (*Hippophae rhamnoides*), whose berries are used in Scandinavian sauces for fish. Barberry (*Berberis vulgaris*) would also make a hardy, if rather prickly, standard. The roots make a fine yellow dye and the berries make a tasty jelly, high in vitamin C and soothing to a sore throat. If you have space for it, a fairly large hardy deciduous standard could be made of almost any species of hawthorn (*Crataegus* spp.), which is a tidy grower, and easily shaped if you can avoid the thorns. The leaf buds make a tasty addition to spring salads and the ripe berries make a delicious jelly. Myrtle (*Myrtus communis*) has a long history of use for dyes, perfumes, and tea and is easy to shape, although it is hardy only to Zone 8. In the desert Southwest, a little lemon tree or kumquat, in a pot or in the ground, would make a pretty vertical accent, or you could use barberry in a cold area or a strawberry tree (*Arbutus unedo*) in a warmer one. In the northeastern states and in much of Britain, the evergreen standard of choice might be some species of juniper, which would take quite a while to grow but be very beautiful when shaped. I know we don't usually think of juniper as a herb, but you can console yourself that the berries are used to flavor gin.

One of the joys of a herb garden is that you can include any of a vast range of plants if the spirit moves. The things we think of as herbs today would seem very limited to an eighteenth century gardener. Old herb gardens contained not just culinary herbs but thousands of medicinal flowers such as foxgloves and primroses, insecticidal flowers such as larkspur and pyrethrum, plants for making cosmetics and scents, and herbs to strew on the floor to scent the air or mask unpleasant smells. (Modern "air fresheners" anesthetize the sense of smell for the same effect.)

Hedging Plants

If you are going to use low hedges in your garden, I strongly recommend using dwarf box or holly rather than things like germander (*Teucrium chamedrys*), santolina, myrtle, or lavender, all of which are much faster growing and shorter lived. For this reason, they are less satisfactory, having a tendency to die erratically, leaving holes in

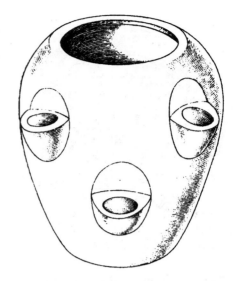

A stawberry jar.
Traditionally used for strawberries, a strawberry jar could also hold a collection of herbs for a tiny herb garden on patio or balcony.

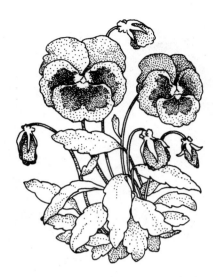

Pansies can be used for decoration in the herb garden. The edible flowers add color to a salad.

your hedge, and to put on so much growth in a season that the long stems flop about in midsummer, which is not the effect you want. Lavender is beautiful when left to grow naturally, in which case it gets too large for a miniature hedge.

Korean box is the hardiest good-looking hedge plant if you live in the North. English box is hardy only to Zone 6. When you buy hedging plants, the cheapest way is to buy seedlings from a large nursery. But if you lash out and buy plants in containers, inspect them carefully before planting. You may find, as I did with a recent batch of box, that you have more plants than you paid for, because the grower stuck more than one cutting in some containers or because some of the lower branches have rooted. Separate these extra rooted stems and use them for every other plant in the hedge and the hedge will look thicker. Plant deeply. Most plants that you buy or grow from cuttings have a length of stem between the roots and first branch because they were not pruned early enough. If you want your hedge to be foliage right down to the ground, you have to bury this extra length of stem.

PERENNIAL HERBS

If you are into herbal teas, the list of herbs you grow is probably much longer than mine. We are *Camellia sinensis* drinkers in this family so we don't grow the vast list of things such as *Melissa officinalis* (lemon balm), *Monarda didyma* (Oswego tea), *Matricaria chamomilla* (German camomile), *Marrubium vulgare* (horehound), *Hyssopus officinalis* (hyssop), *Agastache foeniculum* (anise hyssop), and *Valeriana officinalis* (valerian), that can be used for tea, or at least we don't grow them in the herb garden. People who are into pot pourri and herbal decorations will also grow plants specially for this purpose, but most of these belong in the open garden as well. Enough *Artemisia* to make a few wreaths at Christmas would soon overwhelm a small herb garden. Everyone has a list of herbs they consider indispensable so this one makes no claims to be complete. It includes only culinary herbs and includes a few oddballs that happen to be family favorites.

Bay (*Laurus nobilis*)

When you buy a bay plant you will get a rooted cutting in a pot. It will need frequent pruning once it gets going or you will have a fairly large tree on your hands. It makes a delightful standard. If you haven't yet tried growing your own bay, the improvement in taste over the dried variety will impress you.

Chives (*Allium schoenprasum*)

Like most members of the onion family, chive seeds are slow germinators so you may find it easiest to purchase plants. The grassy leaves make a pretty row or clump in a herb bed and produce attractive lavender (edible) flowers in spring. Chives grow slowly and increase by division. You will probably find you have large clumps that need to be divided every few years unless you eat an awful lot of chives. Garlic chives *(Allium tuberosum)* have wider leaves and a slight taste of garlic.

Use scissors to cut the leaves as you need them for a mild onion flavor. Chopped chives are decorative sprinkled on soups and many other light-colored dishes.

Horseradish *(Armoracia rusticana)*

The horseradish you buy in a jar consists of grated roots of the horseradish plant, bottled in vinegar. A European with large fleshy roots, horseradish tends to be invasive and forms large plants so give it plenty of room. It is propagated by root division and does not seem to be fussy about where it grows, although it won't stand prolonged drought and prefers rich garden soil and at least some sun. To get fat roots, uncover the top inch of root occasionally and rub off any rootlets (branches) that form, then re-cover the root.

Horseradish tastes better after frost so do not harvest it until winter. Then dig it all up, throw the leaves on the compost pile and wash the roots. Cut off the smaller roots and set them aside to replant for next year. Scrape or peel the larger roots to remove dirt and toss them in the blender or food processor with a little vinegar or lemon juice. Scrape the grated roots into jars and store them in the refrigerator or pop them in plastic bags in the freezer.

Take the roots you have saved to replant and cut off all the side roots so that the main root will grow into a convenient single giant root by next year. Replant.

Blend fresh grated horseradish with heavy cream or sour cream to accompany roast pork or sauerbrauten. Add horseradish and a little sugar to white sauce to make Sauce Albert—wonderful with ham or beef.

THOM SMITH'S COCKTAIL SAUCE

Horseradish
Tomato ketchup
Worcestershire sauce
Garlic powder
Lemon juice
Put your prepared horseradish into a bowl and add ketchup until everyone who is going to eat it agrees that the mixture is pungent but not too hot. Add garlic, Worcestershire, and lemon juice to taste.

Use as a dip with raw oysters and clams or freshly steamed oysters, clams, shrimp, or crabs.

UNDERSTANDING THE ENVIRONMENT

PLANT SECONDARY CHEMICALS

The chemicals that give herbs their taste and odor are plant secondary chemicals, chemicals that are not part of the plant's metabolism but serve other functions, usually defense against herbivores that might eat the plant. If an Eastern black swallowtail butterfly lays her eggs by mistake on a mustard plant instead of on wild carrot as usual, the caterpillars will die from the mustard oils that crucifer family plants produce (and which is what we smell when mustard or cabbage are cooked). Garden crucifers, such as broccoli and brus-sels sprouts, have been bred to contain less mustard oil because humans prefer a mild taste of these oils. This is why garden plants are so heavily attacked by things like cabbage white caterpillars, which have evolved the enzymes to detoxify mustard oils.

Secondary chemicals are the reason few herbs suffer much insect damage. They are also the reason it is important to take the right amount of the many medicines made from plant secondary chemicals that are poisonous in large doses. For instance, digitalin from foxgloves, and plant alkaloids such as caffeine, morphine, and strychnine, are useful medicines but will poison even large animals like us if consumed in large amounts.

Mint

Marjoram = Oregano *(Origanum spp.)*

The "oregano" on a grocery shelf is usually a mixture of herbs, running largely to various species of marjoram, dominated by *Origanum onites* (pot marjoram), which holds its flavor better than the other species when dried or cooked. Wild marjoram *(O. vulgare)* is a creeping perennial of dry, especially limestone, areas in Europe. It has a fine taste but the wild type is a nuisance in the garden because it forms a ground cover even lower than thyme and it is difficult to disentangle the marjoram from the inevitable weeds when you want some. Unless you have room to let it roam between paving stones, when it looks very pretty, a bush variety of pot marjoram is better. This is a woody perennial. The variety 'Aureum' has golden leaves but must be grown in shade or the leaves will scorch. Trim long stems from pot marjoram if they appear and you will have a bush up to two feet high. Greek oregano *(O. heracleoticum)* also forms a handsome mound if you keep it trimmed. The most delicate flavor or all comes from sweet marjoram *(O. Majoranum)*, but delicacy may not be what you want to flavor a tomato sauce. Pot marjoram or Greek oregano are spicier. You can buy marjoram seeds, but it is usually easier to propagate by division or cuttings.

Mint *(Mentha* spp.)

There are many species of mints with slightly different flavors. The common spearmint used to make mint jelly or mint sauce, traditional accompaniment to lamb, is *Mentha spicata*, introduced to Britain by the Romans. The various species of mint hybridize readily so if you want to keep them separate, plant them far apart.

If you are in doubt about whether mint is invasive in your climate, don't risk it. Grubbing mint out of a bed is an almost impossible task. You are sometimes advised to grow mint in a pot sunk in the ground, but those long roots have no trouble penetrating the drainage hole in a pot so if you do choose the pot method, pull the pot up occasionally to make sure the roots are not escaping.

Use mint leaves in mint juleps, chopped with sugar and vinegar as traditional English mint sauce, in tea, and chopped with cucumbers and sour cream for a lovely salad.

Pineapple sage *(Salvia rutilans)*

A lovely tender perennial with fragrant leaves and red flowers. Sprinkle the flowers on a salad for a touch of color and novel taste.

Rosemary *(Rosmarinus officinalis)*

Rosemary—traditional accompaniment to lamb or pork—is another of those Mediterranean shrubs that likes lime and dry soil, although it is not really fussy as long as the soil is well-drained. It has handsome straight branches with leaves that look like short fat pine

Rosemary

needles—a tip off that it is a true xerophyte and very drought-tolerant. It will grow into a sizeable shrub if you let it and produces blue flowers in January in Zone 8. Love it for its looks and for those magnificent pork chops.

Saffron crocus (Crocus sativus)

What could be more exotic than your own saffron to flavor a paella in autumn when this attractive plant blooms? You can grow saffron from seed, but it takes about three years to bloom. Easier to plant bulbs in very dry sandy soil. Like many herbs, saffron is happiest in an almost desert environment. When it flowers, immediately remove the stigmas and dry them in the sun; then store them in a dark place in an airtight container.

Sage (Salvia officinalis)

Sage is a hardy, woody perennial that grows rapidly into a shrub about three feet high. Prune it fairly often to achieve an attractive shape if you live in Zone 5 or thereabouts, where sage grows rapidly. There are many attractive varieties with yellow and variegated leaves to add a decorative touch to the herb garden.

Sorrel (Rumex acetosa)

Sorrel is a leafy perennial (and a common weed in many areas). The young leaves impart a lemony taste to salads, soups, and sauces. Sorrel sauce is the traditional accompaniment to shad (and shad roe), that delicious seasonal delicacy. Sorrel is high in Vitamin C but

---

 **SORREL RECIPES**

COLD SORREL SOUP

5 cups chicken broth
1/2 lb washed and chopped sorrel
4 egg yolks
2 cups light cream
Juice of half lemon

Heat the chicken broth to boiling. Add the sorrel, remove from heat and purée in the liquidizer (or pass through food mill). Sieve. Return to saucepan and gently beat in the egg yolks and cream. Cook until slightly thickened, stirring frequently, over very low heat or hot water. Do not allow to boil. Add lemon and salt to taste and refrigerate until cold (Serves 4-6).

JANUARY SALAD

One of our favorite winter salads is young spinach, leaf lettuce, sorrel leaves and parsley served with poppy seed dressing.

SORREL SAUCE

1 Tb butter
1 Tb flour
1/2 cup clam juice or chicken broth, hot
1/2 cup light cream, Juice of 1/2 lemon
1 cup sorrel leaves, stemmed, washed and finely chopped

Melt butter over medium heat. Add flour and stir until mixture foams. Cook one minute. Add hot liquid and stir. Add cream and reheat. Stir in sorrel and lemon juice. Blend if you prefer your sauce without sorrel bits. Serve with trout, shad, flounder, bass, shark.

also in oxalic acid. Some people are allergic to this and large quantities of it are said to encourage bladder stones and gout so don't consume large quantities of sorrel unless you are sure it agrees with you.

Sorrel is easily grown from seed and likes rich, well-drained soil with a slightly acid pH. In the Deep South, it has to be planted in deep shade to survive the heat of summer. If you live where it is happier, sorrel may be invasive, so cut off seed heads when these appear to prevent it spreading through the garden. If sorrel threatens to take over, you can often kill it by sprinkling it with lime. The old leaves are tough and unpleasant but need to be picked off if you want to keep the tender young leaves coming from the center of the plant. French sorrel *(R. scutatus)* is less bitter and more popular for that famous delicacy, sorrel soup.

Tagetes lucida

This marigold species is a substitute for tarragon in areas too hot for the real thing. You can grow *T. lucida* as an annual further north (it has pretty orange flowers), but I can't imagine why you would want to if you can grow tarragon.

Tarragon *(Artemisia dracunculus sativus)*

Don't let anyone sell you Russian tarragon. The kind you want is French tarragon, which does not come true from seed so you have to buy plants. This is a narrow-leaved plant up to three feet tall. It likes dry shade, although it is perfectly happy in the sun in cool parts of the world. It doesn't like the heat in Zone 8 and points south.

Thyme *(Thymus* spp.)

Thyme is the quintessential herb, essential to the well-ordered kitchen and a beautiful mat-forming plant in the garden. Wild thyme *(T. serpyllum)* is the culinary species, a shrubby perennial of northern Europe where it grows in dry, poor soil. This essential ingredient of bouquet garni, cosmetics, perfumes, mouthwashes, toothpastes, and pot pourri is easy to grow in dry soil in sun. Garden thyme *(Thymus vulgaris)* is a bit stronger and dozens of varieties and hybrids are sold for decorative use in the garden. Thyme is lovely creeping between stones or over walls, where its tidy foliage and white or purple flowers can be enjoyed.

Vita Sackville-West planted a thyme lawn at Sissinghurst, a tapestry of different colored varieties. It would not be difficult to produce the same effect in one bed of a home herb garden. Come to think of it, the beauty of thyme, wild strawberries, and other low-growing herbs is another argument for building the herb garden out of stone or wood rather than low hedges, which tend to hide attractive low-growing plants.

Wild strawberry *(Fragaria vesca)*
Not really a herb, but I cannot imagine a herb garden without a bed edged with *fraises des bois* to nibble on as you weed. These tiny strawberries are native to Europe and eastern North America and much tastier than the domesticated variety. 'Baron Solenmacher' is reputed to have the best flavor, but I love 'Alpine Pineapple Crush' (try Parks Seed), a long yellow berry with a succulent flavor of pineapple that bears for several months.

ANNUAL HERBS
If you want to add a little color to the herb garden, it is easily done by including some of the annuals and perennial flowers that are good in salads. You may not want to plant dandelions to use their leaves in salads, but nasturtium, dame's rocket, and pot marigolds *(Calendula officinalis)* are all attractive. Eat the leaves and flowers of nasturtiums, the flowers of pot marigolds, and the leaves of dame's rocket *(Hesperis matronalis)*.

Basil *(Ocimum basilicum)*
There are now dozens of varieties of basil including Thai basil for oriental cuisine, one with purple leaves that makes an attractive addition to a border, and a dwarf globe variety that can be used for temporary hedges, although it needs quite a bit of pruning. Plain old large-leaved sweet basil is the best variety for most cooking needs.

Borage *(Borago officinalis)*
Borage is beautiful, with leaves and 18-inch stems covered with white hairs and blue star-like flowers for much of the summer. The young leaves have a cucumber-like taste and are used to flavor drinks. Borage is used as a pot herb and often grown near bee hives. Bees make a delicious honey with it. Borage grows rapidly from seeds sown in spring and may well self-seed where it is happy—in dry stony or sandy soil with a fairly high pH.

Cilantro=Coriander *(Coriandrum sativum)*
Cilantro leaves have a pungent taste that is an essential ingredient in Indian and Mexican cooking. The seeds are the spice coriander. If you are growing cilantro mainly for the leaves, try a variety that is slow to bolt because the wild type sets seed and dies very rapidly when hot weather arrives. Fresh cilantro contains a remarkable 6000 units of vitamin A per 100 grams so it is very nutritious, in case you care.

Dill *(Anethum graveolens)*
Dill is a Eurasian native, naturalized in North America. The seeds are used in pickles and the leaves are a traditional flavoring for fish dishes—delicious with cold salmon. The plant grows rapidly from seed to as much as six feet. If your garden is windy, you will be

Dill

happier with a dwarf variety, less likely to fall over. The feathery foliage and flat clusters of yellow flowers make dill a very handsome presence in the herb garden.

Parsley (*Petroselinum crispum*)

Parsley is a European biennial that is easy to grow almost anywhere. Curled parsley is usually used to decorate food. It is rather coarse and tasteless. Flat-leaved Italian (French) parsley has more flavor and a better texture in salads.

Parsley is easy to grow. It needs no fertilizer or special watering. But it grows extremely slowly and is, therefore, easy to lose in the weeds. In the Deep South, plant seeds in the sun in early winter and then transplant a dozen plants into the shady herb bed before hot weather arrives. Plant seeds at least once a year to keep the supply coming. We don't bother to thin parsley but merely transplant it in clumps, like chives. Crowded like this, it makes a handsome mini-hedge of its own.

FRUIT TREES

I think it is a pity that we have lost our grandparents' habit of sometimes planting a fruit tree when we just want a tree. If you have ordinary, fairly fertile soil, you can grow fruit trees for their shapely branches, lovely flowers, and even for their fruit. It is true that there are several barriers that make it easier to plant a maple or flowering cherry. One is the intimidating barrage of literature that tells you fruit trees need to be sprayed with every imaginable chemical and pruned with scientific accuracy if they are not to succumb to diseases with long names; whereas you know that you can just plant your flowering cherry or maple and leave it to fend for itself.

The literature also tells you fruit trees are short-lived and you have visions of having to replace them if you stay in the same garden for twenty years. This is misleading. While fruit trees (including your flowering cherry) do not have the lifespan of climax trees, they don't usually drop dead after 20 or 30 years. But they do start to bear less fruit. An apple or cherry tree may have a life span of less than 20 years in a commercial orchard, but in a home landscape it may well live for a century, becoming gnarled and interesting as it ages.

If you have had experience with growing fruit in the past you may also have concluded that it is a little too environment-friendly. The local raccoons, woodchucks, opossums, bears, and at least 50 species of birds are up before you every morning in search of whatever's ripe and, dearly as you love them, you are fed up with weeding strawberries and pruning blackberries for the benefit of the wildlife. This is a very real problem with soft fruit. Indeed, if you are going to go into soft fruit production in a big way, it is worth

Apple blossom and fruit.

building a netted cage to keep the wee beasties out of your raspberries. But it does not apply to most fruits that grow on trees unless you are very parsimonious about sharing the bounty. You are stuck with a certain amount of loss, anyway, if you garden environmentally. The viceroy butterfly attracted by your butterfly plantings may well leave its caterpillars on the leaves of your apple tree, as may the attractive red spotted purple butterfly *(Incisalia augustinus)*, although the caterpillars will not harm the fruit. You will lose some fruit to this and that, but not all of it. Pears and bananas, for instance, are picked before they are ripe and ripened indoors, and few animals are interested in unripe fruit so they eat mainly the overripe fruit that falls to the ground. There are exceptions. I met howler monkeys in Costa Rica that threw half-eaten unripe mangoes at us—which was when I learned that unripe mangoes are even tastier than ripe ones, making a marvellous salad served with a sweet-sour dressing.

A final deterrent to planting fruit trees is that you may once have purchased a fruit tree that just sat there and stared at you. You know there are hundreds of varieties out there and that you got the wrong one, but where do you turn for advice on finding the right one? Tanya Denckla's *Gardening At A Glance* is one easy place to start, but you also need local advice.

Cherries

FINDING THE RIGHT VARIETIES

The answer is to find a fruit tree grower in your area. Books like *The Mail Order Gardener,* list almost every grower in the country. In upstate New York, we were not far from Millers of Canandaigua. In Savannah, TyTy Nurseries propagate fruit trees in our area. The first move is to study the catalogue of such a nursery. If you can also visit these places and pick their brains, so much the better, but you can also do business by mail. Don't forget, when ordering fruit trees, to check pollination requirements. Some varieties are self-fertile, but many need another plant somewhere in the vicinity so that they can cross-fertilize.

As an environmental gardener, I like to start with native fruits, such as American grapes *(Vitis labrusca)* and naturalized apples in New York, persimmons in Georgia. But you want the tastiest, easiest, most pest-resistant varieties. (In the case of persimmons, this means going with oriental persimmons, *Diospyros kaki*, which are actually not native, but I am no purist.) Apples (descendants of *Malus pumila*) are native to the north temperate zone and easy to grow in most parts of it. I was heartened to find that old favorite 'Granny Smith' recommended as one of the best apples for the South.

Temperate natives for northern gardeners to start with are sour cherries *(Prunus cerasus)*, marvellous for pies, peaches *(Prunus persica)*, much better adapted to Missouri and points north than to the South, despite popular misconception to the contrary, and apricots *(Prunus armeniaca)*. I had no idea apricots could be drip-down-your-chin juicy until I found a roadside stand in Ontario that sold peerless apricots the size of peaches.

PRUNING AND TRAINING

Don't prune a fruit tree when you plant it. It will have been correctly pruned at the nursery. Unless you are using it as a shade tree, you probably want to stop the tree getting so tall that the fruit is impossible to pick. The usual way of doing this is to encourage an arched shape in which branches that head up or down are removed and ones that point outward are retained. After the second or third year of pruning, the final shape of the tree is established and you should have only three or four main branches whose side branches will produce most of the fruit. Make sure that these main branches point upward at about a 60 degree angle to the trunk and are well separated. Where two branches cross or touch remove one of them, and of course remove any dead or diseased wood. A cherry tree usually needs nothing more than this light pruning every winter. Pears, peaches, and apples tend to produce lots of internal branches, however, and need more pruning to open up the inside of the tree.

Researchers have recently discovered that pruning is the best way to control the bacterial disease fire blight in apples and pears

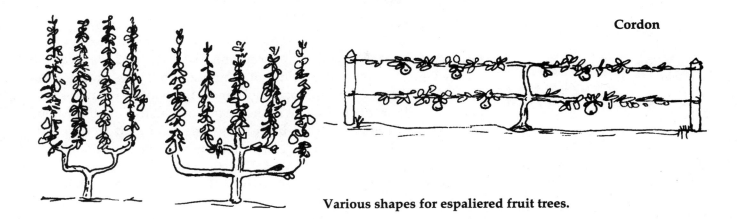

Cordon

Various shapes for espaliered fruit trees.

(although resistant varieties really are quite resistant). Fire blight turns a branch black or brown as if it had been scorched and reddish, water-soaked lesions develop on the bark. The secret is not to fertilize, to let grass grow right up to the tree to slow its growth, and to prune whenever you detect fire blight. Cut the diseased limb at least 12 inches below the infection, sterilizing your shears with bleach between cuts. This is not such a major task as it sounds since fire blight nearly always occurs in thin new shoots that are easy to remove.

Espaliering Fruit Trees

If you are not planting an orchard, consider espaliering fruit trees up the walls of the house or in low cordons or high fences along paths or around the vegetable garden. Walls with plants on them give a house that been-here-for-centuries look for which foundation planting is no substitute. Espaliers bear more fruit than ordinary trees of the same size because pulling the branches down induces them to produce more side shoots that flower and fruit. The warmth of the wall also often induces the tree to bear earlier than it would in the open and an espalier insulates the house, reducing energy costs.

Start an espalier by constructing a sturdy framework to which you can tie branches. Then, each year, you select the branches to keep, tie them to the frame, and remove other branches. Many people tie bamboo canes to the branches to be trained. This spreads the strain on a tied branch over the whole length of the branch and the canes can be removed after a year or two.

Of course there is an easier way than this to grow a tree up the side of a house if you have an informal sort of house, such as an old farmhouse or a cottage in a village. Just plant the tree and prune off all branches that grow in the direction of the house or out away from the house, retaining those that grow in the plane of the wall. This will probably be all the pruning the tree ever needs.

UNDERSTANDING THE ENVIRONMENT
FUNGI AND BACTERIA

While contemplating fire blight in pears, it may have occurred to you that fungus diseases are more common in plants, bacterial diseases in animals. There is a reason more fungi parasitize plants than animals. Most fungi, like animals, need air for respiration, so they do better in the bodies of plants, which are full of air spaces, than in the bodies of animals, which are not. Fungi that do attack animals, like ringworm and athletes foot, nearly all live on the surface where there is plenty of air. Yeasts used to make wine and bread are exceptional; when deprived of air, they make alcohol instead. Many bacteria, in contrast, are anaerobic and can survive inside the bodies of animals, where many of them cause disease.

Thinning Fruit

Whether you are growing a standard or an espalier, apples, pears, plums, and peaches will bear more and larger fruit if the fruit is thinned after it has formed. Without thinning, some trees produce so much fruit that it may even break a branch. Some of the young fruit naturally fall off the tree early in the year. Keep an eye open for this "June drop." After it is over, inspect the trees and start to thin the rest of the fruit by hand. Don't thin all at once, because some of the remaining fruit will fall off by itself as the summer progresses, but by the time the fruit approaches full size, you should have completed the thinning. Apples, peaches, and pears should be thinned so that the fruit is about six to eight inches apart; apricots and plums to about three inches.

EXOTIC FRUITS

Bananas are monocots so they are not real trees. They love wet soil although they will grow without it. They are pruned completely differently from ordinary trees. After each stalk bears fruit, you cut it to the ground. New stalks continually sprout from the steadily growing rhizome. Wild type bananas are tropical and take about 18 months to bear fruit from the time a stalk starts to grow. But breeders have shortened this period so that you can now buy varieties that bear in about 10 months. This is long enough to produce fruit most years in Zone 8, where a banana may be cut back to the ground by frost. If you live in the South and have always viewed your banana as a foliage plant, do try one of the new short-season varieties that may produce edible fruit for you. Some of them are much tastier than the commercial banana and there are also varieties with red leaves that make attractive accents in the garden. Bananas will grow in shade, although they may not produce as many fruit as in the sun. I have one growing in the dry shade of two evergreen oaks. It is not growing as rapidly as the ones with more water and sun, but its pale green, tropical looking leaves are a striking accent.

Figs (*Ficus carica*) are about the easiest fruit to grow since they need no pruning or fertilizing to bear heavy crops of fruit. However, if you have never grown figs before, be warned that they don't grow in the predictable small-tree fashion of apples and plums and they are not really suitable for formal areas. Most of them grow six to twenty feet tall and about the same across, depending on the variety. Sometimes they produce new stems from the roots or very low on the trunk, and sometimes a branch goes off at a right angle for no obvious reason. Their roots also tend to travel to places where you don't want or expect them. If you can give them enough space to let them do whatever they are doing, they make handsome contorted trees with large, tropical looking leaves. They like moist clay soil, although not standing water. Figs do not seem to have any pests, although most birds are fond of figs. If you live where figs are marginally hardy, it's worth knowing that trees that are never fertilized are much hardier than those that are. Figs bear for more than 50 years and each produces about 50 pounds of fruit a year. You cannot propagate most fruit trees from cuttings because they are grafted, but figs are an exception and easy to propagate from twelve-inch twigs stuck deeply into the ground in winter.

BERRIES AND FRUITING SHRUBS

"Soft fruit" are things like blackberries, and blueberries that are soft when ripe and grow on shrubs or herbaceous plants rather than trees. They also include currants and gooseberries, attractive shrubs with fruit that makes marvellous jelly and pies, not to mention gooseberry fool. Currants and gooseberries harbor white pine blister rust, a fungus that causes damage where white pines grow, so check with your county agent that it is legal to grow the fruit in your area before planting these two.

Mulberries are worth planting in an attempt to keep birds from attacking soft fruit. New mulberry varieties are much improved and even tasty for people to eat straight from the tree. Even if you don't like the taste, mulberries are one of the very best wildlife plants. Mulberries are generally grown as shade trees and cursed for dropping purple fruit on the sidewalk which people then tread in and traipse into the house. Plant a new variety of mulberry at the end of the orchard as the settlers did, or somewhere where dropped fruit doesn't matter, and enjoy the birds and animals that visit you.

Quince don't fit into the soft fruit category because they are not soft, but, on the other hand, they grow on shrubs rather than trees since a quince seldom grows more than ten feet tall. If you like quince jelly, you can buy various varieties for the home orchard, but you can also make very good jelly from the Japanese quince (*Chaenomeles*) in the shrub border.

Blueberries *(Vaccinium)*, like quince, grow on handsome well-behaved shrubs that are happy in the shrub border. Make sure you buy the right variety for your area and plant them where they get plenty of sun since blueberries are plants of the open hillside rather than the forest floor. Since they need acid soil, they do best in the eastern United States and the northwest coast as far south as northern California. Keep a thick mulch around blueberries at all times—up to eight inches on older plants—and prune them in winter because the largest berries are borne on new wood. Prune out dead wood and the oldest, thickest branches.

Blackberries, boysenberries, loganberries, dewberries, and youngberries *(Rubus)* are all thought to be derived from plain old wild blackberries, which have undergone extensive breeding. You

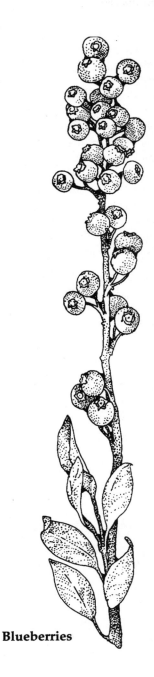

Blueberries

Strawberries

can buy varieties that are hardy from Zones 3 to 10. Breeders have finally taken the most useful step of all—producing thornless blackberries, which I consider a horticultural triumph. Blackberries are not for the faint of heart because if you neglect the pruning, you have a jungle on your hands which will bear little fruit and take a lot of sorting out. If you are not the totally organized type, make life easier by buying a thornless bush variety rather than a vining type. Blackberries produce new canes from the roots each year and the canes bear fruit and die in their second year. This means that every winter you need to prune out all the canes that have borne fruit— which are usually easy to tell because they bear the remains of fruit and are thicker than the younger canes. Then thin the younger canes to about ten inches apart, to give each some space and to prevent the plants growing into nearby paths and beds. Now prune side branches to about 18 inches long and give the plants a thick mulch. In the spring, when new shoots are about three feet high, cut off their tips to induce side branches.

Raspberries are perhaps the most valuable soft fruit for the home garden because they are so soft they travel poorly. There are several varieties, hardy from Zones 3 or 4 to 7 or 8. Prune them as you do blackberries and don't wash the fruit after you pick it as this dilutes the flavor.

Strawberries are probably the most popular fruit crop for home gardeners, with varieties that grow in all areas. They come in day-neutral varieties that produce for most of the summer and June-bearing varieties that produce one heavy crop in early summer. The eight inch plants grow from central crowns which produce runners whose management is the most awkward part of strawberry culture.

To manage the runner problem, you need to know that a strawberry plant produces fruit in its second and third years of life and then needs to be replaced by a plant grown from a runner. So it is easiest to treat strawberries as biennials, getting rid of most of the oldest plants each year.

For June-bearing strawberries planted in spring, plant in double or triple rows with the plants about eight inches apart and three feet between rows. Half of the crown should remain above ground when you plant. You will get a modest crop of fruit the first year and the plants will send out runners to either side of the row. When you pick, remove all but six runners from each plant. In cold winter areas, spread a mulch over the bed for winter. Next year, the first-year plants will produce their best crop and the bed will then need renovation. After the final picking, mow the bed with the blades set high enough to remove leaves but not touch the crowns. Now, dig or till under the middle half of the bed that contains the oldest plants. Thin the remaining plants to eight inches apart and mulch with straw or grass clippings. Next year, runners will grow into the area you have tilled. This year when the harvest finishes, till under the outer half of the bed, and so on. Strawberries need regular water in July and August.

Grapes on an arbor are a decorative addition to the garden, especially in autumn when large bunches of purple grapes, we hope, hang down from the roof. This desirable sight is not achieved without a fair bit of work, however. For starters, the arbor, whether free-standing or attached to a building, has to be very sturdy because grape vines get big. It also needs to be high, to make room for people as well as those bunches of grapes.

Choose varieties suitable for your area, which will almost inevitably not be the best wine grapes, however tempting the notion of setting up a home winery may be. The experts are still arguing vehemently about the best ways to prune grapes so I won't presume to tell you how to do this. The main thing to understand is that unless you prune most of the plant away in winter, you will be lucky to get any fruit. The time to prune is invariably February, even in the frozen North, and how anyone ever gets through February, which is a short month anyway, what with all the roses, grapes, and fruit trees that have to be pruned then, is a mystery. For the rest of the year, the only pruning you need to do is to tie up or cut off the strands of vine that hit you in the face when you walk through the arbor.

Kiwis, in contrast to grapes, need a lot of water and fertilizer. This is another plant that forms a vast vine (to 50 feet) and needs strong support. It will cover an arbor even faster than a grape and has handsome foliage. It is sometimes grown up a wall, but this requires some pretty impressive trellising. In Zones 8-10, you grow the tropical kiwi, *Actinidia chinensis*, which is the kiwi you find in the store. You need one of each sex. Further north (to Zone 4), grow hardy kiwi (*A. arguta)*, or *A. kolomikta*, which is hardy to Zone 3. *A. arguta* now comes in self-fertile varieties so you may or may not need a pollinator. Tropical kiwi is one of the few fruits that will produce even in part shade. Although it prefers reasonably fertile soil, kiwis are less demanding than grapes, and may be grown from southern California to Nova Scotia.

COMPANION PLANTS
Organic gardeners use companion planting to reduce disease in the garden. There is sound sense behind this. Many of our pest problems come from the fact that we plant large areas of a single species—which makes it very easy for pests that specialize in that species to find their food plants. In nature, the plants would be scattered around among other species and harder to find. Companion planting is an attempt to make life more difficult for the pest by

filling air and soil with secondary chemicals from other species that may even kill the pests, but at least repels them.

There is no question that the theory behind companion planting and crop rotation is sound. What is not as clear is precisely which plants are useful companions to other species, since not much research has been done. The best-documented example is the use of marigolds to reduce populations of nematodes in the soil. Look for nematode-repelling marigolds, which produce particularly large quantities of the relevant secondary chemicals. Most of the other companion plantings you may see recommended come from anecdotal evidence, but it can't do any harm to try them. For instance, coriander and dill are reported to attract beneficial insects to orchards—usually wasps that parasitize the caterpillars that eat fruit tree foliage and fruit; chives are said to deter Japanese beetles and black spot.

CHAPTER 12

Vegetables

When the rest of the garden is looking gray and neglected on a dismal January day, I get great pleasure from trotting into the vegetable garden to pick a salad of baby lettuce, spinach, parsley, sorrel, snow peas, and onion leaves. With sweet poppy seed dressing, and fresh boiled shrimp with cocktail sauce from our own horseradish, this is a meal fit for a king and queen. So is a favorite summer lunch of sliced tomatoes warm from the garden with chopped basil and a drizzle of olive oil.

Even a small kitchen garden of vegetables, fruit, and herbs, can keep you supplied with tasty food year round. You may not save much money, but nothing can compare with the taste (and nutritional value) of goodies fresh from your own garden. You can keep a family of four in vegetables from a plot as small as 20 feet by 20 feet if you choose the right varieties and plant closely.

DESIGN

Despite the virtues of edible landscaping, with food plants scattered around the property, I am devoted to the appearance of a well designed, well kept kitchen garden. Perhaps this is a hangover from my childhood, when I roamed a large, tidy garden, its high walls espaliered with fruit trees, its hot beds and cold frames bursting with good things (the whole thing tended, I may say, by three gardeners), which supplied vegetables for the Welsh estate where my grandfather worked. Perhaps we remember the beauty of old kitchen gardens that have been restored, like those at Mount Vernon and Villandry. Wherever the urge comes from, a vegetable garden can be a beautiful, and comforting, feature of your property, even if it is tiny. The aesthetically pleasing vegetable garden is a result of careful thought. It usually includes structural elements such as brick or wood edgings, miniature hedges or topiary, as well as flowers to add a touch of color.

There are many possibilities. Do you want a circular garden so that a sprinkler in the middle can reach all parts of it? Will there be a fence round the garden? If so, could it be made of trellis or wire netting and used to support vining vegetables? Or will you surround the garden with cordon fruit trees to make a fence only a foot or two high (although it always seems a miracle that these don't get tripped over at regular intervals). If you want flowers and formal accents, will they be pansies around pillars of yew or holly, or standard roses like those at Villandry?

Decent paths are important in a productive vegetable garden. Even if you are not out there digging when the soil is wet, you will probably be harvesting or improving the soil, so you need dry footing and room for a wheelbarrow. On sandy soil that dries rapidly, you may not need to make permanent paths at all and this has the design advantage that you can move beds around at will. But most people will want some permanent paths of grass, gravel, brick, or whatever, that provide access to a few main beds. If your paths are grass, edging them with wood, stone, or brick looks good and saves time in the long run because the edging helps to keep grass and lawn mower wheels out of the beds.

Most books tell you to locate herb and vegetable gardens where they will get at least six hours of sun a day. This may be fine for those in Britain or the northern United States, but in the sunny South, many vegetables grow better and use less water in the shade. The best location for a southern vegetable garden is an area that gets full sun in winter but is partly shaded by deciduous trees in summer when the sun is hotter.

Making the Most of Space

If you are short of space, or even if you merely want to have less ground to weed, it helps to grow things upward in the garden, and not just the things like pole beans and peas that need support to produce good yields. Cucumbers are actually better climbers than peas. I don't know why anyone ever lets the vines straggle on the ground when the cucumbers stay cleaner and the crop is easier to weed if you grow them on a trellis. Melons also grow up fences with aplomb.

Another space-saving technique is to grow vegetables in patches, or blocks, instead of the traditional rows. The snag is that it is harder to hoe between vegetables planted in blocks so you generally have to weed by hand. It then becomes helpful for your blocks to be small enough so that you can reach them when kneeling in the nearest path. Even if you want to keep things in rows so that you can weed with a hoe or tiller, you get more vegetables from the same space if the rows are wider than usual. You can plant lettuce seed in a band six or nine inches wide without noticeably increasing the amount of hand weeding.

GROWING PERFECT VEGETABLES

The object of growing food crops is to produce food with excellent taste and the maximum yield in as little space and as short a time as possible. To this end, the plants must be kept happy, growing rapidly so that they do not become tough with old age and so that pests do not get the chance to ravage the crop. In flower borders or shrubbery, neglecting to water or improve the soil may do little damage. In the vegetable garden, it may lose you a crop—which may not be the end of the world but is certainly a waste of your time in planting it.

Soil and Water

Since most vegetables are in and out of the garden in short order, you have to prepare the soil before you plant because after you plant is too late. If you have an endless supply of high quality compost, you can improve the soil in small areas, by digging masses of compost into a single row where a previous crop has been harvested. But it is much easier if the whole garden is not continually planted. Then you can improve the soil in a largish area in a leisurely fashion. Green manure is one of the best ways of improving poor soil and getting rid of persistent weeds and you cannot plant it unless you can free some of the garden from vegetables for long enough to grow the cover crop.

The convenience of having the soil empty of crops for part of the year is one reason many Americans plant the whole vegetable garden at a time. In country districts, "I've put in a garden this year," may mean precisely that: the gardener has spent a few days or months improving the soil and then planted the year's vegetables, as seed or transplants, one sunny Saturday in May. Of course all the beans mature at once but, before the family has rebelled against beans, the whole crop is harvested and frozen. To those raised in other traditions, this seems like an odd way to garden, but it is an efficient way to feed a family in this era of freezers. Its main disadvantage is that you do not have fresh vegetables for many months of the year. If you keep planting throughout the year, you can have fresh vegetables all the time, even where the garden is deep with snow in midwinter.

What goes for soil improvement and weeding, goes for watering: you cannot afford to neglect it. Seeds will not germinate unless they are continually moist, and leaf vegetables get tough and bitter if they don't get enough water. Even if you don't have an irrigation system in any other part of the garden, it is worth installing something satisfactory in the vegetable garden and burying the hose, if any, so that it doesn't spoil the view and get in the way. I am going to get around to this any year now. If you live in a damp part of the world, you may need nothing more than a rain barrel and watering can. I like those rain barrels with lids to keep out debris and taps built into the side so that it is easy to fill a can. You install them under a downspout from a gutter

Many people use drip irrigation, but this tends to be a time-consuming solution because the hoses and pipes run along every row of vegetables and have to be moved, or at least get in your way, whenever you weed or plant. If you are gardening on arid clay, you can dig sunken beds straight into the ground and water them with a bubbler head on the hose. Never water anything in the garden with water that has been through a water softener. The salts from a water softener are quite toxic to plants.

Salt Tolerance

For gardeners with saline soil, it is worth researching the salt tolerance of vegetables before you plan the garden. Most plants are least tolerant of salt when they are seedlings. You can often grow plants that don't tolerate salt if you can provide a lot of water to wash salts out the seed bed and during the plants' first few weeks of life. Among the species that tolerate high salt levels are beets (including sugar beet), kale, asparagus, spinach, and sea kale. Radish, celery, and green beans do not tolerate salt well (although many shell beans are not as picky). Vegetables with moderate tolerance for salt include broccoli, cabbage, peppers, cauliflower, lettuce, sweet corn, tomatoes, potatoes, carrots, onions, peas, squash, and cucumber.

Thinning Seedlings

You have been told many times that no plant can grow to perfection unless it has sufficient space. Then you are told to thin your five seedlings to eight inches apart, carrots to five inches, and so forth. This would be all very well if you always wanted to grow your vegetables to perfection, but often you don't. For instance, I sow lettuce seed thickly because the plants are not going to remain in the garden for long enough to form mature plants. We pick lettuce whenever we want it, no matter how tiny the plant. On the other hand, broccoli and pepper plants will be in the ground a long time and grow to large size before the harvest rolls around, so these must be properly spaced to do well.

Hot Vegetables in Cool Climates

It takes a certain amount of ingenuity to grow heat-loving vegetables if you live where summers are not. Here are some of the techniques used to stretch the season, or push the vegetables.

Alaskans have these techniques down to a fine art and grow magnificent vegetables in a very short, cool growing season.
• Start plants early indoors.
• If you don't have a greenhouse, it is very useful to have some way of giving vegetables extra protection. In the old days, the method of choice was a hotbed, which was a cold frame heated from beneath by decomposing manure. Even without the extra heat, a cold frame is useful. Cloches also do a good job; so do gallon milk jugs with the necks cut off over each tomato plant.
• Warm the soil with black plastic for a month before planting and plant through slits in the plastic.
• Plant against a south wall that will reflect heat onto the vegetables and hold heat after dark, releasing it at night. A cucumber trellis makes an attractive addition to the wall of a house.
• Use bottles filled with water around plants for the same purpose—to absorb heat from the sun during the day and release it to the plants when the sun goes down. The gadgets that surround the plant with a wall of water contained in a plastic bag also work.

PESTS

When you find insects on your plants or observe bad insect damage, the proper procedure is to identify the insect and then control it with the least dangerous pesticide that will do the job. Since you are going to eat these plants, you cannot use toxic pesticides. When you shop, look for biological pest controls and read the labels carefully, since even "biological" or "organic" pest controls are often toxic if ingested.

There are several measures you can take that reduce the chances of disaster from pests.
• Keep your plants healthy. A healthy plant is more resistant to pest damage than one that is barely alive. A plant will usually grow new leaves as long as it has plenty of water and fertile soil. Keep the compost and the water coming and a pest attack will seldom prove fatal.
• Weed frequently. Weeds provide hiding places for insects that can rapidly invade your plants. Go through the vegetable garden at least once a week with a hoe.
• Hand pick caterpillars, stink bugs, or anything large enough to handle. You have to repeat this frequently, but it is very effective. Squash any bugs you hand pick. (I can't think why some people recommend dropping them in cans of kerosene and other noxious substances that need a hazardous waste permit to dispose of.)
• Time planting to avoid pest populations. Insect reproduction is fairly predictable. Insects lay eggs that hatch on or around particular dates—the date when their food plant is likely to be newly leafed out and has not had time to synthesize secondary chemicals that make it more difficult for an insect to eat. Note the dates that

you plant things in your garden diary. If this year, the melons are decimated by caterpillars, planting three weeks earlier or later next year may avoid the problem completely.

• Try out some of those strange-sounding remedies, such as using saucers of beer to catch slugs and planting nematode-killing marigolds. Local remedies often do work, despite the doubts of outsiders. I read an article in the *New York Times* a few months ago about the strange superstitions of Southerners, who actually believe that Avon's Skin-So-Soft (which is a bath oil) repels sand flies (gnats or no-see-'ums), those tiny members of the mosquito family that can empty a golf course in milliseconds and make life an itching hell in cool weather in the southern United States and the Caribbean. Let me bear witness to northern skeptics that Skin-So-Soft is the cheapest sand fly repellent there is and they are welcome to perform a controlled experiment on the matter in my garden any balmy spring or autumn day. Don't be deterred from trying out your grandmother's patent cure for flea beetles. It might just work.

Crop Rotation

Crop rotation is a pest control method as old as agriculture. It means moving crops around so that you don't always grow the same crop in the same spot every year. In some relatively pest-free parts of the world, it is not essential to rotate crops in the early years of a garden. But most people, sooner or later, find that pests attack a particular crop more and more viciously with every year that passes if they continue to plant it in the same patch of soil.

To reduce a population of soil-borne pests you usually have to plant something else in the soil for two or three years, which means you ideally need a four-year rotation. This is not easy to achieve except in a very large garden. The problem is compounded by the fact that the same pests attack most members of any one plant family. It is no good rotating cabbage, broccoli, Brussels sprouts and kohlrabi because these are all members of the same species, *Brassica oleracea*, and attract most of the same pests. I have never managed a complete four-, or even three-year rotation. The best I can manage is not to plant tomatoes and carrots in the same spot until the soil has had two years to recover. These are our most pest-ridden crops; yours may be different. I don't bother to rotate lettuces and peas because these are seldom attacked by anything. A crop of green manure is a good way to speed up pest control. Digesting green manure encourages new populations of organisms in the soil that will help crowd out whatever has been attacking the tomatoes or carrots. Most commercial crop rotation works on a three-year cycle: two years to different crops and then one year of green manure. This may be the way to go for your susceptible crops.

Floating Row Covers

If you feel like spending all the money you save by not using pesticides, you might like to try floating row covers. Originally from France, these sheets of fabric are so light that the plants push the cover up as they grow. Row covers let in light and water, but they keep out insects that would otherwise lay their eggs on your plants. Leafy things, such as spinach, carrots, and beets, develop faster and with less insect damage under floating row covers than in the open. Row covers raise the temperature around the plants, so don't use them in full sun in midsummer or you may bake your plants. And you have to remember to remove the covers at flowering time from things that need to be pollinated by insects, such as cucumbers and melons. Leaf crops are ideal for floating row covers because they do not need to be pollinated so you can leave the covers on all the time.

CHOOSING VARIETIES

The first rule of choosing what to plant is not to bother with things your family hates or that are cheap and equally tasty in the shops. That seems so obvious it's ridiculous, but I know many gardeners who merrily plant carrots each year although no one in the family, including the gardener, can stand the taste of them. Having said that, I must confess that we grow for fun or novelty a couple of things, such as horseradish and ginger that are almost equally good and and not particularly expensive in the shops.

Since the number of vegetables the family would be happy to eat is almost unlimited, the next rule is to start by planting the things *you* really love and to go on to less desirable things or other peoples' passions when you know you have time and space for them. It is easy to start a huge vegetable garden in the first flush of spring fever, but you may regret it when you find yourself weeding the back forty on a sweltering August day.

Don't let yourself be snowed by other people's taste. Even if 5000 highly trained runners did give 'Gardener's Delight' highest marks in a tomato tasting, if you and yours prefer 'Sweet 100' then that's the tomato for you—although if you don't know 'Gardener's Delight' it couldn't do any harm to try it after coming upon this statistic. Varieties that are selected for awards by national committees are not necessarily the most tasty. For instance, the All America Selections each year are tested by amateur gardeners all over the United States, and only those that do well in almost every region pass muster. Any plant that grows well in every biome in the United States is devoting a lot of its genes to being as tough as nails and not to tasting good. A cucumber that is sweet and delicately flavored in Seattle may become tough-skinned and bitter in southern heat. It will never make the All America Selections, but it may be the tastiest variety that you can grow in Washington. Often, though by no means always, the tastiest varieties are locally adapted.

One of the most important developments in vegetable breeding in recent years has been improved pest resistance. With pesticides ever more expensive, ineffective, and dangerous to the environment, amateur and commercial growers are calling for pest-resistant crops. Techniques such as tissue culture and genetic engineering are making production and testing of new varieties faster than ever, so it is well worth keeping your eye out for new varieties. You may find that your favorite 'Sweet 100' tomato has transmuted this year into 'Sweet Million VFFNTA' with the same delicious taste as well as resistance to tomato pests that you have battled for years. New mainly-male asparagus, day-neutral strawberries, and thornless blackberries can't be all bad either, as long as the breeders haven't sacrificed flavor for these advances—which they sometimes have.

And don't omit to do your bit for genetic diversity by planting any heirloom vegetables that may be around and ordering a few seeds from a seed savers' group. I try to order a few things from each catalogue each year to keep the catalogues coming. Some companies strike you off the mailing list next year if you don't order anything this year—which may be short-sighted of them, but there you are; they have costs to control (and if some of them would teach their computers not to send three identical catalogues to our house, they would have found a better way to do this).

PERENNIAL VEGETABLES

Artichokes

The globe artichoke (*Cynara scolymus*) is a close relative of cardoon (*Cynara cardunculus*), which also has edible flower buds. The plants are exceedingly handsome, with exotic gray foliage, so they are often grown in the flower border instead of the vegetable garden. Artichokes are usually propagated by division in spring and bear edible buds the second year. They grow well on the Pacific Coast and in Britain, but they cannot stand much frost so they are not perennial in the North. Nevertheless even people who cannot provide the conditions artichokes really prefer sometimes grow artichokes as annuals. Like asparagus, artichokes prefer sandy loam. They rot if the soil is too wet and in hot humid weather. California gardeners throw out plants after four years, replacing them with plants grown from root suckers. Artichokes don't like the humid summers of the Deep South and I have never had much luck with them, but give them a try before you decide they are not for you.

Asparagus

Asparagus-growing has changed from the days when everyone planted 'Martha Washington' in trenches. Now we grow more productive varieties, planting the roots only two inches deep. Male asparagus plants are more productive because they don't waste their energy producing seed (the black balls on asparagus at the end of summer) and yield much more than older varieties. Actually, you still cannot buy asparagus that is guaranteed completely male, although you may be able to by the time you read this. The main thing is to buy plants with as many males as possible.

You can't grow all male asparagus from seed, so buy roots in winter or early spring, when they are dormant. One-year plants seem to get established faster than the larger two-year plants. Dig in lots of organic matter and add lime until the pH is at least 6.5.

Plant the roots two feet apart, spreading them out in a fan, and covering them with two inches of soil. Give them one inch of water a week for a few months, but after that don't bother, since asparagus likes dry sandy soil.

For the first two years, harvest only a few spears—which are the stalk and leaf buds. The plants need their leaves to grow large healthy roots while they are young. The third year after planting, you can harvest several spears from each plant for about a month. After this, the bed will continue to produce for 20 years or more if well looked after.

Asparagus

ASPARAGUS RECIPES

Elegant fat stalks are best dropped into boiling water for 5 minutes and then eaten as finger food dipped into butter with a squeeze of lemon, or into hollandaise sauce. Less elegant skinny spears, or ones that have begun to leaf out can be made into a delicious soup.

HOLLANDAISE SAUCE

(Serves 4-6)
1/2 lb butter (or half margarine and half butter)
3 egg yolks
Juice of half a lemon
Pinch of salt

Melt the butter over medium low heat until it bubbles and steams without turning brown. Put egg yolks, salt, and lemon juice in the blender and blend at low speed, adding the hot butter very slowly, a few drops at a time, until the sauce begins to thicken. Then add the rest of the butter a little more rapidly. This can be a messy business. Take precautions to prevent the sauce spattering all over you and the kitchen. When you have added all the butter, the sauce should be thick and creamy and is ready to serve.

Hollandaise is also wonderful on broccoli (or on ham and eggs as Eggs Benedict). It keeps well in the refrigerator if you cover its surface with tinfoil or wrap. Reheat it in warm water or at the microwave's lowest temperature. If you overheat it, you will have scrambled egg—which will taste fine but look uncouth.

ASPARAGUS SOUP

(Serves 4-6)
3 Tb butter
3 Tb flour
5 cups chicken broth
1 large chopped onion
2 lb chopped asparagus
1 cup light cream

Melt the butter in a saucepan and stir in the flour. Cook for one minute. Add the chicken broth slowly, stirring to avoid lumps. Add the asparagus and onion. Bring to the boil and simmer for 8-10 minutes. Liquidize the soup in the blender and sieve to remove fibers (or pass through food mill). Add cream. Reheat without boiling. This soup is also delicious cold.

During the month or so of harvest, cut down any leaves and stems that emerge. The plant produces more buds from its roots if it is not allowed to produce leaf stems. It will have all summer to produce leaves and store food. In autumn, when the leaves start to brown and fall over, cut down all the foliage, scatter a few good handfuls of lime on the bed if your soil is acid, and cover this with at least a two-inch layer of compost or grass clippings. In the South, asparagus does best if you can provide it with shade in summer.

ANNUAL VEGETABLES

The list of annual vegetables is almost endless and, happily, getting longer every year. One of the results of feeding the world by intensive agriculture is that we eat many fewer species than our ancestors did. When European settlers arrived, North American Cherokees ate more than 500 species of native plants. The average person today is unlikely to taste more than 50 species in a lifetime and four species (wheat, rice, corn, and potatoes) provide 80% of all human food. The result of this diet simplification is a great loss of genetic diversity and the danger that pests may wipe out a huge proportion of the human food supply. The food supply is safer if we depend on a wider base of plants. The world's germ plasm conservation centers do not have the resources to widen the food base alone. An army of adventurous home gardeners, seed savers, and farmers is their most valuable ally in this important battle.

Winter and Summer Gardens

If you live in a relatively mild climate, you may get two (or even three) crops a year from one patch of soil by planting different crops in the same spot in winter and summer. Most areas have two main seasons for planting vegetables: spring and late summer. Many vegetables can be planted at both times but there are advantages to growing different things in winter and summer.

Vegetables generally divide into those that require summer heat, those that cannot stand it, and those that don't much care. Summer vegetables are those that cannot tolerate frost and need a fairly long warm period to mature. They include tomatoes, cucumber, peppers, tomatillas, melons, sweet corn, jicama, ginger, eggplant, and the squash family. You can get a head start on the season by planting seeds indoors and juggling cold frames, cloches, and the like, but these plants are not really going to do much until warm summer weather arrives—if it ever does.

Winter vegetables are just the opposite: those that collapse when the temperature stays above about 75 °F for any length of time. They include lettuce, spinach, and many other greens, peas, sorrel, and most of the onion family. All of these plants can take a lot more frost than I had any idea until I started gardening in the South. It was a real shock the first day I went into the garden after two days of icy roads and 18 °F temperatures and found everything except the peas apparently unharmed. Even the peas were merely curling at the edges and started flowering again within ten days. New Englanders manage to have fresh salad all winter by planting an insulated cold frame with spinach, lettuce, and parsley in August or September, picking it through the winter, and reseeding in the empty spaces. If you haven't yet tried this, do. Home grown vegetables never taste better than when harvested in a snowstorm!

The in-between vegetables are those that will stand very little frost but are not worried by heat. Potatoes and the green bean family spring to mind. Although beans don't mind heat, the harvest is longer in cool weather because the beans mature over a longer period. So I plant them in midwinter and midsummer, hoping they will mature when the weather is moderate. Sometimes they even do.

Beans

Beans are American natives and, together with corn, were probably the first crops grown in the New World. When Spanish missionaries reached Georgia in the fifteenth century, the local Guale introduced them to these unfamiliar foods. The Guale planted strains of shell beans developed by the Mayans, from seed brought from Mexico by traders.

Shell beans are harvested when the pods swell and dry. They were important before refrigeration because they can be stored for long periods. Nowadays, we tend to buy our shell beans in the store and grow beans to eat the tender pods when the seeds are still immature. Beans grow best between 75 and 85 °F in sun or part shade. You can plant seed before the date of last frost but not in the dead of winter.

Plant beans thickly (about an inch apart), one inch deep in spring and two inches deep in summer. A light mulch of grass clippings over the bed will make it easier for the seedlings to push through the soil. Do not thin. Weed occasionally until the beans are about twelve inches tall. After that the weeds won't have a chance.

Many pole beans grow more than six feet tall so they need a tough trellis. Bush beans are undoubtedly less trouble. But they do tend to mature all at the same time so it is a good idea to plant several short rows a couple of weeks apart. Pole beans mature over a longer period. Keep all beans picked or they will stop producing.

I don't think I gave pole beans a fair chance until a few years ago, or perhaps I now have the perfect spot for them—part of the kitchen garden that is shaded by a tree and gets three or four hours sun a day. Anyway, the yield from a small space is enormous. I plant them in February, about a month before the frost-free date, with bamboos for a tepee trellis. These I stick in the ground in a circle, with their bases about one foot apart, shoving them in as far as I can, and tying them all together just above head height. The first time, I sprinkled all the pole bean seeds I had (which happened to be ancient packets of 'Scarlet Runner' and 'Kentucky Wonder') under the tepee and covered the whole lot with an inch of grass clippings. Two months later, the plants were falling off the top of the tepee and we were eating tender young beans every other day. The harvest went on for more than a month because the 'Scarlet Runners' did not even start producing their decorative red flowers until we'd been eating the Kentucky Wonder (white flowers) for two weeks.

The restaurant mania for serving tiny little vegetables, picked when they are very young, is not an unequivocally good idea. It depends on the vegetable. For many years I thought all edible pod peas should be picked young, but it turns out this is only true of snow peas. Snap peas, such as the incomparable 'Sugar Snap,' are much sweeter when left until the peas fatten. The squash family should all be harvested small, but beans are best left to mature. Even though larger peas and beans need stringing before cooking, they are much sweeter than those picked young.

My grandmother had a gadget for slicing enormous scarlet runner beans before cooking them. First you took the strings off both sides of the beans and then you pushed them through the bean slicer—which resembled a meat grinder clamped to the edge of a table with a handle to rotate the knife. This affair produced thin decorative slices of green pod and red and white bean and they were very tasty when gently steamed. You sometimes find this gadget advertised as a "bean Frencher."

Carrots

It is not easy to grow a good crop of carrots and I never have. First, the seed takes a long time to germinate so you usually find weeds in the seed bed before the seedlings emerge. It is difficult to grow straight carrots in rocky soil, where the roots bend and it is difficult to grow them in sand which is invariably full of root-distorting nematodes.

Size and sweetness depend on the variety you grow, not on harvesting the carrots when they are young. The taste is better in cool weather so you want to plant your last carrots at least 60 days before the last frost. Seed will germinate at temperatures between 50 and 80 °F.

Cucumbers

For many years, American cucumbers were the short fat ones with a rather bitter taste, used mainly for pickles. Now there are dozens of

Cucumber vine

varieties for every purpose. Try a few of the "burpless" ones which lack the bitter gene, and some of the long, thin oriental and European ones, which have thin skin so that you don't need to peel them.

The easiest way to grow cucumbers is up a trellis. Plant seeds just before the date of last frost and every three weeks for another two months. You may lose the early plants to a late frost, but all you've lost is a few seeds, so just plant again. Thin to stand about ten inches apart. If you start cucumbers indoors, do it in peat pots—cucumbers don't like their roots disturbed. When the plants are 18 inches tall, start them up their trellis. You may have to tie them on to get them started, but when they get bigger they will climb by themselves.

Cucumbers are insect-pollinated—usually by bees—so don't use insecticides in the garden when they are in flower. And they need at least some sun to set fruit. A vital part of cucumber culture is keeping the fruit picked. Even if you have so many that you have to throw them on the compost pile, it is vital to pick fruit at least every other day once they start coming. If you let the fruit get big and seedy before picking, the plants will stop producing.

Eggplant

Eggplants come from India and have spread all over the world. There used to be a wide range of eggplants in home gardens, but twentieth century Americans seem to have settled down with large, black, rather seedy, bitter varieties. It's time to rebel and try some new ones. Some of the best eggplants are small, yellow, and almost seedless—and these are easier to grow than the large black ones.

The secret of eggplants is warm weather. While a tomato will survive a 50 °F day, an eggplant may be permanently damaged if the daytime temperature falls below 70 °F. Most people start with transplants as the weather warms up. Set the plants 18 inches apart and side dress them with compost or fertilizer a couple of times. They do not demand much water and in the Deep South they do fine in shade.

Harvest eggplants when they are considerably smaller than those you see in the store. Good fruit is small and shiny. Once the seeds have turned brown, the fruit is so tough it is just about inedible.

Jicama, Yam Bean (*Pachyrhizus erosus*)

Jicama is a Central American vine in the morning glory family that looks much too like kudzu for comfort but is not invasive. It is

Eggplant

grown for the root, which looks like a large turnip. Don't even try jicama unless you have a long growing season. If you do, give it as tall and tough a trellis as you can. Seeds planted about the date of last frost are followed by fifteen-foot vines, which burst into gorgeous purple pea-like flowers in later summer, followed by large pods which contain the seeds. From late in the summer, dig up a vine or two and eat the root. Wait till after the first frost has killed the vines and then dig up the remaining roots.

Jicama has a crisp texture and slightly sweet taste. Peel and slice and serve with a squeeze of lemon, a little salt, and a salsa dip. Use them raw in salads for a touch of crispness or toss them into a stir fry at the last moment.

Melons (Watermelons or cantaloupes)

Melons are for when you have lots of space. The vines spread over many square feet when they are healthy and happy and each plant produces no more than three or four melons. But remember that you do not need to cultivate all that soil. Many people grow melons and squashes in the middle of the lawn or in a corner of the garden. Pile compost, leaf mold, or fertile soil in large heap on the lawn and plant a dozen seeds one inch deep in the heap. Keep them well watered until the seeds germinate. When the plants are about six inches high, thin to the sturdiest four or five plants. Spread a thick layer of mulch (pine needles, leaves, wood chips) on the lawn around them. As the vines grow, keep them spread them out over the mulch so that they are growing away from each other.

Most melons are ripe when the fruit comes away from the plant without tugging, but this depends on the variety so be sure to check the directions given on the seed packet.

Okra (*Hibiscus esculentus*)

Okra is a warm weather staple and very easy to grow in the South. It also has the advantage that it produces over a relatively long period. As a member of the hibiscus family, it has handsome flowers. When the harvest is finished, you can leave the woody stalks in place and grow peas up them during the winter.

Sow seeds when the soil is warm and thin the plants to a final spacing of about 12 inches. It is important to pick okra when it is small—and it grows rapidly so check it every day. Pick it even if you don't want to eat it or it will stop producing.

Steam or boil okra for five minutes and serve with butter and lemon juice. Or try out some of those gumbo recipes. Tomato and okra is a natural combination. Sauté okra, tomatoes, garlic, a chopped ancho pepper, and a chopped onion in bacon fat or oil for five minutes, cover and simmer for another ten minutes and you have a delicious combination.

Okra

Squash

The squash family includes zucchini and pumpkins, winter and summer squash. You grow them like melons. I am very fond of the little pattypan squash, delicious steamed with baby zucchini and tossed with herb butter.

The difference between summer and winter squash is that summer squash is for eating immediately, whereas winter squash survives well in storage so can be kept in the root cellar for use in the winter. Butternut and Hubbard are winter squash.

Sunchoke, Jerusalem artichoke, girasol *(Helianthus tuberosus)*

This American sunflower was cultivated by American Indians and introduced to France in the seventeenth century. It is propagated by division of the edible roots and produces rampant six foot stalks with cheerful yellow sunflowers on top. The roots you can buy in the supermarket grow perfectly well. Plant them in full sun and dig up the roots when the stems die down in autumn. You will never manage to dig up all the roots and those that remain in the ground will provide next year's crop.

Scrub the roots thoroughly with a brush to get rid of dirt in crevices. There's no need to peel them. Use sunchokes uncooked for a crispy texture in salads or substitute them for chestnuts in oriental recipes. The traditional method is to cook them like Yorkshire pudding: toss them into very hot drippings from a roast for about five minutes.

Sweet Corn

I have never grown a perfect crop of sweet corn. I am always defeated by the pollination problem and assorted pests. Choosing the right varieties is also complicated. The not-so-new varieties seem to be easiest for the home gardener. The new sugar-enhanced and supersweet varieties need buckets of water, fertilizer, and tender loving care to produce well. If you live in the cool mountains, Bay Area, or Britain, try a short-season hybrid such as 'Early Sunglow' which will nevertheless take twice the advertised 60 days from seed to maturity. In windy areas, choose varieties with short stalks and hill the earth around the stalks for extra support. In any case, you should plant several varieties of corn so that it does not all mature at once.

Corn doesn't do much until the soil temperature is 60 ℉. Plant seed in a block, not a row, in deep, fertile soil. A common mistake is to crowd corn. Rows should be three feet apart and plants at least ten inches apart when you have finished thinning.

Corn is a heavy feeder. Most farmers fertilize with a fast-acting fertilizer such as sodium nitrate when they sow and sidedress with

SUNCHOKES IN CHEESE

(Serves 8)
2 lb sunchokes
1/2 cup grated Parmesan cheese
2 Tb butter
Salt and pepper to taste

Clean sunchokes and boil for 15-18 minutes until tender. Slice thinly and lay in ovenproof dish. Add salt and pepper. Cover with cheese and dot with butter. Bake at 375 ℉ for 7-10 minutes until browned on top.

6-12-12 when the corn is four inches high and again when it begins to tassel. Corn should get at least an inch of water per week. Keep it weeded and give the plants a bit of extra support by hilling them up (dragging soil up around the stalks) or planting in a four-inch trench and piling soil around them as the seedlings emerge. If suckers form at the base of a plant, leave them alone. They are merely adventitious roots and removing them is supposed to reduce the yield.

The pollination problem arises because each kernel in an ear needs to be pollinated and the pollen is windborne. Small patches of corn in the home garden tend to suffer from "edge effect" whereby the plants on the edge of the patch do not receive enough pollen. This is why you are advised to plant corn in blocks, rather than in long thin rows. All I can say is plant as big a block as you can, and good luck.

When you can feel the ears fattening, you can pull back the husk and peak to see if the corn is ripe. Corn loses sugar rapidly after it is picked. So when it is ripe, run, don't walk, to the kitchen, husk the ears, pop them in a pot of boiling water for five minutes and eat them smeared with butter and salt—there are few finer treats.

Corn borers and earworms are the main pests. Planting early helps to reduce the chance of attack. A small hole in a developing ear is the warning sign. Squeeze the hole to squash the worm and dust with carbaryl.

Peppers

Nothing grows better in hot weather than peppers—sweet bell peppers, hot chili peppers, and everything in between. In warm summers, they even grow happily in shade. You may lose a few plants to unknown pests, or to known pests such as cutworms, and you may find that production slows down in midsummer, but in a long warm summer you may still be harvesting succulent peppers toward the end of November even if you haven't given the plants any attention since June.

Peppers cannot grow new roots until the soil is warm. Researchers say not to plant until after the soil has reached 50 °F for three days running. Start your plants from seed or buy them locally so that they are ready to go into the ground shortly after the last frost. If you plant them 12 to 18 inches apart, they prop each other up and do not need staking.

Like tomatoes, young plants must be protected from cutworms. Cutworms emerge at night and eat the stem. Next morning, you find your seedlings felled at soil level as by a Lilliputian logger. The easiest preventative is toothpicks—a couple of toothpicks touching the stem and pushed partly into the soil seem to foil cutworms. Aside from this, peppers have few pests that I know of.

Bell pepper

You can pick and eat peppers at any stage of development. You improve the later crop if you pick your first peppers when they are tiny. That way the plant can put its energy into growing more leaves to support later fruits instead of into ripening the early peppers. In fact your total yield will be greater if you pick off the first set of blossoms and prevent them from setting fruit. Nearly all bell peppers are much sweeter if they are allowed to ripen fully—until they are red. So, especially after midsummer, leave some fruit on the plants to ripen.

Tomatoes

Tomatoes

Tomatoes are the most popular vegetable in the home garden, probably because the fender-benders in the grocery store are so tasteless. The reason is simple: tomatoes lose most of their taste unless they ripen on the vine but vine-ripened tomatoes are too soft to ship. Breeders are working to develop tomatoes that will survive shipping after they have ripened on the vine (as well as square tomatoes that take less space when packed!) Until they succeed, growing your own is almost the only way to have tasty tomatoes.

There are hundreds of varieties. Some grow well in one part of the country and not in others, some are tasteless types bred for shipping, some are tiny plants bred for containers. If you buy plants or seeds of unknown varieties, you will make some mistakes. But, on the other hand, you have to experiment. The varieties that we would not be without are 'Sweet 100' (or 'Sweet Million'), 'Big Girl,' 'Quick Pick,' and something in the Supersteak series. The letters after the varieties indicate disease resistance. A VFNT tomato is resistant to Verticillium wilt, Fusarium wilt, Nematodes of various kinds, and Tobacco mosaic virus.

It is traditional to grow tomatoes in the sun. But studies in Florida, not to mention my garden, show that tomatoes grown in the shade in the South produce more fruit than the same variety in sun. Your first fruits will be later in the shade, but the plants will produce over a much longer period.

Tomatoes are heavy feeders, so prepare the planting area with lime and lots of organic matter or give them a shovelful of compost in the planting hole. Tomato plants are often tall and leggy before you get them in the ground. Give them a better start by digging a trench to bury most of the stem in the ground where it will form new roots. Don't try to stand the plants up in the trench. Leave them on their sides and they will stand themselves up in a few days.

For the very earliest tomatoes, plant an early variety, before last frost, in full sun, and train it to a single stem. This involves pinching out all side branches, which start as buds in the angle between a leaf and the main stem. Be careful not to pinch out the flower buds, which arise from the stem between the leaf branches.

Staking tomatoes is an undoubted pain. One popular method is to use a wire tomato cage around each plant. Commercial cages are only three or four feet high, which is much shorter than most healthy tomato plants. One way to use them is to prune the plant to a single stem and tie it to the cage until it reaches the top of the cage and then just let it flop over the top. Some people pinch out the top of a tomato plant when it is about five high and let side shoots develop.

The first fruit will not set until the temperature is above 55 °F for at least part of the night. Night temperatures above 75 °F prevent fruit set. The problem you are most likely to encounter is blossom end rot, revealed by black scars on the bottom of the fruit. Blossom end rot is apparently caused by calcium deficiency brought on by various factors. It is fairly easy to prevent by avoiding too much water and fertilizer. Fertilize only with organic matter after the plants have been in the ground for a month and give the plants no more than an inch of water a week.

VEGETABLES FOR COOL WEATHER

Many cool weather vegetables will not even germinate when the soil temperature is high so you have to time them carefully. Hoping for a head start on my winter spinach one year, I planted them in late August, when the temperature was still high. They never even germinated and the ones planted a month later did no better. Next year, I am going to germinate spinach in the house under air conditioning in an attempt to have spinach by the New Year. Even in New England, it is hard to get spinach that you plant in spring to a decent size before it bolts under the influence of warm weather and it is best planted in the autumn. Lettuce is a bit faster and most Northerners can grow a spring crop if they get the seeds in the ground well before the "ground can be worked" as the books say. All you have to do is sprinkle seeds on the surface so there is no need to work the ground at all.

Broccoli and Family

Broccoli, cabbage, Brussels sprouts, collards, and their relatives are members of the brassica family, sometimes known as cole crops. All of them are fairly slow and grow best in cool weather, although they will germinate in hot weather. In the South, put out seeds or transplants in August through November. In the North, start them in early spring. Even in New England, brassicas survive the winter and you can often dig into a snow bank for Brussels sprouts for winter meals when it is hard to believe anything is alive in the vegetable garden. For this, however, the plants need to be well grown before the snow flies, which can be achieved by putting out transplants in September. If you are a bit late, the plants will probably survive the winter and mature with the first warm weather in spring. Cole crops in winter will suffer little pest damage. If you try them in spring, you will probably need to control cabbage worms.

Broccoli heads are the flower buds. Perfect temperature control is needed to grow the big heads of broccoli you see in stores. For the home gardener, it is easier to grow sprouting broccoli, which produces smaller heads over a longer period and is more tolerant of temperature variation. Good varieties include 'Calabrese', 'Purple Sprouting', and 'Italian Green Sprouting'.

Harvest broccoli with a sharp knife, cutting just below the head. New heads will keep forming from side shoots all winter. In warm weather, broccoli, like mustard and lettuce will "bolt" sending up tall stalks that flower. The flowers are quite decorative. Try them with redtip or Japanese maple leaves in a copper pot in the fireplace.

Cabbages and Other Greens

Cabbages bolt and split in warm weather so they are best grown in autumn or winter in areas with warm summers. Try some of the Savoy leaf cabbages so popular in Europe. They have decorative leaves (like kale, which they resemble) and many of them make great salad greens. The restored eighteenth century decorative kitchen garden or *potager* at Villandry in France gets its color and design mainly from standard roses planted in beds of decorative cabbage and kale. It is gorgeous!

The only greens that will stand summer heat are collards. For the fall garden, plant seeds of greens in the garden any time after mid-August. You'll need to water once or twice a day to keep the soil moist until the seeds germinate in this heat. Plants are best set out after mid-September. The flavor is better after some frost.

You can grow a patch of greens by sprinkling seed over a three or four foot area. Thin as you harvest. If you want large leaves from collards or kale, thin the plants to about a foot apart. (Mustard usually goes to flower before its leaves are more than six inches long.) Pick small leaves as they grow, without uprooting the plants. Cook greens by steaming briefly and serve them with a bottle of hot-pepper vinegar.

The name Chinese cabbage is used for a number of mild-tasting "greens," some of which form heads and some of which do not. Pick leaves at any stage and let the plant continue to grow. Cook them very lightly in stir fries or use them instead of collards or cabbage.

Chard (Swiss)

Chard is much more heat tolerant than most greens so it can be planted at any time of year. It is a very decorative plant with heavy white or red ribs in the older leaves, so it is often planted in the flower bed. You harvest it a leaf at a time at any age.

Chard is said to taste like spinach but I find it too strong to eat without cooking. Prepare young chard leaves by washing and

BETH MARKS'S SPINACH SALAD

SALAD:

Torn spinach (with ribs removed from older leaves)
Crumbled crisp-fried bacon
Mushrooms
Onions (red ones if possible)
Something red: sweet red pepper, pimento?
2 hard boiled eggs, sliced

DRESSING:

1/3 cup sugar
1/2 cup vegetable oil
1/2 cup ketchup
3 Tbs vinegar
2 Tbs Worcestershire sauce
The dressing sounds improbable, but this odd collection of ingredients merely has to be mixed together until the sugar dissolves to make a go-to-meeting dressing that will impress your guests. Pour it over the salad just before you serve it.

drying them. Chard contains a lot of water so it does no harm to let the leaves dry to the point of wilting before you cook them. Treat them like collards or any other greens. They are excellent chopped up and sauteed for two minutes in a little butter or olive oil. You can add a sprinkle of garlic, Parmesan cheese, or cream as well if you like. Chard leaves eventually get very large—several feet long. At this stage the leaf ribs are so tough they need longer cooking. Separate leaves from ribs, cut the ribs into one-inch slices and sauté them for four to five minutes before adding the chopped leaves at the last minute.

Leek

Leeks are another slow-growing member of the onion family, prized for their subtle flavor (and staggering price in the shops). Sow seeds outdoors after the soil has warmed to 60 ˚F or, in warm areas, after it has cooled to that temperature in autumn. Sow in rows two inches apart or broadcast at about one seed per inch. Transplant baby leeks into trenches when they are about six inches tall—at which point they are like wisps of grass and it is hard to believe that they will survive the mangling they receive, but they do.

UNDERSTANDING THE ENVIRONMENT
THE DEPRESSING HISTORY OF ENVIRONMENTAL PHILOSOPHY

Many believe that the cultural background of western civilization is part of the reason for our present environmental problems of over-population, resource depletion, and pollution. For instance, the 1990 *National Arboretum Book of Outstanding Garden Plants* starts with this quotation from Genesis:

> And God blessed them, and God said unto them, Be fruitful, and multiply, and replenish the earth, and subdue it: and have dominion...

It is disturbing to a biologist to find this quotation as an introduction to a gardening book when most of the problems on earth today are direct or indirect results of our multiplying much too fruitfully and subduing the earth all too effectively.

That quotation reflects seventeenth century notions of the human species as above and against nature, entitled to rule it as a tyrant, which was formulated into a philos-ophy of progress by people such as Francis Bacon, Galileo, and Descartes. These worthies marveled at the infinite vastness of the natural world created by God for human delight and exploitation. During the nineteenth century, even biology was used to support the right of humans to deal with nature as they chose. Darwin's theory of evolution was transformed into the "survival of the fittest," interpreted as meaning that only the fittest had the right to survive.

Western philosophers have asked several questions about the relationship of people and their environment. One is to what degree people have changed the earth from its original, "pure" condition. Another is whether their particular environments have shaped the social and moral natures of human cultures.

The the effect of environment on people has been of most interest historically. For instance, European settlers in the Americas viewed the native Indians as shaped by their savage environment of desert and forest into amoral rogues. The Spanish, treating the local

The reason for the trench is that you want to blanch (whiten) as much of the stem as possible. You do this by surrounding it by soil. Any part of a leaf that is in the light will become green and tough (which is all right for soups but not what you want when serving leeks as a vegetable course). Competitive leek growers dig a mighty trench two feet or more deep and a foot or more wide. An eight inch trench is adequate if you are not trying to win prizes for the size of your leeks. Add several inches of rich compost to the bottom of your trench then transplant seedlings about four inches apart in a double or triple row down the trench. About once a month, put an inch or so of soil or compost into the trench with a little nitrogen fertilizer if you're feeling energetic. Try not to get soil into the fork where the leaves branch out or the leeks will be a nuisance to clean when you harvest them. Make sure leeks get the standard one inch of water a week or they get thin and dry.

Leeks eventually stop looking like buried onions and get several inches thick. Some leeks begin to thicken in July or August, others not till September or October. (It seems likely that they are sensitive to daylength as onions are.) Once they start to thicken up, they are ready to harvest. Leeks do not get tougher as they mature, so you can leave them in the ground and harvest them when you like.

inhabitants with more respect than the later-arrived British, induced the Indians to settle down in villages. There the Spanish could teach them Christianity and agriculture: the way of life which the missionaries believed to be civilized and which they had brought from their own "superior" environment. So certain were the missionaries that theirs was the only knowledge worth knowing, that few of them bothered to learn from the Indians. As a result, the Indians forgot their hunter-gatherer skills and starved with the Spanish when the harvest failed.

Historical discussions of the effect of people on their environment are few and far between, except for an early realization that deforesting land caused soil erosion and flooding. Not until the 1920s did a significant number of scholars search for an alternative to environmental destruction in the name of progress. In the 1920s and 1930s, Harlan Barrows and Carl Sauer led an influential campaign against destructive exploitation of nature, recognized the environmental skills of primitive peoples, and warned of the need for conservation. In the Soviet Union, although Karl Marx had adopted an environmentalist point of view in *Das Capital*, nature was still viewed as waiting to be conquered. The 1948 "Stalin Plan for the Transformation of Nature" envisioned massive assaults on the environment in the name of economic progress. We are just beginning to learn of the economic and environmental disasters that ensued, which included mass starvation as well as pollution with radioactive and toxic waste to the point where large areas of the former Soviet Union had to be evacuated as unfit for human habitation.

With this kind of philosophy alive and still with us today, it is not surprising that the speed with which the environmental crisis has developed has caught us sleeping, morally and intellectually. Who could have predicted a century ago, that the most useful value we could have taught people if we want the human race to survive is that they should have no more than two children? Most scientists think that it will take a revolution in philosophy and economics to get us out of the environmental mess we are in today.

GREEN PEAS AND SAUTEED JICAMA

(Serves 6-8)
1 medium jicama
1/4 cup butter
2 lb green peas
Salt and pepper to taste
Peel jicama and cut it into small cubes. In a saucepan, melt butter and add green peas, stirring until they are coated with butter. Add jicama and seasonings and simmer over medium heat (uncovered) for 4 minutes.

Lettuce

There is no reason to buy lettuce when you can have dozens of delicious varieties in your own garden except in the heat of summer. Lettuce is completely hardy. Ours survived 15 °F in December, 1989.

Sprinkle a little seed on the ground every couple of weeks to keep the lettuce coming. Do not cover it because lettuce needs light to germinate. Thin the seedlings as they grow and eat the seedlings. When the plants are a reasonable size and about four inches apart, stop pulling them and merely harvest a few of the largest leaves from each plant. They will keep growing new ones. We sometimes grow some extra seedlings in pots and plant them in the ground as the lettuce row gets thinned by harvesting.

Lettuce seed will not germinate if the soil temperature is above 70 °F but some people manage to grow it in spring and summer with a little effort. You might germinate seeds in an air-conditioned room for planting in late spring. Most lettuce gets bitter and bolts when weather gets over 80 °F but some varieties stand up to heat better than others. It may be worth experimenting with lettuce in shade in summer. In colder weather, it grows faster in sun.

Try red-leaved lettuces for colorful salads and garden rows. If you do, however, wear your glasses when you prepare the lettuce or the family will complain about oak leaves in the salad. Don't bother with iceberg, which requires special conditions. Buttercrunch is our favorite for winter. Or plant 'Chef's blend' for a mixture. Cos or romaine lettuce is delicious and the main ingredient in Caesar salad. In the South, Romaine does best in shade in spring. It will grow in sun in a mild winter.

Mesclun

Mesclun is the yuppy thing to serve as salad. It's the name for the bunches of young mixed greens you find in French markets. Snobby American restaurants charge you five dollars an ounce for mesclun salad.

I don't recommend planting seeds labeled "Mesclun," however. The packet will contain some things like corn salad (roquette) and chervil that always die for me. (The same goes for fashionable radicchio. It's a beast to grow.) In addition, the French version contains some pretty pungent specimens which are less than delightful to most Anglo-American palates. Better to remain a hick from the sticks and invent your own salad mixture of delicious greens that grow well in your garden. On second thoughts, if you invent your own, easy-to-grow version of mesclun and give it a fancy French name, you might be able to do a deal with an upwardly mobile restaurant.

Peas

Multiplier Onions, Shallots, and Garlic

I've never had much success growing onions although we live in Vidalia country and should be able to grow these mild beauties. But I have recently become a convert to multiplier (Egyptian, or potato) onions, as well as shallots, and garlic, which are grown in the same way. Multipliers have been grown in the Middle East for more than 3000 years and were brought to the United States by early settlers. They are now available commercially thanks to the rescue of many heirloom varieties during the 1980s by Jeff McCormack of Southern Exposure Seed Exchange.

Multipliers almost never flower. They are propagated by the bulbs, each of which divides into two to twelve bulbs in a growing season. The smallish bulbs are good keepers and will last through the winter if properly stored. The leaves make the tastiest green onions I have ever encountered, adding a delicious touch to winter and spring salads, sandwiches, and sauces.

Multipliers can be planted in autumn or spring. Planted in late October, they will overwinter as far north as Wisconsin if you give them a straw mulch. Farther south, they are planted later, preferably after the first frost. Within a week or two, green tops appear. Harvest these with a light hand so as to leave the plant plenty of leaf surface for photosynthesis. In summer, when most of the leaves have died and fallen over, dig the onions, remove the larger bulbs for eating and save the smaller ones to replant.

Peas, Green (English, Snow, or Snap)

Peas grow exceedingly well in winter or long cool springs and there are some delicious varieties. Scrape a trench about six inches wide and fill it with compost, grass clippings, or any other organic matter you can find, because peas are heavy feeders. Plant the seeds quite thickly (two inches apart or less) in the trench, cover them with an inch of soil, sprinkle some more grass clippings on the top, and wait for the harvest. Don't thin peas. If the weather is mild, peas will grow steadily through the winter. If it is cold, they may not even germinate for several months, but they will be up and climbing with the first hint of spring weather.

The first time you plant peas or beans, it is a good idea to dust the seeds with legume inoculant when you plant them. This inoculant contains the bacteria that fix nitrogen. Legume inoculant will last for two years in a sealed container in the refrigerator and the bacteria survive for three years in the soil after legumes have been removed. The take-home message is to make sure you plant peas or beans in every part of the garden once every three years and to use the rich soil left when you remove spring peas for tomatoes or peppers in the summer. A 1989 National Research Council study found that crop yields on land planted to legumes the previous year were up to 20% higher than on other land—with the same use of fertilizer.

Frost while plants are in bloom can ruin a crop. We have never had this happen, but it is easy to take precautions against it: start late and early varieties at the same time so that one will make it. This also helps to overcome the problem of all the peas maturing at once. Several varieties will extend the season.

The tastiest and most productive pea varieties get very large and need support. (Peas aren't such vigorous climbers as beans so it's no good trying to grow them up slippery bamboos; they need something to hold onto near the ground.) Breeders are working on the support problem by developing leafless peas. These are all tendrils and no leaves and the stiff tendrils support the plants. For shorter varieties, you can use pea brush, stuck in the trench when you plant the peas. (Don't use fresh willow or you will have a row of willow trees by spring.) We have a permanent length of trellis in the garden that we use for peas in winter and cucumbers in summer.

The names of the main varieties of peas and beans are pretty confusing, and vary in different parts of the country. Southerners have a tendency to call things that I would call beans, peas. In general, shell beans are things you grow for the dried seeds (like kidney and pinto beans); limas have inedible pods but you eat the beans green, green beans (which divide into pole and bush beans) are ones where you eat pod and all, and peas divide into English peas (including *petits pois*) where you eat only the peas when they are mature, snow peas where you eat immature peas and pods, and snap peas where you eat peas and pod, but not until the peas are mature. Got that?

VEGETABLES AND NUTRITION

We all know, don't we, that one of the best things we could do for ourselves is to increase our intake of fresh and lightly cooked vegetables. According to the National Academy of Sciences, this would help us reduce fat in the diet and increase our intake of fiber and of complex carbohydrate (which means carbohydrates other than sugars).

Vegetables lose minerals and vitamins, not to mention sugars and flavor, when they sit around in the store or refrigerator or are overcooked. So enjoy the boiled-to-death cabbage so beloved of Britons and New Englanders if you like, but find tasty ways to consume most of your vegetables raw or lightly cooked. Steaming is probably the best way to cook vegetables. Steam vegetables until they are slightly tender and then toss them in a little butter, herb butter, or olive oil for that finishing touch. You could learn to love it and we should all live forever, *quod Deus avertat.*

Sources

A & D Peony and Perennial Nursery, 6808 180th S.E., Snohomish, Washington 98290.

Antique Rose Emporium, Route 5, Box 143, Brenham, Texas 77833. Old roses.

Bay View Gardens, 1201 Bay St., Santa Cruz, California 95060 (Pacific coast irises)

California Gardens, 18552 Erwin Street, Reseda, California 91335. Bulbs, succulents.

Caprice Farm Nursery, 15425 S.W. Pleasant Hill, Sherwood, Oregon 97140. 503- 625-7241. Peonies, etc.

Chiltern Seeds, Bortree Stile, Ulverston, Cumbria LA12 7PB, U.K.

Country Garden, Route 2, Crivitz, Wisconsin 54114. Perennials.

Gilbert H. Wild and Son, Inc., P.0. Box 338, Sarcoxie, Missouri 64862, 417-548-3514.

Gladside Gardens, 61 Main Street, Northfield, Massachussetts 10136

Harris Seeds, 961 Lyell Avenue, Rochester, New York 14606

Heritage Rose Gardens, 16831 Mitchell Creek Road, Fort Bragg, California 95437

Honeywood Lilies, Box 63. Parkside. Saskatchewan SOJ 2A0 Canada. 306-747-3296; 306-747-3776.

Johnny's Selected Seeds, Foss Hill Road, Albion, Maine 04910.

Klehm Nursery, Rt. 5, Box 197, Penny Rd., South Barrington, Illinois 60010. 800-553- 3715. Peonies, etc.

Lamb Nurseries, 101 East Sharp Avenue, Spokane, Washington 99292. Uncommon perennials.

Louisiana Nursery, Route 7, Box 43, Opelousa, Louisiana 70570. Daylilies, magnolias, etc.

Marshalls Seeds, Wisbech, Cambridge PE13 2RF, U.K.

McLure and Zimmerman, 1422 West Thorndale, Chicago, Illinois 60660. Bulbs, corms, and tubers.

Mr. Fothergill's Seeds, Gazeley Road, Kentford, Newmarket, Suffolk CB8 7QB, U.K.

Nuccio's Nurseries, P. O. Box 6160, Altadena, California 91003. Camellias and azaleas.

Park Seed, Cokesbury Road, Greenwood, SC 29647

Perry's Water Gardens, 191 Leatherman Gap Rd., Franklin, NC 28734.

Pickering Nurseries, 670 Kingston Road, Pickering, Ontario L1V 1A6, Canada. Old roses.

Pine Heights Nursery, Pepper Street, Elerton Hills, Queensland 4053, Australia.

Plants of the Southwest, 1570 Pacheco Street, Santa Fe, New Mexico 87501. Natives and grasses.

Reath's Nursery, 100 Central Boulevard, Vulcan, Michigan 49892. 906-563-9321.

Roses of Yesterday and Today, 802 Brown's Valley Road, Watsonville, California 95076.

Seeds Blüm, Idaho City Stage, Boise, Idaho 83706. Specializes in heirloom seeds.

Shepherd Iris Gardens, 3342 W. Orangewood, Phoenix, Arizona 85051. Pacific coast irises

Shepherd's Garden Seeds, 30 Irene St. Torrington, Connecticut 06790.

Southern Exposure Seed Exchange, P.O. Box 158, North Garden, Virginia 22959.

The Daffodil Mart, Route 3, Box 794, Gloucester, Virginia 23061,

The Fragrant Path, P.O. Box 328, Fort Calhoun, Nebraska 68023. Seeds.

The New Peony Farm, P.0, Box 18235, St. Paul, Minnesota 55118.

Thompson & Morgan, London Road, Ipswich, Suffolk IP2 OBA, U.K. or P.O. Box 1308, Jackson, New Jersey 08527, U.S.A. Excellent selection of seeds.

Tischler Peony Gardens, 1021 East Division St., Faribault, Minnesota 55021, 507-334-7242.

Ty Ty Plantation, Box 159, Ty Ty, Georgia 31795. Especially useful for those in Zones 7-9.

Van Ness Water Gardens, 2460 North Euclid Avenue, Upland, CA 91786.

W. Atlee Burpee & Co. 300 Park Avenue, Warminster, Pennsylvania 18974.

Wayside Gardens, Hodges, North Carolina 29695

White Flower Farm, Litchfield, Connecticut 06759, 800-888-7756. Choice perennials.

William Tricker, 7125 Tanglewood Drive, Independence, OH 44131. Water gardens.

Woodlanders 1128 Colleton Avenue, Aiken, South Carolina 29801. Plants adapted to the South.

References

Aiken, George D., 1935, 1968. *Pioneering with Wildflowers.* Englewood Cliffs: Prentice-Hall, Inc.

Appleton, Bonnie Lee, 1988. *Landscape Rejuvenation: Remodeling the Home Landscape.* Pownal, VT: Storey Communications, Inc.

Armitage, Allan M., 1989. *Herbaceous Perennial Plants: A Treatise on their Identification, Culture, and Garden Attributes.* Athens, GA: Varsity Press, Inc.

Denckla, Tanya, 1991. *Gardening at a Glance: The Organic Gardener's Handbook on Vegetables, Fruits, Nuts and Herbs.* Franklin, WV: Wooden Angel Publishing.

Duncan, Wilbur H. and Marion B. Duncan, 1988. *Trees of the Southeastern United States.* Athens, GA: University of Georgia Press.

Hill, Lewis and Nancy, 1988. *Successful Perennial Gardening: A Practical Guide.* Pownal, VT: Storey Communications, Inc.

Jekyll, Gertrude, 1908, republished 1983. *Colour Schemes for the Flower Garden.* New York: Penguin Books.

Nuese, Josephine, 1970. *The Country Garden.* New York: Charles Scribner's Sons.

Ortho Books, 1984. *Landscaping with Wildflowers and Native Plants.*

Pereire, Anita, 1988. *The Prentice Hall Encyclopedia of Garden Flowers.* New York: Prentice Hall Press.

Phillips, Harry R., 1985. *Growing and Propagating Wild Flowers.* Chapel Hill: The University of North Carolina Press.

Phillips, Judith, 1987. *Southwestern Landscaping with Native Plants.* Santa Fe: Museum of New Mexico Press.

Phillips, Roger and Martyn Rix, 1988. *Roses.* New York: Random House.

Phillips, Roger and Nicky Foy, 1990. *Herbs.* New York: Random House.

Proulx, E. Annie, 1987. *The Gourmet Gardener.* New York: Fawcett Columbine.

Sackville-West, V., 1986. *The Illustrated Garden Book.* New York: Atheneum.

Schinz, Marina and Susan Littlefield, 1985. *Visions of Paradise: Themes and Variations on the Garden.* New York: Stewart, Tabori & Chang, Inc.

Strong, Roy, 1989. *Creating Formal Gardens.* Boston: Little Brown.

Verey, Rosemary, 1989. *A Countrywoman's Year.* Boston: Little Brown and Company.

Welch, William C., 1989. *Perennial Garden Color.* Dallas: Taylor Publishing Company.

Wilder, Louise Beebe, 1918, reissued 1990. *Color in my Garden.* Garden City, NY: Doubleday. (Originally published as "Colour in my Garden")

Wright, Michael, 1984. *The Complete Handbook of Garden Plants.* New York: Facts on File.

Glossary

A

acantha (Greek) spine, thorn, prickle.

acid 1. A substance that releases hydrogen ions (H^+) in aqueous solution. 2. A substance that accepts electrons.

acid rain (acid precipitation) Rain containing pollutants that give it an acid pH, usually of less than 5.0. The most common pollutants with this effect are oxides of nitrogen and sulfur which form acids when they dissolve in water.

adaptation 1. Process by which populations evolve to become suited to their environments over the course of generations. 2. Characteristic that increases an organism's evolutionary success.

adaxial In a plant, the upper surface of a leaf, petal, or other organ. Literally, the side facing the stem or main axis.

adventitious In plants, used to describe organs growing in unusual places, e.g., a root growing out of a leaf.

aerobic 1. Requiring molecular oxygen (O_2). 2. in the presence of molecular oxygen.

alkali (= base) A substance that releases hydroxide ions (OH^-) in water or that accepts hydrogen ions (H^+) or that gives up electrons.

alkaline Having a (basic) pH of more than 7.0.

ammonia NH_3; produced naturally during the decomposition of proteins; used in the manufacture of fertilizers, dyes, explosives, and drugs.

amphibian Member of the vertebrate class Amphibia, e.g., frogs, toads, salamanders, newts, and their relatives.

amyloplast Plastid that stores starch. Abundant in cells of a potato.

anaerobic 1. Without oxygen. 2. Not requiring molecular oxygen for extraction of energy from food during respiration. (*noun*: anaerobe)

angiosperms Flowering plants. Most advanced and recently evolved group of vascular plants characterized by production of seeds enclosed in tissues derived from the ovary.

annual A flowering plant that grows from seed, flowers, sets seed and dies within one year.

anther Organ in flowers that produces pollen.

anthocyanins Pigments of red, blue, or purple hue, commonly found in vacuoles of plant cells.

Anthophyta Plant division containing the flowering plants (= angiosperms).

antibiotics Substances that kill microorganisms.

apical meristem Area of dividing cells at the root and stem tips of a plant.

apical Of the tip of something.

arboretum A collection of trees.

arid Dry; of areas where more water leaves the ecosystem each year (by evaporation and transpiration) than enters it (as precipitation).

arthropods Members of the phylum Arthropoda: segmented animals with jointed appendages, and stiff chitin-containing external skeletons; e.g., crabs, lobsters, barnacles, insects, spiders.

axil In plants, the angle between the stalk (petiole) of a leaf and the stem. (*adjective*: axillary)

B

bacterium Member of the phylum Monera, containing organisms without nuclear envelopes around the single, circular DNA genome; most are very small, unicellular or forming colonies of independent cells. (*plural*: bacteria)

basic solution (=alkaline solution) A solution with a pH of more than 7.0.

beneficial insects Insects beneficial to humans because they attack other organisms that are considered pests.

bicarbonate ion HCO_3^-

binomial A Latin, two word name given to each species of organisms.

Conventionally underlined or italicized. e.g., <u>Homo sapiens</u>, *Homo sapiens*.

biodegradable Capable of being broken down by living organisms into inorganic compounds.

biodiversity The number of different species of organisms found in an area.

biogeochemical cycle Description of the geological and biological processes that affect the movement of an element among different components of an ecosystem.

biological pest control The use of naturally occurring chemicals or organisms to reduce the populations of pest organisms.

biomass Amount of material that is part of the bodies of living organisms.

biome Major type of terrestrial community of organisms; defined by the local climate, which determines the type of soil and vegetation. e.g., tropical rain forest, desert,

biosphere Total of all areas on earth where organisms are found; includes deep ocean and part of the atmosphere.

bromeliad Member of a large family of mostly epiphytic plants, including pineapples and Spanish moss.

bulb A fleshy underground organ formed by many members of the Liliaceae and Amyrillidaceae families. A bulb is a highly modified part of the shoot system. Fleshy scales around the outside of the bulb may develop into new plants.

C

Ca Chemical symbol for the element calcium.

calcareous Composed of, or containing, calcium carbonate ($CaCO_3$).

cambium Meristematic tissue that produces new cells which increase the diameter of a woody stem or root. (*adjective*: cambial)

carbohydrates A class of compounds whose members have the general formula (CH_2O) and contain at least one double-bonded oxygen.

carotenoid Accessory photosynthetic pigment that usually appears yellow, orange, or brown.

carpel A female flower part.

carrying capacity Of an area for a species, the number of individuals of a species the area can support indefinitely.

cellulose Polysaccharide that makes up a large part of the cell walls of plant cells—proably the most abundant organic material on earth.

cereals Those grass species of the plant family Gramineae which make up the bulk of human food.

chaparral Dry shrubland biome of temperate coastal regions such as California and the Mediterranean.

chlorophyll Green pigment that traps light energy during photosynthesis.

chloroplast Green plastid (containing chlorophyll) in which photosynthesis occurs.

chlorosis Pale coloration of a plant in poor health, e.g. due to mineral deficiency.

clay Mineral particles with a diameter of less than 0.002 mm consisting of salts of aluminum and silicon.

climax community The community of organisms found in an area if the area is left undisturbed for long enough.

CO_2 Chemical symbol for carbon dioxide.

compound In chemistry, matter that is composed of two or more different kinds of atoms chemically combined in definite proportions.

conifer Member of the plant division Coniferophyta: cone-bearing gymnosperms, including pines, spruces, etc. (as well as junipers and yews, whose reproductive structures do not resemble cones).

conservation Careful use and management of resources, so as to maximise the benefit from them now and in the future. Methods include preservation, reducing waste, recycling, reuse, and decreased use.

consumer 1. In ecology, an organism that eats other organisms. 2. In economics, a person who buys goods or services.

corm A swollen underground stem found in plants such as crocuses and gladioli. At the end of a season, the corm withers and one or more new corms form above it at the base of each flowering stem.

corymb A short and broad, more or less flat-topped inflorescence in which the outer flowers open first.

cotyledon A seed leaf of a plant embryo.

cover crop (=green manure) Crop planted on bare ground to act as green manure or to prevent soil erosion by holding the soil in place with its roots.

cultivar Cultivated variety of a plant species or hybrid.

cuticle Layer of waxy waterproof substance secreted on the outer surface of an organism.

cycad Palm-like gymnosperm; member of the division Cycadophyta.

D

DDT Dichlorodiphenyltrichloroethane, a chlorinated hydrocarbon that has been widely used as a pesticide.

deadhead To remove dead flower heads from a plant.

deciduous Of plants that lose their leaves during one season of the year; not evergreen.

decomposer In ecology, an organism that feeds on the dead bodies, body parts, or wastes of other organisms, thereby breaking down and recycling the nutrients they contain.

deforestation Removal of trees from an area without replacing them.

degradable Capable of being broken down by natural processes (usually by decomposer organisms).

depletion The using up or destruction by pollution of a significant portion of a natural resource.

detritus Molecules and larger particles of dead organic matter that sink to the bottom of a body of water.

dicotyledon (dicot) Member of the group of flowering plants whose embryos have two cotyledons.

dissolved oxygen (DO) The amount of oxygen dissolved in a given volume of a body of water; used as a measure of water pollution.

division A taxon of plants or fungi equivalent to a phylum in the animal kingdom.

DNA Deoxyribonucleic acid, the genetic material of organisms and of many viruses.

dormancy Inactive state during which growth and development is deferred and the metabolic rate is low.

double flower Flower having more than the usual number of petals; usually the result of a genetic mutation that transforms stamens into petals. Flowers in which carpels have also been transformed into petals are termed 'flore pleno.'

drought Period with less than average precipitation.

E

ecology Study of the relationships of organisms with other organisms and with their physical environment.

ecosystem All of the organisms present in a particular area, together with their physical environment.

embryo A multicellular developing plant or animal still enclosed inside the parent's body or in a seed or egg.plant.

endemic (*adjective*, sometimes used as a noun) Peculiar to a particular population or locality where it originated.

enzyme Protein that catalyzes a particular biochemical reaction involving specific substrate (reactant) molecules.

eutrophication Process in which organic debris accumulates in a body of water, making it richer in nutrients and hence in organisms, until eventually it fills in and becomes dry land.

evapotranspiration Method by which water leaves an area by transpiration from plants and evaporation from all sources.

evolution 1. Descent of modern species of organisms from related, but different, species that lived in previous times. 2. Change in the gene pool of a population from generation to generation.

exfoliating Peeling off.

extinction Of a species, its disappearance from earth when its last surviving member dies.

F

fastigiate Upright

fermentation Anaerobic breakdown of food molecules to release energy, in which the final electron acceptors (and end products) are organic molecules.

fertilization 1. Union of an egg with a sperm. 2. Supplying nutrients to crop plants.

fix In chemistry, to incorporate into a less volatile compound.

foliar feeding To fertilize plants by spraying them with a solution of fertilizer.

forb A herbaceous perennial flowering plant other than a grass.

forest Region where trees grow as a result of adequate temperature and annual precipitation of 75 centimeters or more.

frond A leaf, usually highly divided (usually applied to ferns or palms).

fruit Structure that develops from the ovary of a flower, surrounding one or more seeds.

fugitive species Species that occurs in an area for only a short time.

Fungi Kingdom of organisms containing eukaryotic, unicellular (yeasts) or multicellular heterotrophs feeding by absorbing nutrients through their cell walls.

G

gene A length of DNA that functions as a unit.

gene bank An collection of plant material stored in a viable condition. Usually seeds are dried and frozen in sealed containers. Some plants have seeds that will not survive this treatment and they must be maintained as growing plants or in tissue culture.

gene pool All of the genes present in a population of organisms.

genera Plural of genus.

genetic engineering The isolation of useful genes from a donor organism or tissue and their incorporation into an organism that does not normally possess them.

genetic information The information, encoded in the nucleotide sequence in DNA, that dictates protein synthesis and other features of cells.

genus The taxon above species in the hierarchical classification of organisms. The genus name is the first word of the binomial for a species; e.g., *Ursus* is the generic name of the grizzly bear, *Ursus horribilis*. (*plural:* genera; *adjective:* generic)

germ plasm Term used by botanists for genetic material, especially that contained within the reproductive (germ) cells.

gibberellins Plant hormones that stimulate cell enlargement.

glabrous Of plant parts, not hairy.

green manure Crop grown to be plowed or dug into the soil, where it will decompose, increasing the fertility and water-holding properties of the soil.

green plants Photosynthetic organisms that give off oxygen during their photosynthesis; used to include cyanobacteria and all photosynthetic eukaryotes (protists and plants).

greenhouse effect Heating of the earth caused by gases in the atmosphere that trap infrared radiation from the earth and prevent it escaping into space.

gymnosperm ("naked seed") Nonflowering plant that produces seeds, e.g., pines, redwoods, cycads.

H

H Chemical symbol for the element hydrogen. H^+ is a hydrogen ion.

halophyte Plant adapted to living in saline soil.

heel in To store plants temporarily by shading them and covering the roots with soil.

herbaceous Of plants with non-woody stems.

herbivore An animal that eats plants or parts of plants.

host The organism upon which a parasite feeds.

humus Soft, structureless, black or dark brown material in soil derived from decaying plant and animal remains.

hybrid Offspring of a mating between genetically different individuals.

hydroponics Technique of growing plants without soil in aqueous solutions of fertilizer.

I

indicator plant Common, well-studied plant characteristic of a plant hardiness zone or ecosystem.

insect Arthropod with three distinct body areas (head, thorax, abdomen); adults with three pairs of legs, and usually two pairs of wings, attached to the thorax.

insecticide A substance that kills one or more species of insects.

insectivore Insect-eating. (*adjective.* insectivorous)

internode Portion of a plant stem between sites of leaf attachment.

invertebrate An animal that lacks a backbone; e.g., earthworm, snail.

L

lateral 1. (adjective) Pertaining to the side. 2. (noun) A side branch or branch root of a plant.

laterite A hard crust that may develop when vegetation is removed from the surface of soil containing metals such as aluminum and iron in tropical regions with wet and dry seasons. In the dry season, soil solution rises to the surface by capillarity and aluminum and iron oxides accumulate and combine to form the crust. Laterization produces an infertile soil called latosol.

LD$_{50}$ (lethal dose 50) The dose of a poison that kills 50% of a sample population.

leaching The washing out of soluble substances by water passing down through soil. Leaching occurs when more water falls on the soil than is lost by evaporation from the surface. Leached soil has lost mineral nutrients which have dissolved in rainwater running through the soil and away into streams.

leaf nodes Areas of plant stem at which leaves are attached.

legumes Members of the plant family Leguminosae, including beans, peas, peanuts, alfalfa, clover, acacia.

Lepidoptera The order of insects that includes moths and butterflies.

lichen A symbiotic pair of organisms consisting of a fungus and an alga living in a symbiotic realtionship.

litter Plant remains (mainly leaves) that have fallen on the surface of the soil.

littoral Of the shallow part of a lake or sea where rooted plants are capable to growing.

M

mammal Warm-blooded vertebrate with lower jaw consisting of only one bone (the mandible) on each side, with fur or hair, with young nourished by milk from the mammary glands of the female parent; e.g., humans, rabbits, cattle.

manure Feces of an animal, often mixed with the wood chips or hay that has been used for the animal's bedding.

meristem Region of dividing cells in a growing area of a plant. (*adjective* meristematic)

metabolism All the chemical reactions taking place within an organism (often measured as the amount of energy or oxygen the organism uses in a given time).

methane Gas (CH_4) produced by the metabolism of anaerobic methanogen bacteria.

Mg Chemical symbol for the element magnesium.

mineral Any naturally occurring inorganic substance having a definite chemical composition, and a particular crystalline structure, color and hardness.

minimum tillage farming farming while disturbing the soil as little as possible, usually by planting seeds without plowing the soil beforehand and growing the crop without cultivating the soil.

mites Small arthropods in the class (Arachnida) that includes spiders. Mites have eight legs, and the body is not divided into two parts as it is in spiders.

Monera Kingdom containing all prokaryotic organisms (bacteria).

monocot *See* monocotyledon

monocotyledon (monocot) Member of the group of flowering plants whose embryos have only one cotyledon; characterized by parallel, rather than branching, veins in the leaves; includes palms, lilies, narcissus.

monoculture Cultivation of only one plant species on an area of land.

mutation Change in the genetic material (DNA) in a cell that is sufficiently permanent to be inherited by the cell's offspring formed by division of the cell.

mycology Study of fungi.

mycorrhiza Mutualistic association between a fungus and the roots of a higher plant; the fungus takes up mineral nutrients from the soil and passes them to the plant, receiving some organic (food) molecules made by the plant in return. (*plural:* mycorrhizae)

N

N Chemical symbol for the element nitrogen.

nematode A roundworm, member of the phylum Nematoda.

nitrogen fixation Conversion of gaseous nitrogen (N_2) to ammonia (NH_3); carried out in ecosystems mainly by bacteria of the genus *Rhizobium*.

nondegradable Not broken down by natural processes (or broken down only over a time-span of hundreds of years).

nonrenewable resources Natural resources that can be used up completely or else used up to such a degree that it is economically impractical to obtain any more of them.

nucleic acids Class of macromolecules, made up of nucleotide monomers, that contains the genetic information of organisms; DNA and RNA.

nutrient Any chemical which an organism must take in from its environment because it cannot produce it (or cannot produce it as fast as it needs it).

O

O Chemical symbol for the element oxygen.

oligotrophic Of a body of fresh water that contains few nutrients and few organisms.

omnivore Animal that eats both plants and animals.

orchid Member of the largest plant family, the Orchidaceae.

organic compound Any compound containing carbon; usually used to exclude very small molecules such as carbon dioxide.

osmosis Movement of water through a membrane down a water potential gradient–from a weak to a more concentrated solution.

oxidation A chemical reaction involving removal of electrons or hydrogen atoms, or addition of oxygen.

ozone O_3. Poisonous gas, a common pollutant in smog; also formed by the action of sunlight on oxygen in the ozone layer of the atmosphere.

P

P Chemical symbol for the element phosphorus.

parasite Organism that feeds on another living organism, usually without killing it.

pea brush twiggy branches pruned from deciduous trees and shrubs and used to support other plants.

pedicel The stalk of an individual flower.

perennial Living for many years and surviving normal seasonal changes.

petiole In plants, the stalk of a leaf.

pH Logarithm to the base 10 of the hydrogen ion concentration of a solution; a measure of how acidic or basic a solution is, on a scale of 0 to 14 (0=very acidic, 14=very basic, 7=neutral).

phloem Tissue in plants that conducts food from sites of synthesis or storage to sites where food is used or stored.

photosynthesis Process whereby plants, and some bacteria and protists, capture solar energy and store it as chemical bonds in carbohydrate molecules, using CO_2 to build the carbohydrate.

pigment Molecule that differentially absorbs particular wavelengths of visible light and so appears colored.

pioneer species Species adapted to life in a recently disturbed habitat. e.g.

the first species to appear in an area after a landslide, fire, or volcanic eruption.

pollen grain Immature male gametophyte of a gymnosperm or flowering plant; it will produce the sperm nuclei that fertilize the egg.

pollination Deposition of pollen on or near the female parts of a gymnosperm or angiosperm.

pollution A change in the physical, chemical, or biological properties of air, water, or soil that can adversely affect the health, survival, or activities of humans and other living organisms.

predation Consumption of all or part of one organism by another; used by ecologist to include parasitism and herbivory.

predator Animal that feeds on other organisms (usually animals); ecologists often use the term to include parasites and herbivores as well as carnivores.

prick out To separate crowded seedlings and plant them farther apart, usually in separate cells.

pupa Stage between larva and adult in insects with complete metamorphosis, e.g., butterflies, flies, beetles.

R

raceme Unbranched, elongated inflorescence with pedicelled flowers.

renewable resource Natural resource whose supply can be depleted in the short term but is normally replaced because it is continuously produced by natural processes. e.g., wood, fresh water.

reptile Vertebrate with dry scaly skin and eggs laid on land, e.g., snakes, lizards, alligators, turtles.

rhizome An underground stem of a vascular plant that grows horizontally and branches to form new plants.

rodents Members of the mammalian order Rodentia: rats, mice, and their relatives.

S

S Chemical symbol for the element sulfur.

saline Salty.

salinity Saltiness.

salt An ionic compound whose cation comes from a base and whose anion comes from an acid.

salt marsh A wetland containing salt water in which the dominant species of angiosperm is cordgrass, *Spartina* spp.

sap Mixture of water, minerals, etc., conducted in xylem tissue of plants.

saprobe Organism that absorbs nonliving organic matter for food. Fungi are saprobes.

secondary chemicals Chemicals produced by plants, usually for defense. e.g., milkweed produces cardiac glycosides that are toxic to many herbivores.

secondary succession In ecology, series of changes in the populations of organisms inhabiting an area after a disturbance that does not destroy the soil (or bottom sediment of a body of water); culminates in production of the climax community.

seed coat Outer covering of a seed, developed from the outer layers of the ovule.

seed Dispersal unit of gymnosperms and angiosperms, consisting of a seed coat, embryonic plant, and food supply.

self-pollination The transfer of pollen from male flower parts to female flower parts on the same plant.

shoot system The part of a plant consisting of the stems, leaves, and any reproductive structures borne thereon.

sidedress To apply fertilizer, lime, etc. to plants by placing the substance alongside the plant where it does not touch the stem.

solute The material dissolved in a solution.

solution A homogeneous mixture of two or more substances in a single phase.

solvent The medium in which a solvent is dissolved to form a solution.

species A group of individuals sharing the same gene pool because they are descended from a common ancestor. Also, a taxon to which individuals are assigned on morphological grounds. A difficult concept.

species diversity The number of different species in an area.

spore Reproductive cell that can grow into a new individual without fertilization; produced by meiosis in plants, by meiosis or mitosis in fungi. Bacterial spores form when an individual cell encases itself in a protective covering when conditions are unfavorable for growth.

stigma Tip of female flower part, usually sticky, allowing pollen to adhere to it easily.

stoma In a plant, a pore between two guard cells through which gases are exchanged between the plant and the air. (*plural*: stomata)

subtropical Lying near to, but not within, the tropics.

succession In ecology, process in which the inhabitants of an area that has been disturbed change with time in a regular sequence; succession finishes when the organisms of the climax community of the area have become established.

succulent A plant with fleshy, water-storing stems and leaves, adapted to desert conditions. Succulents are found in many different plant families.

sustainable Capable of continuing indefinitely in approximately its present form.

symbiosis Close association between members of two or more species (*See* mutualism, commensalism, parasite.) (*adjective*: symbiotic)

T

taxon Any one of the hierarchical categories into which organisms are classified; e.g., species, order, class. (*plural*: taxa)

taxonomy Study of the classification, identification, and naming of living organisms.

temperate region Region of the earth that is neither tropical nor arctic.

thermal pollution An increase in water temperature as a result of human activity that has harmful effects of aquatic organisms.

tomentose Of plant parts, covered with short wooly hairs.

tracheophyte Vascular plant.

transpiration Loss of water by evaporation through pores (stomata) in the shoot system of a plant.

tropics That part of the earth lying between the tropic of Cancer (at latitude 23 degrees 27 minutes north of the equator) and the tropic of Capricorn (at the same latitude south of the equator). These latitudes mark the limits of the sun's apparent movement north and south during the year.

troposphere Layer of the atmosphere which contains about 95% of the earth's air and extends about 12 kilometres up from the earth. The troposphere ends at the tropopause, the point at which atmospheric temperature starts to increase instead of decrease as one moves further form the earth.

tuber A swollen part of a stem or root, modified for storage. New tubers are formed each year. Stem tubers can be told from root tubers because stem tuber bear buds, called "eyes."

U

ultraviolet radiation That part of the electromagnetic spectrum (from the sun) with wavelengths shorter than those of visible light (below 400 nm) but higher than those of x-rays (about 100 nm), with sufficient energy to break hydrogen bonds and disrupt the structure of many biological molecules.

V

variegation The presence of patches and streaks of different colored tissue in a plant organ, usually a leaf.

vascular tissue Tissue that conducts water, minerals, and food from one part of the plant to another.

vegetative reproduction Reproduction by growth of an individual's body or fragments of its body; reproduction without production of gametes or spores.

vermiculite A mineral product made from mica that is used for insulation and as a medium for starting seeds and cuttings because it contains large air spaces.

W

wetland Land that remains flooded with fresh or salt water for all or part of the year.

wheat A cereal, the most widely grown type of human food plant, usually *Triticum aestivum* or *T. durum*.

wild type In genetics, the phenotype, genotype, or allele (if there is one) that is most prevalent in wild populations of the species. At a single locus, alleles other than the wild type are often called mutations.

wood Secondary xylem.

X

xerophyte Plant adapted to living in dry conditions caused by lack of precipitation or by heat and high winds. Xerophytes are found in deserts, on sand dunes and windy moors, etc. Some store water (e.g. cacti); some have leaves rolled up to reduce transpiration; some have hairy leaves that trap moisture (e.g. *Stachys byzantina*); some have stomata sunk in grooves that trap moisture (e.g. pines).

xylem Plant tissue that conducts sap from the roots to the leaves.

Index

Art Prints

Some of the flower illustrations in this book are available as a limited edition of prints, hand-colored by artist Thom Smith. Send for the color brochure for more details.

Mail to:
Halfmoon Publishing
P. O. Box 30279
Savannah, GA 31410

Pocket dictionary

A Brief Dictionary of Biology and Environmental Science

Please send me:

		Price
_____	Color brochures describing art prints	FREE
_____	Copies of *A Brief Dictionary of Biology and Environmental Science* at $4.95 each.	_____
_____	Copies of *Environmental Gardening* at $23.95 each.	_____

Halfmoon Publishing pays shipping and handling.

TOTAL _____

I enclose a check for:
Charge my credit card, but not until the books are mailed.

Mastercard/Visa number: _ _ _ _ _ _ _ _ _ _ _ _ _ _ _ _

Expiration date: _____ Signature: _____

Name: _____

Address: _____

_____

Notes